Expendable and Necessary

Expendable
and Necessary

▲ ▲ ▲

Ralph Harris

© 2017 Ralph Harris
All rights reserved.

ISBN: 1546771980
ISBN 13: 9781546771982

CHAPTER 1

Expendable? But Necessary

▲ ▲ ▲

NOVEMBER 1968 TO NOVEMBER 1969. One year, that's all it was, just one year. I had no idea how that one year would impact my life. But much of my life had been charted long before then.

When my parents gave birth to me, in Cleveland, Ohio, in 1948, they could not have anticipated the future challenges their black son would be presented with. But a black man's experience in America at any time in history has always been difficult.

My parents, John and Jennie, for example, had their own set of challenges. They were born and grew up in rural Alabama and Georgia, in the 1920s and '30s, where tenant farming was one of the few sources of income. Working on someone else's farmland for little or no money didn't offer much of a future. Sometimes the rent left them actually owing the farmer at the end of the year. It's no wonder they left the first chance they got, vowing to never move back. To my parents the impoverished inner-city section of Cleveland, Ohio, was the promised land. To their credit they worked, owned their own home, and kept me and my brother fed and well dressed.

Then there were my sets of grandparents, Sam and Minnie Marchman and Willie and Mozell Harris, who were born and grew up in the rural South in the late 1800s. They faced even greater challenges. Both sets of grandparents learned parental skills and life lessons from my great-grandparents, who were slaves. The world for my great-grandparents was the plantation, where the slave owners controlled every aspect of their lives. I cannot imagine the

Sam & Minnie

Willie Harris

challenges they must have faced. It took courage, determination, and diligence just to stay alive and keep their children safe.

But this was the 1960s, and I thought that if I worked hard, maybe I could purchase a home around here one day. Housing discrimination didn't bother me. Everyone and everything that mattered to me was close by. As for future dreams, my prospects were limited. I must admit the pimps and hustlers my friends modeled themselves after gave the appearance of a glamorous life. But it seemed they were either sitting in, wearing, or carrying their entire fortune in their pockets. They were just one stickup from financial ruin, and there were many in the neighborhood who would do the stickup. I once saw the same TV being stolen three times in one day.

Those same acquaintances would rob me as well. As the saying goes, "Keep your friends close, but keep your enemy closer."

At the start of the year, everything was going well. I had graduated from high school two years earlier. Shortly after graduation my uncle got me a janitorial job at a General Motors plant. The only time I left my community was to drive into to the suburb where the plant was located. Leaving the city was always a challenge. Like most young black men, driving through the suburbs resulted in my being frequently stopped and questioned by police. I was never accused of breaking any laws. The police seemed to believe it was their duty to see if I had stolen the car and if I was employed in the area.

But that was a small price to pay. That job made me a success story and a good catch for the ladies who had less options than I did.

My older brother did suggest that I to go to college, as he was doing. That advice fell on deaf ears when he was borrowing my money and driving my new car.

But there were events going on beyond Cleveland, and I was about to be violently and unwillingly drawn into the melee.

My immediate problems were right outside my door. Established civil rights organizations were slowly and methodically gaining ground. However, legislation still segregated blacks in schools, in employment, and in society. Now rumblings from more aggressive groups were becoming a roar.

The homes purchased by African Americans like my parents were sold to them at inflated prices by the whites who were moving into the suburbs. The housing projects that offered affordable living weren't being given the routine maintenance required. The small factories that offered the manual labor jobs were moving out of the city. Soon, lack of job opportunities caused many to turn to social services for survival. Those from my generation who could afford to move were denied access to the developing communities where people believed that black residents would bring down the property values.

This is what differentiated the northern protest from the South. In the South, blacks were protesting the Jim Crow laws that denied access to buildings, services, and businesses all over the city. In the North and other major cities, African Americans were confined to deteriorating conditions and inferior schools with little opportunity for improvement. The police were looked upon as jailers, with many of them patrolling the city limits like prison guards. The urban riots could be compared to prison riots. In fact, one of the first riots happened in Cleveland, the year I graduated from high school. The press called it the "Hough riots" after a Cleveland neighborhood. Civil unrest continued over the years. In 1968 there was the "Glenville shootout" occurring in another Cleveland neighborhood.

These and other riots quickly turned public sentiment against the inner cities, prompting heavily armed National Guard troops to be deployed in our neighborhood. Now even nonviolent protests like the symbolic protest by John Carlos and Tommie Smith in the 1968 Summer Olympics brought condemnation.

Politics was also breaking the country apart. Richard Nixon, a man widely recognized for his animosity toward minorities, was elected using the "southern strategy." The vote was largely a protest against the liberal cities perceived as causing that unrest. When you combine the assassinations of two vocal advocates of peace, Robert F. Kennedy and Martin Luther King, you get the sense of how pivotal 1968 was in American history.

Add to this the unpopular Vietnam War. The country was already turning against the war, but the Tet Offensive launched by the North Vietnamese in January 1968 shocked the nation. There was a total loss of innocence when the Mỹ Lai Massacre took place a month later.

How naïve I was at the start of the year. With the television images and newspaper and magazine articles, I still didn't consider myself a part of the turmoil, when all I had to do was look out my front door. I was poor, black, and uneducated. It was a perfect storm. At nineteen years of age, I was classified as 1-A. The draft notice that followed got my attention. I was called to join the fight to preserve the rights, freedom, and privileges granted me as an American citizen. Privileges, what privileges?

Now I was ready to pay attention to the civil-rights issues. I decided it wasn't my fight. I was ready to march, get on the bus, sit in, go on a hunger strike, even quit my job and go to college full-time. But it was too late; I could find nothing to turn this around besides going to jail or Canada. Neither of those options appealed to me.

Finally, on the day I was to report for induction, I made my act of defiance. I got drunk, doped up, and then passed out. I was hoping I would wake up and find it was all a dream. It wasn't; my brother found me unconscious, in a seedy hotel. He put me in the car with a packed bag and drove me to the induction center.

My disheveled appearance and verbal disapproval of the army personnel who seemed to be in charge might have been the motivation behind moving me to the group designated for the marines. By the time I slept off my high, I was in South Carolina at the Parris Island Marine Corps Base.

It was my first time out of Cleveland, well beyond my comfort zone. All the bravado I'd exhibited had turned to submission. My only connection to home while on Parris Island was Ellis, a brother I met at the induction center who was from Youngstown, Ohio. He was as scared and confused as I was.

The drill instructors, who terrified us all, were responsible for turning a diverse group of teenagers from across the country into a cohesive fighting unit. They seemed to have succeeded. Upon graduation we were calling ourselves "a mean green killing machine."

There was a high proportion of black recruits slated for the infantry in 1968, and we were no exception.

After basic training there was infantry training, then a short leave to go home to say good-bye to my family, especially to my number-one girlfriend, Elaine. With public sentiment growing against servicemen, my arrival and departure weren't met with great fanfare. Not wanting to be called a sellout to the man, I kept my military participation low-key. Perhaps the rise of drug usage in my neighborhood ex- plained why some of my buddies didn't know I had left in the first place.

Elaine & Me

When the brief leave of absence was over, all marines ordered to Vietnam as replacement troops were arriving at the San Diego military base. It was the first time we could freely mingle without the watchful eye and close supervision of instructors. Most of us were recently out of high school, and it showed. There was no age limit on drinking in the clubs on base, and we all took full advantage of that. Some would go into San Diego, where the prostitutes and drug dealers were waiting at the bus stop. Others would take one of the limousines into Tijuana, Mexico. There the decadence moved to another level.

But this was a good time for marines from all across the country to get to know one another. Soon we would be depending on each other for survival. In less than a week, the journey began. It started on the walk up the boarding ramp, thinking I might be taking my last step on American soil. Once seated, I braced for takeoff, consumed with thoughts of the past and anticipating an unknown future.

I watched intently from my window as our plane began its ascent into the heavens. It would be commonplace for those on the ground to see a passenger airplane passing overhead leaving its telltale white streak across the sky. But this flight was different.

On board was a precious yet deadly group of passengers. Precious because we were beloved sons, brothers, husbands, fathers, nephews, cousins, and friends who had someone waiting for our return. Deadly because we were marine infantrymen whose job would be to hunt and kill other men and women. The stewardess who served us smiled at the precocious flirtations, encouraged laughter, and listened intently to those who engaged her in conversation. When not on duty, she would sit alone, eyes closed, deep in thought. She had also made the return trip and knew that for many, this would be one-way, and those who survived may be physically or emotionally changed forever. At the very least, they would lose the innocence and naïveté that she found so endearing.

Among the many passengers on board was a confident-looking man in his midtwenties. In spite of his youth, he was considered an old-timer, a sergeant, several pay grades above the men he oversaw. What distinguished him further was that he was once a drill instructor. Before receiving orders for a second tour in Vietnam, his job was to prepare ragtag groups of teenagers to be marines. He was looking us over like a coach taking his team to the big game.

If ever there was a group of young men representative of America, it would surely be those who were assembled on that military aircraft. Black, white, Hispanic, Oriental, Jewish, Native American, most cultures were represented. The most noticeable division was between the black and white marines. Those racial tensions exhibited across America were just as strong among the marines on board that plane. The drill instructor's job was to erase those distinctions. The men were trained to think as a cohesive unit. One for all, all for one, as the saying goes.

Sergeant Jones had no problem teaching that, as long as a proud white American like himself was in charge.

The sergeant wasn't a blatant racist, just a third-generation marine who had grown up with stories of the old glory days when diversity was a Catholic and a Protestant sharing a foxhole, and a black marine was a contradiction in terms.

What puzzled the sergeant was the effort the black marines went to distinguish our ethnicity. It was "brother this, brother that," the clenched-fist salute, the elaborate handshake. *Why,* he thought, *do black leaders and liberals push to erase racial distinctions and get blacks the opportunity to be involved? Then we let them in, and they separate themselves.*

Those thoughts were going through his mind as two of the black marines, Ellis and Dura, timidly approached. As recent graduates of the notorious Parris Island Marine Corps boot camp, where drill instructors were both feared and respected, they had never engaged a drill instructor in a casual conversation. "Hey, Sarge," asked Ellis nervously, "what's Okinawa like?"

Knowing he still held the fear factor over the inexperienced marines, the sergeant first gave them a look of disdain; then he proceeded to answer.

"You'll like it there," he said before turning away. "You'll get three meals in the chow hall, a clean place to sleep, and cheap whiskey at the base clubs. Those numb nuts that have money left can go into town and buy pussy. You broke asses gonna keep jacking off and having your wet dreams." Ellis, Dura, and those within earshot let out a loud laugh like kids hearing a dirty joke. Becoming more serious, Ellis then asked, "What about Nam?" Sarge arched forward, speaking like a father admonishing his sons. "If you stay away from drugs and do as your superiors tell you, you just may become decent marines." Then he sat back in his seat, a clear signal he was done with the conversation. Agitated by the attitude of the sergeant, they returned to their seats.

Schultz, the marine sitting next to the sergeant, was of equal rank and experience with those who had walked away, but Sarge reacted to him differently. He felt that with the proper mentoring, Schultz would advance quickly. "You think those black guys will make good marines?" Schultz asked the sergeant.

"Those who learn their place," he replied sarcastically.

"The white man with a gun is what made this country what it is. All this civil rights, antiwar Commie shit pisses me off. Me and my buddies in Missouri would have just nuked those motherfucking gooks in Nam,"

Shultz said, with Sarge nodding in agreement. "But what is Okinawa like, Sarge?"

"Well, Marine," the sergeant proceeded to tell him, "enjoy the break; it will likely be the last time you'll have to relax. You see, the marines use it as a staging area for troops going to Nam."

"Is it a big place?" Schultz asked.

"Okinawa is one of the Ryukyu Islands in the East China Sea, about an eight-hundred-sixty-nine-square-mile area. The Japanese controlled it before World War II, but once we kicked their ass, we took control. That's why we have these military bases here. Now we use it for staging our troops going to Vietnam. We have barracks, military stores, and everything that is on bases in America. Eventually America will give the islands back to the Japanese, but how they gonna survive then? Most of them make a living working on our bases."

"What about Nam?" Shultz asked.

"Stick close to the officers and sergeants," he advised. "Let them know you're a leader, not a follower." They talked for hours with Sarge outlining the dos and don'ts of combat, establishing a clear bond between the men. The conversation was interrupted by an announcement from the plane's captain stating that the plane was about to land in Okinawa.

The sergeant stood in the aisle and commanded the attention of the men. "Listen up," he bellowed, "stay in your seats until we land. When you exit, grab your duffel bags and assemble inside the terminal. We'll get our barracks assignment and transportation. Good luck, men."

The plane landed. Then, as Sergeant Jones had told us, we assembled in a military formation. A lieutenant from the base informed us that we were part of a troop buildup that would be on the island for a few days and then transported to Vietnam. Next we were given barracks assignments. Sergeant Jones, being the senior-ranking noncommissioned officer, was in charge of one of the barracks. Each barrack housed about fifty marines. There were about fifteen African Americans, two Native Americans, and the rest Caucasians in the barrack with Serge. More marines would continue to arrive on a daily basis.

We were assigned to two-man cubicles. When left to the discretion of the men, we would usually pair by racial makeup. At this point I was leaning toward self-isolation. So when Chief, a Native American from Arizona, seemed to be getting left out, I offered to share a cubical with him. It seemed like every Native American was called Chief. I was as ignorant as everyone else, because I never asked his real name. Schultz shared a cubical with Sarge. By the end of that first day, we were totally exhausted. At night the snoring was so loud you would have thought the roof would blow off. Our only concern for now was to remain physically prepared for combat and wait for orders to deploy.

We exercised for one-hour sessions two times a day. When we weren't doing the physical training, we cleaned the barracks and the outside area. Life was good; after 1400, marines were off duty. The base was like a small city. There were stores, or PXs as they are called; a movie theater; a cafeteria; and bars for drinking that had no age restrictions. But there is only a limited amount of freedom on a military base, and the class structure applied to everything. The officers had a club located near the officers' living quarters. The sergeants had the noncommissioned officers' club, and those below the rank of sergeant filled the overcrowded enlisted men's club. By the third day, many began to venture off base. We were required to be back on base by 0600 for roll call. We were young men in a foreign country for the first time, looking for fun and adventure. There was plenty to be found on Okinawa.

When we took the twenty-minute cab ride to the city, it was like we had entered another world. The city had everything a young man could hope for. It didn't matter if they came from the mean streets of New York, the coal mines of Virginia, the suburbs of Wisconsin, the cotton fields of Mississippi, or a farm in Idaho; we were all thrilled and amazed.

There was a slight language barrier, but the Okinawa people knew how to communicate the things marines wanted to know. Everything was set up to accommodate military personnel and to get their money. There were convenience stores that sold liquor, snacks, and souvenirs. There were clothing stores, barber shops, restaurants, and bathhouses where women would offer a private bath. Massage parlors and houses of prostitution, or skivvy houses as they were called, lined every street. The biggest attraction was the many fortune tellers. The fortunes were generally the same. According to them, except for a few superficial wounds, everyone was going to survive the war.

If blacks thought they were escaping racism being so far from home, they were sadly mistaken. Racism was in Okinawa just like in America, The white guys had a secret they kept among themselves. Through a mass of alleyways guarded by tough-talking locals were skivvy houses that only serviced whites. They were much cleaner and had what were considered younger and more attractive women and less police presence. The brothers protested and some tension occurred, but the system was in place, and they felt there was little they could do to change it. To pacify the African Americans on Okinawa, there was another town a short cab ride away that catered to the brothers. It was called Four Corners. The women were slightly past their prime, and skivvy houses were smaller, but it didn't bother the brothers. The clothing stores, music, food, alcoholic beverages, and barber shops were more culturally based. The locals even attempted to dress and talk like they were in the inner city. Brothers from Los Angeles, Chicago, or New York would laugh and reminisce at the sight of an Okinawa prostitute with an Afro wearing a miniskirt. "Step off!" they would say to the brothers, who thought their game was more valuable than money. "You no got money, I no got time!" The brothers accepted the segregation; in fact, the town of Four Corners was a happy compromise.

Two days became two weeks. By now everyone was running out of money and spending more time on base, where food was free and liquor was cheaper. Marines were spending long hours sitting in the barracks smoking reefer and dropping barbiturates and tabs of LSD. The polarization among ethnic groups began to subside.

The men were beginning to socialize, and cross-cultural alliances were starting. From small towns to the big cities, stories and experiences were shared. Soul music, country music, and hard rock filled the air.

Chief and I were avid bid whist players, so our cubical was always filled with bid whist players. Jackson and Hare, from Mississippi and Georgia, respectively, were frequent card players. Mines, the "Chi-Town Brother," as he called himself, was perhaps the best card player. Mines was from the mean streets of Chicago. At twenty-four, he was older than most of the men, bringing some maturity to the group. I would usually hang out with Mines, and we would frequently travel to Four Corners. Mines also made some connection to Sergeant Jones and frequently encouraged him to join in the games. At first the brothers seemed uncomfortable with Sergeant Jones, but over time the barriers came down.

The new marines had many questions for a former drill instructor. They had long suspected drill instructors played mind games on the raw recruits. The sergeant confirmed it. Most came to recognize that the physical and emotional abuse was necessary in boot camp. I might have been the exception. Having been punched in the stomach by a drill instructor in boot camp made it difficult for me to separate the man from the job. But I got over it. I had no choice.

As time passed, the military structure was fading. The men in the barracks were starting to resemble a sports team, complete with a coach, a captain, and key players. But the game for this team was war, and the team was getting eager to get the game started. By the middle of the third week, alliances and loyalties would be put to the test.

The night started routinely. I was playing cards with Mines, Ellis, and Dura, and we were getting thoroughly intoxicated. About ten o'clock, or 2200 hours, Mines decided to go to the Four Corners. The night before, we had been briefly arrested after an altercation with a couple of army personnel. I felt the arrest was racially motivated and vowed not to spend another dime there. Instead I went to the enlisted men's club, hoping for a less eventful evening. Ellis and Dura would leave for the club a few minutes later.

Sergeant Jones was at the enlisted men's club drinking with Schultz and his two companions. A couple of brothers, Hare and Jackson, were also at the club thoroughly intoxicated. The club was full to capacity. Normally the four Okinawan barmaids had no problem keeping patrons supplied with drinks; this night they just couldn't keep up.

To the satisfaction of most customers, country western music was blasting over the loudspeakers. Everyone had to shout just to be heard. Hare and Jones were sitting at one of the many tables, with Schultz and his companions at a table next to them.

Both Hare and Jackson obviously had had too much to drink, but no one could have told them that. Hare called for another round of drinks for him and his friend. Maybe the barmaid couldn't hear him, or maybe she felt he had had enough. Whatever the reason, she didn't respond to his calls. Feeling ignored, he shouted a string of rude comments to get her attention. Jackson laughed and encouraged his friend to be even more belligerent.

Schultz came to the defense of the barmaid and was joined by his friends, who began to threaten Hare. Jackson's laughter had now turned to anger, and words were being exchanged between the two tables. Sergeant Jones, sensing the confrontation building, left the table and called the military police station. Two MPs showed up. After taking Sergeant Jones's statement, they promptly arrested Hare. Jackson erupted in anger when his friend was dragged out in handcuffs and threatened Schultz, challenging him to a fight. The sergeant attempted to defuse the situation to no avail. To his credit, Schultz was attempting to cool things down. But one of the other marines who accompanied Shultz was not going to let it go. Now you had two Mississippi natives with opposing racial pride refusing to back off. The sergeant left, fearing the incident could damage his career. The dispute was to be settled in the alley beside the club.

Starting a racial dispute when thoroughly intoxicated and overwhelmingly outnumbered was not a wise decision on Jackson's part. But his anger and alcohol clouded any sense of reason.

The fight wasn't even close; Jackson was so drunk he would have fallen without a punch being thrown. The crowd was disgusted at the spectacle and urged him to stop. Some of them walked away. Jackson was constantly knocked down, but he would not stay down. He would stumble to his feet, attempt to throw a punch, and go down again. Schultz and his remaining friends were trying to stop the fight by pulling Jackson away. His response was to attempt to punch them. At that point the fight was almost comical, an incident they might have laughed about the next day. But as fate would have it, I was walking past the alley on my way to the club. When I saw a group of marines running out of the alley, I rushed to see what was happening.

It appeared that Schultz and his friends were holding Jackson while he was being pounded on. Seeing this brought back memories of my arrest the night before. I casually walked through the crowd, drawing little attention, and went straight for the marine beating on Jackson. After first taking a fighter's pose, I delivered three blows to his head, sending him backpedaling. As he stumbled to gain his footing, my heel slammed into his nose. Blood shot out as though I had burst a balloon. Whether it was the viciousness of the attack or the sight of blood, the crowd attacked me like a school of piranhas fighting over a meal. Jackson tried to come to my aid but was immediately thrown to the ground.

Fortunately for me, Ellis and Dura arrived on the scene. They came in swinging. Jackson let out a yell that set off a whole series of events. "Race riot," he yelled at the top of his lungs.

Within moments the barroom crowd came rushing out. Responding to Jackson's repeated call, the multicolored group began taking color-coded sides.

Some of the men seemed to be running away in retreat. However, as the crowd began to grow from around twenty to approximately seventy, it was apparent they had gone for help. Sergeant Jones had also broken away from the fray, heading for the military police station. The MPs had underestimated the situation, sending about four MPs to gain control. They found themselves immediately overwhelmed and called for backup.

Fighting spread like a shock wave. The bar was no longer the center of the action but the fringe. Groups of whites were going into the barracks attacking blacks. Groups of blacks were seeking whites to attack. The cross-cultural friendships that had begun to form were shattered. The scene was reminiscent of the riots that were taking place in the large cities in America.

The MPs were now out in full force but were still unable to gain control. They began to separate the crowd into smaller groups. This tactic seemed to be somewhat successful. Dura, Ellis, Johnson, and I, along with about a dozen other black marines, were the most destructive group. The MPs decided to target us. When exiting one of the barracks, we were confronted by a wall of MPs. Dura, the largest and most physically powerful in the group, stepped to the forefront and urged everyone to come out swinging. Ellis stepped forward extending his arms in an attempt to hold the men back.

"Hold it!" he yelled, "Those are all brothers out there." He was right; the first wave of MPs were all black.

"Fuck it!" Dura responded. "Those Uncle Toms can go down too."

"God dammit!" Ellis yelled. "This isn't what this is about. If we fight them, we're just a bunch of niggers beating each other up." Perhaps it was the use of the "N" word that did it. Whatever the case, the crowd stopped. The MPs were still poised to attack. Some of them were edging the brothers on, but the black sergeant in charge stopped them. He approached alone. "I'm glad you brothers are going to back off," he said. "I don't like this no more than you, but you see what's happening. If you guys come at us, we all lose. We can stop this now," he said, "with the least amount of damage." The rioters nodded in agreement. The MP sergeant proposed a solution.

"We are going through the barracks one at a time. The men will be escorted to the barracks they were assigned to. If no one resists, there will be no arrests tonight. I can't guarantee what they will do tomorrow. Pick your fights carefully," he cautioned, walking away and flashing the clenched-fist salute.

After about an hour, everyone was back to their assigned barracks. The overturned bunks were uprighted, trashed property put away, and cuts and bruises attended to. Hard looks were exchanged, but few words. The night held an eerie silence with little sleeping taking place. The men were lying on their bunks consumed in their own thoughts. They were thinking perhaps of the shattered friendships that may never be repaired.

This was particularly troubling to Sergeant Jones, who knew these men would soon depend on one another for survival. Animosity and feuds may cost lives. He also had to come to terms with his biases in the conflict; he was by no means a neutral party, as witnessed by the cuts and burses he had sustained. Men who were normally in awe of him had pounded him to the ground.

Mines returned about 0200, excited and bursting to tell about the riot that had taken place in the city. Everyone, to his surprise, was in their bunks with none of the usual all-night chatter taking place.

"You should have seen it!" he tried to tell me. "The brothers trashed those raciest hoe houses. There was fighting everywhere. Did you hear me?" he tried to tell me. "There was a race riot in the city. Most of the city has been declared off limits!"

He got no reply; I was clearly fighting to restrain my emotions. At that point Ellis entered the cubical. "You're preaching to the choir," he whispered to Mines. Concerned that a riot might restart, he took Mines outside and told him what had taken place on base. "Damn!" you could hear Mines repeat, as Ellis recounted the night's events. In time they returned to the barracks, and Mines showered and then went to bed. To the satisfaction of everyone, he didn't rekindle the emotions.

The next morning we were awakened by the usual reveille. We were assembled to a special formation. Some of us were selectively taken in for interrogation. We would return to the formation with no exchange of thoughts or concocted alibis. It became evident that there was no finger-pointing or informing on one another. The inquisition was eventually dismissed due to lack of riot leaders being named.

However, there were repercussions. The colonel delivered some unexpected news. "So you marines want to fight?" he said. "Well, we are going to give you your chance. Your orders are being processed. Pack your gear. Tomorrow we will begin shipping troops to Vietnam. I am confident you will make your country proud. May God be with you."

True to his word, at 1100 hours the next day, troops boarded the planes for the one-and-a-half-hour flight. "Next stop," Ellis called while going up the ramp of the plane, "Da Nang."

CHAPTER 2

Da Nang
November 1968

▲ ▲ ▲

AN HOUR INTO THE FLIGHT, no one was talking, and I was having a panic attack. I was sweating and squirming in my seat. *Damn it! Damn it! Damn it! I can't believe this shit. I'm actually going to war. I never thought I'd really have to go to Vietnam. Now there is no way around it. We either land in Vietnam or the goddamn ocean. Why should I go? I don't owe this country shit.* Grabbing my armrest, I made a final decision. *I'm not going! They are gonna have to pry my black ass out of this seat.* It only took about five minutes for the restricted blood circulation in my hands to cause me to loosen my grip, along with the idea of resistance. I calmed down for a moment, holding on to the hope that the commanding general would spot me and say, "That marine is special. We are going to keep him at headquarters to do intelligence work."

Why not? I thought to myself. *I'm a fast learner.*

Ellis, who was sitting in the window seat next to me, shifted forward trying to see out of the window, but there was only blue sky above and clouds below. "Oh shit!" he called out. "We may be flying over enemy territory. What if we get shot down? Where do they keep the parachutes? How do you work a parachute? Which way do we go when we hit the ground?"

I looked at him with a condescending smile. "Don't sweat it, brother," I said, as if I were unfazed by the circumstances. "They wouldn't fly over the enemy, and there are civilians on board." I didn't know any more than anyone else, but somebody had to keep a cool head.

The comment brought Dura, who was sitting on my right, into the conversation. "Hey, man," he shouted out, "the airport may not be secure; what if we come under fire? I hear about people getting shot when they first land."

"That's when they land in the bush," Ellis said, taking his turn at sarcasm, "not in a commercial airport."

There were a few more moments of silence. Ellis was the next to speak. "Did you notice that the brothers on Okinawa leaving Nam didn't have many medals?"

"Or rank," I interjected. "Maybe we won't have to do the dangerous shit," I said with a laugh. There was continued silence as the marines again retreated into their own private thoughts.

The clouds were so thick it seemed you could walk on them. Flying above them was a peaceful, heavenly experience. One could dream, fantasize, and recall good times from the past. It was the future, however, that consumed our thoughts. The door to that future would open no matter how much we feared what was on the other side. Everyone knew we were flying over the beast, and soon it would open its mouth and suck us in. The pilot broke the silence with an announcement.

"Gentlemen, fasten your seatbelts. We will arrive in Da Nang in approximately fifteen minutes." The men did as instructed and extinguished their cigarettes. Within five minutes the plane began its descent through the thick clouds. It looked like a rug had been lifted and the dirt underneath was being exposed. It wasn't that Da Nang was an ugly sight. A military installation is not designed to be astatically pleasing.

Da Nang was on a coastline. Flying above, the passengers could see naval gunships, poised for battle. Just inside the coastline was a military installation with a web of airstrips. Beyond that, we could see mountains and jungle terrain. As the plane got closer to the ground, more detail came into focus.

The plane touched down on the runway. Outside, objects were whizzing by. All eyes on board were glued to the small windows, focusing, trying to make out the objects. This was certainly no American airport. There were no colorful advertisements or billboards. Just cumbersome-looking military vehicles painted to look like the surroundings.

As the airplane slowed to a stop, the faces of the people could be distinguished. Everyone was military, even the Vietnamese. Until that moment most of the young marines had only seen the Vietnamese people on television, in newspapers, or in movies. Now the South Vietnamese were all around, alive and in person. "Wow," said Ellis, wide-eyed with his nose pressed to the window, "I wonder what the North Vietnamese will look like?"

The airplane finally came to a rest, and the marines began to disembark. The four stewardesses stood on each side of the aisle. This allowed time to give each man what we needed at that moment, a smile and a reassuring hug as we exited. When stepping off the plane, the tropical heat almost drove us back. It was like an oven door had been opened, and we tried to avoid the initial blast.

We continued down the walkway and then across the runway. The intense heat continued to consume us. Everyone was wet, not damp, soaking wet. Steam was actually rising from the runway. The heat and steam seemed to wrap around us, impeding our movement. Everything seemed to be moving in slow motion.

Servicemen and civilians in the immediate area seemed to stop their activities and stare at the terrified marines as we stared back at them. The people appeared to have blank expressions, as though they were looking straight through us. Then a tough-talking marine staff sergeant pushed his way through the crowd. His uniform was starched, his hair was neatly cropped, and his chest was full of medals.

Speaking with a southern accent, he bellowed out commands. "My name is Staff Sergeant Williams. You will do what I say, when I say it. Go to the cargo hull, pick up your gear, then fall out back here in formation." We complied without responding. While searching through the mountain of duffel bags, we noticed another airplane about fifty yards away obviously waiting for passengers to be taken out of Vietnam.

Soon a convoy of buses arrived carrying the passengers who would board that aircraft. It was obvious this plane was transporting hospital patients. After initial emergency care, they would be transported to a hospital in Germany or the United States for specialized and long-term care. The scene was reminiscent of television news programs. Young men in wheelchairs, most still teenagers, with blank expressions. Others were in hospital beds, unable to sit up, with IV bottles hanging like spider webs. There were men with legs or arms missing. Others were horribly disfigured. The moment was surreal. One of the wheelchair-bound marines was making eye contact, and he was crying. With all of the life-altering physical and mental injuries he had to deal with, he cried for the replacements. He understood that he had survived the life-and-death game, and many of the men whose faces he searched would not.

We were at a loss for words. Finally Dura spoke. "We must be in hell," he said meekly.

"OK, men," the staff sergeant said, "pick up your duffel bags and follow me." We walked in a procession to the awaiting trucks. Each truck held twenty marines and their gear.

It was a rough ride. We were being thrown around when the truck hit the trenches and potholes caused by the torrential rains. It made for a short but eventful ride to the housing unit. The road was like one big mud hole with high spots. The monsoon season created an odd combination of heat and rain, prompting continued complaints and bickering. Climbing out of the truck, Dura commented, "I feel like that truck kicked my ass."

"Quit your bitching," the unsympathetic staff sergeant snapped. "You guys take the top floor," he said, motioning to half the group. "The rest take the lower floor. In one hour everyone assemble in that building to our left."

"Do you mean that one?" responded Dura, pointing to one of the buildings.

Without warning the staff sergeant charged at Dura, yelling at the top of his lungs. "As long as you are in Vietnam," he yelled, voice trembling, "don't you ever point your finger!"

"What was that about?" Ellis whispered.

"I don't know," I replied, "but I won't be pointing my finger." We went into the barracks and stored our gear. Ellis, Dura, Schultz, Mines, many of the marines who shared the barrack on Okinawa, and I were together.

Later at the assembly, another sergeant addressed us. "Listen up, Marines; we have your orders. The names will be read alphabetically; when you receive your orders, you can leave." All of the marines were infantry, riflemen, or grunts, as we were called. The orders would inform us of the unit we were assigned. Once we were at the regimental headquarters, we would be assigned to a company. No one knew one division or regiment from another. We were just looking to see who would be together. Once we were back in our barracks, we compared notes. Ellis, Dura, Schultz, about a dozen other marines, and I were assigned to the First Division, Second Battalion, Fifth Marine Regiment. Mines, Sergeant Jones, Chief, and other marines were assigned another regiment. The rest joined other units.

Sergeant Jones left without comment. Mines stopped to say good-bye. After a brief good-bye, we gave Mines the power handshake. "You brothers take care of yourselves," he said while walking away.

"You too," we replied while giving the raised clenched fist.

Da Nang was the largest city in South Vietnam and the military hub for the allied forces and all branches of the military. Troops were constantly entering and leaving through Da Nang, so the men there represented a broad range of experiences.

First Marine Division, Fifth Marine Regiment, they read on the orders. The three of us spent the day walking around Da Nang looking for anyone with information on our unit.

Soon we encountered a marine with a First Marine Division patch who was a part of the artillery unit. He had been in Vietnam for three months and was en route for R and R.

Our stateside uniforms and attitude, or lack thereof, made it obvious we were just arriving. Sensing our reluctance to approach him, he came over and introduced himself.

"What's you brothers' MOS?" he asked. (MOS stands for Military Occupational Specialty.)

"Oh three one one," we replied simultaneously.

"Damn! All you brothers are grunts?"

We nodded yes.

"You brothers twins?" he said, referring to me and Ellis. This wasn't the first time someone had commented on our physical likeness. Other than eye color, I saw little resemblance.

"Hell no!" we replied with a laugh.

He then looked at the orders we carried. "I see you brothers are in the First. That will put you in the south. The Third Marines operate more up north." That meant nothing to us. "Well," he went on to say, "the North Vietnamese Regulars operate more up north, and the Viet Cong are more in the south. The NVA are soldiers; they're organized and follow orders. The VC are sneaky, hit and run, and set a lot of booby traps."

"I guess I'd rather deal with the VC," I replied.

"Dead is dead," the marine shot back. We were beginning to get into specific questions regarding the experiences we would encounter. The artilleryman stopped them.

"You need to talk to some grunts, not an artilleryman. You especially need to talk to brothers. I'm not going to bullshit you; there're black and white issues here, just like in the world."

"The world," Dura asked with a surprised look. "Where's the world?"

"The world is America," he replied. "Hell would best describe where we are now."

As if on cue, two black marines in jungle uniforms and a cocky attitude were coming down the street. "Those brothers got to be grunts; run it by them," he said, walking away. "Take care of yourselves."

We walked toward them and then hesitated, realizing the approaching marines were handcuffed together. It was an awkward moment followed by a long silence. One of the handcuffed marines broke the silence. "What's up, brothers?" he said while giving the clenched-fist salute. He then eyed the stateside uniforms and continued to speak. "You brothers must have just got here." Stunned by two black men chained together, we were at a loss for words. So we just stood motionless. We did, however, manage to nod.

The two marines were friendly toward us, and heavily drugged. The reefer smoke was so strong you could get a buzz from the secondhand smoke. "You got any drugs?" one of them asked. We three marines were totally confused and convinced that one of them was the police, so no one was going to risk it. Then Ellis, who was usually the most cautious, reached into his pocket and pulled out a joint. The handcuffed marines lit it up and gave the power handshake. They then pulled out a handful of joints, handing them to Ellis. "Try these," one of them said. After a couple joints, Dura got up the nerve to ask, "Why are you brothers handcuffed together?"

They suddenly broke out in laughter. "We were wondering when you were going to ask. I'm going in for court-martial," one of them explained. "My partner is escorting me in." They laughed and gave one another the power handshake.

"It gets me out of the bush," the apparent jailer said. "If you're a grunt, you get out of the bush whenever you can."

"Besides," the prisoner interjected, "I wouldn't try to escape and leave my partner to do my time." Again they exchanged the power handshake.

"Where you brothers assigned?" the jailer asked, changing the conversation.

"First Marines, Second Battalion, Fifth Regiment; we're grunts," Dura answered.

"That figures," the imprisoned marine spoke out.

Ellis spoke up after another awkward silence. "It's good to see some brothers."

"You'll see plenty of us when you get to the bush. That's why they want to lock me up!" The jailer put his hand on the prisoner's shoulder to calm him down and perhaps stop him from discussing his pending case. Changing the conversation again, he filled us in on the drug flow.

"When a grunt gets wounded, takes a prisoner in, goes on R and R, whatever brings you to Da Nang, you pick up some number tens," he said, pulling out a small container of pills. "This can help you sleep on those rare occasions you are able to. Or one oh ones, like this," he said, pulling out a joint. The reefer was prerolled in packages of ten, the diameter of a typical cigarette, only longer.

"Wow," I commented. "How much do they sell for?"

"A dollar a ten pack," the jailer said.

"Wow," we said in unison.

A jeep with MPs was approaching. "We got to go," the jailer said as they headed toward the jeep. Their last words to us were, "Take care of the brothers; we need you in the world." As they rode away in the police vehicle, they gave one last clenched-fist salute, with the hands that were chained together. It was a moment we would later recount.

It was time to go back to the barracks. We needed sleep for the next leg of our journey, the trip to our regimental headquarters, which would start early the next morning.

Most things were blacked out at night in Da Nang so as not to present a target for North Vietnamese artillery. That included the barracks. The men sleeping in the barracks were an interesting mix. There were marine and navy personnel in transit, either going into the country or leaving. It seemed the men were in groups bound by shared experiences.

All incoming marines were very interested in having conversations with the marines who had completed their tours, but the experienced marines seemed devoid of emotion, with no interest in discussing the war, at least not with the men who had not been there. It was like they were in a special club that was not interested in new members.

But when we began to discuss America, the veterans would move closer and listen, smiling for the first time, amazed at the changes that had taken place during their year-long absence. There was one marine pretending to be asleep, but we could tell he was hanging on to every bit of information we shared about America. I had tried to engage him in a conversation when we first met, but it was obvious he wished to be left alone. He did share that he was a grunt rifleman who had served thirteen months in-country, in the Fifth Marines. The same unit we were assigned to. In spite of his experience, he was a private first class, the same rank a marine leaving boot camp would have. The marine only had the basic ribbons and decorations, except for a purple heart, signifying he had been wounded. This was an angry man who chose not to tell his story but did have a quiet dignity that everyone respected.

Soon all the talking ceased, and the men gradually went to sleep. I was self-conscious about my snoring. So I was one of the last to sleep. Soon I realized I wasn't the only one who snored. The room was filled with a symphony of grunts, snores, wheezes, and a varying level of hums. *Hell, they won't hear me anyway,* I thought before dozing off.

At about three in the morning, on our second day in Vietnam, we heard our first sounds of war. Boom, swish, boom, boom, boom, boom! Five explosions came from the runway; beautiful but deadly fireballs lit up the night. The sound was deafening, like listening to thunder while standing on a mountaintop. By the third explosion, most in the barracks were on their feet. The runway was over five hundred yards away, but to the uninitiated, it was combat.

"Incoming!" someone yelled, although it wasn't necessary; everyone was already fighting to get out of one of the two exits. Within seconds the doors were jammed by a rush of men trying to squeeze through the narrow opening. Ellis was among the first to attempt to exit. He made it through the door to the landing of his own volition. By the time he reached the steps, he rode down among the wave of bodies. Our buddy Dura was a part of that force, reaching the ground seconds later. I tried for the window but became concerned that I would be pushed through. So I went for the door.

After I squeezed through the door to the landing, three more artillery shells hit the runway. Unable to get past the panicking men on the steps, I made a hasty decision. "Fuck this!" I called out before leaping over the guardrail. This was a second-story leap and could have been disastrous for me. Fortunately, no one was below, and there was about two feet of mud to cushion the fall. My feet landed and got stuck, causing me to fall forward and land on my hands and face. I was now spitting mud from my mouth, trying to wipe my eyes with muddy hands. Seeing me flopping around, Ellis grabbed me and pulled me into to the bunker.

"Damn, brother," he said, "did you fall out the sky?"

"I took the shortest route." I laughed. Dura arrived equally covered in mud, somehow seeing more humor in my situation. There was a tremendous rush among the men who were taking shelter in the bunker. Their first taste of combat, and the only physical damage occurred while fighting to get to safety. After about five minutes, the all-clear signal was given, and the men returned to the barracks.

The men went to the shower immediately, except for me. The marine who was returning home was still in his bunk. I hesitated, not wanting to disturb him, but was concerned that he might not be alive. I stood there looking for movement; then I moved in to shake him. Before I could, the marine spoke up. "I'm not asleep," he said.

"Did you know there was an artillery attack?" I asked, continuing to wipe the mud away from my face.

The marine turned to face me and laughed after seeing my mud-covered body for the first time.

"They just wanted to damage the runway and shake up the new boots."

"It worked," I laughed.

The experienced marine, for the first time, engaged in a minor conversation. "You're joining the Fifth Marines. This is about as safe as you're going to be for the next year. Enjoy the time. You'll be able to look back on it. If they put you in G Company, look up a brother named Carl. He is a good man. Tell him Joe said to look out for himself. You do the same, brother." He then turned over and went back to sleep.

We showered and then went to sleep. The next day the men went separate directions. The incoming marines assembled on the helicopter landing pad for the marine outpost roughly seventy-five miles northwest of Da Nang. The destination was An Hoa, the company headquarters and the base of operations. We were going deeper into the belly of beast.

CHAPTER 3

Into An Hoa
November 1968

▲ ▲ ▲

THE THIRTY-MINUTE RIDE INTO VIETNAM took us over jungle and flatlands. If there was a danger attached to the helicopter flight into An Hoa, it was overshadowed by the aerial view of the picturesque landscape. We had taken short practice helicopter rides in training, but none could compare with what we were experiencing

The beauty of the landscape was certainly not a part of the inner-city or suburban experience of the passengers, which is perhaps what made it so exciting for us. In the flatlands the farmers cut their rice paddy fields as uniformly as checkerboards. Some had cut the fields in patterns that resembled a mosaic or stained-glass windows. The resourceful farmers had dug trenches from the bomb craters to irrigate sections of the fields. The bomb craters in fact seemed no more out of place than the swimming pools in the backyards of suburban homes.

The pilot avoided dense jungle terrain, but he did fly over clusters of wooded areas. The trees varied so little in height; it appeared they had been trimmed. It was like viewing a garden of the gods.

 Just outside of An Hoa was a South Vietnamese village called Duc Duc. The people who lived there worked on the marine base. It was a rather large village protected by the marines. The village consisted of ramshackle huts and bustled with activity. Any black-market items could be obtained there.

As the helicopter approached An Hoa, our eyes were shocked by the contrast between it and the countryside. The vegetation was scraped to reveal the barren, well-worn ground. The only appearance of vegetation was painted on everything to disguise it or draped over artillery guns and tanks so their positions weren't disclosed. Beauty was cast aside for power.

The five of us assigned to Gulf Company disembarked from the helicopter. The landing zone was at the center of the Fifth Marines regimental headquarters. The layout of the base camp was the shape of a spider web. We landed in the center with signs directing us to specified destinations. We followed the arrow pointing to G Company.

The stateside uniforms made it obvious we were newly arriving "boots." The white T-shirts drew the biggest taunts. The most repeated comment was, "Why don't you just wear a target?" Our terrified expressions didn't help. There may as well have been a neon sign above our heads. Gulf Company had six tents. All but two were empty. We looked into the first tent. Two white marines were in it. Schultz and his friend went in. I went to the last tent with Ellis and Dura, where six marines had been watching us approach.

The three of us stepped in but ventured no further than the doorway. The tent was dark with a sheet that separated the back section. A heavy cloud of marijuana smoke hung overhead. We knew not to venture there unless invited. There were four black and two white marines; all twelve eyes were glaring at us. Although young, they had a look of experience and were obviously annoyed.

The silence was broken by an aggressive brother with a short, to-the-point manner of speech. His introductory words were, "Who the fuck got on that stinking-ass Jade East?" Ellis and Dura seemed relieved they weren't the target of his aggression. They stepped back and looked at me as if they were seeing me for the first time. It was the kind of question that has no easy answer, so I just shrugged my shoulders and gave an apologetic smile. It was also the last time I would wear Jade East or any other aftershave. Those scents would draw flies, mosquitoes, and Viet Cong.

As we walked around looking for a cot, the marines followed our every move. Ellis tried to initiate a conversation, finishing every sentence with a nervous laugh, but we knew they only wanted us to leave so they could continue to get high. We were rushing to get out of the tent, although we had nowhere to go.

Then I remembered I had a carton of Kool cigarettes, or "Looks," as they were called. All the brothers smoked Looks. I pulled out the carton and broke it open. "Anybody want some cig-motes?" I said.

"Yeah, bro," they said in unison. "We ain't had no Looks for boo-koo time." We learned a valuable lesson that would serve us well in the bush: share what you have.

The aggressive brother spoke up; he actually smiled. "You an all right brother," he said, extending his fist for a power handshake. "My name is Carl; I'm from Cleveland, O-H-Ten."

"Me too!" I yelled out.

"You mean your name is Carl?" he said with surprise.

"No," I laughed, "my name is Harris. I'm from Cleveland."

Damn, I thought, *we just met the infamous Corporal Carl, and he is from Cleveland.* One by one the brothers gave the power handshake, followed by the city they represented: Carl, from Cleveland; Marsh, Chicago; Meets, Atlanta;

Carl   Meeks   Louie   RC   Davis

and R. C. Davis, from Detroit. Then there were the white brothers, who had a whole lot of soul. Oaks was from LA and had a twin serving in another part of Nam. The last marine was from Philly.

These marines had seen some serious action. But with the exception of Carl, who had made corporal, they hadn't moved far up the power chain.

Then Carl pulled back the partition leading to the inner sanctuary. Drugs were piled high on the table. African artifacts were everywhere, with the clenched fist the most dominate figure. Posters were displayed of Malcolm, Martin, and Mohamed Ali. Meeks reached down and popped in a tape of combined songs by The Four Tops, The Temptations, the Supremes, and Smokey. There was even semicold beer. This was as close as we'd felt to being in the world since leaving California.

The vets weren't interested in talking about Vietnam. They only wanted to know about what was going on back in the world. "What are the brothers and sisters saying about us? Is there still rioting? What are the sisters wearing? Is Ali still the champ?" The questions were endless. We brought out the smoke we had gotten in Da Nang and then chipped in money so more could be purchased from the Vietnamese the next day. The brothers filled us in on what the company was doing. We also got information on G Company's activities.

The regiment had just finished Operation Mowie Peak. In that operation, they were the assaulting force and had a bloody standoff with the NVA. The numbers of dead and wounded weren't discussed, because even one would have been too many.

Currently they were about a week into Operation Meed River. The battles would take place in an area called Dodge City, about ten miles south of Da Nang. Dodge City was about five miles wide and three miles long. The area was called this because it was a shoot-up area crisscrossed with rivers and streams, with plenty of caves and tunnels. There were also plenty of bamboo and thorn hedges. Our regiment would block. The objective of this operation was to trap the enemy trying to cross the river. The terrain was thick, so the company could only reach the destination by foot. Reinforcements and supplies would have to be flown in by helicopter. So we would have to wait until that was possible, which was fine with us. They were in no rush to combat. In fact, we hadn't been issued the weapons, war gear, or jungle clothing we would need.

The next day was relaxing for all. We were starting to feel at home sitting around the tent enjoying the music and atmosphere. Then on the night of the third day, we heard a sound we would learn to fear. It was a high-pitched double click, the type of sound a child's toy would make. But the look on the bushmen's faces made it obvious that it was not a child's toy. "Those are AKs!" Marsh yelled. "Get down." The return fire from the marines' positions on the perimeter was almost simultaneous. The experienced marines grabbed their weapons and ran toward the perimeter. They were smooth and sober, and they moved as if they were reading one another's minds.

We had no clue what to do. So we began running to the lines with the other riflemen. "Go back!" Carl yelled to us. "You don't have any weapons." Dura stopped suddenly, causing us to run into him. We were running around like the Three Stooges when Carl told us to get our fool asses in the trench and stay down. We crawled to the trench like crabs while Carl continued rushing toward the perimeter. The fighting on the lines only lasted a few minutes, and none of the three of us was willing to stick our head up to assess the situation. It was silent except for a rambling conversation between us.

"What's going on?" Ellis whispered.

"Fuck you; I'm not sticking my head up," I replied.

"What's going on?" he said, turning now to Dura.

"I'm not sticking my head up either," he replied.

"Anybody got a rock or something on them?" I asked.

"What the fuck is a rock gonna do?" they shouted back.

We were so involved in conversation that we didn't notice the marines standing above the trench. "What the hell you dudes talking about?" they heard Carl say.

"Come over here," RC called to Marsh. "Check out our replacements." There was more laughter and sarcastic remarks as they walked back to the barracks. It seemed to bring comic relief to the situation.

"What happened out there?" I asked RC.

"The VC tried to get through the lines."

"Did any get in?"

"No, but they always try. The men guarding the lines usually stop them. We move up just in case someone does get through."

Once back at the barracks, Carl began to share some wisdom with us. The three of us hung on to every word. "The thing I like about you brothers is that you stick together. That's going to mean a lot when you get to the bush." There was a long pause in the conversation. Carl composed himself and then continued. "I had a partner, and we hung together from day one." Ellis and I glanced at each other, remembering that we had met in the induction center. "Little Joe," Carl said with a broad smile. "There will only be one Little Joe. About a week ago, a sniper got him with one shot. Damn," he continued while lowering his head, "just like that. One second and everything can be changed. What I'm saying to you is in the bush, friendship is all you'll have, but it can come at a heavy price."

Seeing that the veterans were uncomfortable talking about deceased friends, I changed the subject. "Do the Viet Cong try to get into the camp often?"

"Maybe once a week," RC answered. "Sometimes they fire a few mortar rounds."

"How are they stopped?"

"The parameter is surrounded by five feet of barbed wire. On this side of the barbed wire, marines are on guard. They set up two-man positions about twenty-five feet apart."

"The same ones all the time?" I asked.

"No, whoever happens to be on base. It could be supply, motor transport, artillery, marines in transit, or a company between operations."

"Oh, that is why the pop-ups."

"Yeah, that illuminates the area. Everything is blacked out so they can't get a fix with their artillery. Always be aware of the location of the trenches. When the shit hits, that's where you go."

With that, we drifted off to sleep. The second day in-country had come to an end.

The next morning a sergeant from the supply unit woke us up and then took us to pick up our gear. On the way to the supply tent, the supply sergeant informed us that three dead Viet Cong had been pulled out of the barbed wire. "It's a good thing you guys didn't have your war gear last night," he said. "You may have been closer than you wanted to be."

Once at the supply tent, we were issued the items we would need for the bush.

Personal items were toothpaste, soap, a toothbrush, a comb, needle and thread, candy, C rations, a pencil and paper, envelopes, cortisone tablets, cigarettes, and a first-aid kit.

Clothing was two pairs of green socks, two green T-shirts, a green towel, green shorts, a camouflage bush cover, two camouflage uniforms, jungle boots, a flak jacket, a helmet, and a helmet liner.

Comfort items were a poncho liner, a rubber lady, and a backpack.

The utility items were a Ka-Bar, a machete, an E tool, rifle cleaning equipment, a canteen, a canteen liner, and heat tablets.

Then there were the defensive weapons and equipment, trip flares, and two claymore mines.

Last but not least, we got the offensive weapons. That consisted of an M16 rifle, four hundred rounds of ammo, forty magazines, one rocket launcher (LAW), and six grenades. We were now ready to do battle.

Our assigned unit, G Company, was ready for us. The company had completed the first part of their objective, which was to reach Meed River. They could now be supplied and take on replacement troops. We were the replacements.

Before leaving, we stopped to see our new friends and to say good-bye. Although most marines returning home had all been wounded at least once, the fact they had survived was encouraging to us.

"Here," RC said, handing Dura a ten pack. "Take this with you. Our hookup," he explained, "was one of the dead VC pulled out of the barbed wire, so we couldn't get a bigger supply."

"Take care of yourselves," the vets again reminded us. "We'll see you back in the world."

We five replacements packed our gear and assembled at the helicopter pad. After three days in-country, we were about to see the bush.

CHAPTER 4

Meed River
November 1968

▲ ▲ ▲

THE HELICOPTER TRANSPORTING US TO the bush was the same type that had transported us to An Hoa. However, as evidenced by the demeanor of the flight crew, the danger level was increasing. The pilot constantly communicated with ground troops, while the machine gunners' eyes searched intently for a target. This was not a routine flight with a familiar destination. We were now a vulnerable target.

We were also scanning the ground below. "What you looking for?" Dura asked.

"The goddamn enemy!" Ellis shouted back.

"Not me," I interjected, "I'm looking to see which way to go to get back to An Hoa if we get shot down."

While An Hoa was easily identifiable from the air, the jungle revealed few distinguishing landmarks. The terrain was so thick that the only way people would be seen was if they wanted it that way.

The view from the air was breathtaking. The seven-foot elephant grass and tropical growth looked like a still painting you might find in a prestigious art gallery. As the helicopter began its decent, the grass began to swerve the way seaweed does in shallow water.

At first we were hesitant to exit the helicopter, seeing no signs of human activity. Then, at the moment the helicopter touched ground, marines in camouflaged uniforms appeared from the jungle, swarming the vehicle like ants after crumbs at a picnic. They eagerly unloaded the supplies that were on board, ignoring the new replacements.

Next to appear from the surrounding jungle were the men in charge. They immediately let their authority be known. First was the company's gunnery sergeant, a stout Hawaiian with the standard loud voice. Flanking him were two Caucasian staff sergeants waiting to show their authority.

"Get your motherfucking asses over here!" yelled the gunnery sergeant. "You dipshits are replacements for Second Platoon. You and you," he said, pointing to Ellis and one of the other marines, "go to First Squad. You and you," he continued, signaling to me and Dura, "go to Second Squad." Schultz, the remaining replacement, went to Third Squad. The two staff sergeants proceeded to rant and rave the standard "you are a worthless piece of shit, I'll kick your ass if you fuck up, and you better do as you're told" rhetoric.

The gunnery sergeant, not wanting to be outdone, proceeded with more intimidation. Somewhere in the cursing and insults, the men were told the dos and don'ts of bush life. Everything could have been put into one statement: "Do as you're told."

He then asked if there were any questions, as if he expected an answer. "Wait here for your squad leaders," he said in conclusion.

We did exactly as told. Our feet never left their original spot. "I wonder why they are so pissed off?" whispered Dura.

"I don't know," I responded. "We might as well change our names to Motherfucker." The group shared a nervous laugh.

Then the two marines who had first unloaded the supplies approached. The body odor of the bushmen was getting progressively worse. You could almost see it. They were of closer rank with us, so the conversation was more cordial. They were black marines and directed their comments more to Ellis, Dura, and me. "My name is Louie," said the short, stocky marine. "I'm from Philly."

"I'm Holmes. My home is Alabama," said the chubby, taller marine. They then exchanged the power handshake. Both seemed extremely high. Holmes perhaps more so. "Where you from?" he asked.

"I'm Harris from Cleveland, OH-Ten," I called out.

"Ellis from Youngstown, OH-Ten. That's the city in the middle of Ohio. Round on both ends and high in the middle, and I'm from the middle."

"Are you two brothers?" asked Louie.

"Hell no!" responded Ellis with a laugh.

"Well, my name is Dura, and I'm from Atlanta, George I-A, and I keep that road show in line," Dura added, pointing to us.

"What is happening in the world?" asked Holmes, eager for news. The three of us again told of the riots, protests, music, and clothing styles in America. As usual the bushmen listened, hanging on to every word.

When that subject seemed exhausted, Louie asked, "Who is in Second Squad?" Ellis and I raised our hands. "Watch out for that squad leader," warned Louie. "He kicks his people's ass. So don't fuck up."

I was bothered by that, so I pushed for more information.

"Why would this brother go around kicking his own people's asses?" I asked.

"Well," Louie continued, "he's a good man, but he lost a lot of his close friends. Speedy, Little Joe, and Carl were tight."

"Yeah, I heard about Little Joe," I said.

"Where you hear about Little Joe?"

"From Carl, we saw him in An Hoa."

"Carl left a few days ago with Oats and Meeks. I was hoping the brothers were on the way to the world by now."

"Well, they are in An Hoa, so they should be OK," I assured him.

"People die in An Hoa too," Louie responded angrily. "You're not safe until you leave the country."

Feeling I was provoking some irritation from Louie, I backed off. Ellis was still interested in hearing more about Carl and Speedy, so he picked up the questions from there.

"How come Carl didn't make sergeant?" Ellis asked. "He seemed like he knew his shit."

"He did," answered Louie, "but that don't necessarily move you up. You got to blindly follow the lifers. Carl was a tough street brother who tried to keep marines alive. He as well as Speedy would kick your ass if it kept you straight. The lifers liked that. But then they fucked him over," Louie said sadly.

"How?" I asked.

"He had a lady in Cleveland that he always talked about, the mother of his daughter. The brother regretted not marrying her before leaving, but he was going to hook up when he got back. That sister kept him alive. Then she was in an automobile accident. She hung on for a while, probably waiting to see him. But since they weren't married, he couldn't get a leave. The news tore him up, but not being able to see her almost drove him over."

"What did he do?" I asked after a pause. Then Louie responded.

"He got a 'fuck the Marine Corps' attitude. The lifers didn't like it. They think the corps comes before anything. But fucking with Carl wasn't a smart move. Win or lose, you gonna get a fight. So they took away his authority and kept sending him up front. Carl didn't give a fuck, and the bushmen respected him for that. Little Joe got salty too. You fuck with his partner, you fuck with him. So they sent him out front too; he was killed on point."

"What about Speedy?"

"He took it different," Louie said. "He don't want to see more people die. The brother just became mean."

At that moment, three other marines were approaching. "You are about to meet your squad leaders. Good luck," Louie said in closing.

The first to speak was a tall, blond marine of German descent. He was an athletic type with his bush cover blocked like a cowboy hat, and he spoke with confidence and authority. "I'm Corporal Snarr," he said like a quarterback to fellow team members. "Who is in Third Squad?"

Schultz stepped forward. "That would be me." They exchanged smiles and then walked off together.

Then a short, stocky black marine with a Louie Armstrong–type grin spoke up. "I'm Lance Corporal Rhone," he said with a southern accent. "Who gets to be in my squad?"

His comic demeanor eased the tension. Ellis and the other quiet replacement seemed happy to announce they were to be in his squad. "Let's go," he said to the two marines. Ellis looked over his shoulder at his remaining friends with a relieved expression.

Then there was an eerie silence. The remaining stocky, hostile-looking marine circled the last replacements. He looked us over like a mugger in a subway station. We knew who he was. His next sentence confirmed it. "My name is Corporal Washington. My friends call me Speedy. You call me Corporal Washington."

"Yes, sir," Dura and I said in unison.

"You do as I say, you might stay alive. You don't, and we might be hauling your ass out in a body bag. Any questions?"

"No, sir!"

"You give me a hard time, I'll kick your ass."

"Yes, sir!"

"That's right; I'll kick a motherfucker's ass no matter who he is. Any questions?"

"No, sir!"

"Come on," he said, walking in front of us.

Dura and I followed like children following an abusive parent. Occasionally we would glance at each other and mock Washington's demeanor, being careful not to let him see us doing it.

Washington led us down a trail for about three hundred yards from where the helicopter had dropped us off to a riverbank. The jungle was very thick, and we had to constantly brush the vegetation and tree limbs aside. "This," Washington said, motioning toward the river, "is Meed River." For the first time, we were meeting our fellow squad members.

There were other battalions and regiments involved in the operation, and each had a specific role. All replacements were being informed of their roles and the strategy of the operation.

Foxholes about four feet in diameter and four feet deep were dug along the riverbank about fifteen feet apart. Two men shared each foxhole. Replacements would have to dig our own foxholes.

The squads were stretched out along the riverbank. At the backs of the positions along the riverbank were the positions of the platoon sergeants and platoon commander. They made up the command post. A small force surrounded the command position. The entire company was there to block the enemy from crossing the river.

On the other side of the river, H Company and other companies from the regiment were acting as the assaulting force. For two days they had been locked in a fierce battle with a company of North Vietnamese regulars who were now being pushed toward Meed River. The river was only about seventy-five yards across at its widest point. The enemy was being forced to stay and fight or get past the companies acting as the blocking force. A showdown was inevitable.

The North Vietnamese were sending out recon patrols. They would fire across the river probing for an unprotected spot. We were warned to always be on alert.

We picked out a spot for ourselves and began to dig foxholes. As we began to dig, a message came over the radio alerting the company of an approaching supply helicopter bringing fresh water. Each platoon was to send a work crew to pick up their water rations. As the newest members, we were given the task. I had the unfortunate distinction to be the first from the group to break the cardinal rule in the bush: never leave your weapon. Feeling it would be easier to carry the ten-gallon water cans without my weapon, I left it behind. As we were walking away, a Communist weapon began firing in our direction.

Whether ascending or descending, helicopters make a tempting target for snipers.

Experienced combat veterans are accustomed to this and generally show little reaction. New replacements, however, will generally panic. Everyone but me immediately dropped their water cans and ran for cover. I was not encumbered by a weapon, so I managed to run a few yards further but eventually dropped my cans and ran for my foxhole.

But there was no foxhole available, because I hadn't dug it. Frantic to get my body below ground, I tried to jump into my squad leader's position. That didn't go over well with Speedy. "What the hell you doing over here!" he yelled. "And where is your weapon?" I glanced at my weapon sitting about thirty yards away. "Get the fuck out of here!" Speedy yelled.

Everyone at that point was convinced the sniper was long gone. Everyone, that is, but me. I dropped, rolled, bobbed, and weaved, dodging imaginary bullets all the way to my weapon. Once I got it, I realized the other marines were looking and laughing at me. I continued digging my foxhole pretending I wasn't bothered. The episode would, however, be rehashed many times. We had survived the first day unharmed. The night would provide an awesome air show.

The assaulting forces had boxed in the enemy, so the night would belong to the navy and air-force pilots. From dusk to dawn they would pound the supposedly trapped enemy. The awesome power at the Americans' disposal would be demonstrated.

First the B-52 pilots dropped their deadly one-thousand-pound bombs. It was like it was like a pattern of thunder. The concussion from each blast nearly lifted the men out of their foxholes. They were so jarred by the blast that their joints began to ache.

Next it was "Puff's" turn. The name comes from the children's story about Puff the Magic Dragon. It's actually a high-flying attack helicopter with attached machine-gun turrets capable of firing over four thousand rounds per minute. It has the ability to cover every square inch of a football field with one round in less than two minutes. Ducking such a volley of bullets would be like avoiding water in a rainstorm. Many have described it as a roaring eagle pissing fire.

The fear provoked by Puff and the B-52s could only be matched by the napalm bombs that struck the final blow. Napalm, a liquid fire, could cut corners and flow into holes that might shelter a fleeing victim.

The relentless air attack finally stopped in the early morning hours. Those who thought the enemy was done were in for a rude awakening. They had only been pushed closer to the river. The NVA made their presence known when pockets of them fired across the river. The marines held their fire, waiting for orders. Again and again the NVA would fire across the river, still no response from the marines.

Then the gunnery sergeant gave the order: "Open fire!" The marines opened up with every bit of small arms fire at their disposal. Perhaps it was the suddenness of the burst of gunfire, or maybe just a nervous reaction, but Dura went into the foxhole we shared headfirst like an ostrich burying his head. "What the hell you doing down there!" I laughed.

"I'm looking for my knife. I'm gonna stab them motherfuckers if they try to cross," responded an embarrassed Dura.

"Man, get up here!" I said, pulling my frightened friend up. It took a few seconds, but Dura got through the moment. The sound was deadening, and the smell of gunpowder made it difficult to breathe. Those brave enough to expose their arm above ground would throw a grenade. New marines were squealing with joy, enjoying every minute. What a story this would make when we got home.

Then with the same suddenness with which it started, the firing stopped when the order to cease fire was given. The men were breathing heavily but remained quiet. Dura and I would look at each other and grin, like children spying at Christmas. "There must be some dead bodies over there," Dura whispered, with me nodding in agreement. The remaining hours of darkness were silent. We would have to wait for daylight to confirm the causalities.

The next morning Rhone, the leader of First Squad, came along with his men on the way out on patrol. Ellis showed both excitement and fear as he passed on his first patrol. They would have the gruesome task of surveying the damage. The marines were dug into positions and suffered few causalities. The marines in G Company experienced only superficial lacerations, most of which were incurred while scrambling for cover.

Second Squad would spend the day cleaning our weapons. Finally we were going to meet and interact with the other squad members.

Dura and I were sitting in our foxholes cleaning our weapons when some of the other squad members approached. We were in the same squad, but Speedy had assigned us to different fire teams. Walters, a thin white guy from a small town in Indiana, was my team leader. Perrish, whom we had met in An Hoa, was Dura's leader. The two of them were accompanied by Johnson, a black marine from Detroit. All the squad members with the exception of Speedy and Walters had all been in-country about one or two months.

CHAPTER 5

"The Hunter" Walters
December 1968

▲ ▲ ▲

WALTERS, WHO HAD BEEN REARED in a small town in Indiana, couldn't help but notice that most of the new people coming in were black.

Walters came over to introduce himself.

"My name is Walters. How you guys doing?"

"OK," Dura and I answered.

"How long you brothers been in Vietnam?"

"About a week."

"You came at a good time. Things have been calm for a few days. Shit, I ain't killed nobody in over a week," he said with a sly grin.

"We saw some shit last night," Dura added.

"That wasn't shit!" Johnson interjected in a condescending tone. "That was like shooting fish in a bowl. I was in more danger going to school in Motown. I hear you're from Cleveland," he said to me. "That's a good place to be from, not a place to go." I smiled. That smile brought a puzzling outburst from Perrish.

"You motherfuckers seem to think this shit is fun. Well, it ain't. You ever killed anybody?" he said, looking at us.

"No," we said, looking at each other.

"When you do, then you can smile about it."

Walters brought an end to the interrogation choosing to unify us on common ground. He told Johnson to bring out the Motown sounds; then he told Perrish check to see if any lifers were around and the direction of the wind. Concluding the wind was blowing away from the command post, he broke out a ten pack of 101s. While we cleaned our weapons, he explained how to track the enemy.

"I love to hunt man. Growing up, that's what I lived for. War seemed to be an extension of that hobby. If you can sneak up on an animal, you can sneak up on a man." For Dura and me, this was the first time someone was actually relaying practical combat skills. The men listened intently as Walters explained tracking, cover, shadows, and wind direction. As Walters talked, he prepared to dissemble his weapon for cleaning. "Damn, there is a round stuck in the chamber of my weapon!" he shouted out. "I can't get it dislodged." Walters pointed the weapon toward the sky and struck the rifle butt with a hard blow. The hammer slammed down on the cartridge, causing the weapon to fire. Everyone was startled and looked around frantically to see if anyone had been hit. Fortunately everyone was all right. "Oh shit. I fucked up," he said with a frightened expression.

Speedy came running over to the men, looking them over to see if anyone was injured. Seeing they were OK, he demanded to know what had happened. Walters looked him with embarrassment and fear. "I struck my weapon, and it accidentally discharged. I should have checked to see if it was on safe."

Without warning, Speedy struck Walters on the left side of the face. The blow was thrown with such force that it sent Walters stumbling backward. Walters attempted to regain his balance, but he was being so savagely beaten that he lost consciousness. This didn't deter Speedy. He was now kicking and stomping him. Finally, he stopped as abruptly as he had started.

Turning defiantly to the men, he offered a challenge to anyone who chose to get involved. "Mistakes like that get people killed!" he shouted to the men. "I don't want to tell your family members you were killed because of someone's stupidity." With that, he turned and walked away. The men were left standing, mouths open, with shocked expressions.

We all showed compassion and offered first aid. Walters remained dazed for a few minutes, bleeding profusely from the mouth. We all knew why Speedy had done what he did, but he should have respected his team leader enough not to do it in front of his men. He clearly wanted to send a message to all that he was a man to be feared.

None, including Walters, condemned Speedy for the attack. Everyone seemed to share an unspoken agreement that carelessness could not be tolerated. We acted as if nothing had taken place. As the evening progressed, the men returned to their own foxholes, leaving Dura and me in our position.

Near the end of the day, First Squad returned. Ellis ran to our position to tell us about the patrol.

"Man, there was ten bodies over there. Some were shot so many times their clothes were torn off. I know some of those bullets were mine," he said, smiling.

"Did you see any burned-up or blown-up bodies?" asked Dura.

"No, they were further out. First and Third searched there."

"What did you guys do with the bodies?"

"A chopper came in to medevac them."

"Well, what took so long?"

"We chased blood trails. It was some ugly shit."

The three of us continued to talk until the sun began to set. Ellis was now the most experienced of the three, and he relished the attention. That night Speedy sent a listening post out to guard the rear of the platoon's position. He decided Walters would share the position with Dura. There was speculation that the enemy would circle around and attempt another approach.

"Dura," Walters said, going over to him, "Speedy wants us to share a position in the rear. We will sit, conceal ourselves, and listen for any enemy movement. These posts are going to be spread further apart, so we won't see any of the other marines. Let's head out." Dura was very nervous sharing a lone position with Walters, perhaps concerned about Walters's ability after seeing what Speedy had done to him. But it didn't take long for his confidence in Walters to surface. Walters's skill was evident in the way he camouflaged their position, making no alterations to the surroundings. Dura could hardly see Walters, and he was standing next to him.

They took two-hour shifts, with Dura being on guard around 0200 while Walters slept. The silence was broken by a call from the distance.

"Help."

Dura listened intently, not sure if he had heard correctly. Five minutes later, a call again came from the distance.

"Please help me."

Dura reached over to the sleeping Walters, touching him gently on the shoulder. Walters's eyes opened immediately. "Listen," Dura whispered. "I think I heard something." It was pitch-black in thick jungle terrain, so the visibility was only a few feet. Five, ten, fifteen minutes passed with no sound. Then a voice called again.

"I need help, please."

Quickly, Dura turned to Walters, sure he had heard the call. Walters had gone back to sleep. Again, Dura nudged him. "Did you hear it that time? I think a marine is out there." Again they remained silent and listened. Dura continued to look at Walters, making certain he didn't go back to sleep.

"Help me."

This time Dura was certain Walters heard the call.

Slowly, Walters leaned closer to Dura, whispering into his ear. "That's Viet Cong. They are trying to find where we are."

Dura was petrified with fear.

"Don't take the safety off your weapon, but put your finger on the trigger and be ready." There was no radio at their position, so they couldn't make contact with other marines. Therefore they remained silent. The hours before daybreak were long and terrifying. Dura gained a great deal of respect for Walters that night, as Walters remained totally calm while listening to the distant calls.

At daybreak, Perrish and I came out to escort Walters and Dura back to the lines.

"Did they try to rattle you?" Perrish asked sarcastically.

"Yeah," responded Walters. "I hope I can get some sleep later." The experienced marines seemed to take the encounter in stride, but Dura felt uneasy with the enemy having been that close.

When he returned to his position, he was noticeably silent, except for an expression of admiration for the enemy's courage.

I was becoming anxious, because now I was the only one who had nothing interesting to relate. So when Speedy returned with a planned mission for the squad, I wanted to take part in it. But Walers wouldn't have it. They were sure to engage in enemy contact, and it's impossible to predict how a person will react in his first small arms engagement. He just didn't want me or any other inexperienced marine to come along.

Speedy gathered the men for a briefing.

"Second Platoon from E Company had engaged a squad of NVA," he explained. The marines had overpowered them, causing them to take flight. The NVA had no choice but to try to cross the river. The most likely point of crossing was a bend in the river where it narrowed to about forty yards across. This was the river's shallowest point, perhaps waist-deep. The men looked at the map, but it wasn't necessary. The spot was only about a half mile from our current position, and they knew the area well. It was imperative that they reach the position first before the enemy, so they saddled up immediately. Walters didn't want me along, so he pulled Speedy aside to talk.

"Speedy, you shouldn't take Harris," he implored him. "There is gonna be some shit, and Harris isn't ready." Speedy seemed to resent interference, but he respected Walters's opinion. But after some thought, he made a decision. "I need to see how he handles fire," he finally said. "He's going." I was beaming with excitement. We gathered our weapons and went toward the ambush site. If the NVA had gotten across before we could stop them, we would be the ones ambushed.

The squad reached the position without incident. Speedy quickly assessed the situation and positioned the men. I was given the most secure position, a culvert that offered both cover and concealment. Walters was positioned at the furthest point, with Perrish, Johnson, and another marine concealed along the river. Speedy positioned himself in a tree, giving him the high round. "We want as many of them in the water as possible," he stressed. "They will have no cover while in the river, so no one fires until I

Expendable and Necessary

do." The men nodded an acknowledgment, took one last deep breath, and then settled in for the wait.

Except for me, the ambush was routine for this marine unit. I was regretting having come. Ambushing an experienced, well-armed opponent requires patience, self-discipline, confidence, and tenacity. All the attributes that come from experience. Something I totally lacked. I was quickly reaching a state of panic.

This was nothing like I thought it would be. Lying on my back, the only thing I could see was the sky above me. And the only sounds were the rushing water a few feet away. Each second seemed like a minute; each minute was like ten. After about ten minutes, I felt we had been there an hour. I could only imagine what was happening. Soon I was overwhelmed by my imagination. Thoughts were flashing through my head.

Had the enemy gotten to the river before us and systematically killed the others?

Had the marines run off and left me?

Had I fallen asleep and not heard Speedy give the order to retreat? Soon I realized I had not taken the time to get a thorough visualization of the area.

Was the enemy to my front or back?

Where were the other marines?

Suddenly the silence was broken by a hushed but much-anticipated announcement from Speedy. "Here they come. Stand by."

I was in panic before; now I was off the chart. I could hear the approaching enemy sloshing through the water. I stared at the clouds and shook violently, anticipating the enemy to be standing over me any second. Again the questions ran through his mind.

Was the enemy running across the river or slowly wading across?

How many were they?

What kind of weapons were they carrying?

It's me against the world, I thought, *and I'm not going down easy.*

I slung the barrel of my weapon over the embankment and fired three shots. There was the sound of men scrambling. Obviously they were running to get out of the water. Then came more silence. After about a minute, I slowly raised my head over the embankment like a mouse peeking out of a hole. I was hoping to see dead NVA soldiers, but that was not to be. There was nothing, only continued silence.

Speedy broke the silence. "Who the fuck blew the ambush?"

Oh shit, Walters thought, *Speedy is going to kick Harris's ass.* He rushed over to stop him. "Give him a break, Speedy. You know he wasn't ready."

Speedy seemed to calm down. Reluctantly, I answered, "I panicked, man. I'm sorry it happened, but I panicked." At that point I was standing, slowly circling Speedy. I didn't want to be a stationary target.

"I should kick your ass," Speedy said sternly. I relaxed somewhat hearing the word *should*. To everyone's surprise, Speedy backed off, ordering the men to pack up and return to the base camp.

Once the men returned, as was protocol, the squad leader would report to the captain upon returning from an ambush. Hoping to avoid a future confrontation with Speedy, I attempted to bring some resolution to the incident. "Look, man," I said, "I know it won't end this simply. You want me to do some push-ups, guard duty, a work detail, or something?"

Speedy hesitated a moment, knowing he was about to be interrogated by the lifers and needed to save face. He reached down and picked up a three-ounce peanut-butter can and tossed it to me. "Dip the water out of that bomb crater," he said, motioning to a hole about one foot deep and four feet in diameter. I knelt down and proceeded to dip out the hole. Other marines would walk by and tease me. I would smile and remark, "Speedy don't take no shit." The punishment seemed to appease everyone, and the incident was allowed to pass.

CHAPTER 6

The Pointer
December 1968

▲ ▲ ▲

THE MAJORITY OF THE FIFTH Marine Regiment was searching the area for the elusive NVA regiment. Elements of the NVA regiment would attack and then vanish. Golf Company, as a blocking force, spent a great deal of time guarding the defensive line. The next week was routine. The men were spending a lot time talking.

The heat was so overpowering that it seemed to restrict movement, with sanitation almost nonexistent. The river was stagnating in most places, and bathing in it made the body odor even more offensive. Flies and mosquitoes seemed to be drawn to our bodies as if sugar had been poured over us. Despite the discomfort, we enjoyed the relaxed time.

Joe Perrish continued with his war stories, always making himself the central figure. He would also stress his preference for hanging with the brothers. "Yes," he would say with pride, "I did hang with the chucks, but they don't party. The brothers like to do the drugs and screw the sick little girls."

"What!" I shouted, taking offense at the comment.

"That's what the Vietnamese call the prostitutes," laughed Johnson, while turning down his music. Johnson then went on to explain key terms every bushman needed to know: boo-koo, tee-tee, dee-dee, dee-dee-mow, mama-san, papa-san, and baby-san. Soon the language was familiar.

Walters began to give perhaps the most useful information needed in the bush, how to hunt and track. His skills as a hunter were useful at the task at hand: patience, persistence, and understanding the prey, all the attributes needed in combat.

"Yeah," injected Perrish, "my thing is pointing. That's where you need real skill.

"I'm getting sick of hearing your bullshit," Johnson snapped at Perrish. "These brothers need to know straight scoop. The truth is your ass ain't seen shit, so let it go." Perrish was upset, and it seemed a fight was about to ensue.

"Your ass got here after I did, and since then your nose has been so far up the lieutenant's butt, we hardly see you," he shouted at Johnson.

"That's because I got a plan."

"What fucking plan?"

"A plan to move up and stay alive."

"If kissing ass is your plan, then you're good at it. I just thought a brother from Detroit had more pride."

"A brother from Detroit knows how to stay alive."

Walters stepped in to put a stop to the confrontation before it escalated to a fistfight. "Why don't you go back to your squad," he said to Johnson.

Speedy then approached the group, having just left a meeting with Lieutenant Hannahan, the platoon commander. "Listen up," he said sternly. "The company is going to be flown out a few clicks south so they can search for a NVA regiment. Second Platoon is the point platoon. Our squad is the point squad." Speedy then took Walters aside for a private meeting. Walters's team would point for the company, and they were deciding who the pointer would be. As they talked, they were looking over at the team members. Perish, Ellis, Holmes, and I made up the first fire team. One member of the team would have to point, and we all hoped it wouldn't be us. Speedy decided it would be Ellis and me.

Walters came back with the news. "It's time for you brothers to show what you have," he said, looking at us. "Harris and Ellis are gonna be out front." We were in shock. Why, we thought, would they put two people who had never been directly shot at in a position where it was sure to happen? It was our hope that it was because they didn't expect enemy contact. In any event, we listened intently for more information from Walters.

"Listen up," he said. "We will travel light. The fight is expected to be short and decisive. A recon plane spotted what they believe to be a NVA platoon. We will find them and take them out. The birds are on the way to fly us out. When they drop us off, our fire team will go in first. Harris, you'll take point. Ellis, you're second in line. Every fifteen minutes or so, the two of you will rotate duties. I'll be behind you, then Speedy with the radioman. The rest of the squad will be behind us, and Second Platoon will follow. The command post will be next with the machine-gun and mortar section. The remainder of the company will be after them. Are there any questions?" There were plenty, but the key players, Ellis and I, didn't know what to ask. So without further discussion, we collected our gear and rushed to the rally point. The transportation helicopters were appearing on the horizon.

On the ride out, we were continuing to glance at one another with an uneasy look. Our expression, in a word, would perhaps be fear. When the helicopter landed, the marines piled out. The jungle was thick, with visibility being only about twenty yards. Walters gave the final instructions.

"Harris, take off in that direction, and keep a fast pace. The enemy knows we are here, so we have to confront them as quickly as possible. Glance behind you from time to time; I'll be giving instructions to Ellis. He'll tell you when to switch and when to change directions. As thick as the terrain is, you probably won't have contact with anyone but me. Just remember, there is a company of experienced combat marines behind you." He reached out and grabbed my arm firmly. "Pay attention to what is going on around you. There may be an ambush. Now move out!"

An experienced and competent pointer is invaluable to a patrol. They are the eyes and ears and serve as an early warning for the men who follow. An inexperienced pointer can be disastrous to the patrol. If they fire without provocation, they will expose the patrol, giving up any element of surprise they may have had. If they fire randomly, they might hit their own people.

I had to recall the lessons that were told to me.

The point position, whether on a patrol, ambush, or kill team, is a respected but highly volatile position in the formation. He is the "lead dog." When an ambush is sprung, the pointer is the prime target. In most cases, he will be dead never knowing he was attacked.

The pointer has no friendly forces to his front. Therefore, he is the only person on the patrol whose weapon is unlocked. He has a 180-degree killing zone. That means he can shoot to kill anything he perceives as a target. If ever there was a dead man walking, it's the pointer.

When on point, the jungle, though teaming with life, can be a lonely place. All of your support is behind you. A backward glance will divert your attention. So it must be done quickly and deliberately. You can't allow anything to escape your attention.

As told to do, I followed the major trail. The Viet Cong would booby-trap the roads that a patrol would likely follow, so I would carefully avoid any debris or objects I passed. I did notice the trail had what looked like small paths leading off of it. Like a centipede with hairlike legs running from its sides.

I was ordered to move quickly so enemy could be surprised. But the small paths were troubling to me. I stopped and motioned for Ellis to move up.

"Something doesn't look right," I whispered to Ellis when he approached. "See if we should check it out."

Ellis turned to pass the request to Walters. Within a couple minutes, he returned.

"The lieutenant wants you and me to follow a trail off the road for a short distance and report back," he whispered.

We did as told, approaching what appeared to be an out-of-place bush. Gently brushing it aside, we looked behind it. We got our first glimpse of an NVA-dug foxhole. The hole was geometrically different from the ones the marines traditionally dug. It was round rather than rectangular, and considerably deeper. Looking at the other bushes around us, we realized this was one of many positions. We went back to the road, and Ellis took the suspicions to Walters, who passed it back. In a few minutes, Ellis returned with orders. "The lieutenant believes the positions were dug for longtime use, but since they aren't occupied, we should move on. Speedy wants me to move up now, so you can drop back."

"Watch yourself," I told Ellis as I pulled back.

It wasn't long before Ellis sensed something out of order. He looked back at me, motioning for me to come up. "That log shouldn't be lying across the road," Ellis whispered.

"You smell that?" I said, sniffing the air. "That smells like water. In fact, I think I hear running water." Ellis nodded in agreement.

I turned and crept back to Walters and Speedy, who were waiting. After listening, Speedy told the radioman to report to the lieutenant that the four of us would move forward and investigate. The trail led to a shallow river. The riverbank on the far side was slightly elevated with a patch of dry land between the two banks. "Wait here," Speedy told us. Then he returned to report the findings to the lieutenant. About five minutes later, he returned with the remainder of the squad and a machine-gun team. Ellis and I felt some relief feeling someone with experience would be taking over. We were shocked by the next orders.

"You two," he said, referring to Ellis and me, "go over and check it out. We'll provide cover." We were terrified, but we did as ordered.

We entered the river together and then split apart. Ellis went to the left, and I went about ten feet to his right. The rocks under our feet were slippery, but the current was mild, so we had little trouble with our footing. While in the water, we were vulnerable. I thought of the ambush we had attempted the day before, hoping an inexperienced Vietnamese would give away their position and we could escape like the enemy had done. We could not decide if we should rush across to the other side and take cover or continue to approach with caution. Once we reached the halfway point, I decided to make a fast break for the opposite riverbank. Ellis followed closely.

We were now on our own, like two men stranded on a deserted island. Ellis wanted to stop and call the marines across. I, perhaps wanting to exercise my independence, wanted to explore the area further. I climbed to the highest point to get a better view. Convinced the area was safe, I motioned to Ellis to call the other marines over.

Ellis gave the signal, and the marines rushed across the river. The entire company filled the area. Once in, they fanned out and began a thorough search. The lieutenant and gunnery sergeant took charge. They never acknowledged me or Ellis, except to tell us to join our squad. This annoyed both of us, and we began to feel that maybe the two of us were just being overreactive with our concerns. But then Johnson, who was on the radio for the squad, came over and confirmed our suspicions.

"I got to give it to you brothers. You walked right on in. You got some balls."

"What do you mean?" Ellis said with surprise.

"The NVA base camp."

"What base camp?"

"Didn't you know this was a base camp?"

Although both Ellis and I would have liked to take credit for boldly walking into an enemy stronghold, we were shocked.

"Didn't you notice the markings on the road and the worn paths?" Johnson continued.

"Yes, but the lieutenant told us to keep moving," I said.

"What about the machine-gun positions in the river and in the high ground?"

"We saw it, but we weren't sure that was what it was."

"Look!" he said, kicking a clump of dirt. "That's some trash the NVA covered up."

We were now looking at the area with a less naïve vision. Suddenly we noticed the charred wood indicating that troops had camped in the location for a prolonged period. The grass was also pressed in spots, indicating movement.

"Where are they?" I asked, gazing around the area.

"They saw you coming and pulled out," responded Johnson. "They knew there was a large force behind you. If they thought they could take us, they would have blown you away when you started down the trail."

"They should have checked the shit out before they sent marines in," Ellis said in anger.

"They did," Johnson said with a laugh. "That's why you two were sent in first. The lieutenant and sergeants are too valuable to walk into a set-up." That was of little consolation to us. We now knew they considered us expendable.

Looking around, all the men marveled at how efficiently and strategically the camp was set up. It was obvious they were facing a disciplined and skilled force.

"Johnson," Speedy called out, "get over here." For the next few minutes, the radio personnel were busy over the airways. The lieutenant and sergeants were coordinating the next move. First, Third, and Fourth Squads continued to search, allowing Second Squad time to rest.

Within fifteen minutes the order came for the marines to pull out and return to the LZ to be air lifted back to our positions on the river. We left in reverse order, with Ellis and me being the last to exit the base camp. "Ain't that some shit!" Ellis commented with his usual sarcasm. "When they think the shit is in the front, we go first; when they think it's in the back, we go last." I nodded in agreement. The lead dogs get it both ways.

The marines returned safely and took up their usual two-man positions. That night was uneventful. The next morning, after returning from a briefing, Speedy informed us of our next move.

"Recon planes report the enemy is boxed in," he told us. "Headquarters is going to give them a chance to surrender. For the next twenty-four hours, communications planes will offer them a window. They will speak in Vietnamese and English. We are just going to hold our positions. They expect some Viet Cong to give up, but the NVA will likely try to break out. So don't shoot anybody trying to surrender."

The following twenty-four hours were very tense for all involved. Particularly the surrendering Communists. Movement across the narrow river was monitored, but the men did hold their fire. From time to time, the call of "Chu hoi" could be heard across the riverbank. Once acknowledged, a terrified and cautious Communist would appear with hands raised high above his head. One Viet Cong was killed by Second Platoon Some suspected he was trying to surrender. Four Viet Cong and one NVA soldier did manage to surrender to Second Platoon. The total number that surrendered to the regiment was unclear.

When the predetermined period had elapsed, the marines took cover with orders to kill anything that moved on the other side of the river. For the next few hours, the Americans unleashed an awesome volume of firepower. Some of the five-hundred-pound bombs were landing so close that shrapnel showered down on the marines.

After a day of heavy bombardment by the offshore navy gun ships and aerial drops, napalm bombs came in to close the show. The marines, who did a later search, reported dead, charred, and mutilated bodies throughout the area. It was later revealed there were elements from seven marine battalions, roughly five thousand marines, participating in the three-week operation. In that time, 108 marines were killed, and 513 were wounded. We had 1,325 confirmed NVA and VC kills with an additional 300 obliterated from the artillery bombardment. Only six surrendered.

Although the operation was deemed a success, within a matter of weeks NVA forces had reinfiltrated the area.

The high volume of kills warranted a special rewarded for us, in-country R and R on China Beach.

Before that could happen, the company was flown to a point about three miles outside of An Hoa, and we would force march to headquarters. The purpose of the march in was to clear out any enemy troops that might have been outside of the base. It was a grueling, fast-paced march and resulted in no enemy contact.

CHAPTER 7

Fun in the Sun
December 1968

▲ ▲ ▲

AFTER A SHOWER AND SHAVE, the men of Gulf Company climbed into a truck convoy for the two-hour ride into Da Nang to the area called China Beach.

China Beach was primarily a field hospital with a secure area set aside for the men to come in from the field to relax. It was about as safe as you could get while in Vietnam. Guards patrolled the area to keep the enemy and prostitutes out. They also kept the marines in and away from the villages that supplied the drugs and women.

Transporting a company of marines through a war zone is a dangerous venture. We were heavily armed as always, and motor transport people carried their own firepower. Fifty-caliber machine guns were mounted on jeeps between every third truck. Air gun ships circled the convoy the entire trip, and marine patrols were pulled in toward the road for added protection. This safe time gave me time to think and feel sorry for myself.

Even though I had been gone less than two months, I was feeling homesick. I was a part-time college student with a good job, money, women coming after me, a new car, and all the drugs I wanted. Damn, I had it made. All I had now was the same ten dollars I'd had for two weeks with nothing to spend it on. I did have one joint, but it wouldn't go far with all those potheads. I didn't even have anybody to complain to.

Johnny & John

Back home, I would at least have had a family to talk and listen. My father always talked about how much he hated the army. Shit, if he hated the army, the marines might have pushed him over the edge. He didn't show his feelings much unless he was drinking, but I knew he cared. I would sometimes hear him bragging about me. "Big Bad John," he called himself, the baddest motherfucker in Cleveland.

What was that he would tell me? Oh yes, "He who knows not and thinks he knows is a fool. Shun him. He who knows and knows not that he knows is asleep. Awaken him. He who knows and knows that he knows is wise. Follow him." I'll keep that in mind, Dad.

I wished I had taken more time to know and understand my brother, considering he was the only one who consistently wrote me. When I got home, I would let him know how much I appreciated the letters. "Yes, my brother seems to be a very troubled man. I hope he will finally find some peace."

My mom seemed to always worry about my brother, although she would never admit it. In fact, my mother was very guarded of her thoughts. "Shit, I don't even know how she feels about me. Maybe I'll find out when I get back. Getting back is so far off I shouldn't think about it. A year in hell is a long time."

The convoy was finally reaching Da Nang. The closer we got, the more secure the area, so the helicopter support pulled away, and the men on the machine guns began to relax.

The mood was changing. The men on the trucks were getting restless and envious of the servicemen who were stationed in and around Da Nang. The villages on the outskirts of Da Nang had soldiers, sailors, airmen, and marines wandering about.

"Look at that shit!" Corporal Snarr called out. "These motherfuckers walk around like tourists while we crawl around in the jungles fighting for life." The resentment started to build among the men on the truck, with mounting talk of jumping off and kicking some ass.

But, to our surprise, the servicemen showed us great respect. They cheered and greeted us like conquering heroes. To many on the convoy, it was the first time we realized other servicemen respected us for what we were doing. We waved back.

Then an unexpected but comical thing took place. A little Vietnamese boy came running out of one of the hooches with a pair of trousers. An American soldier, naked from the waist down, was in hot pursuit. He was followed by a Vietnamese woman pulling her pants up. It was obvious the boy had tried to steal his trousers and wallet while he was engaging in sex.

Corporal Snarr jumped off the truck to help the soldier retrieve his pants. Seeing he was about to be cornered, the boy tossed the pants and ran into the jungle. The soldier retrieved his trousers and waved to the passing convoy in which the marines laughed but showed little sympathy.

Finally we reached China Beach. A guard opened the gates, and we entered what we considered to be an island paradise. Three days of beer, music, movies, and one five-minute phone call home. For three days we didn't have to worry about being shot or blown up. Man could not live on beer alone. So the streetwise Ellis quickly found a drug supply through the guards. Women, however, could not be obtained, at least not by the enlisted men.

I wanted to make a call home, but it had to be timed right. If no one answered, I would miss my only chance. The platoon was housed in separate barracks. The officers had an area to themselves, as did the sergeants. This was an opportunity for us boots to get more survival information from the bushmen. Since we had the drugs, the bushmen would make the time.

Louie from Philly was in the hooch alone. We walked over to him and gave the power handshake. Ellis then pulled out a ten pack. Louie offered some beer he had on ice, which we accepted. "I'm going to show you the most important thing for a bushman to know," he said, "how we smoke over here." Louie pulled out a large paper bag, as we watched in amazement. Louie lit the joint and then put the bag over his head and continued to smoke it. They could see a faint glow from the joint as he took long, hard drags from it. The bag pulsated each time he took a drag like a bellow. Soon, thick white smoke escaped from under the bag like a pressure release. It seemed if the smoke hadn't come out, it would have burst like an overfilled balloon. Several times we were about to come to his rescue; then he would take another drag. Then the bag came off, and Louie emerged with a wild look resembling a man who had escaped from a burning building seconds before death. His eyes were a bloodred with tears streaming down. His nose was running, and spit shot from his mouth each time he coughed. He rolled back on the cot and then held the roach up in triumph. "That's how to smoke a joint," he finally said between gasps.

I should have known better, but I had to represent Cleveland, so I lit the joint and put the bag over my head. When I exhaled and took the second drag, I knew I'd made a mistake. It was like being in a chamber of death. My survival instinct was to rip the bag off and go for air, but pride drove me to hit it again. At that point, I wanted the bag off, but I was so disoriented that I panicked and tried to run for the door in search of fresh air. With that bag over my head and smoke in my eyes, I ran like a chicken with his head cut off. Predictably, I stumbled over what was probably a cot and hit the floor. I was thrashing so wildly I ripped the bag apart. Ellis finally came to my rescue and took me toward the fan. I struggled so hard for fresh air that my lungs hurt. Finally, I was able to breathe normally, so I sat on the edge of the cot waiting for my head to clear. When it didn't, I realized it wasn't the lack of oxygen but a concentrated high I was feeling.

Louie was still laughing hysterically while Ellis leisurely enjoyed smoking a joint between sips of beer. "Fuck that," he said with a sly smile. "I'm gonna enjoy my high."

Louie lit another joint and opened a cold beer. Ellis then began to question him about his combat experience. "So you're the grenadier?" Ellis asked. "How did you get to carry the M79?"

Louie stood up and flexed his muscles; then he went on to explain. "Well, when you're a short, stocky motherfucker like me, that's the best place for you." He pulled out two large canvas sacks that held the rounds he carried. "Check out how heavy they are," he said as I lifted them. "It's like carrying around a sack of rocks. A short motherfucker like me don't have to lift them too far. This is the best weapon to have."

"I don't know," Ellis said, testing the weight. "This is some heavy shit to be carrying around in an ambush."

"A shotgun is just the weapon when the enemy is close," Louie told him. "Hey, man, if I get ambushed, this buckshot will take care of business. And at seventy-five yards, this high explosive round will get attention. But you have to make sure the distance is right. If the round don't turn enough rotations, it won't explode. One marine got hit with one in the eye that didn't explode, and the medics had to remove it with flak jackets and helmets on. Of course, they would have lost their arms, hands, and face if it exploded." We cringed as we tried to envision it. "All kinds of shit can happen to you over here," he said, drawing our attention to a Korean marine on the far end of that hooch whom we hadn't noticed.

"That's Hoe. He's been here for eight months." We looked at the marine, who was huddled in a corner staring into space. He had the expression you might see on a person who had survived a car crash. "Hoe was a rifleman like you two, but he was caught in one too many ambushes. Now, when fighting breaks out, he just falls to the ground, covers his ears, and cries."

"Maybe he should be in a psychological hospital," I said, feeling compassion for his situation.

"Fuck that coward-ass motherfucker," Louie shouted out. He then went over to Hoe and slapped him on the head, causing Hoe to drop to the floor and cover his head as if an explosion had occurred. Ellis smirked and looked at Hoe with disdain, obviously agreeing with Louie.

Johnson then stuck his head into the hooch and announced it was our squad's turn for a five-minute call home. We knew it was the only chance for a call home, so we all ran to the tent where phone lines were set up.

Each cubicle had two phones. Ellis and I shared one of them. There was a time difference between Vietnam and Ohio, and we didn't know what time it would be there, but we had to try. A sign above the phone told of the five-minute time limit and warned us not to reveal any information over the phone in case the enemy was listening. "What the hell do we know?" I said to Ellis, who responded with a shrug.

I hesitated before making my call. With a five-minute time limit, there was no time to search for words. Ellis wasted no time relaying his number to the operator, but his excitement began to diminish as his call continued to be unanswered. Soon the operator announced to him that his party probably wasn't there, and he could try later. Ellis knew he would not likely get another opportunity. I watched him leave his station with tears beginning to well in his eyes. My line was ringing, but I was beginning to feel I would have the same fate.

Ring-ring-ring. "Hello." It was my father's voice. I was so stunned hearing a voice from home that I could just listen with disbelief. I thought of our father-and-son relationship, good times and bad. Most of all how good it was to hear his voice. "Hello! Hello!" my father said, becoming agitated.

"Hi, Dad," I finally answered. "This is Ralph."

He was so excited that it seemed he wanted to come through the phone. "This you, Buster? This you?" Before I could answer, my father went on. "Where you at, boy? You back home?" The operator, who was obviously listening, broke into the conversation.

"He is in Vietnam, sir." The strange voice startled us both, but we continued as if we were in our own private world.

"Your mom ain't here, boy. You should call back when she gets home from work."

"I can't, Dad. This is my only chance. Besides, I can talk to you." I could almost see him grinning with satisfaction over the phone.

"When you coming home?"

"Dad, I just got here," I said, laughing.

"Boy, you have been gone almost two months. I wish your mom was here. She sho' miss you. Everybody talks about you." He went on to tell me how other people missed me. He would never admit it, but I knew he missed me too. I could have listened to his voice forever, but I knew my time was running out, and my father really needed to hear my voice as well. So I searched for a conversation.

"How is my car running, Dad?"

"OK, I guess. Your brother has it."

"How is Johnny doing?"

There was a slight pause before he continued. "That boy always keeping things messed up." I expected him to go on about my brother, but he seemed to hesitate.

"Is his grades OK? How about his health?" My father seemed to have an awkward pause. Looking at the clock, I knew my time was almost up, so I had to end the conversation. "Dad, tell everybody I said hello, and I will be home as soon as possible." We then said our good-byes. I sat for a few moments with memories swirling through my head, knowing my father was doing the same on the other end. The conversation brought both sadness and joy. I don't know which was greater. Whatever the case, I was glad to have made the call.

From there I went to the beach for a swim. This was a first-time experience for a young man from the inner city. It was like a scene from the "Beach Blanket" movies popular in the '50s. Exhausted from the swim, I pulled myself to the shore and lay in the sand. The warm sun felt soothing, and for the first time since arriving in Vietnam, I settled into a restful sleep.

I awoke to the setting sun. Looking around, I noticed other marines lying about sleeping off drunks. So I went to the supply tent for leftover food before getting more beer. Darkness was quickly approaching, and I could finally enjoy the dark. In the distance I could see the war was still going on. Tracer rounds and mortar explosions dotted the distant landscape.

At that point, I had an inexhaustible supply of beer, a pocket full of reefer, food, soda pop, cigarettes, everything I needed to be happy. I settled back and watched the show before finally drifting off to sleep. From a distance, war can be beautiful.

The sun in my face was the wakeup call. Off to the mess hall for my first real breakfast: bacon, eggs, sausage, pancakes, down-home grits, orange juice, and brewed coffee. Once my stomach was stuffed, I got the most recent issue of *Stars and Stripes* and headed for the portable johns for a leisurely bowel movement. After another nap, the men organized their own entertainment. In the middle of the compound was a stage that was used for USO shows. The men from G Company were assembling with their favorite musical tapes preparing to put on our own show. Everyone was eager to pantomime their favorite groups. There was no discrimination in the music selections. If they had a tape and the courage to get on stage, they got a chance.

Sweet sounds filled the air: soul, R and B, country, rock and roll, blues, folk. It was all there. The enthusiasm would not have been greater if the actual stars had been there. For two days, the war was forgotten.

At the end of the day, we got word we would leave for an urgent mission, cutting the leave a precious day short. The following day, it was back to work.

CHAPTER 8

CAG (Civic Action Group) December 1968

▲ ▲ ▲

THE NEXT DAY THE MEN slept late. We knew orders would come, so why rush? Ellis, however, was unable to sleep. His head swirled with thoughts of home.

"I'm not going cry about being here like the rest of these chickenshits," he said. "I might even be able to walk away with some seed money for a business or something." While Youngstown was his home, he was determined not to spend his life working in one of the factories there. After talking to marines from New York and California, he knew there were opportunities beyond his factory town, and he was determined to take advantage of them. Maybe, he thought, there would be something good in this.

Then we noticed Speedy approaching. "Here comes the bad news," he said. "I'm beginning to hate that brother." Speedy came into the hooch after attending his meeting with the lifers. Everyone listened intently as he outlined our next assignment.

"We got our orders," he said. "Our next mission is to protect a CAG unit." Most of us weren't aware of the CAG units, so Speedy went on to elaborate. "The marines have six-man units embedded in the friendly villages around the outer perimeter of Da Nang. They are called Civic Action Groups. They teach, build, acquire supplies, and give medical attention or any assistance needed. It's a sort of public-relations unit. Patrols out of Da Nang check on them daily, and they keep radio contact. It's good duty and highly sought after. They do carry small arms for protection, but they are not a combat unit and are vulnerable to attacks.

"In fact, a recon team operating in the area spotted a large Viet Cong force. Our company," Speedy went on to explain, "is going to look for them. We will use the village as a base while we patrol the area. After clearing the area, we will march back to An Hoa. Walters will take the first fire team, Perrish's got the second, and, Harris, take the third. If you have any questions, take them to Walters. Inventory your gear; then go to the supply tent to replenish or to add to what you have. The trucks will take us to the outer perimeter." He then left to coordinate the movements with the other squad leaders.

I was uncomfortable with the responsibility, so I spoke up. "Excuse me, but why did he put me in charge of a fire team?" I asked Walters.

"Because they want you, Ellis, Dura, and Hoe to work together," he explained. "Next time Dura or Ellis will take some responsibility. Just keep Hoe out of trouble."

Ellis, the undisputed people person of the group, wanted to alleviate any guilty feelings I might have had for being put in charge. "Being team leader don't mean shit to me," he assured me. "The less authority, the more I can fuck off." Dura agreed. We picked up our personal gear that we had stored under our bunks; then we went to the supply hooch to replenish our war gear: 250 rounds of ammunition, 6 grenades, a claymore, a Ka-Bar, a machete, and a LAAW. Everyone was strapped for battle as we rode the forty-five-minute convoy ride to Da Nang's outer perimeter.

It was about a one-hour march to the village. First Platoon broke up into squads and patrolled the surrounding area. They then set positions in strategic locations. Third and Fourth Platoons set up an outer perimeter. Second Platoon would secure the command post, with the company commander and platoon commander at the center. We started by interviewing the CAG members. First, Second, and Third Squads established an inner perimeter around the village. I shared a position with Ellis, Walters, and a Hispanic

CAG member by the name of Chico. Each of us took a turn digging a two-foot-wide, six-foot-long defensive trench.

While taking his turn in the dig, Ellis noticed a foul odor beginning to emit from the trench. A few more picks with the E tool and the odor was becoming even stronger. "What is that?" I asked him.

"I don't know, but damn, it stinks."

"Well, cover it back up. It's making my eyes water."

"Wait, man, it seems like a tree root. Hand me a machete," Ellis said. He took the machete and began chopping into it.

"Man, cover that shit up!" I yelled.

Ellis may have listened in combat, but he was quick to tell me he knew how to dig a hole. "It must be a rotting tree," he called up before reaching down to pull it out. Suddenly, he let out a girlish scream and threw something into the air.

"That's a hand!" he yelled, jumping out of the trench. Unfortunately, the hand landed on me. I attempted to run but slipped back into the hole, landing on Ellis. In our haste to get out, we unearthed other body parts.

We rolled around on the ground trying to rub the stench off. Walters dumped water on us while Chico threw dirt back into the hole, reburying the recently departed. All the while he was trying to calm us down.

"It's just a body, man," he said in a reassuring voice. Soon things settled down, and we just chalked it to another in a growing list of the bizarre experiences.

That night Chico and Ellis took a watch together. They were in a location safe enough for a low-volume conversation.

"Is your name really Chico?" Ellis asked him.

"No, when you are Hispanic, people assume your first name is Chico, Carlos, or Jesus, so I let it go."

"What do I need to know, my fellow dark-skinned brother?" Ellis asked.

"Just the usual; if you're a brother, Hispanic, or anything but white, you're considered more expendable, so watch your ass."

"How did you get this sweet job?"

"I did the college thing. It helped to land an administrative job."

"I'm happy for you; this is sweet."

"I can't bitch, but I think some bad shit is gonna be coming down. The VC can come through here any time they want."

"How long does it take for them to get reinforcements to you?"

"That depends on how close the marine patrols are when called. But for the most part we are secure."

"Where you from?"

"East LA. My own part of the world. All my people are still there. When this shit is over, I'm going back, and I'll never leave the block. What about you?"

"Youngstown, Ohio."

"You any relation to that brother?" he said, pointing to the sleeping me.

"No, Harris is from Cleveland, Ohio. They say we look alike, but I say I'm much more handsome. How short are you?" ("Short" referred to time left before going home.)

"Two months, and I catch the bird. I have a family business to get into."

"What was home like when you left?"

"Like everywhere there is protest. I might even join them. But I really just want to get my life and see my lady who's waiting."

"Wow, that don't happen often."

"Well, I might be fooling myself, but after this shit some things just aren't that important. My people like her, I've known her since grade school, so the last few months, we will just erase."

"I'm not there yet, but I can see it coming."

"Here," Chico said, handing Ellis a ten pack.

"How sure are you about the Viet Cong unit in the area?"

"Oh, they are around. They will lie low until you guys move out. But we might hold them off until help can get here."

They had a nice chat over the course of the night. The result of the conversation was that Ellis came to respect the loyalty among Hispanics. There weren't many Hispanics in Youngstown, so this was another good cross-cultural experience.

At one point, they exchanged addresses after promising to contact one another once they returned to the world. The next morning, everyone said our good-byes to the CAG unit members. Then we saddled up for the patrol around the area and the sweep west toward An Hoa. It was expected we would reach it the next night.

Hoe was still a part of our four-man fire team. He was with us for his own protection. Not from the enemy, but from other marines.

After we left the village and rice paddies heading for the mountains, the terrain began to get thicker. Rain was a constant. Pockets of water would accumulate throughout the mountains. Soon those water pockets would overflow and create streams down the mountain. This would very often create small ponds at the mountain's base. Second Squad was pointing for the platoon, so they would be the first to cross the first of a series of small ponds we would cross that day. This pond was shallow, about four feet deep. This would be Dura's first up-close and personal encounter with the enemy. The experienced marines had constantly reminded Second Squad of the skill level of the enemy. What the NVA lacked in equipment, they would make up in manpower and determination. For example, they didn't have the communication equipment the marines had, but with the aid of the Viet Cong, the playing the field was leveled. Viet Cong soldiers, who would often be from the area, would conceal themselves at strategic points and monitor the marines' movements and troop strength. That information would be transferred to the NVA. Sometimes they would strike and then disperse into the jungle when an opportunity presented itself. This day, they allowed the marines to get too close. Two Viet Cong observers were keeping a safe distance. Either they moved a little too slow, or the marines traveled faster than they expected. Whatever the case, the marines were too close for one of them to make it across the pond, so he ducked down and tried to stay submerged until they passed.

Second Squad was leading the platoon and was the first to cross the river. Hoisting our weapons over our heads to keep them dry, we entered the water.

Determination, no matter how committed, is no match for the body's instinct to survive. One of the VC popped up like a cork from the bottom of a water-filled tub. Two factors saved his life that day. First, he had no weapon. Had he been holding one, he would have been immediately killed. Second, most of the marines surrounding him didn't panic.

He emerged a few feet from Walters, who barely flinched while pressing the barrel of his weapon to the enemy's forehead, ordering the soldier to surrender.

The calmness of the marines was reassuring. The other VC made it out, but he was later captured. Ellis was in awe seeing live Communist soldiers only a few feet from him. They were just children, no more than fourteen or fifteen years old. With their black pajamas, they looked like junior-high students who had overslept and left home before dressing for school. Killing them would have seemed to be a crime, but to hesitate at the wrong time might have cost lives. Compassion was a luxury we couldn't afford.

The prisoners were immediately bound and gagged in preparation for the helicopter that would fly them to battalion headquarters for interrogation. For me this was a noteworthy event. For the bushmen, it was a chance to rest. Once the prisoners were airlifted, the patrol proceeded.

The order of the formation was changed. Second Squad was moved to the end of the patrol. My fire team, which was one of the three in the squad, was now on tail end. Traveling on tail end offers a different set of dangers. Aside from being ambushed or picked off by a sniper from the rear, scavengers would trail the patrol. Sometimes a tired marine would drop ammunition to lighten his load. That same ammunition could be used against them. I had placed Ellis at the end of the patrol, so along with watching for an attack from the rear, he had to watch for discarded ammunition. Hoe, the timid Korean in the fire team, was a double threat. He was certain to run if a fight ensued, and he would be the likely one to drop equipment. To keep an eye on him, Hoe was the first in the fire team; his only job was to keep in eye contact with Perrish, who was the last member of the fire team we followed. The terrain was now so thick that we traveled single file, sometimes turning sideways to squeeze through. The danger of getting separated was heightened; eye contact was now extremely important. Hoe would sometimes collapse, causing Dura, who was behind him, to push him forward.

Hoe began to complain about the weight of the machine gun. Dura took the gun and carried it along with his own war gear. A few minutes later, Hoe complained of being unable to carry the machine-gun ammunition. I carried it for him. Still he complained, looking to me to carry his backpack. Against my better judgment, I carried it as well. All of us were becoming visibly angry. The anger reached the boiling point when Hoe tried to hand Ellis his helmet. I took the helmet and struck him in the chest. At first Hoe fell to the ground and appeared to be too injured to get up. After I pounded his face into the dirt a few times, Hoe mustered the strength to rise to his feet. The patrol continued with Hoe crying and trembling like a child.

Then we reached a clearing carved by a stream. We were still in a tight space only about five yards across, but there was enough space for two, possibly three men. Perrish stepped out of the clearing into the dense jungle. It looked as if he had gone behind a curtain. "Make sure you keep eye contact with Perrish," I told Hoe, who nodded in agreement. Hoe then sat on a rock and buried his head in his hands.

We enjoyed being in the clearing, but after a few minutes, we became uneasy. "See if Perrish is there," I told Dura, who moved out of the clearing into the dense jungle.

When he didn't return immediately, we knew something was wrong. When Dura returned, he confirmed it. "That motherfucker let the platoon move on without us." We were furious.

I reminded them that we had a more immediate situation to deal with. We were cut off from the platoon in Viet Cong territory with no radio, and a Viet Cong patrol was likely tracking us. To make the situation even worse, the only one with any real experience had his face buried in his hands, crying uncontrollably and mumbling something in Korean.

Instinctively, we formed a circle with weapons pointed outward. I remembered the smoke canisters we carried and reached for a yellow one. "I'm going to pop a yellow smoke!" I said in a barely audible whisper. The men nodded in agreement. It was to let the marines know friendlies were following them.

As soon as the smoke popped, I told them to move in the direction the platoon had gone. At first, Ellis objected; then he realized the enemy would also spot the smoke.

After traveling about fifty yards, we began to question if we were going in the right direction. "Do those look like tracks?" I said, pointing at what appeared to be impressions in the thick brush.

"It looks like tracks all over the place!" Dura gasped.

Now I was truly getting scared, and it showed. "Those motherfuckers have to know we aren't behind them. Why the fuck aren't they looking for us?"

"Hell yeah!" Dura yelled.

Calmly but assertively, I told them to shut up and look out for the platoon. My agitation showed in the manner I was dragging Hoe around by the shirt collar.

Then we saw a faint cloud of yellow smoke in the direction we were heading. Our first instinct was to run in that direction shouting our presence, but I reminded the others we didn't know who had popped the smoke. Cautiously, we approached the smoke cloud. Throwing caution to the wind, Hoe began screaming for help. Fortunately for us, it was Second and Third Squad. Walters was the first to reach us. Hoe continued to sob out loud, prompting me to muffle his mouth with my hand. "Stop that goddamn noise. We're in enemy territory!" I demanded.

They escorted the errant team to the platoon where the lieutenant and gunnery sergeant were waiting. Then unexpectedly even to myself, I struck Hoe in the jaw. Dura and Ellis joined in beating the Korean down. "This ain't the time for this!" Speedy said, pulling us off him.

Once we reached the platoon, the lieutenant called for me to give a report. When I explained the situation, the lieutenant, while not condoning our actions, offered no reprimand.

During the brief pause in the march toward An Hoa, Walters approached Ellis with some disturbing news. "We got the word that the CAG unit we were with the night before has been overrun by a Viet Cong unit. They're all dead. It looks like your partner Chico was right."

The company continued the march. The CAG unit was never mentioned again. Ellis tried not to think about the men in the demolished unit, reminding himself that while this was the first, it wouldn't be the last friend he would lose. We didn't know it yet, but this was the first phase of Operation Taylor Common.

CHAPTER 9

Operation Taylor Common
December 1968

▲ ▲ ▲

When we reached company headquarters, Hoe was removed and sent stateside to be processed for a medical discharge. This was best for all involved.

We were told we would be in An Hoa for the next two days. Our company was rarely at the base for that length of time, so the men viewed it with mixed feelings. The grunts often harbored resentment toward the administrative and support personnel serving their time on the base. Very often their attitude was condescending. Generally, the feeling was mutual.

When at headquarters, we were often assigned tasks by the administrative personnel. There were fewer of them, and they generally outranked the majority of the grunts, so they were in a position of authority and would exercise the authority at every opportunity. The typist and clerks took delight in ordering killers around. The proud warriors were forced to burn feces, sweep offices, file papers, cut grass, and do any other meaningless task that could be thought up.

The grunt officers and NCOs would rarely step up in the defense of the men they commanded. While the men under them were ordered around like children, they spent the time relaxing among themselves. They also took advantage of every privilege available. The animosity from the grunts was obvious; if looks could kill, there would have been bloodshed. I must admit we were seldom penalized for our drunkenness. When not in combat, most of us were usually drunk.

Another bright spot for the grunts was the chow hall. Thanks to the mess sergeant, there was always more than enough good food served when we arrived. The mess sergeant must have been a grunt at one time. He always pulled out plenty of bottles of steak sauce and hot sauce at each meal, which we promptly pilfered. Then at the next meal, the tables would be restocked, and the cycle would repeat itself. Those sauces would turn a bland boxed field ration into a savory feast in the bush. We knew this and showed our respect for the mess sergeant. The respect was for the man, not just his authority.

The first day we woke at five, ate in the chow hall, and went on the demeaning work details. It actually wasn't bad. That evening we played basketball. Then we partook in one of the bushmen's greatest pleasures, getting high. The lifers said to stay off drugs to keep your mind clear and the body healthy. Whether they practiced what they preached is doubtful. We were physically fit. Being healthy don't mean shit if you're shot dead.

In an attempt to make the best of the situation, Walters had to consider aligning himself to a particular clique. All groups had advantages and disadvantages connected to them. Walters was intelligent enough to know that being a Caucasian American gave him certain advantages. But many of the Caucasian marines, particularly those from large urban areas, couldn't see beyond his Appalachian lineage. Walters was proud of his rural small-time background and resented being painted as a backwoods hick. But the brothers would also keep him at arm's length, primarily because they didn't trust him. This was the '60s, and blacks were banding together rather than attempting to socialize with white America. What they didn't understand was that Walters was also ostracized by the system and mistrusted authority. The brothers seemed to live our lives as if we had nothing to lose, and he was coming to that same conclusion about his situation.

Walters didn't want to be black. He just wanted to exercise his rebellious side and not be put down. He attempted to get close to Speedy, but Speedy was a loner. Besides, Speedy had nearly broken his ribs, so he should have avoided him at all costs.

Ellis seemed to be the person everyone liked. Hooking up with him, Walters believed, would bridge all groups. When he saw the brothers in the hooch getting high, he walked in with Ellis. But before he could enter, Speedy walked up.

"Hey, Walters," Speedy said as he approached. "I just got a briefing about our next mission, and I wanted to brief the team leaders before the men. I thought you would be in the tent with the rest of the chucks."

"No, I was going to hang with the brothers. Why don't you brief me and let me pass the word to them?"

Speedy spent the next few minutes briefing Walters; then he left. Now Walters was able to go into the inner sanctuary and get our full attention. When he first entered, all eyes turned. The good news was that it would be a few days before we would go back to the bush, so there was no need to stop the party.

"Speedy wanted me to brief you guys, and you don't have to put up the shit," Walters said, referring to the reefer. "In fact, pass it on.

"Our next mission might turn out to be a tough one. The People's Army of Vietnam [PAVN] have a base area one twelve, which has a number of battalion, regiment, command, and support bases. Located in the Arizona Territory. We are going to fly in and take a suspected NVA base. Marines from other battalions will be dropped on other hills to search for bases. They aren't sure of the size of the units or how entrenched they are. Whatever the case, we're taking it from them. These are regulars, and they won't give it up without a fight."

"What do we know at this point?" the experienced Louie asked.

"Very little; a recon team was dropped in last night. They will gather whatever information they can. They will be picked up in a couple of days. When they return, it will be our turn. For now, let's just get fucked up." Other squad members joined us; we were a mean green drunken machine.

We had at least two days before the fight, which, in some cases, was a lifetime. The beer, reefer, country western, and Motown sounds pushed the coming mission out of our minds. As nightfall approached, the base followed the routine blackout, and headquarters personnel manned the parameter. This allowed the bushmen to fall deeper into our drunken stupor.

Around 2200, Speedy came into the hooch carrying two gallons of cheap wine. "Anybody up for Mad Dog and the Bird?" he said, waving the wine around. After some hesitation, everyone, except me, accepted the challenge. It looked like Friday night on an inner-city corner. The drunker the men got, the more I belittled them. "I don't drink that cheap shit," I proudly boasted. "The way you drunk motherfuckers look reminds me why." I laughed.

I knew my remarks would bring ridicule, but I couldn't resist. "We drink the good shit in Cleveland." An untruth I managed to say with a straight face.

"Bullshit!" Ellis said, pounding his chest. "You Cleveland brothers are just a bunch of wimps. Even that moonshine-drinking Walters can handle the Mad Dog."

I just couldn't accept the insult. I grabbed the bottle and turned it straight up while my fellow marines chanted encouragement. Soon they stopped chanting and stared in disbelief. Even the most hardened drinkers couldn't believe anyone could drink that amount of alcohol without stopping to breathe. When you combine that with all the beers and smoke, I must have been close to poisoning myself. I stumbled around the room grunting like a pig before letting out a disgusting burp; then I passed out on the nearest cot. It was clear I was destined for the mother of all hangovers. There was little doubt food would not be welcomed in my stomach for some time. Speedy raised my unconscious arm, proclaiming me the undisputed drunk. He stumbled back to his hooch, leaving the men of Second Squad to fall into a deep alcohol-and-drug-induced sleep.

Somewhere around 0400, the platoon commander, Lieutenant Hannahan, burst into the tent. "Listen up!" he said while violently shaking each man in the tent. "Recon is under fire. We're going in to get them out now! Get your shit and assemble outside!" He then exited as abruptly as he had arrived to inform the other squads.

Speedy came in and hustled everyone along. They were surprisingly coherent considering the amount of alcohol they had consumed. Everyone, that is, except me. I was so lifeless that Speedy had to shake me to see if I was alive.

"Harris is out cold," Walters told him.

"He ain't no good to us," Speedy decided. "They'll have to fly him in tomorrow." The squad assembled outside as the lieutenant had ordered. When the squad exited the tent, the lieutenant immediately noticed I wasn't with them.

"Where's Harris?" he asked impatiently.

Speedy spoke up. "Sir, we were drinking, and, unfortunately, Harris accepted a challenge to finish off a gallon of Thunder Bird."

"Throw some water on him; then bring him!" the lieutenant ordered.

"Sir," Speedy said, "he's unconscious."

"We need every man; drag him if you have to. Bring the motherfucker out now!" the lieutenant demanded.

Speedy sent Walters, Dura, Ellis, and Johnson to get me. Fortunately, I was dressed, so they only needed to make certain I had all my war gear. "Get him out here now!" the lieutenant yelled into the tent. Still I was not coherent. They would carry me a few feet; then I would walk about two steps and collapse. It was a difficult but coordinated effort, and we finally reached the helicopter.

The platoon was to be flown out in two helicopters, two squads in each. Speedy was in charge of Second Squad. Brantley was in charge of First. Before boarding, the squad leaders briefed their men.

"Recon is on the run," Speedy informed us. "First Platoon is going to locate them and assist in the extraction. Second is to take the base."

The best points would get the call. Brantley, the First Squad leader, informed Bodfield that he would point for their squad. He then gave his men further instructions.

Speedy addressed Second Squad. "We will take a V formation. Walters will point for the squad. When we get to the drop point, Walters will be the first out. Harris is gonna follow. Ellis will flank to the right, Dura the left.

I'll be in the center with the radioman. We are going to push the NVA out, so don't stop until I give the word."

Walters, Dura, and Ellis were worried about having me cover them while I still was in a drunken stupor, but they had to trust me. "Load up!" Speedy ordered.

The marines lined each side of the chopper, feet facing outward. They weren't sure how thick the terrain would be, so it may have been necessary to rappel down the rope. "Anybody here ever rappel down a rope?" Perrish asked, looking around. Everybody shrugged their shoulders. "Ain't that a bitch!" the radioman laughed, "none of you motherfuckers know how to rappel."

"It's a ladder, goddammit," yelled Speedy. "Just climb down! Walters, you better be concentrating on getting your backup sober."

Walters threw water in my face, getting only a slight response. They hastily tied me in as the chopper ascended.

As we approached the hill, we could see the rifle muzzle flashes from the firefight between Recon and the pursuing NVA. The choppers carrying First Platoon headed in that direction.

Soon rounds began to zip through our helicopter. We had been spotted, and the NVA were trying to bring us down. The chopper gunner opened fire, trying to make a hole. The noise was deafening. I looked down at the NVA directly below firing up and yelled, "Goddamn, we going to be dropped on top of them." The NVA began to disperse as the chopper started our descent. Suddenly, I began to throw up. When I raised my head, I was as sober as a judge.

The clearing was narrow, so the pilot slowly descended while the gunner frantically fired at the enemy backing away. "This is a motherfucking flying coffin!" Ellis yelled. "Let's get the fuck out!"

The sentiment was shared by everyone. The chopper was still about five feet in the air when we started jumping out.

When Walters hit the ground, he charged into the darkness. He was at his best, and he needed to be. The enemy fought back with a vengeance, determined to halt our advancement. Walters was faced with a wall of enemy gunfire. Walters was a defensive fighter, not an aggressive alley fighter. His instinct was to drop to the ground and hold his position. But we were still in the open, so I ran right past him, taking cover beside a tree and positioning myself for a good shot. I felt as if I were possessed and chasing a demon.

The elusive enemies were like shadows in search of a body. They appeared, disappeared, and then reappeared. The gunpowder smell burned the nose and throat, and the noise was deafening. There were dead and dying all around, but it wasn't clear whose side they were on. The only secure target was the muzzle flash from the enemy's weapons and the distinctive sound their weapons made.

My running past Walters returned him to his rightful position, that of team leader rather than pointer.

"Slow down," he called to me. "Don't get to far out front; you could get shot in the back!" That slowed me down, but I still fired fiercely into the darkness.

"Hold your position!" the platoon sergeants called out. "Hold your positions." As more troops landed, they would continue to expand the perimeter.

Then there was a burst of enemy gunfire on the left flank. "That's Ellis's position!" I yelled, moving in that direction. We were concerned the enemy had pounced on him. Then we heard him return fire and rushed to join him, encountering a brief firefight on the way. The enemy quickly pulled back.

"Ellis! Ellis!" I called. "Where are you?"

"Over here!" he responded. As black as the night was, they could see him coming out of the darkness. His eyes were as big as fifty cent pieces.

"Man, he was right in front of me!" he said, still in a daze. "I killed that motherfucker."

"Could you see his face?" I asked like a ten-year-old schoolboy quizzing his buddy who had seen a girl in the shower.

"I didn't want to see his face," Ellis responded.

"Where's the body?" I asked, looking around.

"His people came for him, and I fired a few shots and got the hell away. I wasn't going to die over a dead body."

"This ain't no time to shoot the shit!" Walters snapped. "Let's pull back!"

We pulled back to the perimeter the platoon had set up and prepared for a counterattack from the enemy. Firefights continued at other positions, but the fiercest fighting was taking place in the valley. With helicopters circling that area, they surmised the recon team and the dead and wounded were being extracted.

The remainder of the night was intense but largely uneventful. By the light of day, we were able to assess the situation.

The remnants of a base camp made it evident that the enemy had occupied the area; however, their casualties would not be known. In spite of the amount of blood, there were only a few dead and no wounded enemies left behind. We had no deaths in our platoon that night, but we did have six wounded. There were causalities among other marine units anticipating that night, but we weren't given the numbers. I came to learn that losses are rarely presented to the troops. We were now ready to settle in for the long haul. More causalities would surely follow.

CHAPTER 10

Quiet after the Storm
December 1968–January 1969

▲ ▲ ▲

THERE WAS STILL SOME UNFINISHED business to clear up after the initial contact. Gulf Company was now responsible for providing security for the engineers who would build what was to be called Firebase Pike. Other units would establish smaller firebases. This would require securing a roughly a half-mile area with a hill at the center. After about two days of search-and-destroy patrols, the marines felt confident enough to have the engineers flown in. Once there, it took them all of two weeks to clear the area of trees and rocks. Then the heavy earthmoving equipment was brought in. NVA and Viet Cong units were likely observing the progress, so the marines anticipated they would attempt to sabotage the area once it was further along.

First, Third, and Fourth Platoons established positions in the surrounding hillside, with Second Platoon actually on the hill. There were only two causalities in Second Platoon during that two-week period, but it was nonetheless an interesting time.

The first causality was job-related, coming from the ranks of the combat engineers. It came about while they were clearing trees and earth with the combat explosive C-4. One of their own was killed by flying debris in this dangerous process.

The second death in the two-week period was a marine who died from malaria. He might have been saved had the captain given permission to medevac him sooner. He was black, so the brothers felt that weighed heavily in his decision not to seek immediate medical attention. The captain was later punished for the action with a transfer to another unit. They also gave him a citation for his leadership in taking the hill. With that citation, there would likely be a promotion. Some punishment, the brothers would scoff.

The two-week combat inactivity was making the men restless, particularly Speedy. Activities were becoming routine. Dig trenches, guard the perimeter, or patrol by day. Go on an ambush, man a listening post, or guard lines at night. Speedy warned the men that to get careless could cost lives. He seemed to feel Walters should have been more responsible in keeping the men alert. He, in fact, became physical with Walters, thinking it would motivate him. The marines under Walters seemed annoyed at this; perceiving him as the underdog, we were beginning to sympathize with him. We were also growing impressed with the combat knowledge Walters shared with us; however, we never mustered the nerve to criticize the abusive Speedy.

There were, however, several incidents that brought levity to the situation.

There was Johnson, the Motown brother who always tried to maintain an air of mystery and purpose. Most felt he was bumbling and nerdish. His greatest distinction was his snoring and inability to awaken from a deep sleep. He was harder to awaken than a bear in winter. In the bush being a heavy sleeper is a definite handicap.

That particular day, Johnson and Ellis shared a defensive trench the squad members had dug.

One would remain alert while the other wrote letters or napped. Johnson decided to take his customary midday nap.

The silence was shattered by the distinctive sound of an incoming mortar round. Ellis instantly pushed Johnson violently, gave the call for an incoming round, and then dived for the trench, which was ten yards behind them. The first round landed roughly thirty yards from where they were sitting, sending jagged shrapnel flying in all directions. I was guarding the lines with Walters, and we had already jumped into the trench. I peeked up and saw Johnson was out front sleeping soundly.

"Somebody get Johnson!" I said, turning to Ellis.

"Fuck you," Ellis responded. "The motherfucker should hear all that goddamn noise!" Everyone silently agreed, including me. I made no attempt at leaving the safety of the trench to awaken the sleeping Johnson. We did continue to yell for Johnson while throwing rocks at his head. In spite of the stinging pain of the rocks, which Johnson only swiped at like they were annoying mosquitoes, and the blast of more incoming rounds, Johnson barely budged. Every time someone prepared to run out to grab him, another round would hit, driving them back.

Speedy now joined the effort, yelling at the top of his voice, "Johnson, get your motherfucking ass up!"

Ellis leaned over to me and whispered with a smile, "Does he think he can yell louder than the mortars?" We shared a mocking smile.

The next round landed so close that it took the levity out of the situation. The percussion was so jarring that it flipped his body over. He landed and continued to sleep in the fetal position like a baby in his mother's arms. Everyone was amazed. Had it not been for slight movement on his part, we would have thought he was dead. That round was the last in the attack. Speedy, clearly agitated, stood up and walked aggressively over to Johnson.

With his customary burst of violence, he came down with three hard blows to Johnson's head. Finally Johnson woke up, still totally oblivious to what was happening. Speedy just walked away with no explanation, leaving Johnson to wonder about the knots and cuts on his body. Disgusted by Johnson, the men ignored him for the remainder of the day.

The lieutenant decided we should clear out more of the vegetation in front of the perimeter, particularly a patch of bamboo. This patch provided a memorable experience for the squad members.

A bamboo patch was a sight that inner-city dwellers, like the majority of the young marines, had never experienced. Walking through it, we behaved like children in a playground maze. Ellis seemed to take particular delight behaving like a giant, unearthing a forest. Of the men present, it could not be argued that Ellis was the least adept at jungle survival. This made it even more outrageous that he would be the one to demonstrate to everyone the technique learned in training to get water from bamboo.

"Does anybody know how to get water from bamboo?" he questioned.

"Hell no!" shouted Johnson, who was still irate over the sleeping incident. "We don't have bamboo in Motown." I was ignoring them, focusing on getting the job over so I could take a nap.

Determined to get attention, Ellis held the pole over his head like a flight attendant about to demonstrate the proper use of a seatbelt. "Watch and learn," he said, positioning the tip of the pole on the ground. He raised his Ka-Bar over his head as he prepared to chop the end of the pole. This pole was unlike the green poles used in the training demonstration. This one was a dull yellow and hard as a tree root. The blade of the Ka-Bar bounced back like it was rubber. Full of determination, he decided his machete was better suited for the job. He now had the attention of everyone in the immediate area, including me. I was sure Ellis was about to do something foolish. Holding the bamboo stalk at eye level and bracing it against a tree, he chopped of the end with one hard swoop.

Those looking for comic relief were not disappointed. Large black ants shot out of the end of the pole and down his arm like carbonated bubbles from a shaken can of beer. "Goddamn it!" he shouted, slinging ants everywhere.

We exited the patch as if a grenade had been thrown. Other dry ant-filled stalks were overturned, releasing a stream of angry, ravenous, roach-size insects. Most escaped relatively unscathed. Ellis, however, was not so fortunate.

Once he removed his clothes to pound the insects that had saturated his trousers, shirt, shoes, and socks, large welts could be seen covering his body. It appeared he had been beaten with the dreaded cat-o'-nine-tails.

The physical damage was minimal. His pride was slightly more damaged. I made certain of that. Had I known of the trauma I was headed for, I might have shown more sympathy.

I was sharing a position with Perrish in the bamboo patch that we had cleared earlier. In doing that, we had disturbed the habitat of the dreaded "bamboo viper."

In training there were a few animals we were warned to avoid. The viper was at the top of the list. These small, green reptiles were said to be aggressive toward intruders and highly toxic. They were called "two-steps." As the story goes, the viper bites you, you take two more steps, and then you are dead. Everyone understood the story was likely an exaggeration, but there was some truth in the danger that the viper presented. Most felt the time it would take to smoke your last cigarette was about right. Needless to say, I was concerned about being in that bamboo patch that night.

Perrish seemed only concerned with getting high sniffing glue. This was one of our survival items. It was used to repair our air mattresses, or rubber ladies, as we called them. He decided to get high one more time. I watched him squirt a stream of the glue into a plastic bag, place it over his nose, and then take about ten deep breaths. Suddenly, he stood straight up, twirled around several times, and body-slammed himself to the ground.

He then looked at me, bag in hand, face devoid of color, gasping for air, appearing to have come back from the dead, and asked if I wanted to try it. I declined, feeling Perrish had given up about a week of life for a ten-second high.

I took the first three-hour watch, hoping that would give Perrish time to sleep it off. Most of the time was spent watching for vipers rather than the enemy. By the time my watch was up, it was completely dark. It was around midnight, perhaps the darkest part of the night. It was, in fact, so dark that if you weren't looking at the stars, you wouldn't know if your eyes were open or closed.

After a day spent removing trees, chopping bamboo, digging trenches, and clearing away large rocks, I was completely exhausted. Finally, it was my time to rest. After waking Perrish and feeling assured that he was sober enough to alert me if the enemy attacked, I dozed off to sleep.

After about thirty minutes, I was jolted out of my deep sleep by an excruciating pain in the right buttocks. It felt like someone had given me a booster shot with a nail and with such force that it penetrated the bone. It was enough of a jolt that it caused my leg to stiffen and my whole body to leave the ground.

Perrish frantically knelt down and asked what had happened.

"A viper bit me!" I panted.

"Where is he?" Perrish said, searching the area, clearly more concerned for his safety than my condition.

"I saw him slither off," I said, not really knowing. Then I said as calmly as possible, "Go get the goddamn corpsman." Perrish gave no verbal response. He just turned and, without the benefit of light, began to feel his way toward the corpsman's position. I could hear him telling everyone he passed, "Harris got bit by a viper! Harris got bit by a viper!" This continued until he was out of hearing range.

Ellis was the first to arrive. His face showed that he was concerned. Moving close, he asked, "Did you get bit by a viper?"

"Yes."

"Are you paralyzed?"

"No."

"Can you move your legs?"

"I don't know."

"Try to move your legs."

"I ain't moving shit. It might make the poison move faster," I snapped.

"Then you're paralyzed."

"Look, man!" I said, moving my foot. "I'm not paralyzed!"

Dura was now approaching, talking as he got nearer.

"Are you dying, man?"

"No."

"Didn't you get bit by a viper?"

"Yes."

"Then you're dying."

Ellis couldn't resist joining in the discussion.

"I hate to tell you this, Harris, but the brother is right; you only get about ten minutes after the bite."

I didn't want to debate if I was about to die or not, so I just remained calm, hoping to conserve energy. Dura made an attempt at showing compassion.

"It may take a half hour for the poison to circulate."

"No!" countered Ellis. "It only takes ten minutes." The two of them seemed to forget about me and continued to debate their ten-minute-versus-half-hour theory. Finally I couldn't take it anymore. "Who the hell are you two, Abbott and Castello? Get the goddamn corpsman!" The rush of energy took my strength, causing me to slump back with exhaustion.

Walters was rushing over by that time. "I heard Harris was dead," he said, seeing me lying motionless. Walters moved closer, looking for movement.

"I ain't dead," I said in an almost inaudible voice.

Moving even closer, Walters asked, "Are you gonna die?"

I didn't respond, but the comment sent Ellis and Dura back to their debate.

While their seeming lack of concern for my imminent demise agitated me, I was reminded that I had just a little amount of time to get my final thoughts in order. Searching through my address book, I began to dictate messages to people back home. "Send a letter to my home. Tell my father and mother that I love them. Let my father know I appreciate him taking over my car note. Ask him to give it to my brother. Oh! Tell my mother I'm sorry I didn't write more often. Things were just happening too fast. You can put some shit in the letter about what a good person I am and how you will miss me. Then I want you to write a letter to my brother at his school address. Let him know that he was the best older brother I could have had. We weren't as close as we should or could have been; had I lived, I would have tried to change that. There were a lot of things I would have liked to have said. I regret I didn't get the chance," I concluded.

"Damn, that is some deep shit," Ellis said while pausing his writing. A sadness came over me at that point. I decided to review the remainder of my life in silence. For the next ten minutes, my friends just stared at me in silence, waiting for me to die. Thoughts about my brother consumed me. Our lives were so different, but that shouldn't have mattered. He was my only sibling. In the last letter my brother had written to me, he said he admired me. In fact, the letter expressed feelings I never knew my brother had. I wished I could have lived longer. Perhaps I could have said what he'd never said to anyone for fear of being called weak. That I did love him.

Johnson joined the group, moving his face so close we were almost touching.

He spoke, "I don't think he's breathing. Can anybody see him moving?" They all began poking me with their fingers.

"I'm not dead," I said, almost apologetic.

"Why not?" Johnson asked. "I bet it wasn't even a viper." The brothers seemed angered by his insensitivity. Ellis was about to strike him when they noticed Perrish returning.

My body was stiff, and I was too weak to speak. But when I didn't see Doc Webber with him, a sudden rush of energy came over me. "Where the fuck is the corpsman?" I demanded to know.

"He wouldn't come," Perrish answered.

"What!"

"He wouldn't come."

"Why not?"

"He said it wasn't nothing he could do. If a viper bit you, you would be dead before he could get here."

"What else does that fat motherfucker got to do?"

"Well, aren't you glad you aren't dead?" Perrish said to me.

Johnson capitalized on the opportunity to clear his reputation. "I told you it wasn't a viper!" he said, walking away. The rest of them were now looking at me with disgust. Trying to salvage my dignity with humor, I looked to the stars with outstretched arms and proclaimed, "It's a miracle." The humor was obviously lost, because each turned and walked away in disgust. The last word came from Perrish, who told me to just go back to sleep.

The stiff leg and sizeable lump on my right cheek left me with little doubt I had been bitten by something, but I would have to wait for the light of day to check it out. This made an anxious night for me. As time went on, I realized I was going to live. It was like I was going to get a second chance at life. What's more important, I would get a chance to recognize what was really important in life. Perhaps this was a good thing. I greeted the first light of day with my pants down attempting to inspect the wound. This would have been impossible for anyone other than a contortionist. I looked like a dog chasing his tail. Having failed every attempt to self-diagnose the situation and feeling it was too personal to allow others to inspect, I went to see Doc Webber. "Well, it must not have been a viper," he commented as I approached. Agitated by his lack of sympathy, I simply showed him the wound. After inspecting it for a few minutes, he acknowledged something had clearly bitten me. He was, however, clearly puzzled as to what it could have been. He reached into his medical bag and gave me an ointment that probably had no medical value whatsoever. But I accepted and applied it. Within a few days, the swelling went down, and the stiffness subsided. Bush life went on.

A few promotions and personnel changes were given within the platoon. Snarr was moved to company radioman. This put him working directly with the captain, a fast track to the top. Brantley and Speedy were promoted to corporal. A member from Fourth Squad, Bencomo, was promoted to corporal and given charge of the squad, replacing Snarr.

Speedy and Brantley had come in-country together, but they couldn't have been more different. Speedy was still the violent inner-city brother from LA, and Brantley was the mild-mannered Mississippi native. They both followed and relayed orders without question, but their leadership styles were opposite. Brantley did show he had a violent side and a strong loyalty to the men under him. Hanson, one of Brantley's men, had left his safety off his weapon. Speedy noticed this and punched him in the face, knocking him down. This surprised everyone because squad leaders don't usually discipline outside their own squads, but no one commented.

When Brantley found out, he went into a rage. This was the first time we had seen anyone challenge Speedy. Brantley let out a banshee scream while charging Speedy, swinging with both hands. It was obvious that Brantley had limited offensive skills. In fact, he looked like an octopus fighting with himself. Speedy was startled. That slight hesitation allowed Brantley to get in his one and only blow. After that, Speedy deflected every punch. Seeing Brantley wasn't going to stop, Speedy went on the offense.

He grabbed Brantley, lifted him over his head, and slammed him to the ground. He then grabbed an arm, then a leg, then twisted him into a contorted position. Speedy obviously respected his old friend, because he playfully slapped him like a cat toying with a mouse. However, the tenacious Brantley never gave up. Speedy had to decide either to seriously hurt his old friend or to apologize. He apologized. Brantley finally backed down when Speedy assured him it wouldn't happen again. It was the strangest fight I had ever seen. One in which the winner was the loser.

With their newfound respect, they collaborated in assigning men. Each would supply one man. Speedy volunteered me, and Brantley sent Little Louie. The observation post was an early warning system during the day; at night it would become a listening post. Care was taken to select the position. It had to provide a range of vision during the day to observe the approaching enemy. Then it had to be at a likely spot where the enemy would approach at night. In both cases, the men on the position had to be able to conceal themselves. There were only three positions outside the lines that suited the purpose, so they were continuously used. The constant use presented a problem.

The men would eat their meals and then bury their discarded refuse. Louie and I stood watch at what was now a garbage dump. I had a closely held secret that would be exposed that night. I had an unnatural fear of mice, topped only by my fear of rats. It was predictable how I would react when confronting the fearsome "bush rat." In hindsight, I should have warned those around me of this, but I naïvely thought rats only lived in the ghetto, so I felt no need to divulge weaknesses.

At dusk we slipped past the men guarding the outer perimeter. When we reached the position, there was just enough daylight light to see the discarded food containers. "Damn!" I mumbled, tossing the debris. "Those motherfuckers ain't nothing but pigs."

"How do you want to set up?" Louie asked.

"Every two hours."

"We won't get much sleep. Let's switch every four."

"No way, man. It's too hard to stay awake for four hours," I answered.

After a few minutes of protest, Louie agreed. We reasoned that if the enemy attempted to infiltrate the lines, we wanted to be as alert as possible. The sun had now set, and I took first watch.

From the corner of my eyes, I saw a black object that looked like a puppy with no legs scurry within a few feet of where I was sitting. I recoiled in a defensive ball. The movement startled the creature, and it darted into the brush as suddenly as it had appeared. "Some kind of animal came out of the brush," I whispered to Louie.

"It was just a rat," responded Louie.

"A rat?" I repeated.

"Yeah, man," Louie said before reassuring me that the rats wouldn't come close to humans. He then went back to sleep. Louie was wrong. Soon more of the vermin came out of the shadows. It was apparent they were attempting to reclaim their territory. As their numbers grew, their boldness grew. I secured a tree limb and pounded on the ground, keeping them away. Each time I would come close to hitting them, they would let out a piercing scream and then scurry back into the shadows. By the end of my watch, I was exhausted, but I kept the rats away.

"Man," I said, waking Louie. "I didn't see any VC, but there some big-ass rats running around. I spent all that time chasing them away."

"Thanks," he said with a grin, "they give me the creeps too." I gave him the tree branch, assuming he would continue to drive the rats away.

Feeling confident of our shared desire to keep the rats away from us, I drifted off to sleep. It was, however, a restless sleep. I was in a semiconscious state. A potential enemy confrontation and the image of the rats wouldn't allow me to fall into a deep sleep.

I felt something wasn't right. It was like I was being searched, like there were hands roving all over my body. My first thought was that maybe Louie was searching for drugs, or maybe there was a side of Louie I didn't know. Either way, I was going to catch him in the act. I raised my head, and, through my partially closed eyes, I could see Louie sitting about four feet away and silently laughing. My sudden movement caused the sensation to quicken. Rustling sounds were in the brush all around. There was pressure on my chest. Less than a foot from my face was a hungry rat trying to get at the food in my pocket. There were rats all over me searching for food. All the time Louie sat there laughing, enjoying it.

Expendable and Necessary

Although I had respect for Louie and looked upon him as a mentor, there are some things that can't be overlooked. Louie had to die.

My first move was to reach for my weapon. I tried to grab for it while keeping my eyes on Louie, but Louie reached his knife first. I knew I would now have to disarm Louie and then take him out with my hands. So I reached out with my left hand, grabbed Louie's weapon, and slung it away. Then I went for his throat. My forward momentum drove Louie to the ground. I was now on Louie's chest with my hands locked firmly around his neck. Louie was clawing, kneeing, and scratching, but I wasn't releasing my viselike grip.

Louie was losing consciousness, and in a desperate attempt to stay alive, he was attempting to pry one of my fingers back. Realizing I was losing my grip, I went for my Ka-Bar. When I got it about halfway out of the sheath, Louie grabbed my right wrist.

This didn't deter me. I managed to dig the finger of my left hand into Louie's throat while banging my head into his. The scene was reminiscent of an action-movie scene. During the entire struggle, Louie was attempting to apologize. To no avail. But what Louie said next changed everything. He put his mouth to my ear and whispered, "Don't move; there is somebody watching." His grip tightened to the point that I couldn't move. If I questioned this as simply a diversion, the look in Louie's eyes told me it wasn't. We released each other and slowly went for our weapons, creeping across the ground, a cat approaching its prey. To make a harder target, we moved apart. Then we lay motionless, listening for movement.

Our eyes searched the silhouettes we had become familiar with during the night in search of any changes. Although the fixed surroundings seemed intact, there was unnatural movement in the distant brush. Even the rats stayed away.

After about a half hour we relaxed, confident the danger had passed. For the rest of the night, we both stood watch for both the Viet Cong and rats.

At daybreak we gathered our gear in preparation for the walk back to the base camp. We would leave when the men who would occupy the position as a daytime observation post arrived. Louie continued to apologize for allowing the rats to run freely in the area. His reasoning, which I found weak at best, was that he didn't believe someone who would face enemy fire would be afraid of harmless rodents. But I wasn't through with it. My anger had subsided only to put the incident on hold.

A call over the radio broke our uneasy silence. "Gulf two, LP, this is Gulf." Louie answered the call.

"Gulf two, this is Gulf two LP."

"Gulf two LP, be advised a Gulf three rover will pass your position in approximately oh five."

"Gulf two, that's a copy."

In about five minutes, as announced, a squad from Third Platoon passed our position. The black marines gave us the clenched-fist salute as they passed. When the squad leader reached us, he halted the patrol to get a report regarding any night activity they needed to be aware of. Louie, being the senior between us, filled him in.

"You guys see or hear anything?"

"We believe we saw some movement, but nothing clear."

"What?" the squad leader responded.

"We thought there were troops in the brush in that direction observing us, but if it was, they pulled back in the same direction."

The squad leader relayed the information to the command post and was ordered to cautiously inspect that area. He confirmed the order and then ordered the men to continue. Louie and I continued to gather our gear for the short walk back to our line, taking a few moments to clear the garbage. What we didn't toss down the hill I buried. After about five minutes, about the amount of time it would have taken the patrol to travel about one hundred meters, there was an explosion of gunfire from Communist weapons. The marines had walked into an ambush.

We couldn't see them, but they were close enough for us to hear those wounded cry out in pain. Almost simultaneously, the marines returned fire. A full-scale firefight had erupted. Rounds were flying in our direction, causing us to take cover. Louie went for the radio, but the radioman on the patrol was already calling for reinforcements. I grabbed my weapon and attempted to charge down the hill, but Louie grabbed me and wrestled me to the ground. "We've got to hold this position and direct the reinforcements!" he yelled into my ear.

The words were barely out of his mouth when a heavily armed squad of marines appeared to assist the ambushed patrol. "That way!" The marines motioned to them as they passed. It was evident when they reached the firefight, because the volume of American gunfire greatly exceeded that of the Communists. Soon, it was only marines firing. It was obvious the Vietnamese had retreated, taking their dead and wounded as always. Three marines were medevacked. Most likely they were dead or severely wounded. Two more marines received superficial wounds, for which they received a purple heart.

Louie and I were debriefed when we returned, and it was determined we acted properly. We never mentioned the fight or our suspicion that the enemy had been observing us. In all likelihood, the enemy patrol had decided not to reveal themselves and to set an ambush that would yield more kills. The issue was never revisited.

CHAPTER 11

The Top Cat, Ellis
January 1969

▲ ▲ ▲

AFTER SURVIVING FOR OVER TWO months, we were beginning to be accepted by the bushmen. Dura was adjusting by keeping a low profile; I decided to do the same. Ellis was a hustler with a likable, outgoing personality. Walters had joined the tight circle, primarily through Ellis, bringing his combat experience into the mix. Had there not been a war going on, we would have been representative of a typical group of young men coming of age.

The average age of the bushmen was between nineteen and twenty-one years. That age group is in the stage in life referred to as sex, drugs, and rock and roll. For the brothers, the music was R and B.

Although it was rarely discussed, self-gratification was the primary sexual activity in the bush. Occasionally a patrol would run into a prostitute who would take your mind off your troubles for a mere five dollars. The prostitute was likely a plant by the Viet Cong to delay a patrol or to spread venereal disease. That was a minor detail to the precocious young bushmen.

Occasionally a marine returning from R and R, the hospital, or some sort of leave would bring in a fresh supply of drugs. But the supply was running low. As was the food.

In spite of our live-off-the-land survival training, all of the food came out of a can or a pouch. Food and water was delivered on a regular basis and stored in a guarded area among the artillery personnel. Three meals per day were distributed to the riflemen. The energy-burning marines could eat that amount of food in one sitting. Because the area was deep inside enemy territory, resupply was difficult. The men went from three meals a day to only two. Anger was mounting toward the officers and artillerymen who were suspected of hoarding the limited supply.

Second Squad was sitting around discussing the food shortage when Walters came over with his newfound friend. "This is Hansen!" Walters announced. Hansen looked totally out of place among this group of African Americans.

PFC Hansen was a dairy farmer's son from Wisconsin. His blond hair, blue eyes, and freckled face would have made him the perfect American Farmer poster boy. The men gave him a scornful glance, snickered, and then ignored him. Walters introduced him again, this time getting louder and addressing Ellis directly. "Hansen," he said. "This is Ellis the Top Cat, or TC, as we call him."

"Why you bringing super chuck over here?" Ellis snapped at him.

"Hey, man, this is my partner," Walters snapped back. "Why you dissing him?"

"Cause he could be CID [Civilian Investigation Department] checking for drugs."

"Shit, man!" Walters yelled while stomping his foot. "He's been in the bush for four months. How far you think they will go to catch you smoking reefer? Anybody that comes over here can smell it!"

Walters pulled a joint from his pocket, lit it, and handed it to Hansen.

Hansen wasn't very experienced, coughing and turning bright red, but a CID wouldn't implicate himself, so the men were satisfied. However, they still didn't want any part of Hansen, so Hansen took the initiative.

"You guys hungry?" Hansen said in his Midwestern accent.

"Living on one meal a day, as big as my ass is?" Dura responded sarcastically. "What do you think?"

"Come on." Hansen motioned for us to follow him. He took us to a spot near his foxhole that appeared to be a clump of brush. It was actually a camouflage cover. We were shocked to see what it concealed. There were; writing supplies, candy, cigarettes, and a case of C rations. It was as though the marines had discovered a pot of gold.

"Where did that shit come from?" asked Ellis.

"I stole it!" Hansen said with a wink.

"How and from where?"

Hansen went on to explain. "The supplies are brought in by chopper every few days. The artillery people unload the chopper, and then they store it out of sight. We're so preoccupied guarding the perimeter and patrolling that we don't notice the boxes. Those motherfuckers are eating well up there."

"But they keep close watch on the supplies," I interjected. "How do you get the supplies out?"

"I walk right past them."

"If I went up there and picked up those boxes, I couldn't get two feet," I told him.

"Of course not."

"In fact, when they find they are short, they're gonna come search the brothers."

"Of course," Hansen responded with a shrug.

"So you think that is all right?"

"No, but that's what's gonna happen," replied Hansen. I was now clearly agitated.

"Look at me!" Ellis said, turning to me. "Now look at Hansen!" I turned to Hansen. "Who do you think the lifers will be suspicious of?"

The answer was so obvious I didn't bother to respond. So Ellis went on.

"To get what we want, we have to use whatever the situation presents."

Hansen apologized to me for the misunderstanding. He wasn't saying that it was the way it should be, just that it was the way it was. It was dropped, and we enjoyed the food he shared. Hansen, in turn, had made a drug connection.

It was postholiday 1969, and we were getting the traditional holiday depression. The American people tried to lessen the pain of separation with an extensive letter-writing campaign. Massive amounts of letters arrived and were randomly distributed. Most were from mothers or schoolchildren offering a kind word or spiritual solace. There were also many from religious leaders seeking converts.

The most sought-after were the sexually explicit ones. On rare occasions revealing photos arrived. The men would always answer those letters asking for more. Usually the return address was bogus. This didn't bother the men, and they accepted it like a man being stood up. Some would save the letter and photos, being as protective of them as they would of a spouse.

Others would circulate the photos when new ones arrived. They were even more satisfying to the sex-starved marine standing night watch than the *Playboy* magazines that occasionally arrived. The women likely never knew what a service they were doing for the morale of the fighting men for their country.

The Viet Cong soon brought an end to that party when they shot down a chopper loaded with supplies. Most of the attempts to shoot down the heavily armed supply choppers were from crippled old farmers with rusty, antiquated rifles who didn't have a chance. It was more of a suicide attempt on their part. The NVA attempt using RPGs was successful. The next chopper was also hit.

The food situation soon turned desperate. We were now rationed one meal a day. To make the situation even more unbearable, we were short on drugs. So the kids who frequented the camp were upping the price. We had gone from paying one dollar for ten joints to ten dollars for one joint. Then the prostitutes, who sometimes greeted the patrolling marines, also tripled the price. The start of '69 was not looking good.

So Ellis, the consummate schemer, was thinking of a way to turn it around. He turned to the farm boy Hansen.

"The Wisconsin Wonder!" Ellis said as he approached him. Hansen stopped feeding his face momentarily to answer.

"Hey, TC, you want some peaches?"

Not being one to refuse his favorite dessert, he accepted and then struck up a conversation.

"You know we're short on food and supplies."

"Yeah, man, shit's bad, but there is a lot stored on top of the hill."

"What other supplies are up there?"

"Smokes, candy, soap, beer."

"Beer!" Ellis said in astonishment.

"Hell yes, they stockpile that shit. But beer is counted, so it's harder to get."

"How about helping us raid the supplies?"

"What do you mean?" Hansen said.

"Just what I said."

"What's in it for me?"

"Just like the white man, you don't do nothing unless there is a payoff. OK, drugs, I'll get you some one oh ones," Ellis told him.

"OK, but why me? I can only get enough to carry in my pockets."

"You know the layout and the guard routine. Come on." Ellis motioned to Hansen. "Let's talk to some people."

Ellis and Hansen went over to the Second Squad members who were sitting around listening to some music and writing letters. "We've got to figure out how to get more supplies," he said, getting right into the conversation.

"No shit," I answered, while eating a bean and pork slice meal, which I detested.

"I think we can get as much as we want, if we work it out," Hansen said with a smile.

"That's why I brought you here," agreed Ellis.

"We guard the outer lines, so that won't be a problem," Hansen went on. "But we have to get past the inner lines that are guarded by the artillery people. Of course, we aren't supposed to be in the compound at night, and if we were, we can't just walk across the compound at night and take the supplies. But we can slip in from outside the lines and haul it off."

I wasn't convinced until Hansen reminded me of the section of the hill that had a steep drop-off. At the bottom of the drop-off was a listening post that was guarded by grunts from Second Platoon, who would be in on the raid. The artillerymen on the inner perimeter had no reason to suspect the enemy would approach from that spot, so they wouldn't be looking closely. Just in case, they needed someone to be in the position with them. Speedy, as squad leader, was the only one who could do it without arousing suspicion. Walters was the likely one to approach Speedy about it. To everyone's surprise, he agreed without hesitation. As a final precaution, Johnson, who monitored all radio communication, had to know about the plan. There was always a chance some alert marine with night vision would call an alert. With Speedy in on it, Johnson had no choice but to cooperate. With all the details worked out, it was agreed that the raid would take place the following night.

At 0200 hours, the raid took place. All available men from the platoon assembled at the final position before the drop-off. They formed a human chain that went into the supply tent and skillfully completed the task. The raid was a total success. The platoon netted twelve cases of C rations and a case of beer. It was such a large amount that it was immediately noticed. Now concealing it was more difficult than stealing it in the first place.

The lifers were furious. They knew the grunts had stolen the food but couldn't prove it. But rules of law don't apply in the military. They used every means of threat and intimidation they could think of. They even tried to appeal to their conscience by accusing them of stealing from fellow marines. But the grunts shared it with their peers, so that line of reasoning also failed.

The lifers then ripped all the men's gear apart and threw it all around searching for the food. Those tactics only drew us closer. In time even the artillerymen and those who gained no benefit supported the raid. After a while, the helicopters started the supply drop again, and the incident died down.

Then a new group of marines joined the platoon. They were short timers near the end of their tour en route for An Hoa. It was never explained why they stopped on the hill, but they made for interesting conversation. One of the marines was from Cleveland, so he was immediately introduced to me.

When I learned the Cleveland brother had been involved in the battle for Khe Sanh, I was full of questions. But like most veterans, he chose not to discuss it, so I dropped the subject. Since the marine had not been home in over a year, he was full of questions about Cleveland.

More importantly, he knew the neighborhood I lived in. By a strange coincidence, he dated a girl who lived on the same street. This young lady gave him the inspiration to survive his tour. Every letter she wrote him was a cherished possession. He went on and on about how much he missed her and how they had planned to marry upon his return. What he didn't know, and what I would never tell, was that his girl wasn't waiting faithfully as she had led him to believe. She was known around the neighborhood as an easy lay. In less than two days, the marine was transferred to An Hoa. From there he was to be sent home. We all wished him well, but I knew he would be in for heartbreak.

Another concern for me besides rats was my inability to keep from snoring. With the enemy constantly searching for our positions, snoring could not be tolerated. Because I would rarely get over ten minutes of continuous sleep, I tried everything to stop snoring.

First I tried sleeping on my stomach, which only resulted in a muffled snore. Then I tried taping my mouth shut, causing me to snore through my nose. Finely I tried sleeping with a gas mask, to no avail. The snoring was just as loud through the mask. I even tried to tape the exhaust holes shut. If someone hadn't seen me thrashing around trying to rip that thing off, I might have suffocated. I was resigned to no more ten minutes of sleep at one time.

There was another Harris in Third Platoon. I constantly reminded everyone we weren't related and had no characteristics in common. Just like the Korean marine Hoe, he was exceptionally jittery. Most simply labeled him as a coward as we did with Hoe, but he had more serious problems. He could be seen talking to himself as though he had an alternate ego who could watch his back. If people approached him from the rear or woke him from a sleep, he would draw his weapon on them. That brought repeated ass whippings on him. He might have gone on that way if an incident hadn't brought his situation to the captain.

The enemy would constantly attempt to penetrate our outer perimeter. Most often they would be unsuccessful. On one occasion, they did get in, managing to blow up one of the howitzers. Sometime during the incident night, Harris just disappeared. Pandemonium ensued. The hill was thoroughly searched as well as the surrounding area. About eight hours after his reported disappearance, one of the artillerymen came down to report him hiding in one of the supply tents. He was apparently going to attempt to board a supply chopper when it returned to its base. This enraged his fellow squad members. With the support of the platoon commander, they charged up the hill. The entire squad, in plain sight of officers and sergeants, burst into the supply tent. They thoroughly beat the cowering marine. Finally the lieutenant came to his rescue, ordering the men back. Later that day he was medevacked, and sent to be processed for a medical discharge.

Walters, Johnson, and I were sitting around talking. There could not have been three people so unalike. In spite of the fact that Johnson and I came from two predominately black urban areas, Detroit and Cleveland, we rarely agreed on anything. Our view of the marines would always be a bone of contention. I was a draftee, greatly influenced by the civil rights agenda. I never came to trust those in leadership, always doubting their concern for my safety. War seemed senseless. Johnson, a volunteer, was a staunch supporter of the Marine Corps and never questioned the motives of the leadership. He thought that black people should stop separating themselves and join the band. "One leader, one cause, one direction," he would say. "If the officers and sergeants didn't know what was best for us, they wouldn't have been put in the position."

I considered him an Uncle Tom who couldn't be trusted. But I knew his attitude would assure him a promotion. I personally thought getting a promotion that way was a step down. I might have said that out loud, because Johnson abruptly walked away.

Walters stayed out of that conversation. "I'm a white man," he said. "Y'all gotta work that out yourselves."

"And I'm a black man," I said, unsure why I stated the obvious. It's strange how those few words, at that moment, opened a conversation that seldom takes place in America.

We acknowledged neither of us knew much about the other's race. Curiosity perhaps allowed us to openly and honestly discuss the stereotypes we had been told growing up and in some cases believed. It was clear that a true and unlikely friendship was developing.

From a combat standpoint, the whole month was a mild one. The next six weeks proved to be the least action-filled time that G Company had experienced since Ellis, Dura, and I had arrived. There was, however, conflict brewing within the unit.

For a fighting unit, the principal job is to engage the enemy. Absent of that, the men have a lot of idle time. Soon lounging around becomes the primary activity. Those in positions of authority, superiors as they called themselves, lifers as referred to by the men they commanded, felt it was necessary to keep us busy. Conventional military wisdom was that discipline and morale would suffer if the men weren't being pushed to their limits.

Physical and tactical training exercises were developed and then increased. Physical and verbal abuse was encouraged. Corporal Snarr, Fourth Squad leader, pushed his men hard, but he seemed to show some compassion. The other three squad leaders, all African American, used a more hands-on approach. Perhaps they wanted to impress the officers and NCOs. Corporal Rhone, First Squad leader, who was generally mild mannered, was starting to become abusive. He would insist his men keep their gear neat and weapons immaculate. If one of them had anything out of place, he would scramble the entire squad's equipment and then insist they redo it with undue speed.

Not to be undone, Corporal Brantley physically attacked Perrish, one of his squad members, whom he considered a friend. On some occasions he would throw him down the hill. There were times when he came seriously close to injuring him. Brantley would force his men to repeat maneuvers until his men were at a point of exhaustion. All of this was encouraged by the lifers.

Speedy, as usual, was the most physically and emotionally abusive. He attacked Dura, Hansen, and most of all Walters. Johnson escaped Speedy's wrath by endorsing his actions. That left Louie, Ellis, and me, but I suspected the time would come.

Things came to a head when he grabbed Ellis by the collar threatening to pulverize him for not responding to an order quickly. Ellis was generally liked by everyone, so the general feeling was that Speedy was going too far. He had attacked Top Cat.

Little did he know that the series of events he had set in motion would change the attitude among the men of G Company.

CHAPTER 12

A New Gun Is in Town
February 1969

▲ ▲ ▲

It was a relatively uneventful day, which made it unusual to see Ellis in such an agitated state. He was pacing in circles, looking for someone to express his anger to or at. I sat writing a letter. Considering me to be his best friend, he came over to me. Ellis was visibly upset, so much so that he couldn't sit or stand still. He would walk in circles and kick the ground. His anger was continuing to mount. Finally, he punched at the air, frantically swinging and yelling at an invisible foe.

"I'm gonna kick that motherfucker's ass!" he finally announced.

"Whose ass?" I asked.

"Speedy, who else?" Ellis yelled. "That son of a bitch slammed me against a tree. Don't nobody do that to me." I made no comment, just looking at my friend with a sympathetic expression. This seemed to anger Ellis even more.

"What you looking at?" Ellis hollered at me. Again I gave no response.

"Well, say something, goddammit!"

"You're not going to like this," I finally said, "but you can't beat Speedy."

"What! How the fuck you know?"

"Look, I know you, and I know Speedy, and you can't beat him."

"You can't look at me and tell me I can't beat him."

"Yes, I can."

"How?"

"Speedy is bigger than you, stronger than you, and a hell of a lot more vicious. That crazy motherfucker would fight a seven-hundred-pound gorilla just to see if he could beat it."

"What do you mean I can't whip his ass?" To prove his point, Ellis put on a ten-second shadowboxing exhibition. "What you think about that?" he said while gasping for air.

I addressed him like a coach or trainer to an athlete. "You're right-handed, but you box from a lefty's stance. Unless you're a boxing prodigy, you're just a one-handed fighter. And you telegraph your punches."

"What the fuck you talking about?"

"You bounce two times before you throw a punch. Then you pull the punch back before you throw it. Shit, you're a counterpuncher's dream." Ellis threw a couple punches to test the observation and realized I was right.

"What else?" Ellis asked, becoming convinced I was onto something.

"Well, your balance is bad, so you can't get leverage behind your punches. That's why you're throwing all arm punches, which won't even slow him down. If he charges you, which he will, you'll trip over your own feet."

Ellis suddenly became silent, thinking hard about what I was saying. "You know," Ellis said, stroking his chin, "you seemed to handle yourself pretty well in that fight in Okinawa. Did you get into a lot of fights?"

"Not really," I said, shrugging my shoulders.

"I've always been meaning to ask you something. How did you get that scar on your face?" Ellis said, referring to the six-inch pink scar on the left side of my face. The question did trouble me. Others look at your face all the time, but we rarely look at our own. Since no one had ever mentioned it, I had forgotten I had a scar. Ellis now seemed to regret having mentioned it, but now that the cat was out of the bag, he waited for an answer.

Perhaps he was expecting me to tell him I had been in an accident, or that it was none of his business. I decided to just tell him the truth.

"Some dude tried to cut my throat," I finally answered.

"Why?"

"To stop me from kicking his ass."

"I'm sorry for asking. Does it bother you to talk about it?"

"Yeah, but not why you might think."

"What do you mean?"

"I forgot it was there," I finally said.

Ellis's curiosity wasn't satisfied, but he decided to leave it alone. "Look," he said, "it's bad enough that we have to worry about being shot over here, but getting beaten to death by Speedy is becoming a greater likelihood. Since you don't think I can beat him, who can?" I didn't answer, so Ellis asked a more pointed question. "OK, goddammit, can you beat Speedy?"

"Well, I can outbox him."

"That doesn't answer my question."

"OK, I can beat him, but not in a fight."

"What?"

"Fighting is a survival instinct; boxing is a sport," I went on. "Speedy is bigger and stronger. If he grabs me, which would happen in a fight, I'd be in trouble. But if he stands in front of me and tries to box, I'll take him."

"You a boxer?"

"Any motherfucker within twenty pounds of my weight that's not a pro is gonna get their ass whipped. I just got to get Speedy to put on gloves and box."

"We're in the middle of the jungle with no sporting store within a hundred thousand miles. How the fuck you gonna set up a boxing match?"

"I sent for some boxing gloves a week ago. When they get here, I'll challenge him to a friendly match. Speedy will never walk away from a challenge. Especially since he'll have no doubt that he'll win."

"Are you sure you can take him?"

"Yep, I've been watching him from day one, and I know his weaknesses. The key will be keeping him from knowing what's coming."

"How you going to make it happen?"

"The opportunity will come. You just keep from challenging Speedy, and don't tell anybody of this conversation." I went back to writing my letter, while Ellis took a nap.

The next day the opportunity presented itself. The lieutenant was doing an inspection of the marines' positions. Each squad member had dug a foxhole and camouflaged the position with the natural vegetation. The squad leader had his men's position critiqued by the lieutenant. The squad leaders were reprimanded when the men they commanded failed inspection. They, in turn, would take their anger out on the men.

We stood in front of our positions waiting to be inspected. My position was next, followed by Ellis's.

The lieutenant was brutal in his criticism of me. "Look at this shit!" he said, pointing to the rocks in front of my foxhole. "Do you see rocks piled anywhere else on this hill?" Then he ripped down the branches and leaves I had placed around the hole. "Leaves don't grow upside down!" he yelled. "You can spot his position from one hundred yards. Why do you let this motherfucker to get away with shit like this?"

Speedy was thoroughly embarrassed. The lieutenant's admonishment was like an order to physically attack. In fact, he stepped aside to give Speedy room.

Speedy grabbed my backpack off the ground and threw it at my head. I stepped to the side, allowing it to pass just over my shoulder. This was perhaps the first time someone had not allowed Speedy to hit him, and he took it as an act of defiance. As predicted, he charged, swinging wildly.

Speedy didn't give any thought to the fact that being on the downside of the hill put him at a disadvantage. I was able to back up while stepping and turning, making Speedy look clumsy and comical. The men, including the lieutenant, watched in disbelief. Speedy was about to charge again when I pumped four perfectly placed jabs less than one inch from Speedy's nose. It was a warning, and Speedy knew it, stopping dead in his tracks.

He might have tried again had the lieutenant not stepped between us. He could no longer ignore the conflict. He had to take charge. "That is enough!" he said. Only Ellis knew how relieved I was that the lieutenant had stopped it when he did. Speedy was about to grab me, and Ellis knew I would be in trouble.

Ellis took the cue to get involved. "How about a boxing match?" he called out. I could tell Speedy was still angry and could unexpectedly charge, so I moved to defuse the situation. "I don't want to box you, Speedy," I said, deferring to him. "I'll get the foxhole together."

But Speedy's pride wouldn't let it end that easy. There was no way this wiry young underling was going to make him look bad in front of an officer.

Ellis again came in right on time. "Why don't we send for some boxing gloves?"

Speedy liked the idea and adopted it as his own. "OK," he said with a sly smile, "let's hook up a match." I was relieved, but I didn't want to give it away. The lieutenant, who had the final say, was showing some reluctance. But he noticed the men were starting to gather, and excitement was beginning to build. "Listen!" he said with his authoritative voice. "There will be no boxing until the gloves arrive. Then we will have a match under the Marquis of Queensberry rules."

Speedy and I gave each other a confident smile before shaking hands. The fight was on. The thing most exciting about the potential match was that we both were confident we would win.

Later in the day, in a private conversation, the gunny questioned the lieutenant about the fight. "Letting a private box his squad leader may cause moral problems, sir. What if that motherfucker can fight?"

The lieutenant looked at the gunny with a disbelieving smirk. "The men need some entertainment, and that smartass needs his ass kicked. My concern is that Speedy won't cause him some brain damage." They laughed in agreement.

"I guess that means you won't bet," the gunny finally said.

By the start of the following day, the match was all the buzz. Speedy was the heavy favorite. Few seriously believed I stood a chance; however, I did have a small but vocal group of supporters. Ellis and Dura never wavered in their support. The Motown brothers RC and Johnson were slower to join the chorus of supporters. I believe Johnson wanted me to get my ass kicked. Walters wasn't going to risk getting on the wrong side of Speedy.

As interest in the match grew, so too did the resolve of each man. We both began to train. I was the most focused. I stopped smoking, drinking, and doing drugs. I would train for at least four hours a day. Push-ups and sit-ups for the upper body, knee bends and thrusts for the lower body. Each day I would jog ten laps around the compound to strengthen my lungs. The most impressive routine was my shadowboxing. Soon I won over the Motown supporters. "I know the sweet science," RC commented to Johnson. "The brother's got skills." That endorsement began to persuade the nonbelievers.

But Speedy was equally impressive. He was a natural athlete. The twenty pounds he had over me was solid muscle. In addition to the weight advantage, losing was an alien concept to him.

The gloves arrived the next day, and the fight was scheduled to take place in a week. No one seemed to question the fast arrival of the gloves. They were totally focused on the event. Everyone seemed to join in. The engineers built a ring, regulation size with ammo crates for seating.

Sparring sessions began to take place. This was where Speedy's supporters gained greater confidence. He would treat each sparring session as if it were a title fight, pummeling all who stood before him. Gradually through fear, intimidation, and raw power, his sparring partners fell until there were none.

Each time Speedy would spar, I would watch looking for weaknesses. I realized quickly that Speedy was quick to become frustrated and would quickly revert to swinging wildly. Speedy also had no defensive skills. Thus far he had no need of them.

I was more purposeful in my sparring, always coming short of overpowering my opponent. I didn't want the sparring to become a boxing match. I knew Speedy could deliver and sustain a harder punch. But Speedy threw arm punches. My edge would be ring skill, so I worked on my jabs, hooks, uppercuts, and combinations. I practiced circling to the left and to the right and punching while moving backward. It was imperative that Speedy stand and box. If he did, I felt I could frustrate him and then wear him down. Once Speedy tired, the power advantage would shift to me. I knew how to shift my body weight to increase the power of my punch.

I added one more weapon to my arsenal, overt confidence. I actually borrowed the ploy used by the great Muhammad Ali, a hero to most brothers in the bush. I laughed, joked, and treated it as if I had waited for this day all my life. It was rumored that I was either an exceptional boxer or crazy. It was also falsely rumored I was a pro. All of this was starting to break down Speedy's confidence

As the fight date approached, other marines in the company signed on for preliminary bouts. Old grudges would be settled. The card was set: Bencomo versus Johnson. Bodfield challenged Holmes from Chicago. Dura took on a big German squad leader from Third Platoon. Rhone, the First Squad leader, decided he would beat up on Perrish. Ellis challenged Pirra. The engineers and artillerymen suspected the grunts were a crazed bunch of warmongers who would fight each other in the absence of a common enemy.

It would be four three-minute rounds with one minute between rounds. A sergeant from Fourth Platoon would referee, and there would be no judges. The spectators would decide for themselves.

At last, fight day arrived. There was about to be a rumble in the jungle.

None could have predicted the level of interest the match would generate. The confidence displayed by both of us fueled speculation. Some of the men from Gulf Company were betting their whole month's pay. The men from the artillery and engineers company could also be heard placing wagers. The lifers, still unsure if this was within the rules of military protocol, watched from a respectable distance.

Security for the base and area was being maintained, but the majority of the personnel were focused on the fight. Even the Chinese mercenaries and South Vietnamese scouts were vying for a spot in the limited space available. The preliminary bouts were matches proved a matchmaker's dream. Bodfield, the tough-talking street kid from Philly, could back up his words. Homes would have made the brothers from the south side of Chicago proud. The combatants proved equally skilled, so the fight played out like a chess match. When it was over, the spectators agreed it was a draw. The next match was a heavyweight bout between Dura and the German. The match could best be described as a pier one brawl. The blows were so wild and uncontrolled that the referee was afraid to step between them. The men slammed against the ropes so hard that they broke them loose. They continued to pummel one another outside the ring, sending spectators scrambling for cover to escape the thunderous blows.

It took two marines to pull them apart at the end of the round. The pride of the two men had elevated it to an all-out fight. While nursing their wounds between the rounds, they mutually agreed to call off the match.

Holmes's adrenaline was still high after his match with Bodfield, so he challenged Johnson. It was Chi-Town against Motown. Johnson could talk the talk, but he couldn't walk the walk. Homes toyed with him. It was a shock to everyone to see a brother from Detroit who couldn't box. To add insult to his injuries, Ellis, the self-proclaimed lover, not a fighter, was calling him out. Johnson wisely took off the gloves for good.

Next, it was First Squad leader Rhone against Perrish. Rhone, who had bullied Perrish on a daily basis, was anxious to display his skills. Perrish begged him to go light on him, but Rhone insisted on the match. That proved to be a bad decision on Rhone's part. The tough facade that Rhone portrayed was quickly destroyed by Perrish. It wasn't that Perrish had great skills, Rhone just had no skills. The round ended with Rhone still talking tough, promising to get vindication, but clearly lacking the ability to carry out the threat.

When round two began, Rhone charged. Perrish stopped him in his tracks with the first punch. Then Perrish showed character and respect for his squad leader. He backed off from Rhone and allowed him to land a barrage of punches. He then faked an injury, giving his friend an honorable way out. Rhone never bullied Perrish again.

Johnson with his clear baritone voice was now taking on the role of announcer. "All those wishing to hold a match, step forward," he called out. There was silence, but excitement filled the air. Then he made the announcement everyone was waiting to hear. "Let's bring on the main event!" The crowd roared and went into frenzy.

Then, like phantoms appearing from the shadows, we emerged from the jungle. Each wore our game face. Speedy's glare was menacing, as if he wanted to kill, clearly trying to intimidate me, a plan that had always worked in the past. But I knew how to play the game. I became the only thing a bully feared, an unpredictable crazed maniac. First I was excited, taunting Speedy, causing Ellis to restrain me. Then I was laughing as if at a party celebration. Several times I alternated between the personalities. Speedy's expression went from menacing to confused, just as I had hoped.

Johnson attempted to state the rules, but neither of us listened, so he went straight to the introduction.

For no apparent reason, Speedy's introduction came first. "To my left, the man who needs no introduction, from LA Ca-li-forn-i-a, Speedy Washing-ton!" The crowd roared.

"To my right, the brother from Cle-ve-land-O-H-Ten, Ralph Harrisssss!" Again there was a roar from the crowd. We touched gloves and then retreated to our corners. There was no bell, just a designated marine who started and stopped the rounds by yelling out "Ding!" Which he did.

I pulled out my first bag of tricks, a mouthpiece. Looking at Speedy, I smiled. Speedy had no time to protest the advantage.

Just as expected, Speedy charged, throwing what could best be described as power hooks. If any of the blows had landed flush, I would have been knocked cold. But I dropped my head and threw a combination of straight left and right punches that stopped Speedy's charge. Speedy did manage to land at least two glancing blows, which I felt but showed no reaction to. To negate Speedy's power, I stepped close and threw short hooks and uppercuts. Speedy attempted to step back to gain punching room, but I continued to crowd him. The infighting, at that point, was an advantage for me.

Speedy's instincts quickly kicked in, and he attempted to grab me so he could wrestle me down. Speedy clearly had fighting skills, but he wasn't a boxer. With the bulky gloves on, he couldn't grab me, and I never stopped punching.

The round ended with Speedy more confused than hurt, struggling to keep control of his emotions.

The next round, Speedy attempted to turn it into a brawl, but I wouldn't cooperate. I was determined to lure him into a boxing match where I would maintain an advantage. I jabbed and circled, consistently landing pesky but effective combinations. Speedy attempted to mimic my footwork, which was perhaps his greatest undoing. Speedy had an awkward bounce and a moment when both feet would leave the ground.

He was off balance with a predictable rhythm that was easy to detect. I pushed off from my right foot and threw all my weight behind a perfectly timed overhand right. Speedy had the reaction of a man who had run into a brick wall. The blow sent him stumbling backward across the ring into the ropes. He was such a physically strong man that, despite being unconscious, he managed to remain standing. He was, however, standing in the middle of the ring with his hands to his sides, an open target. The jaw-dropped crowd was totally silent. No one, including me, wanted to see the proud warrior beaten to the ground. I glanced at the timekeeper as a signal to prematurely end the round and avoid the inevitable.

Speedy didn't go to his corner. He walked over to me and raised my hand. I smiled, embraced him, and returned the gesture. The crowd went wild with excitement. They showed appreciation to both of us for the entertainment. There was no doctor or cut men in attendance, so all fighters had to nurse their wounds.

Later that day I decided to locate Speedy to have a talk. I knew that if we didn't settle things, Speedy might attack me at any time. This was the first time we had an open dialogue. Normally, Speedy held to the military code that forbade fraternization with those you command, but that time it was different.

"How you doing, brother?" I asked timidly. After a short pause, Speedy looked at me.

"OK, champ," he said with a smile.

Before approaching him, I asked, "Are we straight?" Speedy assured me the issue was closed, and we exchanged the power handshake. Speedy seemed surprised.

"Am I that bad?" Speedy questioned me.

"Well, you do have a temper," I said.

"Naw, that's just an act."

I was surprised by Speedy's comment.

"There is a reason I do things the way I do," Speedy explained.

"What's that?"

"I care what happens to the men," Speedy said. "Do you think you have seen some rough action?"

"Yes!"

"Believe me, brother, it's gonna get worse. The only thing that keeps us alive is everybody doing their job and doing it right. In most cases, timing is everything. People can't hesitate when you give them an order, so there must be one voice, and everyone must react without hesitation. Maybe I'm wrong," he said, looking toward the sky as if guided by a divine force. "I just want to keep people alive."

I offered an honest opinion. "You have been here longer than I, but with all the things we have to fear, we shouldn't have to fear each other."

"Let me ask you this," Speedy went on. "Your men are in an ambush, and you want them to move out, and they say, 'Fuck you!' What would you do?"

"Why would they do that?" I asked.

He gave me a list of logical reasons. "Because they are scared and they would rather stay behind a rock, because they would rather run in the opposite direction, because they don't think you know what the hell you are talking about. Shit, there is a lot of reasons not to do what you tell them. You just can't have an open discussion. They do what they are told from either fear or respect. Fear is much easier to control. What would you do if I gave you an order you didn't agree with?" Speedy asked.

"I would do it."

"Why?"

"Because you know more about what's going on, and I trust your judgment. It takes time to win respect, but a person will willingly follow you if you have it."

Both of us made valid points, but there was a slim likelihood we would ever totally agree on the leadership role. After further discussion, we realized we did have something in common. We both questioned the country being in the conflict, particularly the black man, but were helpless to do anything but go along. It was no surprising revelation; this was the Marine Corps, where conformity was demanded and diversity was not allowed.

In truth, our views were more common than those outside the situation were led to believe. There was always controversy and discussion among the lower ranks regarding the role of the leadership and the purpose of the war itself. But it was always silenced by those in positions of power.

It was a surprisingly revealing conversation between two men who had never held a conversation that lasted more than two minutes. Something positive did come from the fight after all. Speedy was clearly uncomfortable criticizing the corps, so he switched the topic, deciding to learn more about the man he commanded.

"I always wondered something," he said, looking directly at me. "Who are you?"

I was hesitant to answer, perhaps because I felt guilty at having set him up. But Speedy persisted. "Look, brother, I know you aren't just some crazy motherfucker who likes to fight. Who taught you to fight?"

"I'm from a big city," I said. "To survive, you either know how to bullshit or fight."

"A big city, you call Cleveland a big city?"

"It's not LA, but yes, it's a big city."

"What's Cleveland O-H-Ten about? We don't get a lot of information about it on the West Coast."

"OK." I was proud to talk about my hometown, so I gave him a brief history. "Cleveland is an old industrial city. It borders on a lake and empties into an ocean. Those waterways and natural resources made it an ideal location for the steel, aluminum, and automotive industries. That means jobs were plentiful. So during the forties and fifties, immigrants and people needing work that wasn't offered in other parts of the country came to cities like Cleveland, Detroit, and Chicago. Well, in Cleveland, like other cities, each nationality gravitated into their own sections. Blacks had the largest sections because most whites sold them their houses, moved to the suburbs, then shut the door."

"That's the way it is in LA," Speedy interjected.

"Then you know we black people have our own turfs in those neighborhoods. We had neighborhoods like Kinsman, Saint Clare, Hough, Cedar, Superior, and a few others. I lived around Superior. My partners and I would stand on one of the corners and watch people going by on the main street. If somebody went by that we didn't recognize and we thought we could take them, we would jump them. There were these five brothers that would jog by every weekday about five o'clock."

"Did you jump them?"

"Hell no!"

"Why not?"

"They would have kicked our ass."

"They must have been some badasses!"

"Damn right. You could tell by their wrapped hands they were boxers. One day I followed them. When they went into a recreation center that one of the area churches sponsored, I followed them inside. I found out, later, they were part of a boxing team from the recreation center a few blocks over. While standing in the hall, a tall, burly man approached me and asked if I would like to learn to box. I told him I would. A few days later, I showed up with the gear he told me to bring. I was late that first day, and when I walked into the gym, all eyes turned to me. At fourteen, I was not only the youngest but, at a hundred and five pounds, the smallest one in the room. To add to the humiliation, I wore the wrong type shoes and trunks. I wanted to walk out, but before I could, the trainer stopped me.

"'My name is Ash,' he announced as though I should recognize him. 'I'm the trainer of the Cory boxing team, the best in the city.' Then he introduced the other fighters, giving special attention to the five fighters I had seen jogging through the neighborhood. 'That's the Parks brothers, Jim and James. They're going to the Golden Gloves tournament this year. Over there are the Malone twins, the baddest middleweights in Cleveland. Over there is Earl Johnson, a third-year pro. He's about to break into a world ranking. I'm going to make a fighter out of you, little man,' he said. 'That is, if you are serious.' I was like a star-struck kid, envisioning myself as the next Muhammad Ali, the newly crowned heavyweight champ. But that was just a fleeting dream for me, and these guys didn't just have idle dreams; they had goals. Ash, the trainer, made it clear to me, if I wasn't serious, not to waste his time. That was the start of my boxing career, or what could have been a career." Speedy wanted to ask about that statement but decided to wait. So I went on.

"The training started with an increasingly strenuous exercise regimen. Then he taught me the proper technique to throw punches. Leverage, balance, timing, head and foot movement, all the skills someone outside the sport might have thought would come natural. Most of the time was spent watching the other boxers and then trying to emulate them. They were also watching me and giving much-needed advice. Around the third week, Ash decided it was time for me to spar. That would be the true test. If a student wasn't serious, the sparring sessions would certainly wash them out. It nearly did. As the smallest and least experienced, I got my ass kicked on a regular basis. My size also made me faster than them. Fortunately, the fighters would ease up when they had me in trouble.

"From time to time, others from the neighborhood would come in, but most wouldn't stay. Sparring with the casual walk-ins showed me I could box."

"How is that?" Speedy asked.

"When boxing someone my size, I could handle them easily. The 1963 Golden Gloves tournament was coming up, and Ash decided that, although I was under the age limit, I was the best novice flyweight in the area, so he wanted to enter me. When I found the only serious competition was a white boy from the West Side, I was overconfident."

"Why?"

"I had gone to the tournaments with the team, and I saw him box."

"So did you kick his ass?" Speedy broke in.

"Well," I went on, "life sometimes doesn't go as expected, especially when you work against yourself. In my mind, I had already won, so the night before I was hanging out with my partners Billy and Bub. We were celebrating my expected victory. We chipped in for a bottle of wine and the extra cost we had to pay the wine head that picked it up. It wasn't long before I was smoking cigarettes and drinking wine along with them."

Speedy cut in again. "You mean to tell me you got drunk the night before a fight?"

"Yes," I responded with embarrassment. Speedy laughed and reminded me of the drunken episode prior to our aerial assault on the NVA base camp.

"You know you can't hold that wine. But I must admit," he said, laughing out loud, "you sobered up when those bullets whizzed by your head. I'm sorry, man," he laughed. "What happened next?"

"We kept drinking until I began throwing up. I hoped that would clean me out. Then I staggered home. When I got there, my parents were asleep, so I got in undetected. My brother was awake. He would sometimes stay up to see if I was OK. He saw I was drunk and tried to remind me of how foolish that was before a fight. As usual, I didn't listen."

"You don't talk about your brother much," Speedy commented.

"I know," I said, almost apologetic. "We were just so different. I hung in the streets living the thug life. He didn't socialize in the neighborhood. His friends were in the rich side of Cleveland. I did the minimum in school. He was the academic."

"But he is your brother."

"I know," I continued, while pulling out the picture of my brother he had sent in his last letter. The picture was taken in his college dormitory. He was dressed in the popular large-collared open shirt and bell-bottom trousers, with a neatly trimmed Fu Manchu mustache, standing by a leather couch. "He is also driving my brand-new canary-yellow Cougar," I added.

"Wow," Speedy gasped. "The brother looks like he's got it together. He is a lover, not a fighter."

"That's true," I said, putting the picture back in my pocket, before continuing with the story.

"The next morning I woke up, and my brother again showed concern, suggesting I withdraw from the fight. Again I ignored him. To help the hangover, I finished the rest of the wine I had saved. To aid my nerves, I smoked on the way to the gym where we would be transported. Inside the closed car, everyone could smell the wine and cigarettes. Ash was pissed. Not only had I broken his gym rules, but I stunk up his new Lincoln Continental. The team discussed whether I should be withdrawn from the fight. Ash, who makes the final decision, decided to keep me in. There was little discussion for the remainder of the ride. The team members were mentally preparing for their own contests.

"When we reached the recreation center where the fights were to take place, I immediately prepared for the fight. The lighter-weight divisions went first, so, at a hundred and eight pounds, I was the opening fight. That wine had me thinking I could whip the world, so I wasn't concerned at all. Ash, who was working my corner, was very concerned. He instructed me to knock him out as soon as possible.

"I rushed him and landed a well-placed combination. He tried to retaliate with two looping punches, which I easily slipped. The crowd went wild. I responded with showboat tactics, burning energy I did not have. After about one minute, I was out of air. It felt as if I had just completed a two-hundred-yard sprint. The fight quickly shifted, with me fighting in spurts and then holding while I gasped for air. I knew what to do and how to do it; I just couldn't. Finally, the first round came to an end.

"When I reached my stool, Ash talked, but I wasn't listening. Strategy was nowhere in my thoughts. All I wanted was some air. But things were getting worse; I was on the verge of throwing up. Man, was I miserable. I needed to throw up, and Ash was sticking the mouthpiece in my mouth before the start of round two.

"At that point, I wasn't too concerned about him knocking me out. I had taken his best punch, and it wasn't much. I was strictly on the defense, throwing punches only to keep him off me. He really made me look like a fool, but all wasn't lost. The little movement I did didn't cause me to expend much energy. There was a chance for a second wind. When the round ended, that was all I could think of.

"Ash was so upset he didn't even attempt to give me instructions. All he did was curse. James kept repeating, 'Breathe deep, breathe deep,' but nothing helped. I was so exhausted I attempted to lie down. My corner was even laughing at me.

"Again, Ash shoved the mouthpiece in my mouth in preparation for the last round. James gave me the final instruction that I'll never forget. 'Don't let that motherfucker knock you out.' Then they shoved me to the center of the ring.

"The fight had digressed to a comedy act. I was so dazed, exhausted, and confused, I would just stand there while he wound up, drew back, and attempted a wild punch. That gave me so much warning I could easily duck the blow, but the second wind I was hoping for never came. Several times I even tried to sit on the ropes, which had to be a first. Hearing that final bell was one of the high points in my life. All I wanted to do was get out of the ring and get to the locker room to rest. Ash was not going to let me out that easy. He held my arm, insisting I not miss one moment of the humiliation.

"Finally, the announcer declared my opponent by a unanimous decision. The judge gave me the first round and him the last two. Ash stormed out the ring toward the locker room, leaving me far behind. James stayed close, sensing I was still on unsteady legs. That was fortunate for me, because I passed out as soon as I stepped through the locker-room door. Ash woke me up by throwing a glass of water in my face."

"What did he say?" Speedy asked.

"He told me if I ever came into the gym like that again, he would kick my ass himself." I dropped my head, ashamed by the whole episode.

Speedy knew that wasn't the end of the story and asked the obvious question. "Then what?"

"I made up my mind, right then and there, that was the last time I would get my ass kicked, and I was going to kick that white boy's ass," I said with a laugh. "The next week I was back training with a vengeance. No cigarettes, no drinking, and eating the right foods. Within a few months of hard training and many rounds of sparring, I was beginning to move ahead in the pack. Ash decided, one day, to put me to the test. Our team was going into a juvenile detention center to challenge their fight club. I overwhelmed my opponent so badly the referee called the fight to a halt in the third round.

"My next fight I got my first knockout. Man, I was hot. Ash took some of us to the West Side of Cleveland for what must have been illegal fights, because we were paid five dollars per round, and the spectators placed bets.

One night I threw a hook at just the right angle, cutting my opponent's mouth wide open. That fight thrust me into the open division without my ever having a Novice Golden Glove fight. It also convinced the trainer of the white boy I was gunning for not to let that fight happen. At sixteen, I found my calling. Hell, I was beating the shit out of grown men.

"Unfortunately, a week before the tournament, I went out drinking with my friends. I figured, with a week before the fight, I could clean my system out. There I was, drinking in a bar, in a neighborhood I knew nothing about, looking for trouble. Well, I found it. A friend got into an argument with a man at the bar, and I somehow got involved. The two of us began to argue, and the bartender ordered us to take it outside. In spite of the age and size difference that favored him, I felt confident.

"Everyone kept telling this man about my fight experience. Personally I would have kept it to myself. Soon he became convinced that he would lose a fair fight, so he decided not to have one.

"He picked up a beer bottle and smashed it on my face about a quarter inch below my eye. The bottle shattered, leaving him holding the bottleneck with a knifelike edge to it. I opened my eyes in time to see him attempt to slash my throat. I pulled back, and he missed my throat but caught the side of my face."

"So that's how you got the scar?" Speedy interjected.

"Yeah, man." I continued, "Blood was gushing everywhere. The nearest hospital was five miles away, and since no one had a car, I had to walk. By the time I got there, I was almost dead from loss of blood. It took sixty stitches to close my face, and I almost lost my eye. The doctor said it would take a year before my face could take punches, and the skin would always be subject to tearing. That ended my boxing career."

"Damn!" Speedy said, using his best Brando accent. "You coulda been a contenda."

CHAPTER 13

The Call
March 1969

▲ ▲ ▲

As the operation drew to a close PAVN forces hit our marine regimental headquarters, An Hoa, forcing troops to be called back to defend it. As the marines withdrew, PAVN troops attacked the lightly defended bases, causing our troops to abandon them. Our base, the more heavily defended, survived. The operation ended when we turned the base over to our counterparts, the Army of the Republic of Vietnam (ARVN) forces. Within days we would be pulling out.

The units defending the smaller bases suffered heavy losses. When the operation ended, according to reports we had 183 marines killed and over 1,000 wounded. The ARVN had 100 killed and 378 wounded. We reported 1,398 PAVN killed and 29 POWs.

In the interim, we had taken a major supply base from the PAVN, complicating the Communist ability to supply their troops in the field. One marine was reported to have received the Medal of Honor.

A company of Chinese mercenaries, under the charge of marine commanders, had been flown in. They would temporarily take control of the base that would later be turned over to the ARVN.

The mercenaries relied heavily on booby traps and quickly set up an elaborate network of them. Ellis, the consummate observer of human nature, watched their tactics closely. Those observations would serve us well later.

Expendable and Necessary

The reefer supply had dried up, so the mercenaries filled the void. They proved to be very shrewd. American currency was replaced with military payment certificates (MPC), which decreased in value on the exchange market. That and the scarcity of drugs had caused the cost of a joint to progress in price from ten cents, to one dollar, to ten dollars.

But money was of little value to us. The absence of women and my aversion to gambling left only drugs as an expense. After the paymasters deducted the small percentage set aside to cover my future R and R expenses, the remainder would go to purchase reefer.

Ellis intercepted me as I approached his Chinese connection. "Man, they don't want money; shit, they already have a small fortune," he said. "Right now they want food." He then opened a bag containing about thirty joints. "They trust that farm boy Hansen," he explained, "so he can get in and steal their food. He gives it to me. I trade it back to them for joints, and that makes it free."

"Sounds good to me." I smiled, accepting a couple joints.

Ellis focused his eyes on a group of mercenaries standing nearby. Motioning for me to follow him, he approached them. Having gained respect among the men following my successful battle with Speedy, I figured Ellis may need me for backup, but I didn't anticipate what Ellis was about to do. Ellis grabbed one of the stocky Chinese men, reached into his pocket, and took his money. He then peeled off twenty dollars, tossed the rest back, and calmly walked away.

"God dammit," I shouted at Ellis once they were out of hearing distance. "You mugged a professional killer."

"So am I," Ellis responded, showing little remorse. "That motherfucker bet me twenty dollars that Speedy would kick your ass. He must have thought I couldn't tell them apart." We laughed and then split the winnings. It was now time for us to join the platoon, who were gathering their gear in preparation for the two-day forced march back to An Hoa.

The terrain was thick, so we marched until it became dark. The next morning we continued toward our company base camp, arriving about noon the following day. When we reached An Hoa, Bencomo and R. C.

Davis received their orders to return home. Each had received at least one Purple Heart. Three African Americans, Herman Dank Smith, Big Moose, and Kitchen, joined the company. All were from the Deep South.

Moose was a 250-pound bully who came in attempting to force his will. Within a day of his arrival, he faced the wrath of Speedy, who hit him so hard with a tree limb that it took fifteen minutes to wake him up. It was a great attitude adjustment.

Herman was a likeable man who always had a smile and an earnest desire to become a good combat marine. Kitchen was very streetwise and immediately bonded with Ellis and me.

The first day was a day of rest; we men showered, ate at the chow hall, got drunk off the beer rations, and visited the skivvy house. The end of the day was spent resting. It was the first night in months that we could get a relatively safe night's sleep.

The following day the platoon was sent out to patrol the area. We were to find a strategic location and set an ambush about a mile out. It had to be somewhere on the road connecting An Hoa and Phu Loc 6.

The well-worn dirt road was the supply route between the two bases. This made it vulnerable to booby traps. It was, therefore, constantly patrolled and swept for mines. That night, with the aid of night-vision goggles, I spotted two VC attempting to set a mine. I got off two shots that missed. Unfortunately, it alerted the VC that the marines were in the area. The platoon moved to another location. Along the way we discovered a large concentration of tracks. They weren't the boots worn by the marines or the sandals used by the VC. The brass concluded the NVA were moving troops through.

They were apparently turning it into a road to move from east and west into and out of the Arizona Territory. For strategic reasons, the Communists tried to maintain control of the area. This was a big part of our area of operation. So again we would have to break up the enemy concentration. We knew we would, as always, face an unyielding assault from the North Vietnamese. The platoon's squad leaders, Speedy, Rhone, Brantley, and a marine whose name I can't remember, were briefed b Lieutenant Hannahan. Speedy later addressed us.

"Listen up!" he announced while unrolling a map. "The rumors you heard about us going into Arizona are true. It will be a search and destroy. This is roughly the area in question," he said, pointing to the map. He slowly paced around the men, carefully choosing his words. "First we will move to a staging area." He drew a dotted line on the map. "We will then muster with the rest of the regiment. They want us to go in hard and fast. Therefore, choppers will pick us up and fly us in one big wave.

"Our platoon will point for the company, and our squad will point for our platoon. Harris," he said, turning to me, "you're on point. Can you handle that?" I gave a confirming nod. Soon after the briefing, a convoy arrived carrying more war gear: ammunition, grenades, motors, water, and C rations.

The men saddled up and prepared to move to the staging area. It was difficult to determine who was more apprehensive; the old-timers who knew what to expect, or the new men who had no idea of what they were about to face.

"Move out!" Speedy called to us. The company was now on the move. We had only moved about five hundred meters when Ellis relayed the command to stop. The squad members waited for future orders in silence.

"What's up?" I asked Ellis without turning my eyes from the front.

"They're looking for a line number."

"A what?"

"A marine with a particular line number."

"Why?"

"I don't know," Ellis answered as he returned to Speedy for more information. After a brief conversation with Speedy, he returned. "A line number is a means the Red Cross uses to identify us in an emergency."

"Why would they identify us in an emergency? Shouldn't they be the ones being notified?"

"No," Ellis went on, "they notify a person if they have an emergency back home."

"What kind of an emergency can someone over here have back home?"

"A death in their immediate family."

"Oh. What's the number?"

"Two fourteen."

"Who's two fourteen?"

"They're checking now." Ellis returned to Speedy, who was now talking to the lieutenant. The squad members were congregating, and the air buzzed with discussion. Ellis returned with what would be devastating news. "It's you," he sympathetically informed me.

The lieutenant, along with Speedy, came up and offered his condolences. "I'm sorry about your family member passing," he said. "You're going home." I was sad and confused, unable to respond. "A chopper is coming to take you back to An Hoa," the lieutenant continued. "Ellis is going back to the base too. Good luck." When he left, other marines gave their condolences to me and encouraged me to find a way not to return. They gave me my space while we waited for the chopper to arrive.

"Are they letting you escort me back?" I asked Ellis.

"No," Ellis answered with a sly smile. "I convinced the corpsman I had the clap."

"Yeah, right," I laughed, knowing the corpsman was likely correct.

"My father, mother, or brother, one of them is dead. How could that be?" I kept repeating. "I dreamed of going home, but not like this." The helicopter came and picked us up while I continued to speculate. "My father," I explained, "is forty-five years old. Aside from a hangover, I've never seen him sick in his life. He has been on his job over twenty years never missing a day's work. He was a heavy drinker, and he did pass out drunk every night, but people don't die without any warning."

"Was he violent?" asked Ellis.

"More talk than action, but yes. Black men from his generation can't stand up against the true cause of their troubles if they want to stay out of jail and keep their job, so they take it out on the people closest to them. The only place they have any real control is in their home, so they demand the discipline and respect they're lacking outside their house. But we have a good relationship. In fact, he always shows me respect and love, which goes both ways.

Expendable and Necessary

My Mother Jennie Harris

"My mother is a typical black mother. Forty-one years old, keeps a clean home, and always threatened to beat the hell out of me if I misbehaved. I've always respected her, so threatening me wasn't necessary. In fact, it drove a wedge between us. I just went out of my way to keep the things I was seeing and doing from her, but I love my mom. I do wonder if the violence between my parents could have gone too far. If one of them hurt the other, I could lose both parents."

After a short pause, Ellis asked about my brother. That was a possibility I had not even considered.

"No way," I responded without hesitation. "He is a twenty-four-year-old college student at Central State, one of the historically black colleges. He is the hope for the family." Ellis interrupted me to give a Black Power salute as a show of respect for my brother. "Even though we live deep in the inner city, my brother doesn't spend any time there. He will catch a bus to the affluent suburbs to hang with friends whose parents have money, social status, and influence. That keeps him away the drugs and violence in our neighborhood. But keeping up with their lifestyle is financially difficult."

"How does he do it?"

"He does it with the help of family, friends, teachers, and me. That is, when I finished high school and got a job. After my brother graduated from high school, he went on to college. His major is accounting, but he is a gifted writer. He is in good health, so I just don't see a reason for him to be deceased. I wish we were closer, but I'll try to reconnect when I get home."

The helicopter landed in An Hoa, allowing us men to disembark. I was so focused on my situation that I turned away without saying good-bye. Ellis called out to me.

"I'm sure this will be our last time together," he called. "It's been a hell of a ride. Do whatever you have to do to keep from coming back. You owe it to yourself." I managed to the man who had become my best friend. Then I wrote down my home address while encouraging Ellis to write and to look out for himself. Ellis made one last request to me on behalf of the brothers who still had time to do. "Tell those sisters in the world that we miss them, and tell everyone what is happening here, and to keep the struggle alive."

It was a sad moment for me as I went to company headquarters for further direction. They directed me to the chaplain's tent.

The initial encounter was not very cordial. The chaplain was a religious leader, more importantly, a marine officer. He would generally break protocol and instruct the men reporting to him to be at ease.

It wasn't necessary. I resented authority and viewed religious institutions with suspicion. I expected to meet a distant, arrogant man consumed with self-importance, and I wasn't disappointed.

"I'm Harris," I said, approaching the chaplain. "They told me to report to you."

"I made no such request," the chaplain snapped.

"This is the chaplain's tent, isn't it?"

"Yes, it is, Private, and who are you?"

"I'm Harris; I was told I had a death in my family and I should see you."

"Oh, you're the marine the Red Cross called about."

"Yes, sir, who died? Was it my father?"

"I'm not sure, Marine," the chaplain responded. "Let me check." After checking the papers, he asked, "What's your father's name?"

"John Harris," I responded.

"I'm sorry; your father has passed. The deceased person is John E. Harris."

I felt a rush of emotion, remembering the last conversation I had with my father when I was on China Beach. I never would have thought that brief conversation would be our last. The chaplain offered counseling and prayer, which I declined. He seemed somewhat offended by having his offer rejected, so he just handed me a copy of my orders. I thanked him and then left.

While heading for my tent so I could prepare for the trip home, I suddenly stopped in my tracks.

"Wait a minute!" I said out loud. "Did he say John E. Harris?" Doing an about-face, I returned to the chaplain's headquarters.

"Sir!" I said with urgency. "Did you say John E. Harris?"

"Yes," the chaplain responded.

"Are you sure?" I again asked. The chaplain was annoyed that I would question him and handed me the papers. After staring at the papers for about thirty seconds, I raised my head and said in an almost inaudible voice, "That's my brother."

The chaplain looked at me with what seemed to be genuine concern. This time he resisted his instincts to converse with me as a spiritual leader and wisely spoke as one man to another.

"How old was he?" he asked me.

"He was just twenty-four."

"Was he sick?"

"No."

"Was he in the military?"

"No, he was in college."

"Were you informed of his being in an accident?"

"No, I thought he was well on the way to a bright future."

"Were there any other siblings?"

"No."

"There is a lot on your shoulders now, son. I pray you find a way to work through it."

Aware that I needed to be alone, he offered perhaps the best advice of all. "Your parents need you, son, and as hard as it may be, they need you to be strong. Go home and help them through this." I thanked the chaplain, and after a brief embrace, I turned and walked out.

Dazed and confused as if I had just walked away from a car accident, I walked to an isolated spot, sat down, and cried.

CHAPTER 14

"He Ain't Heavy"
March 1969

▲ ▲ ▲

Johnny & me

WITHIN A FEW HOURS OF the official Red Cross notification, I was boarding a helicopter for Da Nang. There was a slight mix-up over the serial number on my weapon when I turned it in, but I wasn't concerned. Returning to Vietnam was the last thing on my mind.

The helicopter landed in Da Nang at a landing zone designated for in-country transport. I was only a short distance from the airport. It had been months since I could walk around without fear of being shot or caught in a mortar attack. I could have gotten a ride but chose to walk.

It was an enjoyable walk that allowed me to take my mind off my troubles, although seeing all these servicemen walking around visiting bars, skivvy houses, movie tents, and PXs without a care brought feelings of resentment. I wondered if they thought grunts were dumb because we didn't have technical occupations. Did they think grunts were the most expendable servicemen and therefore put in front? Did they think grunts were hoodlums whose only skill was fighting? Or would they try to build a reputation by beating a grunt's ass? I went into a defensive mode, preparing for a confrontation.

I had totally misjudged my fellow servicemen. Perhaps my arrogance and unkempt appearance made me a standout; they immediately knew I was a bushman. Along the way other servicemen constantly asked about life in the bush and the combat experience. It was as if I had a sign over my head that read, "I've been there; don't fuck with me."

I was polite but chose not to share stories, going straight to the airport to check the flight schedule. After finding it would be an hour before my flight, I slid down in one of the hard metal chairs and reviewed the final correspondence from my brother. I read the letter one word at a time, rubbing my finger over each word. It seemed to bring me comfort knowing my brother had placed emotion as he formed each letter. We had never expressed our feelings toward each other. Somehow putting it on paper was easier. Beyond the customary salutations, my brother wrote that he respected and admired me and expressed confidence that I could survive any situation I was placed in.

Having at least an hour before my flight, I thought about going out to purchase some reefer. But in Da Nang, they only sold it in ten packs, and I might be searched before boarding the plane. *I can't smoke a ten pack in an hour, and I sure as hell won't throw that much away when the plane comes*, I thought. So I just lay back and nodded off to sleep.

A result of my life in the bush was that I had acquired a ten-minute sleep pattern. Any noise or the presence of another in my two-foot comfort zone would also wake me. I woke up on schedule, looked around, and, once satisfied of my safety, settled back for another quick nap. Then it occurred to me that something had changed. Scanning the area again, I noticed a joint in the ashtray that wasn't there before. I palmed it, went to an isolated spot, and smoked it. On the way back, I brought a warm off-brand beer from a street vendor to refresh my dry throat. Settling down again, I pulled out the letter and picture again and began to rethink my brother's words.

He envied me? I thought. *Why would he envy me? He was on the fast track to success. He had looks, personality, brains, ambitions, and talent. If it wasn't for a steady janitor's job in a factory, I'd be standing around on the corner like the rest of my friends in Cleveland. Shit,* I laughed, *that was before I got drafted. Now I'm even*  *worse off. I am a low-ranking marine infantryman on the front lines of a rifle company, with little chance of surviving with my life. How could he envy me?*

Perhaps for the first time in my life, I had to accept the truth about my brother. I never really knew him. I didn't know his friends, his goals, his recreational activities, if he was happy, or how he felt about our parents. I knew none of the common questions siblings should know about each other. Now I would never have the opportunity to find the answers.

I nodded out again, and after my habitual ten-minute nap, I awoke to find another joint in the ashtray. *Life is good*, I thought as I went to a secluded spot to smoke it. This time I had gotten careless and was surprised by a military policeman. "Look, Marine, you can't do drugs on the compound!" he barked. I acknowledged I was wrong; then I moved to a spot where I could see anyone approaching and finished the joint.

Again I went back to my chair in the airport and continued my thoughts about my brother. I went back to the early years when I was about six and my brother was around ten. We were close at that point, Johnny and Ralph. One name was always associated with the other. My brother was a popular young man and a gifted gymnast. The girls were always chasing him. But with our age difference, we had different circles of friends.

One day I was with my friends, and Johnny was with his. When my friends left, I went looking for my brother. I had seen him and two of his friends going behind a garage. When I stepped around the back of the barn, I got a shock that changed our lives forever. Two boys were having sex with my brother. Believing they were attacking him, I flew into a rage.

I grabbed a brick and flung it at one of them, missing him by inches. When that failed, I grabbed a tree limb and was about to come down with full force on his head. My brother stopped me, and, to my surprise, he told me to go home. I was shocked, expecting my brother to join me in beating the shit out of his attackers. "They aren't doing anything I don't want them to," my brother told me. At six years old, the image of the brother I respected and looked up to was permanently shattered. I could only run home crying.

My reaction must have been devastating to Johnny as well. He never again allowed me to see him engaging in that lifestyle. I would never talk about my brother's sexual preference. If Johnny was with one of his partners, they would never interact as anything other than friends. Or if together with  a group of his like-minded friends, they would appear to the outside observer like your typical group of preppy friends.

But Johnny was who he was, and others did notice. To make it easier on me, his younger brother, Johnny would distance himself, becoming an overachiever and associating with a more accepting and liberal group of friends, rarely coming into the neighborhood.

Only through newspapers was I aware of the accomplishments my brother had made all while still in high school. He was a member of the Junior Champs, an academic social club. He was president of a teen club called the Conquistadores who organized social events for teens. *Time* magazine had awarded him a "Certificate of Excellence." While he was perusing his hobby of dress design, his submissions to dress shops in Cleveland and New York had garnered positive responses. Upon graduation from high school in 1964, he was elected class president

When he came around the neighborhood, he would bring around some of the most beautiful  girls in Cleveland and make sure my friends would see them. We developed a great deal of unspoken respect for each other, and I would come to my brother's defense at home, where our father made his life difficult. Our mother, on the other hand, was very protective of her older son.

While in my last year in junior high, I realized I would be facing problems when I got to the high school my brother had attended. The people there were aware of Johnny's homosexual life-  style, and they would surely make the younger brother a target for humiliation. I had developed a reputation for putting up a good fight among the people in the neighborhood, but there would be a group of larger and more aggressive young men in an inner-city high school. I would need an edge.

That thought was heavy on my mind the day I sat on the corner watching the brothers from the boxing gym jogging down the street. I had shown an interest in the sport from an early age. Circumstance would make it necessary to pursue it further. It was then I decided to take up boxing. My brother had inadvertently prepared me for the tough challenges ahead.

But the question of how my brother had died continued to trouble me. Once again, I drifted off to sleep.

Expendable and Necessary

A sudden movement to my right woke me up. There was a marine corporal sitting next to me. He looked at me cautiously. "You all right?" he asked.

I didn't answer; I just nodded, so the marine continued to speak.

"You a grunt?"

"Yes."

"What outfit?"

"Two-Five."

"Wow, the fighting Fifth. You are going on R and R?"

"No, my brother died. I'm going back to the world for his funeral."

"Damn, that's fucked up."

I pulled out his picture, the final one of him, and proudly showed it to the marine.

"Wow, he looks like a heavy brother," the marine said. "I want to offer my condolences."

"Thanks, man."

"You looked like you had some heavy shit on your mind, so I left those joints for you."

"Thanks, they were right on time," I replied.

"You need any more?"

"No, but thanks. My flight will be leaving soon."

"I'm in supply, and I watched you guys coming and going into the bush. I won't ask what happens there. I just know I'm glad I don't have to deal with it."

"Thanks for that," I responded. We shook hands, and my newfound friend departed, respecting my privacy. That encounter went a long way in relieving racial tensions I had within me.

Shortly thereafter I heard my name announced over the loudspeaker. Passage had been secured for me on a nontraditional flight to Okinawa.

There were two planes on the runway. The first was carrying the wounded.

All the evacuees were either in wheelchairs or carried on gurneys. The plane was packed to capacity with shattered lives and broken bodies; some were led away like babies. They seemed to have no knowledge of what was going on. But those were the lucky ones; the plane that awaited me was carrying the dead.

The small cargo plane was packed to capacity with steel-gray caskets. They were three high, three across, and five deep.

The other two passengers, including the chaplain, sat on benches facing them.

On the side of each casket was the name, rank, serial number, and hometown of the unfortunate marine.

We sat in silence reading the names of the fallen marines, each engrossed in his own private hell with the realization of how lucky we were to be alive. The flight also included three crew members, the pilot, copilot, and gunner.

When I got to Okinawa, there was a commercial flight waiting. I immediately boarded it for a direct flight to a base in California. From there I got another direct to Cleveland, Ohio. In roughly thirty-six hours, I would go from walking point in Vietnam to Cleveland Hopkins International Airport.

CHAPTER 15

Home: Cleveland, O-H-Ten
March–April 1969

▲ ▲ ▲

I ARRIVED AT CLEVELAND'S AIRPORT wearing my Marine Corps uniform, having had little interaction with anyone after leaving Okinawa's airport. The war had touched everyone's life in some way. I knew I provoked interest from those I passed. I also knew the uniform would serve as a mask and shield, preserving my individuality and keeping people at a distance.

Even though I no longer had to hide, hunt, kill, or fight for my life, I still felt uneasy. My thoughts would go from the war to my brother's death until I began to approach my old neighborhood.

The cab ride into the city was the first time I faced the effect the civil unrest had on my old neighborhood. Prior to my leaving, it was an ideal community. The city was old, most structures having been built in the early 1900s, but the homeowners took pride in their sanctuaries. The city was polarized. The Jewish, Hungarian, Slovakian, and Polish cultures had left their legacy on the architecture, street names, and businesses they had built. The African Americans, who now inhabited most of the neighborhoods as a result of "white flight," had maintained the area. There were professional offices, clothing stores, drugstores, grocery stores, a theater, and pool rooms. Most businesses were white-owned but employed some neighborhood residents. There was even a street cleaner on duty. The area of 105th and Superior Avenue was a bright smile in the heart of the city.

Some in the community had concluded, perhaps justifiably, that the white business owners and professionals were coming into the community and getting rich off the residents. They felt they were taking that money to their suburban communities and then redlining the blacks who tried to move to the more affluent areas.

As a result, the residents attempted to purge the white businesses from the community. The perpetuators of the violence, most from outside the community, attempted to drive out the outsiders through the use of force and fire.

But the buildings were connected, and the few black-owned establishments, slated to be spared, were also engulfed in flames. That left gaping holes and smoldering ruins that would cause one to turn in disgust.

Many of the homes were occupied by blacks and owned by whites. Those owners wouldn't dare to return to do maintenance, so much of the rental property fell into disrepair. There was no doubt that the image of a bright smile the community once had could never be restored. Perhaps the biggest victims were the residents who were employed in the destroyed businesses.

There was no fanfare noting my arrival. The cab would have only drawn attention if the driver had been white. My house, however, was notably distinct; a large floral wreath was centered on the doorway. After paying the driver, I paused at the wreath and then composed myself before knocking on the door.

My father and mother were home. Elaine, a young lady with whom I was romantically involved, was sitting with my mother. She waited patiently while my parents greeted their lone surviving son. It was an emotional scene, with me showing the restraint typical of servicemen. Elaine then gave me an embrace equally passionate but visibly different from my parents. She then excused herself, understanding that my priorities should be my parents. We agreed to meet later. For the first time in months, I was being referred to by my first name, Ralph. That was comforting for me, allowing me to distance myself from the war.

The strain my parents were under showed clearly on their faces. Having lost one of your only two children, with the sole surviving son at a high risk of losing his life as well, is a nightmare for a parent. The brief moment of joy was brought to an end by my next line of questions.

"What happened to Johnny?" I asked my father directly. My father, while an excellent provider for the family, could never handle stress very well. He simply wouldn't answer, only shaking his head violently. I asked again, this time with more insistence. My father still provided no answer, just placed the blame on everybody and everything. He would go from one subject to another, never ending a sentence or a complete thought. His coping technique was clearly not to discuss the issue. I tried to always be respectful to my parents, but I was losing my patience. "Will someone please tell me what happened to my brother?" I shouted.

My mother, who handled stress by sometimes becoming cold and seemingly uncaring, shouted, "He was killed in a fight!" She then turned away angrily.

"Fighting who?" I pressed on. My mother gave hostile answers, annoyed that I wouldn't let it go. "Somebody in town I don't know."

"Are the police involved?"

"Of course."

"Well, what are they telling you?"

"They don't tell us anything."

"Was he mugged? Was it a robbery? Was it a fight? What happened?"

My mother just walked into her bedroom, refusing to answer any questions. I stood in disbelief at my parents' attitude. My mother returned and slapped a well-worn newspaper article on the table in front of me.

The article was from a local newspaper in the city in which my brother lived. The back-page notice simply stated, "John Harris, a student at Central State University, has been shot and killed." It went on to say that the police were investigating. "That's it?" I shouted. "That's all they had to say?"

"Mrs. Abeck," my mother went on, "is having an investigator look into it. When he gets answers, we'll let you know"

"Who's Mrs. Abeck.?"

"She is an older white lady I met that was helping your brother. She's known your brother for years."

"Helping him, how?"

"Your brother has been acquiring a lot of bills. She helped us and him. You had bills too," she said, beginning to cry. "We had to pay for that new car you left when you got drafted."

"Mom, I can't afford that car on the little pay I get. You should sell it. Besides, it's not doing me any good!"

"You should send money to help on those payments!" my mother shouted back.

Before I could respond, my father joined the conversation.

"God dammit, I told that boy that his car will be sitting in that driveway when he gets home from the war, and that's where it will be."

After composing myself, I made an attempt at an apology. "I'm sorry," I said, "but the system is full of unsolved cases of young black men, and unless you push, they won't even try to solve it."

"We're all under a lot of strain," my mother replied. That offered her the opportunity to end the conversation. She then went to the kitchen, and my father retreated to the bedroom. That left me looking at a copy of my brother's obituary. I scooped it up and went to view his body. I stopped down the street to pick up Elaine, needing some support. She was the perfect companion.

Elaine was a high-school junior, with a close and ordered family structure. School nights meant she was on a curfew, and extended periods away from home were questioned. She seemed to genuinely care about me and kept up with my war experiences through sparse written correspondence and discussions with my parents. Under different circumstances we might have had a fulfilling monogamous relationship. She offered the stability I needed, but my life was too chaotic to accept it. Her family and friends were likely warning her not to become too involved and to focus on high school. They were right, but I hoped she wouldn't give up on me.

I, on the other hand, was a twenty-year-old man who had recently lost his only sibling, and I was less than forty-eight hours from deadly front-line combat to which I would soon return. The next ten days could quite possibly be my last days of life. I was determined to live each of those days as if I had nothing to lose, which wasn't far from the truth.

Wills, the funeral home that handled my brother's body, was familiar to me. It was one of three funeral homes that blacks used in Cleveland. My heart pounded as I approached the casket. I had seen death but never the death of someone so close. In spite of all attempts to remain strong, I nearly passed out at the sight of my brother's body. That was the moment that Johnny's death became reality.

Unlike combat deaths, funeral directors prepare bodies so they appear to be asleep. I reached out and touched him as if I could somehow jar him into consciousness. It was a very solemn moment; neither I nor Elaine spoke. We turned and left the funeral parlor, spending the later part of the evening together.

It was a difficult evening, shifting from passion to sadness as I struggled to deal with conflicting emotions. Elaine struggled with the task of being a lover and a compassionate confidant. After taking her home on what was a school night, I went out to look up my childhood buddies. They would catch me up on what the war had done to the neighborhood.

Billy and Bubble, two of my friends, were now hard-core drug users. When I located them, they were mellowing out from a recent score. They were, therefore, calm enough catch me up on the neighborhood business and to share the marijuana I had brought home from my brief layover in California.

The war had reached in and robbed the neighborhood of its best and brightest. Ronald Hampton, who lived six doors from my parents, had been drafted into the army and recently killed in combat. David Lasiter, who lived a street over, had survived as an army paratrooper only to die from a drug overdose while at home. The neighborhood was replete with similar stories. Even those who had escaped the draft were being destroyed mostly by drugs, the great escape from the troubled times.

The pimps and players, who were admired for their fast life, beautiful women, big cars, big money, and fancy clothes, were now begging for dollars to feed their drug habits. Those who held some integrity, perhaps one step above begging, were supporting their habits through petty theft. The once beautiful prostitutes had shifted priorities and were now dedicated to feeding their drug habit. With their food-caked and rotting teeth, matted hair, malnourished bodies, and soiled attire, they had become grotesque and ghoulish figures.

After less than two days at home, feeling I had nothing to lose, I began snorting cocaine. While riding from a drug house, I passed a young lady I had known prior to being drafted. Her name was Cynthia. I stopped, picked her up, and rekindled the relationship.

She actually helped slow my rapid fall. Cynthia had completed high school, had a job, and was about to move out on her own. She was no stranger to the streets. She could party all night and sleep through the day. There was no place I could take her that would be intimidating. Marijuana, barbiturates, and cough syrup were her drugs of choice, and she encouraged me not to indulge in the heavier drugs. Cynthia was actually looking for an older, more stable partner; in fact, she was involved in such a relationship. Perhaps I was her one last fling before settling down.

Cynthia was operating on the fringes of the emerging African American movement. With her perfectly cropped Afro, dark complexion, large earrings, African style of dress, and proud demeanor, she could have been the poster child for the movement. She was my introduction to some of the local groups. Once I knew where the local groups were headquartered, I was free to operate on my own. There was a smorgasbord of organizations offering direction and solutions to the civil-rights agenda. I approached all institutions with an open mind. If nothing else, they made the community aware that change was needed. I was never drawn to the faith-based institutions. Religion was an excellent method for gathering the masses, but they relied too much on faith. I wanted action, not prayer.

The passive approach to civil rights that was spawned in the fifties was giving way to a more aggressive approach in the sixties.

There was a group that claimed to have ties to the Black Panther party, although it seemed they were making it up as they went along. With the violent confrontations they advocated with police, it wouldn't be long before they were either arrested or dead.

I visited a group based in an abandoned building that once housed the local hardware store. They claimed to be a faction of the black nationalist movement. I knew very little about the movement, so I thought this might be an opportunity to learn more.

The group was highly visible in the neighborhood. Prior to their meetings, the members would form a procession and walk to their meeting place. The brothers and sisters in the group dressed in African attire and addressed one another by African names. Some had legally changed their names. The leader was a onetime street hustler referred to as Cool Daddy on the street. He chose to keep the name, which somehow diminished the group's credibility.

His lady, who was actually his common-law wife and the mother of his children, went by the name of Queen. They had decorated a wicker chair to look like a throne, which he would sit on with Queen sitting at his side. His followers, numbering about fifteen, would sit cross-legged before him while he spouted his wisdom regarding local and world events. They were, in fact, a group of unemployed members of the community with too much time on their hands. They had delusions of grandeur that told them they could establish their own little African kingdom. It's doubtful if they knew anything about the nationalist movement. But they were relatively harmless.

That wasn't the case with a group of teenagers living in a house two doors down from my parents. They were led by a brother they called Black Herman.

Herman, a young man in his midtwenties, had recently gotten out of prison, having served time for a string of petty thefts. After his release, he moved in with a mentally and physically impaired single woman who, with the aid of public assistance, rented the house for her and two children. Herman himself also seemed to be mentally challenged with criminal tendencies. Most in the neighborhood, including me, kept their distance.

He did, however, appeal to impressionable fourteen-, fifteen-, and sixteen-year-olds from around the city who viewed him as a revolutionary leader. They were the principal looters, breaking in and burning down the businesses, leaving militant slogans under the pretext of driving the white man out of the community. They would attack any white persons who wandered into the community. In fact, they were simply opportunists. The teenagers just wanted a place to drink and do drugs, and Herman needed merchandise to boost.

The only thing they really did was keep the police patrolling the neighborhood. It was obvious by the crowd of drunken teenagers who frequented the house both day and night that something illegal was going on. But since no arrest resulted from the patrols, the police likely preferred to have them in one location. But all of this was only a minor distraction for me. I still had to face what was heavy on my heart, my brother.

The funeral was held on my third day home. It was a tremendously sad day, and neighborhood sentiment, or lack of it, was evident. Johnny didn't spend much time in the neighborhood, and few of his peers showed to pay last respects. However, his educational accomplishments gave hope to the community, and the older community members came out. Family and friends from his close circle packed the funeral home. My parents and I were too grief stricken to speak at the funeral. There was some animosity within the family members toward Johnny's friends due to their lifestyle. Feeling uncomfortable, they also chose to grieve in silence. It was beginning to appear that the presiding minister, who didn't know my brother, would be the only one speaking on his behalf.

Then Johnny's high-school music teacher and mentor, Mr. Bennett, stood up. His loyalty, compassion, and respect for Johnny would not be contained. He spoke for those unable to do so in a compassionate acknowledgment. His powerful baritone voice bellowed out a farewell song so full of pain the room shook with emotion. Reggie, Johnny's partner, isolated himself but was visibly shaken. I knew Reggie would be the best source to fill in the missing pieces in my brother's life. I decided to hold that discussion for a future time.

After the funeral, my friend Billy passed a message to me from a young lady by the name of June whom I had also briefly dated prior to being drafted. June seemed to have been on a mission to attract a man with a steady job, have his child, and get married. I was not that person. I doubted her promise to wait faithfully for me to return from the war. The fact that she never wrote confirmed it. A few people, including Billy, who passed the message, told me she was dating other men. Billy's advice was to kick the bitch's ass. But I had been trying to further my relationship with Elaine and held no animosity toward June. So when I called her the following day, I just wanted to thank her for her concern and wish her well.

Her response to my call took me by surprise. She was bursting with enthusiasm, claiming to have been waiting faithfully as she had promised, and was eager to get together. Her reason for not writing, she claimed, was she didn't have my address. When I asked her why she hadn't contacted me, she said she wanted to give me time to be with family. I knew she was playing me for a fool, which was pissing me off. Somehow I managed to contain that anger. Confronting her in person would be a great stress reliever. It would also allow me to save face with my friends.

I spent considerable time composing the right words to humiliate her before calling to arrange to pick her up under the pretext of a date. She claimed to be unable to meet because she was spending time with a cousin. That angered me even more. It was obvious she had another date. But I did arrange to meet for lunch the next day.

She asked me to pick her up on a corner of a street only five blocks from my parents' house. *Damn!* I thought; this was probably the street where her current boyfriend lived. She didn't even go out of the neighborhood.

When she spotted my distinctive canary-yellow Cougar, she ran to it, jumped in, and then tried to passionately kiss me.

I could no longer contain my anger. "You must think I'm a goddamn fool!" I shouted.

"What do you mean?" she replied innocently.

I was so enraged that I forgot my well-rehearsed humiliation speech. The only thing coming out of my mouth was a string of obscenities and threats. My distinctive sports car also attracted the attention of my two neighborhood friends Billy and Bub, who ran up and jumped in the car.

I was too involved in my confrontation with June for a joyride and immediately ordered them out.

"Drive!" they frantically yelled while scanning the area.

Unmoved by their perceived urgency and still hyped up, I yelled back, "Drive, hell. Get the fuck out of my car!"

"Look, man," Billy pleaded, "we just robbed the flower shop, and that motherfucker is behind us with a gun!"

The priority shifted. I had unwillingly become a getaway driver. I knew if I drove forward, I would drive past the floral shop and most likely would be shot, or, at the very least, they would get my license number. So I threw the car in reverse and sped backward down the narrow street. If June's new boyfriend happened to be looking out his window when we passed, he probably would have thought she was being kidnapped.

There was chaos in the car with everyone screaming. "You know this bitch ain't nothing but a hoe!" Bub yelled in his drug-impaired speech. "You want me to kick her ass?" Not to be outdone, Billy was also offering to kick her ass. June was screaming at the two of them to stay out of her business and for me to let her out of the car. I was oblivious to them all. I was totally focused on getting as far away from the scene as possible so I could put them all out of my car.

I managed to turn the car around and race toward a secluded spot. Finally I stopped the car. June immediately tried to get out, but Bub grabbed her by the hair and began beating her. I reached over the seat and grabbed Bub. This gave June an opportunity to open the car door and attempt an escape. Billy, by that time, had opened his door and ran around the car to grab her. I released Bub so I could get out of the driver's door and stop him. Once Bub was free, he jumped out and joined Billy. By the time I reached them, they were beating the poor girl like she was a man.

Jumping between them, I managed to break her free. She ran screaming for dear life with hair all over her head, makeup smeared, and clothes torn. Fearing someone would be coming to her aid, I jumped in the car, threw it in reverse, and sped away, almost killing Billy and Bub, who were trying to get back in. Not wanting to add murder to my list of growing crimes, I allowed them in and took off at about twenty miles per hour over the speed limit.

"Get the fuck out my car!" I yelled while still driving.

"We can't until you stop!" Bub pleaded.

"Get out!" I yelled again after stopping the car.

Seeing I was losing control, Bub offered part of the stolen money. Glancing back, I saw it was just fifteen dollars, causing me to become even more enraged.

I jumped out vowing to drag them out and leave them on the highway. But by the time I pulled one of them out, the other would get back in. During the struggle I kept yelling. "You motherfuckers got me involved in an armed robbery over fifteen dollars!"

"It wasn't an armed robbery," Bub said with a grin. "I just pretended to have a gun." I was at such a loss for words that I just stood silently, shaking my head in disbelief. This was an opportunity for me to calm down.

"Why in the hell did y'all beat up June?" I calmly asked.

"Because she cheated on you," Bub said in defense of their actions.

"We weren't dating," I responded, throwing my arms in the air.

After a long pause, Bub gave a one-word answer. "Oh."

Billy, who had remained silent, was showing signs of withdrawal. "Can you take us to the drug house?" he pleaded.

I could see the need to take them for a fix before they began to freak out.

There were many drug houses in Cleveland. Some streets had two or three. They instructed me to go to one in East Cleveland where the dope was better. This was a house where heroin was being mainlined. Fifteen dollars didn't buy much of a fix for such heavy users as Billy and Bub, but it was the best they could do. I saw another longtime friend there, "Hook Arm" Butch. He lived with his father, stepmother, brother, and sister on a side street near my parents' home. He got the name because of his deformed left arm.

"Did your brother have his funeral yet?" he asked.

"It was yesterday."

"You should have called me so I could have come through."

"You got a phone?" I asked sarcastically.

"Damn, man. You don't have to be so cold," Hook Arm groaned. "You know I got this 'Jones' on my back. I can't think of anything else. When you going back to Vietnam?"

"In a few days."

"Good luck, I'll pray for you." That comment made me laugh. "Can you loan me twenty dollars so I can get a bag?" he asked.

"You still owe me ten dollars from the last time I saw you," I shot back.

"How about splitting a bag?" Hook Arm pleaded, shaking from withdrawal.

I didn't do heroin and certainly not intravenously. But I also wasn't about to continue giving a junky money. I concluded that I would be going back to Vietnam soon, where drug withdrawal would be the least of my problems. Besides, nobody could get hooked on a dime bag. So I took the three of them to the dope house, where I shot up half the bag.

I wasn't prepared for a heroin rush. I nodded a couple of times and then went into unconsciousness. The next thing I remembered was feeling as if I was floating; then it was more like falling out of a tree. I wasn't far off. Billy, Bub, and Hook Arm Butch were carrying me out of the building to a Dumpster in the alley. Fortunately for me, I woke up before being left in such a disgusting and degrading place.

"What the fuck you doing?" I yelled. That startled them so much they dropped me.

"Oh!" Hook Arm said. "We thought you had OD'd, so we had to get you out of the house."

"So when were you motherfuckers going to call for an ambulance?" I yelled. The three of them just looked at each other. Bub finally answered with a laugh. "You don't call the man to a drug house." I stumped down the alley toward my car, cursing all the way.

"I can't believe that I'm with people I've known most of my life, and when they think I'm about to die, they drag my body into a filthy alley and leave me just because they don't want the police to know about this place.

God dammit, they probably know more about this place than you. All they have to do is sit outside and watch the junkies go in and out."

Now that I thoroughly mistrusted my onetime friends, I checked my wallet to discover the obvious. My money was missing. "You even took my money?" I said in total disgust.

"No, man, we wouldn't have done that," Billy said defensively with Bub and Hook Arm agreeing. But when Hook Arm left to return to the drug house, I knew he was the probable culprit. "It was worth the fifteen dollars," I mumbled, "just to get away from that motherfucker. I shouldn't have gone into a den of thieves anyway."

Billy and Bub continued to protest their innocence and proclaim their loyalty all the way to the car. Their credibility was shattered when I reached into my pockets and discovered my keys were missing. "All right," I yelled, leaning against the car, "who's got my car keys?" They answered only with silence. Fed up, I went into a rage and picked up a pipe, deciding to violently end the friendship. Bub went into his pocket acting as if he had suddenly discovered the location of the keys. His only defense was that he didn't want anyone to steal the car.

I snatched the keys and opened the door, with Billy and Bub rushing in grabbing the car seats for dear life. They knew I would leave them there otherwise. All I wanted to do was to get home so I could get as far away from them as possible. I vowed this was the last time I ever wanted to see either of them. When we got to my mother's house, I ordered them out of my car, locked it up, and went in the house to close out another day home.

The following peaceful day was spent with Elaine. She was the only port in my otherwise stormy life.

By the seventh day, I was getting dangerously close to the end of the ten-day leave. The time I spent with my parents reminded me of the stress and chaos that went on within the Harris household. My parents constantly fought, my mother verbally, my father physically.

In a rare moment, I did sit for a lengthy conversation with my mother. She told me of a letter-writing campaign she had started in an effort to get me out of combat. She claimed I was the last surviving member of the Harris bloodline. My mother had contacted our congressional representative and minister, who promised to submit letters to my commanding officer requesting I not be returned to a combat role. I was happy to hear of this. At this point going AWOL had seemed to be my only option.

Then my mother remembered a letter that had recently arrived from Vietnam. It was a frantic letter from Ellis.

"Harris," his letter started, "everything is fucked up. Going into Arizona was like going into hell. I'm sorry about your brother, but he probably saved your life. The squad was hit as soon as we arrived."

I was so shocked that I rose to my feet. I was starting to distance myself from Vietnam, as though it had been a bad nightmare. The letter reminded me it wasn't. Ellis was sure it was going to get worse, so he wanted to wait for the potential list to follow.

Later that evening I called Johnny's longtime partner, Reggie. Reggie was a successful insurance salesman seven years older than Johnny, making him eleven years older than me. I really didn't know Reggie very well. In fact, I didn't know any of my brother's friends. The meeting was awkward for both me and Reggie. When Reggie greeted me as "little brother," it seemed to break the tension. I quickly acknowledged to Reggie that I was not as close with my brother as I should have been and had missed the opportunity. I now wanted desperately to learn more. I found it hard to understand how two people could grow up in the same house and be so far apart.

"You have no need to apologize," Reggie assured me. "If he were still alive, you two would have talked it out. You know," Reggie went on with sadness in his voice, "your opinion was important to him."

"I don't think so, Reggie. He never asked my opinion on anything."

"In the lifestyle he lived, people were constantly judging him. It may have been more than he could bear to find you may be judging him too."

"That may have been an issue when I was younger, but when you know a person your whole life, there are a lot more things that define him. In fact, we never discussed his sex life, so for me it was a nonissue. I do wonder about all the women."

"What women?"

"Man, when we were growing up, there were some fine ladies coming to the house. I always wondered, was that just show?"

"No, everybody liked Johnny," Reggie laughed. "People were drawn to him. He was bright, ambitious, and gorgeous." I let the reference pass without a response. "As he got older, the it's-all-about-me attitude got worse."

"What do you mean?"

"He wanted the good life, and he wanted it now."

"There's nothing wrong with that."

"The good life takes time. He didn't feel he had much left."

"What do you mean?"

"His seizures were getting worse, and his sight was deteriorating. It was probably due to the medication."

"I know. His gray eyes were a source of pride, and he would have had a hard time accepting not being able to see through them."

Reggie continued to tell me how complicated my brother's life had gotten. "He wanted the good life, and he didn't have time to wait. Although your brother was a full-time student, he had a nice apartment, the best clothes, a bank account, and a new car."

"That was my car," I cut in.

"Yes," Reggie went on, "but now it is just another bill that your parents have to pay. People tried to help, but with the bad checks and charge accounts your brother was accumulating, everybody who cared about him was falling into a deep hole."

"Where did he get most of his money?" I asked. "Was he into selling drugs?"

After a long pause, Reggie admitted he wasn't sure. I had always suspected my brother had sold drugs. But I also suspected there was much more to the story.

We were silent for what seemed hours but was actually about five minutes. I could speculate, but that is all it would have been. I even considered asking Mr. Bennett, Johnny's other friend, for answers. In the end, I decided to allow time to reveal the details. Reggie broke the silence.

"You gonna be all right in Nam?" Reggie asked.

"I don't know, but I'll try like hell to stay alive."

"It must be bad over there."

"Yes, I just got a letter from one of the brothers telling me I might have missed a bullet by being home for Johnny's funeral."

"Damn, your big brother might have saved your life."

I was at a loss for words at that moment. In fact, I was on the verge of tears. That was an ideal moment for me to leave. After a slight smile, I turned and left. "The best way to repay him," Reggie called to me, "would be to return alive." Reggie was right, and my brother would certainly agree. I hung out with neighborhood friends, and after more pills, smoke, and liquor, I finally passed out in my parents' house.

Sometime in the midafternoon, my mother woke me up. It was the eighth day of my ten-day leave, and I didn't want to sleep any more of it away. "Linda called yesterday," she informed me. I had to think for a moment. The only Linda I knew was a Linda who lived a street over from my parents.

"Linda, Linda Evans?" I asked.

"Yes, she's in the hospital."

"Hospital?"

"Yes, she left this number."

I was hesitant about calling Linda I hadn't even seen her in over a year. But I did feel some loyalty. We had dated when we were fifteen and sixteen years old. Like all adolescents, we were learning about ourselves and the opposite sex. It might have gotten serious had I not found out she had slept with one of my friends. I could laugh about it now, but at the time I was furious. Linda had professed her love for me to a friend of mine. She told him, in confidence, that we were both virgins and she was concerned she couldn't properly satisfy me. This so-called friend offered to teach her proper lovemaking techniques, and she accepted.

She could not understand my reaction when she proudly proclaimed to me that, after her in-depth lessons from a fifteen-year-old boy and diligent practice sessions, she was experienced and could share herself with me. I concluded she was either promiscuous or unstable. In either case there was no chance of us ever being a couple. Yet, somehow in her mind, we were. So when I called, it was to pay respects to a friend. I was shocked to find the number was to a mental ward of a local hospital, and she was a patient. I checked visiting hours and left for what I thought would be a short visit.

I stopped at the visitor's desk and asked for her room number. The receptionist beamed with excitement. "Are you Ralph?" she shouted.

"Yes," I responded, shocked at the receptionist's reaction. She hurriedly gave me the room number and directions. I looked back as I walked to the room to see her rush to make a phone call. It seemed she was letting someone know I was coming.

When I reached the hall where her room was located, it was clear that was what the receptionist had been doing. Staff and patients were lining the walls greeting me with congratulations as I passed. I assumed they were congratulating me for surviving the war, but I didn't understand how they knew I was even in the war. Then I spotted one of the patients whom I recognized. It was a young man I had gone to high school with. I couldn't remember his name, but it was a familiar face, and that was enough to build some dialogue.

"You gonna marry her?" he asked, pulling me aside.

"What!" I said, surprised at the question.

"I heard you were going to marry her when you returned from the war."

"What!" I repeated, thoroughly confused.

"She was waiting for your return from the war so you could get married, so when she found out you were dead, she had a breakdown."

"Who said I was dead?"

"Well, when that wreath was placed on your mother's house, she assumed you were dead."

"It was actually my brother who died."

"She found that out after the breakdown. By the way, I'm sorry about your brother."

"Thanks," I replied.

I was about to inform him and everyone else that Linda and I were just neighborhood acquaintances when she came running out into the hall with outstretched arms. The scene was reminiscent of the ending of a romantic movie. Everyone was clapping and cheering. At least one patient was on the verge of tears. I decided it was best to just go along. After all, this was the best greeting I had gotten since returning home.

A staff member pulled me to the side and whispered, "Try not to upset her, young man. She's still very fragile. All I ask is that you not let her have any alcohol and have her back by eleven." I hadn't planned for us to even leave the building, so coming back by eleven was an easy promise to make. We left with the patients cheering our exit. "Did you tell everybody we were engaged?" I asked once we had left the building. She smiled but didn't answer, which was an answer in itself.

Linda primarily wanted to visit friends to assure them she was all right. We traveled in different circles, so most of the people we dropped in to see were unknown to me. I felt awkward but enjoyed the attention.

Eleven comes quickly when you start at seven, so the final stop was at Ti-Wan, a Chinese restaurant and one of the few remaining businesses in the neighborhood. The restaurant had a positive history in the community offering real jobs to the otherwise unemployable. For that reason the rioters spared it. The Chinese ambiance coupled with the courteous and professional staff made it the inner-city version of class.

I recognized the gentleman seated at the table next to us accompanied by two attractive young ladies. "Earl!" I called out, recognizing the pro from the Cory boxing team. "Earl Johnson."

It had been five years since we had seen each other, and Earl was on the downside of his career, showing effects of having taken too many punches. He recognized my face but didn't remember my name. "Hey, you're, you're," he said, searching for a name. I decided to help him out.

"Ralph, Ralph Harris."

"I know that," Earl responded as if he really did. "You still boxing?" Earl asked.

"No," I said, reminding him of the deep cut that sidelined my career. Earl reached out and ran his finger down the long scar that ran down my face.

"Yeah," he finally said, "you could have made it."

"How are the other brothers doing?" I asked.

"Well, Neal, Nester, Robert, James, and Ray all turned pro. They are on fight cards downtown. Hey, there is a card next week; why don't you go see them?"

"I wish I could, but I'm going back to Vietnam in a couple days."

"No shit."

"Yeah, man, I got drafted in the marines."

"Damn, you one unlucky motherfucker."

I laughed in agreement.

"Wait a minute," Earl said, considering what I had said. "Did you volunteer to do a second tour?"

"No, I came home to attend my brother's funeral. I have to finish the tour."

Earl could see that I didn't want to discuss my brother, so he stopped the line of discussion. He was also done with his meal, so he excused himself after a manly embrace. "Stay away from that war if you can." That was the last comment Earl would make before leaving.

The two of us were so engaged in conversation that we forgot to introduce the ladies. Linda was annoyed but didn't complain. We had an enjoyable meal, and I got her back before eleven as promised. I left knowing it was unlikely we would meet again.

I turned in earlier than usual, but not before a couple beers to help me sleep. I woke up overwhelmed with the realization following the next day, I would be headed back to Vietnam. To add to my anxiety, I received another letter from Ellis reaffirming the desperate straits the company was in. They were in a daily battle for survival. I decided to exercise my last option: breaking my arm.

I could accept going to Vietnam, but since I had never seen a man in the bush in a cast, a broken arm was the perfect way out of the close combat.

The perfect accomplice would be my old friend Billy. He would have broken his own arm for drug money.

I contacted Billy and asked him if he had a baseball bat after explaining my plan. I picked him up, and we went to an isolated location.

I took one last stiff drink, wrapped my arm in a towel, and then extended it like a condemned man. Blinded by alcohol, Billy drew back the way an executioner would do and came down with a powerful downward blow. There was a large crack. The bat shattered, nearly breaking in two. The jolt was so bad on Billy's hand he tossed it. I fell against a tree grimacing in pain.

After a long silence, Billy spoke. "Is it broke?"

"I don't know."

"Can you wiggle your fingers?"

I held out my arm and struggled to move my fingers in spite of the pain. I then called out in disgust, "God dammit!"

"What's the matter?"

"I can wiggle my fingers."

"Then it must not be broken."

"No shit!"

"You want me get another bat and try again?"

"Hell no!"

On the walk to the car and the ride back to Billy's house, I rattled off a stream of obscenities. It seemed to take my mind off the pain as I headed home for an ice pack.

When I walked through the door, my mother knew immediately what had happened. She had heard of soldiers harming themselves before to avoid combat, and she knew I didn't want to return to the front lines.

"God no, no!" she screamed. She continued to pray as if I weren't even in the room. "Jesus," she cried, falling to her knees, "please stop him from hurting himself."

At first I waited patiently while she continued her conversation with God. Then I finally broke in. "Mom, please listen." At first she refused, holding her hand over my mouth every time I attempted to speak. Finally she paused but clearly ignored my reasoning. I continued to try to persuade her.

"Mom, a broken arm is not a serious injury, and it will keep me from going to the bush. I was there for five months. I've done my share."

"Son," she cried out. "Other boys go to war and come home; you don't have to hurt yourself."

"Mom, I'm poor, black, and a low-ranking rifleman in a front-line marine rifle company. It's not the same."

"Why do you think it's all about race?"

"Because it is!"

"Ralph, it's going to be OK. God is going to look out for you."

"Mom, everybody thinks God is looking out for them. It doesn't work out that way. It's just a broken arm."

I knew death was random and not based on good, bad, right, or wrong. My particular circumstances would put me at greater risk, but I chose not to stress the point. She had just buried one son. My father stood and listened to the conversation, never giving an opinion but clearly troubled. My mother ended the conversation after making me promise not to attempt to break my arm again. Then she reminded me that she had written our congressman asking I not be sent back to the front. I attended to my arm and went to visit Elaine, with whom I spent the remainder of the night. She was the person I needed to be with.

On the morning of my final day, I received a phone call from the local naval recruiting station. I was told to report immediately to pick up my revised orders. To my surprise, our congressman had gotten the marines to review my request for a job in the rear rather than being sent back to the bush. My mother had also gotten letters from her minister and doctor urging authorities to consider the request for religious and medical reasons. I rushed home to tell everyone the hopeful news. My father was the most attentive, and we sat and drank and talked for hours. Remembering the financial strain my parents were under, I implored him to sell the car.

My father was adamant. "I trust your judgment and ability, son," he told me. "You're going to go back, and you will make it. You promise me that, and I promise you that car will be sitting in that driveway waiting for you." I wasn't sure if either of us would or could keep the promise. But, whether he knew it or not, he had said what his son needed to hear.

Family and friends would call and drop in all day. Most would offer prayer and advise me to do so as well. I listened out of respect, sensing it gave them comfort. They actually thought they were contributing to my safety. I knew my best chance for survival was firepower, determination, and luck.

I smiled to myself, realizing how different Cleveland was from my idealistic memories. But those memories are still a part of who I am.

What had my trip home taught me? Well, I loved my brother and regretted not having spent more time with him. There were many things about life I could have learned. My home life was confusing, but my parents and relatives did love me and did the best they could. My neighborhood friendships were lethal. There was no question that if and when I returned, I would have to get away from there.

But there was some stability: a good job and Elaine. But I accepted the reality that if I was physically or emotionally damaged, the job would be gone, and Elaine would likely finish high school and move on. With all the drinking, arguments, and fighting already going on in my parents' home, taking care of me would not be good for any of us. So I would be on my own. That was perhaps the motivating factor for me to come back in one piece.

The next morning my parents and Elaine took me to the airport. These were, without a doubt, the most important people in my life. But I knew that once back in combat, I couldn't split my emotions. My concern would have to be directed at myself and those around me. My parents would understand. I hoped Elaine would understand as well.

After one last photo opportunity, I walked to the plane, flashing one last smile. I wondered if they knew, as I did, that this might be the last time they would see me.

Life flows along like a rushing stream. Some can stand and watch, while others jump in and go with the flow. The river was now flowing toward the West Coast.

Next stop, California.

CHAPTER 16

Treasure Island
April 1969

▲ ▲ ▲

I took a direct flight to the San Francisco Airport. My orders were to report to the Treasure Island Naval Base, which was a short cab ride away. I would now be referred to by my last name as per military protocol.

Treasure Island is an artificial island built in 1939 that became a naval base in 1941. The island is situated in the mouth of the San Francisco Bay. San Francisco is located to the southwest. Berkley is to the northeast of the island. Oakland is located to the southeast. Alcatraz Island is to the west, with the Golden Gate Bridge further west. The location of the base would have made it an ideal tourist spot. It was even more ideal for a twenty-year-old whose life was spinning out of control and who felt he had nothing to lose.

Usually a returning marine would only be on the base for a twenty-four-hour period and then flown to Okinawa to board a flight to Vietnam. But my mother had gotten a request from our congressman for a hearing regarding my duty status. Therefore I would be there for an undetermined period of time. I was in the mecca for the antiwar, social change, and black revolution movements. It was like putting candy on the table before a baby and asking him to choose.

I was immediately assigned to a military barracks designated for marines in transit. The duty officer gave me a locker and told me to find an empty bunk. It was dark, so I had to search for a bunk without illumination. At the time it was one in the morning, or 0100 hours military time,

Expendable and Necessary

so only a few men were at the barracks. The rest would return prior to the 0700 hour duty call.

My Cleveland friends had given me a going-away gift, a bag of barbiturates, many of which I had ingested en route. While I was attempting to transfer the pills from my pockets to a bag to be placed under my pillow for safekeeping, they spilled all over the floor, waking up the sleeping marines. The duty officer, a sergeant, came in and turned on the light. Drugs were illegal in the marines just like in society in general, so with all the prying eyes, I was unsure what would happen next. When broad smiles came on everyone's faces, including the duty sergeant, I knew I was among friends. All I had to do was share.

The next day I walked around the base. As I stepped around a dark corner, the sergeant who was the duty officer the previous night jumped out to surprise me. I nearly clocked him. "Why would you do that?" I said after calming down. The sergeant was laughing uncontrollably. I continued to confront him. Then the sergeant spotted another unsuspecting victim coming along and motioned for me to hide with him. I declined and warned the marine.

I thought the sergeant's behavior was odd but thought no more about it.

The following day I met the rest of the marines housed in the barracks. They were a truly an odd bunch.

One marine would go up and down the steps backward. Another would fight with himself. Still another would take a twelve o'clock nap and have a one o'clock wet dream. You could set your watch by it. Some marines would sneak around at night as if they were in combat. There was also another marine who, like the sergeant, would sneak up and attempt to scare people. My suspicions were confirmed after a conversation with a marine from another barracks. "Most of the people in your barracks are being evaluated for mental or physical discharge," he informed me. "But some of them are putting on a show to convince the psychiatrist." I found that out firsthand when one marine asked me to help him prepare for his upcoming evaluation.

"What do you think about me standing in front of the psychiatrist doing this while he interviews me?" he asked.

"Doing what?" I asked.

"This!" he said, getting agitated.

"What are you doing?"

"Squeezing a ball."

"What ball?"

"Oh!" he said, taking the ball from behind his back. He tried it again, this time with his hands to his sides.

"That will do it," I assured him. Satisfied with his plan, the marine went off to his appointment.

It didn't take long for me to recognize which marines were faking a mental illness, but something must be wrong with a person who tries to convince people he is insane.

Another marine, Marlow, took me to another hospital ward. It was one at which he served his duty assignment.

The patients in that ward were clearly disturbed. It was like a snake pit, a place where the realities of combat could not be ignored. Most would just sit and stare at a distant place that only they could see. The most disturbing patients were the guilt-ridden men who, without provocation, would cry uncontrollably. After seeing that, I concluded I was safe in my barracks as long as I watched my back. The good part was other than keeping the area clean, we didn't have job assignments. Drinking and going to the base club were the only activities. By the fourth day, I was becoming bored, so it was time to go off base.

That first trip was to Berkley. The peace movement was heavy in that city, and hippies were a constant presence. In spite of being a marine rifleman, a major player in the war, I felt great respect for the peace movement. Pressure to end the war, from these spaced-out middle-class white people, might be my best chance for getting home.

I found it comforting seeing college students who looked like me, passing out literature and speaking out on issues that were being fought for in the inner-city streets. My next trip was to San Francisco.

Most of the marines would venture no further than the first off-base bus stop, where each bus arriving with servicemen with a pocket full of money and raging hormones was met by a line of streetwalkers. Other marines had warned me about the heavy homosexual community, but I didn't care. I would have missed a truly beautiful city had I not had a live-and-let-live attitude about people.

San Francisco was an interesting city and, like Berkley, a hotbed for social change. Less than two years earlier, over thirty thousand had come to Golden Gate Park for what was deemed "The Summer of Love." But I had another agenda. When you were in what was deemed the hippy capital of the world, there had to be a good hookup for LSD and reefer. As limited as my money was, I had to get the good stuff. Beyond that, I didn't have money to do much more in such an expensive city. I could walk, look, and enjoy the sights, but no more.

Each day would end in the barracks getting drunk with the other marines, listening to music, and playing cards.

The next city I visited was Oakland. Now that city was more my style. I was the typical serviceman following the same routine. The prostitutes were waiting at the bus stop and quickly enticed the men to a nearby sleazy hotel. There were strip joints and bars all along the way. Every conceivable opportunity was there to separate a man from his money. It was fun, but I quickly tired of being herded around like a sheep. So after the third trip to the city, I decided it was time to venture further into Oakland.

Like most black Americans, I was aware that the Black Panther Party had been formed there a few years earlier. It was now an armed camp, monitored closely by law enforcement and the FBI in particular. All parties were under a cloud of suspicion from all sides. It was not wise to venture into the city without someone known in the community. One marine stationed on Treasure Island lived off base in Oakland. I felt he would be my introduction into the city.

So at one of our evening card-playing sessions, I befriended him. There was the traditional feeling-out process consisting of him gathering information about me. While I wasn't a member of the party chapters in the North and East, I had knowledge of them. After sharing stories of the riots, boycotts, and marches that were taking place in the northern cities like

Cleveland, Detroit, and Chicago, he was finally satisfied that I wasn't FBI. He invited me to go with him the next evening.

The next evening he picked me up, and, after sharing some of the LSD tabs I had picked up in San Francisco, we drove into the city, where he would introduce me to some of his friends. He cautioned me along the way that although he wasn't sure if they represented any particular group other than themselves, these brothers were very serious about what they believed to be an upcoming revolution. And, as a serviceman, I might be perceived as a representative of the system they opposed.

We were driving through impoverished neighborhoods thick with graffiti calling for change and racial unity. But even more prevalent were the signs that identified food distribution locations, legal aid services, and self-help information. *This is where the war is*, I thought.

Suddenly he slammed on his breaks on spotting a car with a couple driving by. "That bitch!" he yelled before accelerating toward the car, almost crashing into the back of it. The car took off with us in hot pursuit.

I regretted having dropped that LSD before leaving the base, fearing that I or my new friend was experiencing a bad trip. "That was my wife!" he yelled. "She's fucking around with that motherfucker she used to date." I was now concerned that this marine, whom I didn't know very well, would kill somebody in a fit of rage. I pleaded to be let out at a bus stop and shown the direction to the base. It proved to be unnecessary. The couple had given him the slip. He was very distraught, rightfully so, and decided to go to a friend's house to decide his next move.

The neighborhood was deep inside Oakland. Everything in sight made it evident that military personnel or any government representative was not welcome. We stopped at a house and exited the car. There was a group of men standing in front who clearly opposed having a stranger in the area. As they approached, my friend stood between them and me. He spoke to them in an inaudible tone for a few moments; then the most intimidating-looking one approached me. His next comment took me by surprise.

"We pay top dollar for guns," he finally said. I knew I was in the wrong place. Calling on my street smarts, I looked for a way out. "I only deal with him," I said, pointing to my fellow marine. The brother paused while looking me up and down. Then he smiled broadly and said, "I understand." We exchanged the Black Power handshake; then we joined the group. The topic was dropped, not to be revisited.

We all went inside the house, where other people, both male and female, were sitting around talking. They were interested in the rebellion among the brothers and sisters in Cleveland and extremely pleased that the brothers in Nam were openly fighting the racism we were experiencing. I gained a level of respect from the brothers because I had been drafted into the corps rather than joining. "To stand up against racism in the Marine Corps," the intimidating brother said, "you got to be a strong motherfucker. Don't let them break you," he cautioned me. There was a universal agreement that it didn't matter where blacks were; it would always be in a struggle. They shared the beer and reefer with me while I watched them play cards. A young lady in the group seemed to be attracted to me. I didn't know who she was or who she was with, so I wasn't about to do anything that would upset anybody.

The more I drank and smoked, the worse I felt. It probably wasn't mixing well with the LSD. Eventually I was becoming nauseous. They pointed to a back door, which led to an alley. I excused myself, lit a cigarette, and went out.

I walked a short distance from the house in anticipation of throwing up. Which I did.

When done, I turned to go back in. Suddenly I couldn't find the door. In fact, I wasn't sure which house I had come out of. I walked up and down the alley for what seemed like hours trying to remember.

Soon I gave up and decided to go for help. In the distance I could see a sign that read "Safeway" and ran straight for it. I felt if I got inside the door, everything would be OK. It was quite a distance away, taking me about fifteen minutes to reach it. Once inside, I realized it was a grocery store. Now all the people in the store stopped what they were doing and stared at me. Then their expressions suddenly changed. They now looked like ghoulish figures. Suddenly they charged at me. I ran to escape the angry mob that seemed to want to devour me. After running for what seemed like forever, I had to stop to catch my breath. Now I was crouched over with my hands on my knees. My heart was beating so hard it hurt my chest.

Then, as I was about to walk off, I heard someone call my name. "Come on, man," he said, "I'm heading back to the base." I ran to him and began to blurt out the adventure, but, to my surprise, he was laughing. He took me inside and asked me to share the story. The more I talked, the harder they laughed. "You only been gone ten minutes," one of them finally said. "You better stay off that acid." I realized I was still holding the cigarette I had walked out the door with, so they may have been right. Now I was laughing at myself. I'll never really know what happened.

We said our good-byes to the brothers and headed back to Treasure Island. I vowed to stay out of Oakland and to never take LSD again.

Time passed, and I was well into my second week. This was OK with me. The more time spent there, the less time I would spend in Vietnam. Then I got the word from the sergeant that my hearing had been scheduled. "You'll have to pick up your orders from the OD." The sergeant laughed. "Some punk-ass second lieutenant." I knew that wasn't going to be a pleasant meeting, and I was right. I headed to his office after getting directions.

The lieutenant's office was a two-room trailer in which his secretary, a marine corporal, had a space twice the size of his. "How you doing, Corporal?" I said, walking in and glancing at her chevron. "You got my orders over there?"

"It's not going to be that easy," she said in a hushed tone, obviously not wanting the lieutenant to hear. "You have to get them from Lieutenant Dennis the Menace." She pointed to the door leading to his office.

I laughed; then, with a complete indifference to protocol, I opened the lieutenant's door and walked in. The lieutenant appeared to be twenty-two or twenty-three years of age. His closely cropped military haircut made him look even younger. "My name is Harris. You got some papers for me?" I boldly asked.

The lieutenant had equal disdain for me. He saw a low-ranking black enlisted man, with a minimal education and disrespect for his authority and therefore his country, standing before him. He jumped up screaming like a spoiled child. "You goddamn piece of shit. You're talking to your superior, an officer in the United States Marine Corps." He expected fear from a marine private, but I wasn't even going to pretend to be intimidated. In fact, if he hadn't been an officer, I would have immediately kicked his ass.

My lax demeanor angered him even more. "Do you even know how to address an officer?" he said, looking at me as I shrugged my shoulders. The naïve young officer actually walked over to the door to demonstrate. "You stand outside the door and pound on it," he said, tapping on the door frame. "I'll ask who's there. At such time you state your name and rank, then ask permission to enter. If I give you permission, you walk to the desk like this." He demonstrated. "You stop, stand at attention, then ask for permission to speak. If I grant permission, you ask your question. Each sentence begins and ends with sir. Now you try it," he ordered.

I stepped outside the door, and after a short laugh with the secretary, I made a half-ass attempt at it. When he was satisfied, he gave me the written orders. It was a two-sentence statement that said I was to report to the review board the next day.

Obviously intent on making my life less comfortable, the jerk informed me that he found no legitimate reason for me not to have some sort of work responsibility. Therefore, he assigned me the job of military policeman at the enlisted men's club. Then he told me to get out, which I was glad to do.

The secretary teased me as I walked out, shaking my head and giving the finger to the childish pencil-pushing junior officer who was likely feeling good about himself.

When I told my friends in the barracks I would be the MP on duty, they knew it was going to be a party that night. Everybody showed up, and I partied along with them. I lasted about an hour on the job before I was stripped of my armband. Now free of my responsibility, I went back to the barracks, changed clothes, and joined them. We partied hard all night. The next morning I woke up with a terrible hangover. After a quick

At the base club with fellow marines

shower, I headed out, anxious to get to the review board, where my fate would be decided.

I was informed there would be five high-ranking marine officers waiting for me that morning. This was their world, and I realized if a junior officer was so adamant about protocol, this privileged group would be even worse. So I attempted to make a good impression. I pounded on the door before entering. "Enter," someone on the other side of the door called out. *These guys must walk around with those ribbons on their chest all the time*, I thought as I marched over and stood at attention. "It must take a long time for them to get dressed."

Before I had a chance to speak, one of the officers began berating me. "How dare you come before a review board in a utility uniform?" he yelled.

I looked down at my uniform. "I didn't know I had to dress up," I replied.

That really infuriated them. "How dare you address your superiors without permission?" a major yelled while rising to his feet. "You're an undisciplined low-life disgrace. You don't deserve to be associated with the Marine Corps."

The major was right about one thing. I was certainly undisciplined, at least by their standards. They were expecting me to keep step in a band I had never asked to join. If there was an attitude change, it would be theirs, not mine. "I was drafted," I said defiantly. That comment destroyed any chance I might have had for a favorable ruling.

Every member on the board was poised to attack, but they deferred to the colonel, whose face was beet-red from anger. "What do you want from this board?" he said with restraint and authority.

"My brother was killed at home, sir, leaving me the last male member of the Harris family and their only child. Both of my parents are under a doctor's care from the stress. I've already spent over four months out front as a rifleman where the chance of survival is slim to none. I'm requesting to be placed in a noncombatant role when I return to Vietnam."

This was no revelation to the colonel. He knew that was the reason I was there in the first place. That only gave the arrogant self-glorified blowhard

Expendable and Necessary

an opening for his redundant speech. As a private I had no choice but to listen. "Why, you sniveling little coward," he said with his face inches from mine, "every man in this room has served at least two tours, and we've done it with distinction."

Since I had never seen an officer on point, or anywhere near when the bullets were flying over my head, the colonel could have kept that to himself. "We risked our lives for your freedom and the privileges you enjoy," the colonel went on. "It's time you did your part. This is your country, and you should be proud to fight and die for it if necessary." I was armed with too much information and experience to be affected by what was being said. All the officer's words rang hollow. Everything he was saying sounded like blah, blah, blah, blah. What I saw was four privileged white men who only saw me as an expendable commodity, someone to exploit. What a bunch of bullshit. They expected me to willfully risk my life to maintain their status quo. I was the real marine in that room. I could be wrong about them, but for certain, they were wrong about me.

"Get the fuck out of here," the colonel ordered. I did so knowing the only reason they didn't send me to the brig was because they needed another body in the bush. I cursed all the way back to the barracks, convinced they were now laughing about sending another black man off to die.

Just as expected, my orders to return to my unit were at the barracks before I was. I was to return on the next available flight, which was the next day. "The orders were here before you even went to the hearing," the duty sergeant told me.

"God damn," I shouted after opening them. "Why the fuck did I even have to go through all that bullshit?"

Off-duty leave was canceled that night for me. They were concerned I might not return. That was no problem for me. I just walked around the base having one last smoke and one more drink with my newfound friends. Saying good-bye took the rest of the day. One of the marines had gotten the sough after Section 8 discharge, so they were all going to celebrate with him.

I told them about the hearing, and they shared my frustrations. "Those motherfuckers think I believe I'll be given equal opportunities when the war is over. That's the shit the black men thought when they came home in World War II. I can't stop them from using me, but I damned well won't act like I don't know it."

I decided to leave my remaining LSD tabs. Combat wasn't a good place for a hallucinogenic drug, and it might help those who would be going for a Section 8 hearing later. They just drank liquor purchased at the PX. The military discount made it almost cheaper than soda pop. In Marine Corps tradition, we chugged it down straight. Good-byes were short and sweet in the military. It was an everyday occurrence. I did, however, wake up with a severe headache.

I got up the next morning and located base transportation that took me to the airport. The military commissioned plane taking us to Okinawa was filled with military personnel in transit and military families. There were several families waiting to board the plane. They all had husbands and fathers whom they would be joining in Okinawa. One of the families was African American and from Chicago. The mother was in her late twenties, with two children, a six-year-old daughter and an eight-year-old son. Families with minor children would be assisted by single servicemen who were also on the flight. I was told, prior to boarding, that I would assist that family in the first-class section. This would likely be the only time I would receive preferential treatment, and I loved it.

Nothing in my twenty young years would indicate I was suited for a husband or father role. I did, however, fill it with surprising ease. The woman's husband was a sergeant in the air force. He was a career man, and both she and her children were accustomed to the transient life of a military family. They were very excited about being reunited.

She turned out to be a very kind and perceptive woman. Her husband was an airman who was never really in harm's way. So, in spite of her family's positive experience with military life, she understood my hostility. While the children slept, she listened intently as I expressed my fears and premonitions of an impending doom. Rather than assure me that my fears were unfounded or that prayer would get me through, she placed my chance for survival on me alone. "Your job," she told me, "is to stay alive. You are responsible for your life and the people around you. If you get through this, and I feel you will, the rest of your life's challenges will be a breeze." Her advice was the best I had heard and would always stay with me.

When the children woke up, we played card games and other games the mother had brought along. Rather than have them call me Harris, which was a military thing, or Ralph, which was too informal, she had them call me Mr. Ralph. They were very respectful and well-mannered children. Very quickly, that family became my total focus.

I interacted so well with the family that people in the coach section thought I was the father. We laughed and joked all the way. I was sad when we reached Okinawa. I knew they would leave and I would continue to Vietnam. Once the plane landed, I could see a jubilant air-force sergeant who was obviously the husband and father running alongside.

I helped take her luggage off and assisted with the children. Once on the tarmac, they ran to their father and husband. I headed back to the plane, not wanting to interfere with the reunion, when I suddenly heard my name being called. "Mr. Ralph! Mr. Ralph!" they called, running toward me. They jumped into my arms for one last hug. The woman waited patiently to gently kiss me on the cheek and introduce me to her husband. "Good luck, brother," he said, giving me a firm handshake. "Thanks for looking out for my family. They like you, so be sure to take care of yourself." I looked at them, composing myself enough to tell them that I was the one who owed the thanks. My hardened armor had been penetrated.

In an odd way, I had fallen in love. Not with the woman or her children but with marriage and fatherhood. They had unknowingly given me a goal.

CHAPTER 17

The Good Die Young: Second Time Around May 1969

▲ ▲ ▲

I BOARDED THE PLANE THAT would transport me to Vietnam. Once I landed in Da Nang, I was immediately transported by helicopter to An Hoa to rejoin my unit. Unknown to me, the personnel had changed drastically. My bereavement had been stretched to over six weeks. That was a long time in bush life. Soon after I left for the funeral, the company had faced off with a regiment of NVA around Liberty Bridge. Heavy fighting continued in different parts of the Arizona. A week prior to my return, an area defended by our battalion faced an onslaught of five thousand hard-core NVA. The NVA were trying to retake territory they had lost during Operation Taylor Common. The NVA simultaneously attacked An Hoa, cutting our company off.

Of the original 120 members who were in G Company when I left, there might have been 50 whom I recognized. Most of the marines wounded were permanently disabled. There had been marines who had joined the company and died without my ever meeting them. A corpsman, David Ray, had been killed in his

Memorial for fallen marines

first combat mission. He received the Congressional Medal of Honor. Brantley had been killed and received the Navy Cross. Kitchen was also dead.

Dura was injured too severely to return. Speedy and Rhone were gone. Louie was gone. Moose and Paira gone.

Snarr was promoted and moved on. Walters, Sally, and Froggie were wounded and returned within forty-eight hours. Froggie, due to his mental state, should not have been brought back. Lieutenant Hannahan returned but was soon be moved to a less hazardous position. Ellis was one of the few who hadn't been physically scarred.

The platoon and company sergeants had been changed. The company sergeant was an African American by the name of Gunnery Sergeant Mac. Judging by his weight, Gunny Mac was fresh from stateside duty. The short, round man seemed to compensate for his shortcomings with an exaggerated sense of toughness. His apparent friend and prodigy was another African American by the name of Staff Sergeant Sparks. He was fiercely loyal to the marines, viewing the corps as his life's calling.

First Platoon was headed by a sergeant by the name of Sergeant Bazarr. He looked like the clone of General Custer complete with the bandanna and flowing yellow hair. The three of them thought of themselves as the most important men ever to serve. They all were clear to share their dreams of moving up the hierarchy regardless of whose shoulders they had to stand on to get there. On the day that I arrived, they were in the sergeants' tent discussing how to snap the men in line.

The lieutenant was concerned about how the men had been demoralized by their heavy losses in Arizona. Gunnery Sergeant Mac and Staff Sergeant Sparks believed fear and strict discipline was the way to motivate the men. This was what they had been taught, so they concluded the method was tried and true. They wanted the men to recognize they were now in charge, and they were outlining their vision to the lieutenant, who deferred to their experience.

"It's time those crying motherfuckers quit feeling sorry for themselves," Mac shouted in his characteristic domineering voice. "They've had a whole day to get it together. This ain't the Boy Scouts. It's the Marine Corps; people die."

Sparks agreed, and he wanted to address what he considered a separatist attitude among black marines. "We got to break up this brother shit. They act like they are in some kind of fraternity. I'm 'black and proud' too. I'm a black, proud marine. The only color we are here is green, a mighty green killing machine." Again they agreed.

The lieutenant was reassured to know the black leaders didn't agree with the call for racial division that was growing in the ranks. Sergeant Bazarr added his own two cents. "We should set up a training regimen. Work them; drive them; don't give them time to feel sorry for themselves. We can turn them into fighting men yet." There was a consensus among the group.

While the lieutenant and sergeants discussed their strategies, Walters, who was now a squad leader, was addressing the men in his squad in another tent. Most of his squad were relatively new in-country. Walters was telling them stories of prior platoon members. He laughed as he told stories about Ellis and me, whom he called the Ohio twins. He didn't realize that I had just landed on the base and was walking to the area, and Ellis had just gotten released from the hospital.

A marine came into the tent to alert the men that a new replacement had just gotten off the supply chopper. They rushed out to give the customary harassment. Watching from a distance, they commented on the distinctive walk the marine had, more of a bounce than walk. "Damn, he walks just like Ellis," Walters said to Hansen.

"Or Harris," Hansen responded. All eyes followed as I gradually approached.

They recognized me when I was within about three hundred yards.

"My man, my man!" Walters shouted. "That's Harris." Walters, Hansen, Johnson, and Sally rushed me like linemen charging a punt return. In their excitement we collided, all falling to the ground.

"What you doing back?" Walters asked.

"I couldn't stay away any longer, but I tried," I said, laughing. Looking around, I began questioning them about Ellis's absence. "He's stretching out a hospital stay." Walters laughed. "He's probably banging the nurses right now."

On the walk to the tent, they bombarded me with questions about America. The women, the clothes, the music, civil-rights protests, antiwar protests; they asked about every topic that was being censored in Vietnam. They wanted to see pictures, tapes, magazines, newspapers. Most of all whiskey or drugs.

I could only answer yes to drugs. I had a pocket full of pills and three ten packs I had purchased with my last American dollars.

The whole thing was being observed by the lieutenant and sergeants. They could see the positive reaction the men had given me, and they didn't like an underling having that much credibility. "That's Harris returning from bereavement," the lieutenant said, addressing the sergeants. "Watch him," he cautioned. "He's good under fire, but he's not good at following rules, and he'll polarize the blacks."

"Bullshit!" shouted Sparks. "Not as long as I'm here."

"Good!" the lieutenant said to Sparks. "Marines aren't individuals. We think, move, and act as one. Now you sergeants take control of your men. Tell them how it's going to be. I'll come in later and punctuate the message."

The three sergeants adjusted their neatly pressed uniforms and then took a position in front of the tents. Then the gunnery sergeant, in his commanding baritone voice, ordered everyone to assemble in front of him. We stopped, groaned in unison in anticipation of the customary BS, and assembled outside as ordered.

Once we were in an official formation, the gunnery sergeant told us how it was going to be.

"Why the fuck didn't you report to the command tent?" he shouted at me. "You show respect to your superiors. You don't make a goddamn move unless we approve it." I only answered in silence, which the gunny took as a sign of disrespect, and it infuriated him. "You don't just stand there when I address you!" he shouted into my ear. "You say, 'Yes, Gunnery Sergeant.'" I knew what the gunny was doing and realized it was a no-win situation for me.

"Yes, Gunnery Sergeant," I replied.

"Now get the fuck back in formation," he shouted. He then turned his ire on the men.

"What the fuck are you assholes doing feeling sorry for yourselves? You've had two days to get over it. Have you forgotten who you are? You're United States Marines. You are members of an elite assault force with a proud tradition, not some ragtag bunch of misfits. Our tradition started when we were formed in 1775, one year before our nation declared its independence. Since our formation we have been charged with the assault and seizure of advanced bases. That makes us the first to go into battle. So why be surprised when some of us die?

"When you are dismissed, you will go back to your tents and clean them up and prepare for future orders. Start acting like marines. Is that understood?"

The men responded in unison, "Aye aye, Sergeant!"

Next Staff Sergeant Sparks made his pitch.

"In past wars, America's armed forces were basically segregated and headed by white officers and sergeants. It was a source of pride among career black servicemen to prove we could lead and be competent in combat. Those who came before you pushed for the recognition and promotions that combat would bring. They were torchbearers for the black people and our nation. We will continue that tradition.

"As of today we are going to put an end to that separatist shit. Those motherfuckers in the States can go around talking about Black Power, White Power, peace, and love. The only power color we have here is green. We're one big green killing machine. We represent one country with one goal. That is to destroy our enemy or anyone that threatens our freedom. You assholes don't know anything about black pride. Hell, I'm from Compton, California. If you want to express pride, show that you are just as loyal, courageous, and dedicated to our country's causes as any American ever to call himself an American. Don't diminish the memory of the Americans of all colors that have died to get the freedoms you now enjoy. If one of you motherfuckers waves a clenched fist at me, I'll break it off. Is that understood?"

The men answered him in unison, "Aye aye, Sergeant."

Then the lieutenant came out and addressed the men. "As the gunny and staff sergeant have stated, the marines have a proud tradition. That tradition is a tradition of success. That success comes from our ability to follow the orders of our superiors. Every leader here is a decorated veteran. We are fortunate they have been assigned to our company. These are the men who have proven they can lead and have the wisdom and experience to do so. You are told what to do and when to do it. When you complete the task to the best of your ability, you will be rewarded with the promotions and commendations that accompany your actions. Are there any questions?" The men responded with silence. The lieutenant dismissed us and ordered us to clean up the area and await further orders.

The sergeants and lieutenant were satisfied that they had commanded the respect of the men and therefore boosted the morale of the unit. Satisfied, they went into the NCO tent.

"What do you think about the sergeants' speeches?" Walters said, turning to me.

"Those motherfuckers need to read more than *Stars and Stripes* so they will know what is going on outside their own little world," I said with a laugh.

Walters wisely put the situation into perspective. "I'll be the first to admit I don't know much about the civil rights movement or racial injustice. My world never went further than ten miles from my home, before joining the marines. I do know that our immediate future is Vietnam, and if we don't survive, nothing else will matter. So for better or worse, we are drawn together."

Walters continued to go over changes that had taken place. He was promoted to corporal; Hansen and Donahue were promoted to lance corporal.

"The white dudes got promoted, big surprise. What else is new?" I scoffed.

"Brantley got a medal, then a promotion, and Johnson got promoted to corporal and moved to company radioman. They are black."

"Brantley had to die before he got recognition, and Johnson is a Tom. So what's your point?" I responded sarcastically. My comment understandably brought Johnson to his feet with anger.

"Black people can't stand to see a black man move up; fuck you," he shouted, storming out of the tent.

"I'm going to have to put you and Ellis on point more often," Walters went on. Before I could give my predictable angry response, Walters justified the move. "We're getting some new people in the squad. I have to justify making you and Ellis team leaders; then they have to promote you. You weren't in Arizona, Harris; to gain respect from those who were, you have to prove yourself."

"I don't have any problem pointing; fuck the promotion. All I care about is staying alive and getting an honorable discharge so I can get my job back when I go home."

"Without some promotion, every time someone comes in with higher rank, whether they have combat experience or not, they will be in charge of your life," Walters assured me.

Sergeant Sparks burst into the tent. We were prepared for more verbal abuse but were pleasantly surprised when he announced we would be transported to Phu Loc 6 for a USO show.

After a formal memorial service for the recently deceased members of the company, we were transported by truck to Phu Loc 6. This was a long, harrowing ride over a road vulnerable to ambushes and land mines. Other marine units were assembled along the truck route to provide security, and there were several firefights and detected mines along the way. But with a great deal planning and luck, we safely arrived at Phu Loc 6. For an added bonus, an Australian entertainment company was there providing the entertainment.

Ellis also managed to work his magic and joined the company shortly after our arrival. When he stepped into the tent, my depression subsided, especially when I saw his full beard. "How in the fuck did you manage to get them to let you grow a full beard?" I asked. "Even the officers can't do that."

"I convinced the doctor in Da Nang that I have a strong allergic reaction to shaving, so he gave me this no-shave shit."

"What is that?"

"That's an order that exempts me from shaving. Not bad." Ellis laughed while stroking his beard. We had a good laugh about Ellis's ability to make things happen. The team from Ohio was back together.

Ellis could see that I was depressed, having gone home to bury my brother. I had seen my girlfriend, family, and friends and then had to go through the separation over again. In addition, I saw the turmoil the war was causing in America. "How was home?" he asked. I was about to tell him of all the fun I'd had when Ellis stopped me.

"Don't bullshit us, man; what are you feeling?"

In truth, I was feeling guilty talking about any fun times considering what they had gone through. Eventually we all agreed we had all experienced a different kind of hell and should focus on the future. The immediate future was a USO show.

Phu Loc 6 was a very dangerous place. It was likely the enemy was at a distance watching the same show. It's hard to express the gratitude we felt toward the entertainers who would put themselves in such danger to entertain us.

That night we would forget about our troubles and eat a good meal, laugh, sing, dance, and talk while enjoying the show. The entertainers were outstanding. They had a band, a comedian, and scantily clad women who mingled among the men and didn't complain about the touching.

Reefer and number tens were cheap and easily accessible. To wash it down, each man got two beers. Prostitutes were even snuck into the compound. It was a night the men of G Company would remember for some time. We would need it, because the next day we would start a new and deadly task.

CHAPTER 18

The Face of the Dead
May–June 1969

▲ ▲ ▲

THE NEXT OPERATION INVOLVED A search-and-destroy mission.

Controlling Arizona was essential for both sides. The North Vietnamese needed it for a staging area to move troops and supplies from the Ho Chi Min Trail to Da Nang. Our regiment was responsible to disrupt and eliminate. Because we launched our operations from Phu Loc and An Hoa, they would continually attack those bases. So the tug-of-war battles in and around Arizona were ongoing.

The NVA were hitting with heavy artillery, and their strength seemed to be growing. Intelligence reports suggested the NVA were mounting for an attack. Fox and Gulf were to defend Phu Loc, Fox from within, Gulf from without.

Although Phu Loc 6 had fewer personnel, it was more heavily fortified than An Hoa. It was equipped with an artillery unit, a tank company, a motor transport company, and a field hospital. Because it required such a large mass of land and was so heavily defended, it was difficult to camouflage. The base relied on the marines stationed there and the regiment's rifle companies for security.

Our company was lifted to An Hoa. We would turn around and walk back, clearing the area surrounding the road connecting the two bases of booby traps and enemy positions. It would be a two-day trip.

My squad, Second Squad, was a mixture of experienced and inexperienced men. Walters was the squad leader. Donahue, who had been in-country roughly two weeks, was on radio. Ray, a brother from Virginia, was on machine gun. His actions in Arizona had gotten him the nickname Crazy Ray. I was a team leader who would often walk point. Ellis would also point. Kartis, a new recruit, had just joined the company.

I spotted what I thought was a booby trap the first day. Walters confirmed it, and the engineers blew it up. That night we set up an ambush at what we believed to be a likely spot for an enemy crossing. The unsuspecting NVA patrol was spotted going toward the road. The plan was for the riflemen to force them toward Ray, who would cut them down with the machine gun. The plan failed when an overambitious Kartis fired prematurely, causing the VC to scatter.

On the second day, Walters received good news. His orders come through for R and R. Everybody was happy for him. His choices were Hong Kong, Bangkok, Australia, or Hawaii. The brothers usually chose Bangkok. Their stories probably influenced Walters's decision to go there. I was left in charge of the squad.

Second Squad was to work as a kill team on that day. We would flank the marines on the road, traveling incandescently about two to three hundred yards. We were responsible for stopping enemy troops who might be trying to approach the moving column. At night we would maintain that distance, which made us vulnerable to a night attack. For added protection, we would set up claymore mines to our front. If detonated, these six-by-twelve-inch weapons of destruction would rip an unfortunate victim to shreds. The downside was that it had to be set at least forty yards out. In thick, possibly booby-trapped terrain, that was a dangerous forty-yard walk. I sent Kartis to put it out with Alameda, a man brought in to replace Walters, providing him security. It went without a hitch. In fact, it turned out to be an uneventful night.

The next morning I sent them to retrieve it. First Squad, who maintained a position to our right, did the same. Suddenly, there was a loud blast. When people expect an explosion, they brace their bodies for it. When it happens without warning, the shock rather than the concussion knocks people off their feet. Then they curl themselves up in a ball for protection against the shrapnel. Those who did watch the blast saw a portion of a marine's severed leg flying through the air. That was understandably followed by an agonizing scream. The Viet Cong had set booby traps during the night.

The men in the squad were paralyzed with fear, especially Kartis and Alameda. They looked at me with fear in their eyes, hoping that I wouldn't send them back out. All while this was going on, the members of the squad with the wounded marine had retrieved him and his foot and were desperately trying to stop the profuse bleeding. Johnson, the company radioman, immediately called for an emergency evacuation for him. I didn't like being a squad leader at that moment, but I had to make a decision, one that Ellis didn't like.

"Fuck it!" I said, grabbing my helmet and flak jacket, "I'll get the motherfucker myself."

"What the fuck are you doing?" Ellis yelled, jumping in front of me. "You're the squad leader; send somebody else." Without answering, I started out. Ellis cursed and then picked up his weapon and joined me. The gunnery sergeant and lieutenant had joined us by that time and were observing from a distance. The claymore was retrieved without incident. While the squad members appreciated what I had done, the lieutenant and gunny felt it wasn't a wise decision, because it could have left an inexperienced squad without a leader.

That evening we reached Phu Loc 6. We found out immediately that the situation was direr than expected. Although it was heavily fortified, the NVA were boldly shelling the base. It was expected that they were preparing for an all-out attack. We just took positions guarding the lines. That night, fortunately, was uneventful.

Lieutenant Hannahan had done his six months and rotated to another duty. Before leaving, he introduced us to his replacement, Lieutenant Storm. He was much more personable than the departing officer and made an immediate connection with the men. He was also trained as a reconnaissance officer and could teach us surveillance techniques that could prove valuable.

The next morning the new lieutenant took the platoon on a patrol circling the surrounding area to evaluate the terrain. The company broke off into platoons. First and Fourth Platoons would stand guard inside the base. Our platoon and Third Platoon would take positions outside the base.

Third and Fourth Squads set ambushes on roads leading into the base; our squad was to do a recon operation. We slipped away from the platoon into the distant jungle to avoid the prying eyes of Communist recon patrols that were likely watching. The commanders concluded that the enemy was using the heavy vegetation to observe the base. The enemy would position their artillery in this jungle. But they could only get off a few rounds before the marine artillery would locate them, so it was most often a suicide mission for those who tried. They might also attack from the surrounding jungle. All artillery personnel were informed of our presence, so it was the only no-fire zone that night. Embedded in the surrounding vegetation, we got a clear view of the base. Now we could observe and relay information back to the base.

Darkness consumed us as evening approached. The only illumination was the faint glow from the moon. It was apparent how the enemy felt lying in the dark observing the base. You could almost feel the awesome power contained in the tranquil-looking micro city. It was a monster waiting to be awakened.

There was a constant change from darkness to light caused by the men guarding the lines periodically setting off a pop-up. The flare would shoot up like a rocket, and then there would be a muffled explosion. When it burst, there would be a blinding light as if a light had been turned on. Then the burning phosphorus would illuminate the area as a small parachute slowed its decent. The changing position of the light would cause the shadow to change, causing stationary objects to appear to be moving. By the time it reached the ground, the phosphorus would have burned off, and others would be launched.

Each time a flare would go off, the men of Second Squad would freeze, moving only our eyes, knowing that while we searched for the enemy, they searched for us. When the area was illuminated, we would take a mental snapshot to use as a comparison. We also learned to close our eyes before the flare went completely out, allowing the pupils to contract. The enemy might use that brief moment of vulnerability to attack. So while most faced forward observing the base, others faced the rear and flanks. I was at the center with Ellis on my right and Donahue, the radioman, on my left.

When we approached our position, we saw the ground was littered with sharp bits of shrapnel from months, possibly years, of marine artillery bombardment. There were spots where we walked over inches of charred metal. We knew to avoid those places if it became necessary to crawl back in the event of a hasty retreat. The razor-sharp edges of the metal would rip us to shreds. We chose our position carefully and then settled in for the night.

Sometime around 0100, one of the men on guard crawled over to me and whispered in my ear. "Why is there so much brush outside the base?"

"There shouldn't be any brush in front of the fence," I responded. Then I told him to make sure all the men were awake.

When I approached Ellis, I found he was counting softly.

"Four, two, seven, and three," he would whisper. Next time it would be, "Four, five, seven, and two." Then he leaned over to me and whispered, "Those groups of brush keep changing."

"Oh shit!" I said, turning to Donahue. "They're closing in on the base. Call it in."

Before Donahue could finish the transmission, a squad of marines sprung an ambush on the road leading into the base. Instantaneously, the marines in the base began to fire, as did the advancing enemy. Then a red smoke grenade was popped from within the base, the signal that the enemy had breached their lines. Huge spotlights came on, shining both inside and outside the perimeter. The enemy was exposed, and they scattered like junkyard rats. All hell was breaking loose, and the enemy was between us and the base, the worst possible position to be in.

If the NVA retreated, they would roll over our small force like a steam roller. If we tried to get into the base during the chaos, we could be mistaken for the enemy by the riflemen. Or some overzealous artilleryman might drop a round on us. Any round within thirty yards would take us out. But the biggest danger was the tanks. They had an antipersonnel round that would explode when leaving the gun's barrel, sending thousands of darts that covered a large kill radius. When I heard that first blast from a tank, I knew we had to leave. Then when a round from a howitzer came dangerously close, I knew it would have to be immediately. "Alert the base of our position and ask for a window," I called to Donahue.

Frantically Donahue tried to alert the base of our position. "Check fire; check fire," Donahue shouted over the radio. "Gulf two in zone eight; check fire." Johnson on company radio responded.

"Gulf two, this is Gulf. That's a copy. Hold your position until further instruction." The commanders were coordinating an escape plan. Minutes later I was handed the radio handset. The lieutenant was on the line.

He informed me that when the order was given, we were to abandon the position and rush toward a narrow ravine that led into the base. For the first two hundred yards, we would be in the open. So for a brief time, all defensive shooting would stop in that quarter of the perimeter. That was our window of opportunity. Once we reached the ravine, the calibrated artillery would fire to our back and flanks.

It was a good plan, but there were inherent dangers. The defensive fire from the base could not be contained for long, so any obstacle that could possibly cause a delay would have to be overcome immediately. But if we met resistance and were forced to fire our M16s, the distinctive sound would alert the enemy to our presence, and they would have a swift and sure response. To add to our troubles, now that the enemy had penetrated the lines, the marines on the base were likely focused on saving themselves rather than saving us.

Once the command was given, we started our frantic escape. The squad had traveled roughly two hundred yards before the NVA noticed the absence of incoming rounds. When they scanned the area and saw our squad racing toward the base, they focused a vicious attack on us. Now we were forced to fire back. All involved now knew marines were outside the base. The ravine we were entering could have been called the valley of death.

The artillerymen on the base were extremely skilled. Mortars were dropped just behind us as we ran to the base. This prevented us from being attacked from the rear. Riflemen were firing to our flanks. Our biggest challenge, at that moment, was not to slow down or to stray to the left or right. Like prizefighters being protected by security while going into the ring at a championship fight, we had to remain focused while madness and chaos took place all around.

When we reached the gate, a squad of marines rushed out to assist us. We burst into the perimeter like lambs that had been wrestled from the jaws of a lion. We were exhausted, frightened, and overjoyed. But there was no time to relax. We immediately joined in the defense of the base.

Now that all friendly forces were inside, or at a safe distance, an intense artillery bombardment was initiated. Shouts could be heard throughout the night as enemy forces that had penetrated the lines were hunted down and killed. At daybreak, the men were able to assess the damage. The majority of kills were outside the lines, left behind by the retreating NVA forces. Some were still entangled in the barbed wire; about a half dozen were found around the compound. The number of marine dead and wounded wasn't revealed.

I was now what might be defined as an opportune alcoholic. That is, I would drink if it was safe enough to do so and there was a cold beer available. I began to casually look at the bodies, approaching a body of a man who appeared to be my age. Most participants in war dispense death at a distance, so they are detached from the destruction they bring. But an infantryman has no such luxury. He is forced to face his demons up close. In a macabre way, I was giving respect to my fallen foe.

I visually searched the body, looking for the trauma that ended his life. It was clear the soldier was dead, as evidenced by the gaping wounds that no longer bled and the fact he didn't choke on the insects that roamed freely in and out of his open mouth and nostrils. Then I pondered his facial expression.

A dead man's facial expression reveals his final moments. If he had a pained expression, it would indicate he had suffered. If his mouth and eyes were open, it would indicate death was instantaneous and unexpected. He had no time to suffer, no time to reflect, no time to slowly fade out of existence.

Eventually I did what is not recommended. I looked into the eyes of the dead. Some say when you look into the eyes of a dead man, you are seeing the future, for they have started a journey we all will take. Others believe the eyes are the window through which the soul escapes. If there were any of life's secrets held by the man lying before me, they were taken with him into the afterlife.

When I stood and turned to leave, Ellis, who stood nearby, asked what I saw. Without hesitation I replied, "I learned how easy it is to die."

There was a lull in the fighting over the next few days. We followed our normal routine. Patrols and observation posts during the day, ambushes at night that would yield no results. It became obvious that the enemy had pulled their troops back.

Because we were operating out of the base rather than the bush, we could relax in hooches and eat in a chow hall. But the men had a high energy level, and everyone knew tensions would begin to surface if we didn't see action soon. For the moment, however, all was calm. Walters, who had returned from R and R, Ellis, a replacement from LA by the name of Sherman, and I were holding what amounted to a typical adolescent discussion. Sherman, the new man, respectfully listened to the conversation. He had been advised by RC, whom he had met as he was being processed in An Hoa, to establish ties with the men he was sitting with.

Me Walters & Ellis

"You know what I'm going to do?" Ellis said between drags on a joint and sipping beer. "I'm going to go home and marry one of those beautiful Youngstown sisters and have a bunch of sons, then name them all after me."

"You gonna stick some brothers with a name like Robert?" I said sarcastically.

"It's better than Ralph," Ellis countered. "No black man should be stuck with a name like Ralph".

"Who said I was gonna name my son Ralph?"

"Don't you want someone to carry on your name?"

"I'm gonna be the one and only Ralph."

"There has gotta be some history, something to your name."

"Nope."

"You mean you're the only person in your family named Ralph?"

"Yep, only me, so I'm gonna start a new tradition. I'm gonna give my kids African names."

"I can see that." Ellis nodded. "But I'm gonna leave at least one Robert Ellis to carry on. What about you, Walters? Are you going give your kid your name?"

Walters just shrugged his shoulders. He was more focused on enjoying the company of the ladies back home. My demeanor had become somber. I turned to Walters. "You're all right, man, but why are you about always putting me and Ellis on point? Is that some backwoods racism coming out?"

"Why would you say that to me, man? You know that's wrong. Both of you have a lot of time left, and you're gonna be seeing some tough shit before it's over. Now is the time to polish your skills."

"Fuck that," Ellis said, stroking his chin. "I'll make sergeant; then I won't have to worry about pointing."

Walters responded as sincerely as he could. "Ellis, you're a leader, but those sergeants will never move you up until you're willing to follow them, and we know that isn't going to happen. So you need to work on what is gonna keep you alive. Harris, you have the survival instincts and reflexes that keep a pointer alive. Don't fight it. Pass it on."

Before I could protest, which I surely would have done, Sergeant Sparks burst into the tent. Reefer smoke swirled around him, and the men did nothing to disguise it.

"Is this all you motherfuckers do, sit around and smoke drugs? I'll make marines out of you if it's the last thing I do," the sergeant barked.

"If we aren't marines, then why are we over here? Ellis said with a smirk.

"You're a bunch of clowns," Sparks snarled. "You stupid motherfuckers are trying to move all the progress blacks have made backward to when we had colored troops."

The sergeant was beginning to gain some ground until he started talking about stopping a "Communist takeover." I had heard enough. I stood up, rolled my eyes, and huffed out of the tent, mumbling about my high getting messed up.

"That's right!" Sparks shouted, pacing the tent. "While you shitheads were back home shaking your dicks at the schoolgirls, I was out killing gooks."

"Gooks!" Ellis repeated. "Why is it necessary to call them derogatory names?"

"Because they are a bunch of slant-eyed chinks, beetle-nut-chewing gooks, and I hate every motherfucking one of them," the sergeant yelled. "I'll tell you something else. The only good one is a dead one. My reason for living is to kill more of them."

Ellis should have backed off, but it wasn't in his nature. "If you change the name gook with nigger, you would be saying the same thing that is said about us," Ellis countered.

Sergeant Sparks nearly attacked Ellis after that comment.

Ellis didn't back down. "Sarge, I know you believe in what you're saying, but don't you ever question what you are told to die for?"

"Hell no, Private, and as long as you're a United States Marine, you better not question it either." Sarge was beside himself at the impertinence of a lowly marine PFC. He began shouting at Ellis only inches from his face. "Don't you ever talk to a staff sergeant in the United States Marine Corps like that! Do you understand that, Private?" Ellis was clearly upset but understood he was in a no-win situation, so he had to defer to the sergeant.

"Yes, Sergeant," he finally answered.

Sergeant Sparks then turned his anger toward Walters. "Why the fuck are you, an NCO, sitting around with your underlings?"

"Because they are my friends."

"People you command aren't friends. That's why your squad is so undisciplined. That's also why you won't see another promotion." With that, he stormed out of the hooch.

"Why do you piss him off all the time?" Walters asked Ellis.

"Fuck him," Ellis responded while opening a beer.

But just like with any large group, the platoon was made of men with a wide range of ideals and strong personalities. Johnson, a very philosophical man, was a perfect example. He was black and from a large urban city, so he understood that we were all held hostage by a traditional system built on unfairness. But if he could get the system to work to his advantage, why change it? He idolized Sergeant Sparks and Gunny Mac. They were responsible for his promotion to corporal. No one doubted that he was an excellent radioman and deserved the promotion. But his open idealization of higher-ranking marines and his attempts to imitate them was the biggest boost to his career. He may have secretly agreed with Ellis and me, but he knew that if we didn't survive, all those ideological principles would mean nothing. Our bodies would be sent home with the standard salutations and accolades that were given all fallen marines: "Your son or daughter died bravely defending the rights and freedoms of all Americans."

Donahue, a Caucasian protégé of Johnson, also supported the system and felt no need to resist it. Just like Johnson, he was good in his job as radioman, so he just went with the flow. Then two other strong personalities came into the company. The first was PFC Pepin, a marine from the Midwest. Pepin was unique. His father was a marine officer. If anyone could have avoided combat, it was him. But he was truly an American patriot. His volunteering for the infantry was a way to impress his father and to support deeply held beliefs. That loyalty gave him a measure of respect among the men. Another incoming marine was Sergeant Nato, a marine from the deep South. He had deeply held beliefs as well, especially hatred toward blacks, and he didn't care who knew it. The power of his rank afforded him control over all under him. That made him a threat to the survival of the black man. A showdown was inevitable.

While it appeared all the dissention was coming from one squad, consisting of Walters, Ellis, Sally, Sherman, and me, there were many others who felt the same way. When under fire, those dynamic personalities complemented each other.

That presented a challenge for the new lieutenant to get such a devil's brew to pull together. He tried to bring us together by introducing new tactics. He introduced scout dogs on patrols. The effort proved fruitless. Those dogs just didn't want to cooperate, and some of the men were simply afraid of them. He also tried recon techniques that seemed promising. Certain tasks would require a boldness that was difficult to order a man to have. His challenge was to gain control of the men who were aggressive and confident enough to pull it off.

He decided to isolate the rebellious Second Squad members and strip away their credibility, in hopes they would later push to regain favor.

To do this, he promoted inexperienced but loyal men and fast-tracked the newly arriving men into positions of authority. These were men who would relay his orders without question.

Alameda, who had recently joined the platoon, was promoted to lance corporal and given Third Squad. Hansen was given Fourth Squad. Sergeant Nato would eventually take over that squad. First Squad was led by another recently promoted corporal.

Walters was the only experienced squad leader at that point.

We continued to operate out of Phu Loc. Three days later, patrols spotted Viet Cong in one of the surrounding villages, so B-52s were sent in to bomb them. The platoon would surround them to keep any from escaping. Then napalm was dropped. It would be a sanitized victory for the platoon, because they didn't have to actually do the killing.

Hansen with Fourth Squad and Alameda with Third Squad were to go into the village afterward with the lieutenant, gunnery sergeant, and staff sergeant. First Squad would guard the perimeter. Second Squad was excluded and sent on a mission to search out a supposed NVA unit.

When the squads entered the village after the attack, the sight of the charred bodies stopped them in their tracks. The men who drop the bombs and release the napalm have no idea of the carnage they leave behind.

The hooches that housed the villagers were reduced to charcoal. Many of the bodies appeared as pools of bubbling liquid. The smell of burning flesh made the squad members sick to their stomachs.

First Squad members were startled by a partially naked girl who appeared to be eight to ten years old. She was screaming hysterically in Vietnamese. No one could speak Vietnamese proficiently enough to understand what she was saying. But it was clear her emotions were going between distress and anger.

The men concluded she had been away from the village when the bombs were dropped. She seemed to be returning to a sight that no one, regardless of age or experience, should witness. Perhaps she had just witnessed the horrific demise of her entire family. When someone approached her to help, she ran screaming into the jungle. She had become another victim of the atrocity of war. Both squads returned speechless. Those with a conscience had to have been troubled; however, the feelings weren't shared.

If the lieutenant had truly attempted to isolate and diminish the credibility of the rebellious Second Squad, the ploy backfired. There was an NVA unit in the area, and we found them. In perhaps a moment of carelessness, the battle-hardened force allowed us to surprise them. With skill and courage, we decimated our well-armed foe. Then we brought our quarry back for display.

Among the bodies we brought back was an officer whose pay grade was several above our own lieutenant's. The message from Second Squad was clear. We're bad, and you need us.

The lieutenant would draw on that experience as we prepared for the next task. We were to confront the enemy in the flatlands.

CHAPTER 19

Purging the Flatlands
June 1969

▲ ▲ ▲

Although the enemy had pulled back from the base, it was suspected they had dispersed into the surrounding area, which was mostly flatland. Our platoon was sent into that area with Sergeant Bazarr in charge.

To understand the fighting conditions, one must understand the geography of the area. This flat terrain was excellent for the Vietnamese farmers who had farmed it for centuries. The farms varied in size.

Small farms would have plots of land and raise enough livestock and grow enough vegetables to sustain them. Many times families would ban together with other families to form a village. The male village elder was generally responsible for maintaining order.

There were areas for the livestock with larger pens to contain the water buffalo used to cultivate the land. The larger the village, the greater the growing area needed. Rice was the primary crop. It was cultivated for food and trade. The fields were prepared by plowing (typically with simple plows drawn by water buffalo), fertilizing (usually with dung or sewage), and smoothing (by dragging a log over them). The seedlings were started in seedling beds and, after thirty to fifty days, were transplanted by hand to the fields, which had been flooded by rain or river water. During the growing season, irrigation was maintained by dike-controlled canals or by hand watering. The fields were allowed to drain before cutting.

To retain the water, the farmland was sectioned off like a checkerboard. Each section was about twenty-five to fifty meters and restrained with a two-foot dike. To patrol the flatlands, it was necessary to walk on the dikes. Otherwise the men would have had to walk in the rice field through the foot of water or mud, which would have slowed us down. We were an open target for snipers with minimal cover.

When the marines were on the dikes, we were visible from a long distance, which made us susceptible to snipers, a constant threat in the flatlands. When a sniper picked a target, he would typically pick off the one who would cause the most disruption, which was usually the person in charge. The rule of never saluting an officer was so ingrained that it was seldom a concern. Another rule was to not point a finger, which also shows authority. However, many of the inexperienced sergeants in positions of authority couldn't resist pointing their finger when giving directions. This was a bone of contention between me and Sergeant Bazarr, who led the platoon. I was concerned I would be hit by a sniper bullet meant for him.

The men complained so much that the lieutenant had him stay back at the command post with the other NCOs. The squad leaders now had more control over their men. Walters, who was nearing the end of his tour, was frequently allowed to stay back at the base, so I led the squad.

On about the third day, we had an interesting encounter with the enemy. The objective was to see who was actually living in the particular villages. It was suspected that many of the inhabitants were Viet Cong. So if the makeup of the inhabitants changed, the village was targeted. This type of terrain was particularly suited for covering large distances. So the patrols would typically search as many as three to four villages a day.

On that day, Sherman was on point; as squad leader I followed him. Next was Donahue on radio, followed by Ellis, Kartis, Pepin, and Sally, who was on tail end. Before approaching the next village, Sherman motioned for me to come up front.

"I've been watching that village," he informed me, "and it seems like there is just two young women there." That was unusual in a war zone, because women of fighting age were usually fighting on either side. Those who were raising families would have children nearby or elderly parents. I decided we needed to discretely investigate the village.

I took Ellis and Sherman on a recon patrol. The remainder of the squad positioned themselves at a distance that would enable them to observe any approaching enemy forces. We slipped into the rice paddy, keeping on the side of the dike that wasn't exposed to the villagers. We crept along, reaching the village undetected. The women were working in the rice paddies, so we could slip into the huts for a thorough search. Once satisfied the women were alone, we went out and questioned them. They couldn't speak English, and we couldn't speak Vietnamese, so little was gained by the encounter. So we left and joined the squad.

"They must be VC," Sherman commented.

"But why would they be out here alone working the fields?" Ellis pondered.

"Either they are wives or girlfriends of some Viet Cong, or they provide a release for troops passing through the area," I concluded. We agreed that was the most plausible explanation. I marked the map and reported our suspicions when we returned to our base. Fourth Platoon was sent out that night to surround the area.

The next morning, the night patrol returned with four prisoners as well as the two women. "You were right," the squad leader told us as they passed. "They slipped in to get some last night," he said with a laugh. "They were so horny they didn't see us coming in." Ellis had to ask the question that was on everybody's mind.

"Did you let them get some?"

"Hell no!" the squad leader shouted back. "If I don't get some, they sure as hell won't." They laughed at the captives all along the way. The prisoners even seemed to find some humor in it.

Phu Loc had a movie tent maybe fifty by seventy-five feet. We had to take advantage of the luxury. On this particular evening, the movie *Rosemary's Baby* was being shown.

This was a horror movie that had captivated the moviegoing audience in America. It had a universal appeal. Just like the moviegoing audience in America, the marines were looking for an escape from reality.

The thought of a woman giving birth to a child of the devil was intriguing.

If we had been home watching with our wives or girlfriends, we would have been sitting stone-faced with a macho demeanor offering comfort. But this battle-hardened group was behaving like frightened little boys. "Tell me when the shit is over," Walters shouted, covering his eyes.

"How you gonna be scared of a possessed baby when you got that rifle in your hand?" I laughed.

"A bullet won't stop a demon," Walters protested without uncovering his eyes. "It will just piss him off."

The tent was filled with marines from other squads. Greer, a marine who was only days in-country, was perhaps the most vocal. He searched the screen for a glimpse of any naked part of Mia Farrow's body. "I don't care if the bitch is possessed. I'd put a sack over her head!" he called out, pushing people out of his line of vision.

In the middle of a fright scene, a marine burst into the tent and frantically shouted the need for a corpsman. Doc Webber, a navy corpsman assigned to the company, a man the men respected for his ability but distrusted, was sitting in the audience. Again the marine called for a corpsman, this time explaining the urgency. "A marine from motor pool ran over a mine within the compound and is bleeding to death!" he shouted. Doc Webber immediately jumped up and rushed to his aid.

There was a moment of silence in the tent as the men were suddenly reminded of the fact they were still in a war zone. The marines then showed their ability to switch concentration. As if someone had snapped his fingers, our attention switched back to the movie. In less than two minutes from the time the marine burst into the tent with the startling announcement, we were, again, engrossed in the movie. After the movie, we went back to our tent for a restless night's sleep.

There were many theories about how and why a mine had been placed in the compound. The prevailing one was that one of the many kids who frequented the compound during the day had set it. They had been tolerated because they would provide services such as washing clothes, supplying drugs, running errands, and notifying marines when prostitutes would be outside the gate. Command didn't deny them because they weren't perceived as a threat, but after that incident, the colonel banned them from the compound.

The lieutenant and sergeants attempted to give me more authority, possibly setting me up for a promotion. I was given control of the squad for the daily patrols, but the responsibility of the squad was taken away once we were back on the base. So when Johnson informed me early one morning that the gunnery sergeant and platoon sergeant wanted me to report to the command post, I assumed it would be another put-down session.

When I entered the tent, the ranking authority Gunnery Sergeant Mac went first. "Your squad leader, Corporal Walters, has recommended you be given charge of the squad now that his rotation date nears. We have tried to make you a leader, but you have shown yourself to be a terrible disappointment, Marine!" Unfazed, I just sat and listened with no comment. Gunny Mac went on. "You have been put in charge of a squad of fighting marines, and you just let them do whatever they want. Don't you have the balls to take charge?"

I could no longer keep silent.

"Second Squad is as skilled and efficient in combat as any squad here," I said.

"What are you talking about? They just sit around and smoke dope," the gunny responded.

"When the shit hits the fan, Second Squad pulls through," I said in their defense.

That comment brought Sergeant Sparks to his feet. "Goddamn it. A marine is a marine at all times. They don't decide to act like a marine when they choose," he shouted. "You seem to do everything to fuck up your career, Marine. Why don't you stand up like a man and take charge of that band of misfits?"

"I don't have a military career. I have a year left to fulfill my obligation; then I can go back to Cleveland," I told them.

They were livid. "You're going to take the squad out today. After that, a sergeant will take over all duties. Then an NCO will take over," Sparks shouted at me. "You will aid and assist that sergeant and respect all your superiors, or you will end up in the brig, after I kick your ass. Now get the fuck out," he shouted, nearly tossing me out the door.

It took a combination of restraint and common sense. But I left courteously and respectfully. Johnson was waiting outside the tent. "Congratulations, Lance Corporal," he said.

"What the fuck you talking about?"

"You were up for promotion."

"What promotion?"

"They were going to promote you."

"Well, that won't be happening now," I said, walking away.

"How the hell could you lose a promotion before you even got it?"

"They just want to use a black man to fuck over other black men," I said.

"So you think it is better for the brothers if a white man fucks us over?"

"They do it anyway," I huffed, returning to the squad.

We were now down to Walters's final day in the bush. Walters had formed a friendship with a marine from Fourth Platoon. So he took him around to meet the squad members, starting with Ellis and me.

"These are my main partners," he said, "Harris and Ellis." Then he introduced us to Lucky, "a heavy brother from Chi-Town." The men in the company would rarely interact with marines outside their platoon. Control is easier for the sergeants and officers when they keep the men in groups; however, Lucky and Walters had gotten their orders to return to An Hoa in preparation for their rotation home. That connection brought them together.

"You must be the brothers from O-H-Ten," he said while giving us the Black Power handshake. "Damn, y'all look alike. Are you brothers?"

"Hell no, that ugly motherfucker ain't no kin to me," Ellis shouted. To which I agreed.

"Is Lucky a nickname?" Ellis asked.

"No," Lucky replied with his bright smile. "I was named after my father. He was born under a lucky star, and so was I. That is, until I was drafted into the marines," he said with a laugh. "Man, I have been lucky all my life. I've been lucky with women, money, jobs, everything. I can reach into an empty pocket just like this," he said, putting his hand in his pocket, "and pull out a handful of joints." Everybody laughed and accepted a hard-packed 101. The true test of his luck was the fact that he had survived his tour of duty with no wounds. Not even a serious scratch.

We quickly bonded with Lucky; he was as accepted as if he had been with us all the time. We sat and listened to him for hours. Lucky had stories about his life in Chicago that kept us laughing. He also took the time to share combat stories and experiences with Ellis and me, who were eager to accept any knowledge. We were the elders and were given respect accordingly. Walters and Lucky left to pack their gear. Then, Walters returned for one final word with me.

"I'll write you when I get back to the world," Walters promised.

"Be sure you do, "I answered. "Shit, I might even visit you in Indiana when I get back, but not in them damn woods. I'll never get caught in Redneck World," I laughed.

"Well, I doubt I'll be looking in the hood for you," Walters replied. "Let's agree to meet in natural territory."

We began to reminisce about the past seven months and how each had broadened the other's cultural awareness.

"Something I've been meaning to ask you," Walters said. "What motivates you?"

"What do you mean?" I said, looking puzzled.

"Men are inspired to fight by faith, benevolence, duty, honor, reward, coercion, or patriotism. What is inspiring you?"

"Well, I'm here by coercion," I said. "It was Vietnam or jail. I fight because of loyalty to the friends I've made, and I'll fight to the last because

I don't want to die out here in the middle of nowhere. Besides, I'm only twenty-one. I got a good sixty years left; I want to see all of them."

In an attempt to convert me, Walters said, "If I believed in God, that would give me motivation and hope. If I had hope for a happy afterlife, I could deal with whatever I'm faced with."

"Fuck that." I laughed. "I hope to stay alive, and afterlife may be just wishful thinking. Until someone comes back from the grave and tells me something different, I'm assuming death is irreversible. So I'm gonna fight like hell to stay here. Besides, fighting for my life is nothing to be punished for."

"How far will you go to stay alive?"

"I can eventually work through guilt," I told him, before telling him to lighten up and give me some combat wisdom.

"OK," Walters said, switching to something he knew. "The US controls the skies with their air power, long-range artillery, and communications. But you are fighting an enemy in their country on their terms. They are focused on the war, so they won't stop; they have nowhere to go. You focus on the battle, protect yourself and the people around you. Focus on your year. To fight a gorilla, you must think like a gorilla. They know your rules, so don't follow the rules. Break protocol. Don't be where they expect. You must put together cleverness, fearlessness, and an understanding of your opponent."

Then he gave me advice I wasn't ready to accept.

"You got to stop always challenging authority," he said. "Somebody's got to take charge."

"Well," I said without hesitation, "I don't trust none of these motherfuckers to make life-and-death decisions for me. If the lifers want me to prove myself to them, first they got to prove themselves to me. I respect the man before the uniform," I concluded.

"I can't argue with that," Walters told me. "But," he cautioned, "it's all based on trust. If you find men following you, then you have no choice but to lead. That's the greatest responsibility of all."

Walters posed for one last photo and then joined Lucky. The last I saw of them, they raced for the helicopter that would transport them to An Hoa.

We were all happy our old friend had made it out alive. In a few weeks, he would be going home. I waved to him, knowing it was likely the last time I would see him.

For now, we had to attend to the job at hand. Command realized from the many patrols that the enemies were in the area, and we had to make an all-out push to move them out before they could launch another assault on the base. This was Lieutenant Storm's first real task.

Unlike other officers, Lieutenant Storm's leadership was hands-on, sometimes traveling with the squads. Second lieutenants were platoon commanders and would rarely go on patrols with squads. So he was quickly gaining the respect of the men. But he was a career military man, trained in reconnaissance, and eager to prove himself. The sergeants who normally stayed in the command post would now have to take out squads. The truth was, too many sergeants and corporals had joined the company, and there just weren't enough command positions.

To prepare for the hard push that was coming, the lieutenant was attempting to school us in reconnaissance.

Second Squad was taken from me and given to Sergeant Nato. Third Squad was taken from Hansen and given to Sergeant Sparks. Corporal Alameda took Fourth, and the lieutenant took First Squad. He called together the respective squad leaders.

"This is where you will be setting up ambushes," he informed us, pointing to a broad map. "I will be roving the area with First Squad looking for enemy activity. If I spot any enemy, I'll warn the squad leaders. Sergeant Nato," he said, turning to the sergeant, "we'll let Harris take Second Squad. I want you to handle the company radio communication."

The sergeants smiled sarcastically at the suggestion that a PFC should be taking a squad with other such higher-ranking leaders, but they didn't question it. Nato informed our squad of the plans. He also told me I would be in charge. I asked, "What time will the lieutenant be passing near our ambush and from what direction?"

"The lieutenant doesn't want to confine himself to a set time. Besides, he's recon. You won't see him anyway," Nato told me.

"Bullshit!" I said, rising to my feet. "This isn't training. We are out there to kill anything we don't recognize. If they come anywhere near our ambush, we will spot them, and they will be shot."

The lieutenant and sergeants were nearby hearing the conversation. Sparks was clearly annoyed that I would question any direction given to me. He charged over to thoroughly chew me out. But I didn't back down and repeated my concern. Ellis joined in the protest. Not wanting the men to see dissention, the lieutenant called us to the side.

"Never openly challenge the authority of your superiors, and certainly not my orders!" he shouted at me.

I relented and apologized. The lieutenant paused for a moment and then decided to give us more information. Two points were apparent: he would strictly adhere to military protocol, and he did respect the combat wisdom of the lower-ranking marines.

We returned to our squads, and the men began to move out. When we reached our designated spot, I put the men in their positions. Then I put Ellis in charge and took two other men thirty meters further to maintain a listening post. This post would serve as an early warning for our ambush if an enemy patrol passed.

At 2200 hours, the recon patrol approached our position from the west, just as the lieutenant had stated. Then he came over to me and placed his finger to my temple as if it were a pistol. "Bang, you're dead," he said as if he had shot me in the head.

"What!" I replied in astonishment.

"The purpose of a listening post is not to be detected," Lieutenant Storm explained. "It rained all day, and you walked straight from the trail to your position. The tracks lead directly to you." He then turned and left. I was embarrassed and humiliated, but I had to acknowledge the lieutenant was right. I vowed not to make that mistake again.

Squads in the company were periodically engaging in small skirmishes with VC patrols, resulting in causalities.

To balance the experience, when men were killed or wounded, the captain would move the men around. Ellis went to First Squad, where he was the team leader. I would act as team leader for Second.

Expendable and Necessary

Perhaps due to a lack of combat experience or just a personality flaw, Sergeant Nato seemed to show signs of fear. Fear is normal and useful. It keeps the men on their toes, but when the person in charge shows fear, it doesn't instill confidence in the men he commands. But his fear was justified. The flatlands were a buffer for the dreaded Arizona Territory. The company was extending its area of responsibility, which was taking them closer to it.

All squads in the marine company were undermanned. Second Squad had only seven men. Along with Nato and me, there were Sherman, Sally, Donahue, and Pepin. Fredericks from Florida joined the squad, as did a brother from the South by the name of Jackson. His father was a marine gunnery sergeant. Both he and Pepin, whose father was an officer, felt they had something to prove.

VC forces operated mostly in the flatlands, getting supplies from the villagers. After years of conflict, they had plenty of time to dig tunnels. They relied heavily on booby traps. Most were made from marine ordnance, such as hand grenades, claymore mines, land mines, and Bouncing Bettys.

Booby traps generally resulted in maiming and loss of limbs. The best defense against booby traps is experience. So putting me second in line during patrols was a tactically sound move by Sergeant Nato. But to have Sally, Sherman, and Jackson rotating the point position caused the men to suspect racism. That put the African Americans in the front where the greatest chance of death or injury would occur.

On the next patrol, Sherman was put on point. Sherman was proving to be very observant. The patrol was to move through five small villages. As the patrol approached a grassy knoll, Sherman suddenly stopped. He turned toward the squad and motioned me up. When I reached him, Sherman whispered to me as if he was telling a secret.

"It doesn't seem right that an undisturbed plant could be growing in the middle of a well-traveled trail," he said, referencing the healthy plant in the trail. I looked curiously at the plant, knelt down, and then pushed the leaf aside. I suddenly found myself looking at a claymore mine, I was frozen with fear. The wire leading from the back made it obvious this wasn't just a discarded weapon. It was armed and set to be detonated.

We were in the kill zone of an armed claymore mine. The wire led straight to a patch of vegetation located about seventy-five yards away. Sherman was slowly backing away from the claymore, and the squad members were jumping for cover. I knew if a soldier was on the other end of the wire waiting to detonate it, moving a few feet away wouldn't make much difference. A direct blast from a claymore mine from a distance of one foot would not cripple, maim, or disfigure. It would be a certain and instantaneous death.

I had no choice but to disarm it. First I stabilized the grenade attached to it. Then, while holding it with my left hand, I unscrewed the blasting cap with my right. I didn't do this out of bravery; I simply had no choice. Once the claymore was disarmed, I called everyone up to search the cluster of trees that would be a likely hiding place.

Once we searched, we found that the soldiers or soldier had moved on. Sherman was clearly shaken, and so was I. Pepin hadn't walked point, so I motioned him up to take over for Sherman. Sergeant Nato stopped him and sent Sally forward instead. The patrol continued with Nato navigating the movement. I was, again, second in line.

Sally was taller than me, taking longer strides. Donahue, who was behind me, was on radio. This was distracting for both of us. Donahue had to relay information from the command post to Nato, and from Nato to me. Sally was getting too far ahead, especially as we were approaching a hill.

When Sally stepped over the crown of the hill, he was momentarily out of sight of the squad. There was a sudden burst of automatic fire. The distinctive sound was from an American-made M16. I dropped down on all fours and scooted up to join him.

"What you shooting at?" I asked.

"There was a bunch of gooks out there."

"Where?"

"They were just there. I fired to back off; then, when I looked, they were gone," Sally told me.

"There might be 'spider traps' or tunnels," I said. "I'll get it checked out. Stay low. I'm going to talk to Nato." I went back to inform the sergeant, who was taking cover of our suspicions.

Nato went up, took a quick look, and decided Sally hadn't seen anything. Both Sally and I protested, but Nato ordered the squad to move on.

As we were approaching a village, Sally again stopped and motioned me up.

"I saw movement in that village. At least ten people," Sally whispered.

Nato moved up at that point and joined the discussion. Sally filled him in.

Without discussion, he motioned Donahue up and ordered a mortar drop on the village. "Wait!" I yelled before Donahue could call the mortar drop.

Nato was agitated. "We're gonna level that shithole before they can drop their shit on us," Nato yelled.

"You don't know who they are," I said, ridiculing him. "They might be a farming village, with families in there. If they had weapons, they would have hit us already."

"I'll let you have this one," Nato said, rolling his eyes. "Take Sally, Sherman, and Jackson in to check it out."

The men grumbled. Especially Sally. "Every time some dangerous shit comes up, that raciest motherfucker sends black men!" he cursed within hearing distance of the sergeant.

"No shit!" Sherman blurted out. "My mama wants her baby boy back too."

I agreed but knew the focus needed to be on the task at hand. So I attempted to give a motivational talk.

"You brothers are slick enough to do this?"

"Beyond slick," Sherman said confidently, with Jackson and Sally agreeing.

"When I was a young brother, no one wanted to play hide-and-seek with me." I said with pride. "I would hide so well that they would give up and go home."

"You city boys don't know about hiding," Sally said with his country-boy grin. "I could sneak up on a fox."

"Well," I cautioned, "the ragman has a lot more experience than us, so be careful."

With that, we cautiously approached the village. Silently, we moved with confidence and skill, like a well-choreographed dance team.

There were four structures, three of which were empty. The fourth housed a family of four, the grandparents and two grandchildren eating a meal. Holding our breath with Sally standing guard, we peeked through the doorway.

The family didn't seem startled, but they were clearly afraid. Nervously, they continued to eat their meal, glancing at us with their eyes; never moving their heads. They were anticipating we would strike at any moment. We were just as suspicious. All the time we searched, they rarely took their eyes off us. Everyone eyed each other with suspicion, but no one acknowledged the other's presence. After a thorough search, we slipped back out. We returned to the squad to report and to prepare to move to the next village.

Sherman was, again, put on point by Sergeant Nato. "Is this shit gonna stop?" he mouthed at me. About twenty-five meters into the village, Sherman tripped a booby trap. It was a grenade with the pin pulled and the spoon compressed by being wedged between two rocks.

A grenade is designed to be thrown at the enemy. It therefore has a four-second delay from the moment the spoon ignites the blasting cap. Those four seconds were enough to allow Sherman and the rest of the squad to escape. It's amazing how far one can run when one's life is in danger. The thick vegetation also deflected some of the shrapnel. Sherman, being the closest, was in the greatest danger, but he might have traveled the greatest distance. We laughed about it later and gave him the nickname "Rabbit."

It was a harrowing but routine day in combat. The next few were relatively the same. Occasionally, there would be a firefight. Two men from Third Platoon were wounded. The lieutenant decided this was becoming a never-ending battle of attrition, so he wanted to try something different. The plan was to do a large platoon-scale sweep.

With that large a troop movement, a confrontation was expected. Confrontation was also expected because we were coming close to the Arizona Territory. The platoon moved on with our squad on point.

We moved in a V formation, I was placed on point by Sergeant Nato.

Expendable and Necessary

I approached a distant tree line, anticipating an ambush. My suspicions were correct. The enemy opened with a sudden burst of machine-gun fire. Everyone dropped and braced themselves. Lieutenant Storm called for a ten-round mortar barrage on the tree line.

The men counted, and after the seventh mortar was launched, we charged the tree line, which was about one hundred yards away. As the point man, I had a 180-degree kill zone. All friendlies should be behind me. I ran in, looking for a target, posed for a quick kill.

A quick kill requires the shooter to carry his weapon with the safety off, across his chest, with his left hand wrapped around the stock. When a target appears, he points the barrel of the weapon with the left hand and fires two quick rounds. This is done to startle the target and allow the marine to drop to the kneeling position and aim the third round.

As my eyes scanned the area, I spotted a target. I fired the cautionary rounds, dropped down, and took aim. I was looking down the barrel of my weapon, which was aimed center chest at what appeared to be a child around seven or eight years old. If my second round had been a foot lower, I would have shot the child in the middle of the forehead.

There was no time to contemplate, but a tragedy had been narrowly avoided. Not only for the innocent child, who was only satisfying a natural curiosity, but certainly a nightmare for me, who would relive the child's eyes in nightmares for the rest of my days. I stood up and continued. Someone coming later would comfort the child. We searched, but the attackers had escaped.

It had taken roughly four hours to reach the village, so after the search the platoon headed back to the base. I took the opportunity to register my complaints toward Sergeant Nato. But those complaints fell on deaf ears. The lieutenant did move Sergeant Nato, because a corporal was coming to the company who would take over our squad permanently. Then Ellis was brought back to the squad.

CHAPTER 20

The Alamo
June 1969

▲ ▲ ▲

As fewer enemy troops were spotted, the commanders concluded that they had moved out. The captain, therefore, prepared to move the company further north in search of Communist troops, to the edge of the Arizona Territory. With the experienced marines leaving through death, injury, and attrition, a morale problem was quickly developing.

Ellis, Johnson, and I, after only eight months with the company, were becoming some of the most experienced. When Johnson got promoted to company radioman, Ellis and I gained more combat credibility. We were also the lowest-ranking members of the company, with a rank equal to a raw recruit leaving boot camp. Many of the replacements were coming in with more rank. In fact, marines who came after us were being promoted over both of us.

The reason behind it would depend on who you asked. Clearly both of us were antagonistic and insubordinate toward authority. Then neither of us aspired to a Marine Corps career. The officers and sergeants were bound by tradition and would never reward such behavior. We and most black marines saw it as racism. My accusations of racism against Sergeant Nato were common knowledge. Whatever the case, while the troops continued to respect rank, they were loyal to experience of any rank.

The new squad leader, Corporal Roe, arrived. He was an athletically built Caucasian from the Midwest. His appearance, mannerisms, and rapid rise would indicate that he was the ideal person to impose his will on the predominately African American squad.

I was sitting with Ellis when Johnson approached. At this point he had separated himself from the brothers because of his rank, but he would check in with us. "Hi, brothers," he said before giving the power shake. We responded in kind. We sat and talked for a while. Eventually, Ellis left. When he stepped away, Johnson turned to me.

"I need to talk to you," he said, looking at me "You brothers are going into some rough shit."

"More than usual?" I asked.

"Yep," he said, "the command post is going to set up close to Arizona."

"How close?" I asked, reaching for the map.

"Checkpoint three is here," Johnson said, pointing to the map. "That is about a half click inside Arizona."

I looked at it and then pointed to checkpoint four. "I wonder what that is," I said, looking at what appeared to be a cluster of buildings.

Johnson wasn't sure but suggested that it might offer cover if the NVA attacked from Arizona. "The Alamo," he said jokingly. "Let's call it the Alamo."

"I appreciate the warning," I told him. "Keep me in the know. It stays between us." Johnson assured me he would.

Not long after we parted, Lieutenant Storm approached me and ordered that I assemble the men for a briefing. Once we were together, he came to us with the corporal we were expecting.

"Listen up!" he said to us. "The command post will shift for the next operation. Corporal Roe, a distinguished marine, will take over the squad. I want all of you to give your complete cooperation. You, Harris and Ellis, help in the transition. Corporal Roe will brief you on the particulars." With that being said, the lieutenant left.

The new corporal was very tentative in his approach to the men. He took Ellis and me to the side for a private talk. First he acknowledged his inexperience and asked for help. We didn't respond. "Can I be frank with you two?" he then asked. Again we gave no response, which he took as a suspicious yes.

"I want to be honest with you two, and I hope you can do the same with me. The sergeants gave me a long list of reasons why I couldn't trust either of you and ordered I report your every move. They also said you would show me what to do when the shit hits the fan. If you manage to stay alive with all the heat they're putting on you, then you're the ones I need to talk to. I think we can help each other. Help me keep us alive, and I'll take the heat."

The direct, honest approach seemed to work. We agreed to try. Then we returned to the squad, where two more new members had been added. Roe, who had met them earlier, introduced them. The squad members could sense a renewed cooperation as Roe relayed our orders. We joined the platoon prior to boarding the awaiting helicopter. We were being taken along with the rest of the platoon to the mustering location. Once we landed, our squad broke away and started our patrol.

Moving to our first checkpoint, Sherman was on point, then me, followed by Ellis, then Donahue on radio. Roe was next with Doc Webber behind him. Ray, the gunner, was next, followed by Jackson humping the ammo. Then came Judy, Preacher, and a member whose name I can't remember, with Sally on tail end.

Checkpoints one and two were visited with no confrontations. I was uneasy when we entered checkpoint three. There was no line to indicate we had passed into Arizona, but I could feel it. Checkpoint four with the structures was in sight, possibly 150 yards across the rice paddies. The squad did a superficial search, anxious to reach the Alamo.

The villagers in checkpoint three came out of the hooches and silently watched us. We watched them closely, looking for any unusual behavior.

Sherman, who was walking point, suddenly stopped. I motioned the squad to stop; then I approached him.

"Hear that?" Sherman said, cupping his ear.

I was silent for a moment and then answered, "I don't hear anything."

"There were voices."

"Did it sound like adults?"

"I couldn't tell."

I stomped on the ground and then asked, "Do you think they were under us?"

"I don't know."

"Wait here. I'll be back." Then I went to Roe. "Hey, man, Sherman believes he heard voices under him. Maybe we should search this village." When Roe began to ask me more questions, I decided we should both go up and talk to Sherman. The rest of the squad was silent, maintaining a defensive position.

As we approached Sherman, we saw him suddenly go into a panic. "Look!" he yelled, motioning toward the buildings across the open rice paddies. "The villagers are running out of there."

By now all the squad was seeing what was going on. No one, however, could figure out why they were running.

"Viet Cong must be there!" Roe said. "The villagers are probably getting out before we get there. I think we should blast the shit out of them."

"Kids are still coming out," I responded.

"You think we should let the kids out, then call a strike?" Roe said.

I didn't answer. It was if I was listening for a sign. Finally, I spoke up. "I hear voices now," I said. "We should assault that village and use the structures for cover."

"We need to get the fuck out of here," whispered Ellis into my ear. Roe ordered the men to assault the buildings. We entered the rice paddies with Ellis and me on double point, with Ray between us with the machine gun. We were poised to address an anticipated ambush. The squad members followed, approaching with caution at rapid pace. The mud in the paddies was making crossing difficult. Our feet were acting like suction cups.

When our squad reached the midpoint, the anticipated ambush happened. All hell broke loose. It was not from the front as we had expected, but from the village we had just exited. The enemy had been under us waiting to pop up.

There was sheer pandemonium. The entire squad was in an open rice paddy being fired upon by AKs and SKSs, possibly two of the most efficient assault weapons ever made. The only certainty was that we couldn't stay in that open rice paddy. We were close enough to distinguish the bombed-out structures. These structures would offer both cover and concealment to us as well as to enemy forces that might be lying in wait. "Back out of the paddies!" I yelled to Roe. "We'll get Ray and Judy in the village for cover."

Ellis, Ray, Judy, and I assaulted the village. There was blood in our eyes and malice in our hearts. Ellis and I used single shots searching out specific targets. Judy sprayed all hiding places with buckshot, and Ray emptied a one-hundred-round belt in five seconds, the approximate time it took to secure the immediate area. But we were firing at the wind. When the smoke cleared, we found there were no blood and no bodies.

Now we turned to the men still trapped in the open rice paddy. They were putting up a fierce fight, but it appeared no one had been hit.

The dilemma for us was that we couldn't fire for fear of hitting our men who were between us and the enemy. Judy's weapon was designed for just such a circumstance. His weapon could easily launch explosive rounds over the marines' heads with pinpoint accuracy. When the enemy troops broke their fire, the men were able to race into the village, with Ray covering their retreat. Roe then had them set up a defensive line and continue to fight. He had Donahue contact the command post for further orders with Doc Webber at his side. The village was about thirty-five to fifty yards across with plenty of hiding places. Ellis went with me to search.

Each of us was carrying thirty magazines loaded with three hundred rounds, two LAWs, six grenades, a machete, a Ka-Bar, and the skill and will to use it all. We were asking no questions and taking no chances. When we pulled back what appeared to be a discarded basket cover, we discovered a deep hole that was a tunnel exit. Ellis tossed a grenade into it while we took cover. We continued to search and dissect anything that could hide a soldier. We were acting like deranged scavengers searching for a meal. In less than ten minutes, we had searched the entire village. When we reached the far end of the village, we both collapsed from exhaustion. Both of us were happy not to have encountered any enemy but equally confused.

"Something's not right," I commented between breaths. "We should have come across some VC."

"No shit," replied Ellis, looking around. Then, in a distant village, our questions were answered. We could see what appeared to be Viet Cong setting up guns. "This is a trap. That's why the people were running out," I shouted. "We need to get some people back here to cover our rear."

Ellis stayed to defend the back of the village. "I want to bust them up first," Ellis said, unshouldering his LAW and readying it. "Check my back blast," he said before taking aim. His aim was slightly off, but close enough to cause them to scatter. He then lay down in the prone position and fired at any target that presented itself. I went back to the front for help. When I got there, I found the fighting was fierce and Roe about to lose it. The good thing was that he had gotten the men out of the rice paddy. The bad thing was that they were bunched up. He was on the phone talking to the CP, trying to get direction. When I returned, Roe notified the CP that I was giving him an update on the situation.

"We're surrounded," I informed Roe. "I think they drove us into a trap. We can't let the VC in the perimeter, so the first thing we need to do is to spread the men out. The gun team, corpsman, and radioman need to be with you, but the rest of the men need to cover the perimeter." Roe agreed, and I dispersed the men. Sally and Sherman, the most experienced marines, were placed in strategic positions. Preacher, Fredericks, and the other new marine were placed in other positions. The only advice I gave was, "Kill anything you see." Ellis and I positioned ourselves in the center of the village, so we could check all around.

"Our orders are to hold the position," Roe informed us. We listened without comment. Donahue took his ear from the radio and listened intently to the fighting going on around us.

"I don't hear any fighting in those positions," I said, motioning toward spots around the perimeter.

"God dammit!" Ellis shouted, heading out. "They're not fighting back."

I ran to our furthest position, dodging incoming rounds along the way.

When I got to the position, I found Preacher curled in the fetal position, hoping the fighting would just stop. I let him know that the enemy was looking for a weak spot and how dangerous it was for all if he didn't respond. I visually scanned the area across the open rice paddy, looking for VC positions. I saw a Viet Cong infiltrator creeping through the rice paddy toward us. All the while Preacher had his head down with his hands folded in prayer. What Preacher called prayer I called begging for his life. The fool was facing death with his eyes closed. I fired rounds at the approaching enemy, possibly striking him. He scurried back to the tree line. "Motherfucker," I yelled at Preacher, who hadn't even raised his head, "when you call for help, call someone with a weapon in their hand." I returned to the squad's command and brought Ray out to defend the outer perimeter, but that only weakened another spot.

When I got back, Ellis was there reacting to news that Roe was giving him. Sparks told him over the radio that headquarters wanted us to hold until reinforcements arrived. "Fuck that!" I yelled. "We need to get out of here." Doc Webber agreed but remained silent. However, when a bullet passed dangerously close to his head, he joined the discussion. "Somebody better do something!" he screamed in a panic.

The strangest thing was happening to me. In the middle of this chaos, I was whistling, snapping my fingers, and bobbing my head, to no particular tune. No one questioned me, except for Ellis. "What the fuck you doing?" he yelled, getting in my face. "You better say something!"

He was right.

"Those voices Sherman heard underground were VC in tunnels. All these villages are probably connected. If they are, troops are on their way here right now, and we don't have the firepower to take them on. We need to get out now!"

There was no way to know if my observations were correct, but it made sense.

Roe, the consummate marine, reiterated our orders to stay.

"Fuck those orders! They aren't here. We are!" I shouted impenitently.

Roe's rank and position dictated he make the call. His uncertainty diminished his credibility with the men, who were now turning to me for instruction, and I had no problem with it.

"That's their weak spot," I said to the radioman while motioning toward a distant tree line. "We're going in that direction. Plot that position for five mortar rounds when you get the order. Then give them this position for fifteen rounds once we're out. After we've cleared the area, request an all-out strike." Donahue looked to Roe, who confirmed it. Then I took Ellis and went out to bring the men guarding the perimeter in. On the way, Ellis questioned and admonished me about the whistling.

"Why the fuck were you whistling when that shit was going on? There is a time for action and a time for bullshit. That wasn't bullshit time."

I looked around to make sure no one could and told him a secret. "I was so scared I couldn't talk. The only word that would have come out of my mouth at that time was help!" Ellis laughed and thanked me for not sharing that with the other men.

We maneuvered our way to the positions, dodging enemy fire along the way. When we reached the squad command post, Roe told them of the plan and his suspicion that the enemy forces were about to emerge from tunnels any second. Fredericks protested. "We'll be out in the open!" he said, almost in tears.

"You have no choice," Roe continued. "We're abandoning the Alamo. If Crockett and Bowie had done that, they might have lived." Once the men were together, Donahue called for the mortar strike and prepared to abandon the position. "We'll pull out when the fourth mortar strikes," Roe ordered.

The escape had to be executed swiftly and efficiently. Every man had to do what he did best. I was the pointer, an offensive position requiring quick reflexes and the willingness to take calculated risk. Ellis, a defensive taskmaster, was twenty yards behind me to my right. Sherman was twenty yards behind to our left. Ray was between Ellis and Sherman with the machine gun. Jackson was behind Ray with the ammo. Roe, the squad leader, was behind Jackson, with Donahue, the radioman, beside him in constant communication with the CP. Next was Doc Webber, then Judy with the grenade launcher. He was followed by Preacher, then two new marines. On tail end was Sally, who was a specialist on fighting off a rear attack. The brother could run backward almost as fast as forward.

The squad charged across the open field like men possessed. The plan was to discourage any waiting forces with overwhelming firepower. It worked, and the enemy scattered like rats abandoning a sinking ship when we approached.

The command post gave us a general direction the platoon coming to rescue us would be traveling. Three hundred yards away, they would pass a large, grassy knoll. Two hundred yards from that point was the anticipated final destination, another large, heavily vegetated area. Between the two points were several other areas with concentrated vegetation. All of this could act as cover and concealment for the enemy or the marines. Donahue reported this to Roe, who passed it to Ellis, who then signaled to me to stop.

When I dropped to the ground and looked back, the other squad members followed suit. Ellis worked his way to me. After a brief strategic discussion between us, Ellis returned to Roe. "Harris is going for the grassy knoll," Ellis told Roe. "If they've set an ambush, we would be better off hitting them head on. Have Judy hit it with three high explosive rounds; Harris is gonna go after two. When the smoke clears, he'll be in, and we will be right behind." Roe immediately had Judy drop the rounds. When the second round hit, I took off at a full run. All my attention was to my front, like a mongoose with blinders. Having Ellis and Sherman on my flanks, my need for peripheral vision was lessened. They were as reliable as the Secret Service is to the president.

I was firing with my weapon on fully automatic. When I got into the patch of green, I could see enemy troops escaping toward the far side. I was about to continue the charge, but in the excitement, I realized I had expended all my ammunition.

Now I had no means of protecting myself, with concealment but no cover. It was a rifleman's nightmare. Everyone hit the ground, and the momentum of the charge came to a stop.

"You OK?" yelled Ellis, who was about ten yards away.

"I'm out of ammunition," I responded with fear in my voice. The blood, guts, and heart of Ellis came through at that moment. He took his last bandolier from his neck, rose to one knee, exposing his entire body, and threw it to me. It floated through the air as if in slow motion, landing a few feet from me. I grabbed it, removed a magazine, chambered a round, and then continued the assault.

Now Ellis, Sherman, and I were in the vegetation. We did a quick search and saw the enemy running away at full speed in the distance. The overweight corpsman, Doc Webber, was having trouble keeping up, slowing the charge. The men had to constantly double back. After being dragged by his feet for most of the charge, Doc Webber managed to step up his efforts; finally the remainder of the squad entered. But we had to keep moving.

Ellis spotted the yellow smoke in the distance, which marked the position of the rescue platoon. They concealed themselves in the tree line until we got close.

The rescuing platoon viewed us in awe, as if they were fans witnessing their favorite team return to the locker room at halftime. The lieutenant who commanded the rescue sought out the squad leader, Corporal Roe, for a situation report.

"Damn!" said the small brother from the mortar section to Ellis and me. "You must be the bushmasters from OH ten." That startled us. It was the first time we had received that distinguished title. "My name is Woody, and this is Butler," he said, referring to the Caucasian marine standing beside him. "He is in charge of the mortar section." Both of us were impressed with Butler's skill with mortars.

"You do a good job with the mortars, thanks," I said to Butler. "That makes a big difference when the rag man is on our ass," I laughed.

"When the captain ordered a rescue for Second Squad, I knew it was going to be hot, so I had to come with them. I wanted to see the proper way to get out of an ambush," Butler said.

"But we got a little too close," Woody laughed. "The lieutenant had us taking cover in this village. Harris, you were the point. How many rounds did you fire?" he asked me. "It sounded like an invasion out there."

"About seven hundred," I answered after giving it some thought.

"A hundred of those were mine," Ellis laughed.

"And a hundred fifty were mine," Sherman added.

"I guess I do have a tendency to overkill," I admitted. At that point we heard the Cobra attack chopper coming in to finish the job. It was time for the marines of Second Squad to make our exit. The rescue platoon would do the cleanup.

Once we returned to Phu Loc 6, we collected our beer ration from the supply tent and found a secluded area to get high and get a bid whist game going. Butler and Woody were now joining our inner circle.

That night the squad members stood guard duty on the perimeter as we normally did while on Phu Loc. The following morning, as I was leaving the chow hall, Johnson approached me.

"The lieutenant wants to see you, my brother."

"What the fuck does he want?" I asked as Johnson escorted me there.

"They want to debrief you about the ambush."

"They should talk to Roe. He was in charge."

"They did. They also talked to Butler, Donahue, and me."

"What's all that about?"

"Well, their orders weren't followed to the letter, so they want to jump in somebody's shit."

"Fuck that; did they consider we are all alive?"

"You know how that works. Just do yourself a favor; salute when going in and admit you were wrong."

I did give the lieutenant a salute, even if it was a sloppy one.

The men in the tent were standing. Lieutenant Storm was flanked by Gunny Mac and Staff Sergeant Sparks. Sergeant Nato and Sergeant Bazaar were also there. I was cautious, suspecting they were trying to set me up for something.

"What happened out there, Marine?" Lieutenant Storm asked.

I was suspicious, so I weighed my answers carefully. "We were ambushed," I finally said.

"I know that. I want to know why you didn't follow the order to hold the village."

"We were surrounded and being overrun; we needed to get out."

"You don't know the reason for the orders, and you don't question it. You just follow the orders."

I didn't feel I was wrong, so I wasn't going to say so. "If we had stayed, we would have lost some of our men," I said defiantly. That was the insolence Gunnery Sergeant Mac was waiting to jump on.

"God dammit, Private, you don't have the brains or experience to second-guess a superior. And you don't open your fucking mouth when a superior is talking." He continued to curse and belittle me, but I wasn't really listening. When he finished, Sergeant Sparks got in on the act.

"You don't turn and run like a bitch," he yelled. "You charge and kill the enemy. You are a United States Marine. Our job is to kill. Death is just a hazard of the job." I was pissed off and fighting hard not to respond. The sergeants continued to push. Clearly they wanted a response. They finally got one, a condescending smirk.

Sergeant Nato was enjoying every moment. He had always complained about my insubordination. The lieutenant eventually stepped in to put an end to it. "I think the private realizes his mistakes," he finally said. "You're excused, Marine." I gave another halfhearted salute and walked out of the tent bursting with anger and walking past Johnson, who was outside the open door listening.

"I thought you were going to be cool," Johnson said, catching up.

"Fuck those clowns," I snapped, keeping a fast pace.

Johnson shouted back, "I'm doing all I can without being court-martialed, to keep your black ass alive."

"What?" I said with skepticism.

"Look, man, I control all company communication," Johnson went on. "All the way to Division Headquarters. They jumped my ass for not blocking the communications and shutting you down. They jumped Donahue's ass for relaying what they considered unlawful orders. They jumped Butler's ass for not confirming the mortar pattern with them. And Roe was damn near court-martialed.

"No one but the lifers is criticizing you. You were right. That's why we supported what you did. The problem is the sergeants are pissed because you ignored them. In fact," he said to my surprise, "the lieutenant put you in for a promotion over the gunny's objections. I filed the paperwork myself." I stood silently for a moment, surprised by what Johnson had told me. "Unless you give them credit, they are always going to shoot you down."

"What about Ellis?" I asked.

"Well," Johnson continued, "they didn't promote him yet; the beard works against him. But his R and R was approved."

"No shit!" I said. "The brother is going to Bangkok. What about Preacher? The brother's not safe to be around."

"Preacher didn't seem to fit in Second Squad, so he was moved to Fourth," Johnson told me.

I gave Johnson the power handshake and then rushed to tell Ellis the news. The possible promotion was a mere footnote to Ellis's R and R, but all of this gave us an excuse to smoke another joint.

The following day the lieutenant made both the intended promotion and the R and R approval official. For the next week, the company operated without Ellis, who had a lifetime of memories of his good time in Bangkok, Thailand. He even said he "butterflied," the phrase used for having two women at once. Many have tried and failed to do so. The women usually would never agree to this. But I knew if anyone could pull it off, it would be the fast-talking Ellis. So I didn't challenge his story.

This was part of a larger operation, Pipestone Canyon.' In all, 852 enemy were killed; 58 were captured. The marines had 71 killed in action and 498 wounded in action.

CHAPTER 21

The Mountains (Operation Durham Peak) June–July 1969

▲ ▲ ▲

AFTER A WEEK OF NO further enemy contact, the regimental commander now decided to send the battalion into the hills a terrain preferred by the NVA to search for enemy troops.

We were to be flown out the following morning. The mountains would present a different set of obstacles. Or what might be called "a lotta mores."

There were more physical challenges, climbing the mountains and patrolling in heavily vegetation. More hiding places for both the marines and Communist troops. More insects, more forest creatures to contend with, more obstacles for artillery support to overcome, and more challenges when it came to being resupplied, reinforced, or rescued. It might sound selfish, but I just wanted one more day of easy duty. This was, of course, not an option. But I had to try. A resupply chopper was coming to the base that morning. So I devised a plan I believed would give at least one easy day. My laxity in personal hygiene had resulted in a decaying molar. That offered an excellent opportunity for an emergency evacuation. I jammed a sharp object into the center of the decay and broke it off. Blood flowed into my mouth. My face swelled up like a blowfish, and I was in excruciating pain. The navy corpsman was the closest to a field dentist we had, and he knew the task was far beyond his ability. At his recommendation, I was to be flown to Da Nang for emergency dental care.

The captain wasn't happy. But to my surprise, I became a military VIP. I was flown to Da Nang on the return flight of the chopper. When I got there, a dentist was on standby to do an emergency dental filling. "With all this special treatment," the dental assistant commented, "you are either very important, or you pissed your commander off." We both knew which it was. I barely had time to spit before I was hustled back to a helicopter for the return trip.

The pain and suffering only resulted in a three-hour separation from the company. In the flight approaching the landing zone I could see two small mountains in the thick jungle. It reminded me of two camel's humps. I arrived about thirty minutes after the company. I exited the helicopter cursing and spitting blood all along the way.

The lieutenant, who was briefing the men, motioned for me to join them. The captain, he explained, was concerned that the enemy was building an artillery base and mustering forces in the mountains. He wanted a small patrol to search the smaller mountain without detection before the company proceeded to their primary objective. If the enemy was in the smaller mountain, it would afford them a strategic position.

Lieutenant Storm created a squad by handpicking men from each squad. He also assigned the positions in the patrol that the men would take. It was to be a fast-paced, or forced, march. The lieutenant briefed me, telling me I would lead the patrol, and Ray, who led the gun team. "Harris," he said, "you will take the squad up the hill with Ellis on point. The terrain is a triple canopy, so you will have trouble getting through, but push the men hard. We have a time schedule to keep. It is suspected the enemy has artillery set up somewhere in these mountains," he went on to explain. "We will need to find it. We don't want to be hit with artillery as we move further. Our patrol will end on a distant mountain, so we have a lot of distance to cover while we have daylight. I'm giving an hour to reach the top." With his speech still garbled from the excessive Novocain administered by the dentist, I acknowledged the instructions with a nod and started the patrol.

Ellis was an excellent pointer, managing to maneuver through the almost impassable terrain so smoothly that one would have thought there was a marked trail. It was a physically taxing climb, but Ellis was setting a pace that would surely keep us on schedule. Then, about halfway up the hill, he suddenly stopped. I ordered the men to take defensive positions before going up to talk to Ellis, who seemed clearly agitated.

"What's up?" I asked.

"This is bullshit."

"What do you mean?"

"If this is such an important mission, why do we have such a tight time schedule? We should be given time for a thorough search."

"Well, the lieutenant says we have to go up that larger mountain before nightfall."

"God damned they know the enemy can't have artillery in this thick shit. The best they could do is an observation post, and there is no way in hell a small patrol could locate them in an hour. There just fucking with us while they take a rest." I wasn't convinced, so Ellis went on. "Shit, didn't you notice there are no chucks with us?" I acknowledged his point with a sarcastic smile.

While we talked, Jackson, who was acting radioman, approached. "What's up?" he asked.

"Ellis thinks this is a bullshit patrol," I said to him.

"It is bullshit," Jackson acknowledged. "The lieutenant and gunnery sergeant bet we couldn't reach the top in an hour. I heard them."

"Those motherfuckers are back there sitting in the shade while we're getting ourselves cut up and exhausted."

"Well, what you gonna do, Lance Corporal?" Ellis said to me. I smiled and then answered.

"We are going to search the immediate area, set up a defensive perimeter, and then take a break." Then I told Jackson to call in a progress report every ten minutes so the lieutenant would think we were moving.

Once I told the squad of my intentions, they readily agreed. It was a nice, relaxing time out. In fact, we were so relaxed that the time slipped away from us. We returned thirty minutes late. The lifers were very angry, which was an added bonus for us.

The patrol then continued heading for the mountain slated to be the night's base camp. First Squad was on point. They quickly reached the taller hill. As they started up a hill that was to be partially explored, the point made a startling discovery: elephant tracks. Word quickly filtered back to the rest of the platoon members. I was skeptical.

"Can't no big-ass elephants move through this shit." I laughed. We could barely get through.

"They do use elephants to move artillery to the top of the mountains," reasoned Ellis.

The lieutenant checked with the captain for guidance. The captain ordered him to take his platoon in pursuit of the elephant, convinced the NVA had used elephants to take heavy artillery up the hill as Ellis had suggested. The platoon was ordered to find and destroy it. The lieutenant wanted me on point, so he turned the squad back over to Sergeant Nato, who was upset at the extended time it had taken us to explore the previous mountain.

Up the steep mountain we went, following the orders to find the elephant. The higher we climbed, the more ridiculous the mission was becoming.

The tracks took us on ridges so narrow we had to cling to the side of the mountain to keep from falling off. We climbed clefts so steep that Ellis had to first boost me up so I could anchor a rope that was used to hoist the other men up. Still, the tracks continued. At spots, the terrain was so thick that we had to use machetes to chop our way through. It was clear to everyone that a Vietnamese soldier with an elephant foot was leading us on a wild goose chase. Still, the lieutenant, who was ultimately in charge, wouldn't deviate from his orders. After a day of searching, the exhausted men settled in for the night. Finally the captain called off the search.

All along the climb, we encountered land leeches; they would make it a night to remember.

These parasites were about a quarter inch in diameter and two inches long. They were both underfoot and overhead. They were an eerie sight to behold, like spaghetti strings dangling from trees, bushes, and vines waiting for a host to attach themselves to. If any part of the body touched them, they attached to it and then slowly worked themselves to the tender skin. Once they reached a feeding area, preferably a vein, they would bury their head like a tick and begin extracting blood from the host victim. To remove them, one had to use the same technique as with a tick: apply heat, forcing them to retract their tentacles. If one attempted to pull them out, the head would be ripped off. If left alone, they would often self-destruct, bursting when they had ingested more fluid than their body could hold.

The greatest fear was that a leech would attach itself to someone's testicles. This, unfortunately, happened to Greer from Third Squad. During one of the frequent self-checks, he found one. "I got one on my balls! I got one on my balls!" he shouted, running in circles. "Somebody give me a goddamn cigarette." The men seemed more concerned about saving the favored brands, Kools and Salem. The medical assist was delayed as they searched for an unwanted pack of Kents or Camels. No one but a corpsman would dare to touch his private parts, so he had to do a kind of self-surgery. Finally someone lit a camel and passed it to him. The removal was successful, but he had an attitude that lasted for the rest of the day.

Dealing with leeches in the daylight hours was rough, but the night was worse. The leeches could not be seen, so a person might be covered and not know it.

All squads were sent out about one hundred yards from the platoon for an ambush. Sitting on the ground infested with leeches caused our imaginations to run wild. Everyone was squirming and searching for leeches. Soon the fear of leeches became greater than the fear of enemy detection. Cigarettes were lit and used to burn anything suspected of being a leech. All ambush positions lit up as if there was an invasion of fireflies. The lieutenant and sergeants were too far away to intervene. In fact, the same telltale glow was being emitted from the area they occupied. Needless to say, few, if any, slept that night.

The lieutenant was understandably upset when the squad returned the next morning, but he handled it well. We saddled up our gear and continued the search for the elusive elephant. It was beginning to seem more like a safari than a combat mission.

The thick jungle seemed to have never been seen by human eyes. Animals, both big and small, would occasionally be seen in the shadows, leering curiously at the strange intruders. Watching the animals was becoming like a game. Detecting them was difficult, because the animal's survival instincts were what kept them alive. They knew what their link in the food chain was, and their existence depended on that knowledge as they went from predator to prey. However, barring the dangers of combat, the jungle was a peaceful place.

While traveling in the patrol, I felt a sensation on my right arm. A liquid was rolling down my arm, down to my fingers, then dripping to the side. I shook my arm and noticed my sleeve was covered with blood.

"Oh shit, I've been hit!" I yelled. "I've been hit." Everyone dropped and took defensive positions. Ellis was the first to attempt to administer first aid.

"When were you hit?" Ellis asked.

"I don't know, but it must have just happened."

"I don't see a bullet hole on your sleeve."

"I don't care, man; I'm hit. Cut the sleeve."

"But there wasn't any enemy fire."

"Man, cut my goddamn sleeve. Something cut me open."

Ellis did as I asked and then recoiled in horror at what he saw. "What the fuck is that?" he said, referring to what appeared to be a piece of flesh hanging from my arm. It was obvious to both of us that a leech had attached itself to a vein and burst open after extracting too much blood. "Gross!" Ellis pointed this out to Doc Webber, who had finally arrived.

"Do I get a twenty-four heart for this?" I asked the corpsman.

"Hell no!" he replied. "We're not fighting leeches."

"Fuck all of y'all," I grumbled to the laughing marines as the patrol continued.

After about an hour, everyone was getting exhausted. When taking into account the heavy combat gear, the heat, and the rugged terrain, the low grumbling was becoming a loud roar.

I was on point at that time, when I noticed a cave in the distance and pointed it out to Ellis, who relayed the information to the lieutenant. It was significant because it was so isolated and accessible only by a narrow ridge, making it an ideal observation position. Getting to it would involve a treacherous and potentially dangerous climb, but it was doable. The lieutenant decided it should be explored, and Sergeant Nato as squad leader came up and ordered me to do it.

"What!" I protested. "I've been out front all day. Why the fuck don't you send someone else?"

"Because he wants to kill off the brothers," Ellis, who was standing near, shouted.

"Then you can join him," Nato yelled. Ellis was about to refuse, which would have brought a sure court-martial, when I pulled him along.

The two of us inched ourselves along the narrow ridgeline. The platoon watched silently, pleased for the moment's rest. I slowly peered in the cave. Suddenly I backed out of the cave, and Ellis and I scurried back along the narrow path. Then there was a loud blast, and the two of us clung to the mountainside to avoid being thrown off.

Tossing a grenade had taken away any hope of surprising the enemy. The lieutenant was yelling at Sergeant Nato, assuming he had told me to do it. When I approached, Nato began yelling at me for disobeying his instructions. "What do you mean?" I countered. "You told me to do that." Then Nato accused me of lying, which I was, but the lieutenant reprimanded the sergeant for not making his orders clear. He ended it by saying a leader should make his instructions clear.

When I walked up to Ellis, he smiled and whispered, "That stupid motherfucker expected us to crawl into that death trap, didn't he?" I acknowledged him with a sly smile, and we laughed about it and moved on.

By nightfall everyone including the captain was becoming convinced there was no enemy activity in the area; now the primary concern would become the leeches. The best defense, everyone decided, was the bug juice we had been issued. Most would avoid it if possible, because it was so strong it could have fueled a truck. But extreme conditions required extreme measures. We stripped down and saturated our bodies with it. The fumes were so strong that they produced watery eyes and dizziness. Even worse was the rash. The men appeared to be covered with fish scales. But there were no leeches.

Sergeant Bazarr was now at the head of the platoon, and the task of selecting a spot in which Second Platoon would camp for the night fell to him. He assigned Second Squad a spot and then told me where to place the men. Ellis stood at a distance and wouldn't join them, so I approached him. "What's up, man?" I asked.

"That Sergeant Bazarr gets dumber each day," he yelled.

"What makes him dumber today than yesterday?"

"Look around you."

"OK, I'm looking."

"We are on this big-ass mountain that's covered with vegetation, and that fool wants us to camp in the only clear spot."

"Damn, you got a point. Hey, Sarge," I said, calling Sergeant Bazarr over. "Ellis just made a good observation about the position you chose, and I agree. We are exposed here to enemy artillery."

"Oh," he said with disdain. "So you two believe you are a better military strategist than a marine sergeant? Do you really think I asked for a military opinion?"

"No!" Ellis shot back. "It's common sense."

"Well, you better have the common sense to obey my order!" the sergeant yelled.

Lieutenant Storm had reached the position by that time and joined the discussion. "What's going on?" he said to the sergeant.

"Nothing, sir," Bazarr replied in his military manner. "These men are about to take their positions as ordered."

"This is a bad spot!" I informed him. "We are exposed to enemy artillery."

"God dammit!" Bazarr shouted. "Get the fuck over there and put the men in positions."

"Do as you are ordered," the lieutenant reiterated to me. I knew I was in a losing battle, so I complied.

"An order is an order," Ellis whispered to me, "even if it gets everybody killed."

"Fuck that," I grumbled. "I bet they won't put the command post in the open. When it gets dark, we're moving into the trees."

Once we were out of hearing distance, the lieutenant and sergeant continued with their discussion. They talked while circling the entire perimeter. Then they held a discussion with the gunnery sergeant. Finally, Sergeant Bazarr returned and walked up to me.

"Gather the men," he said. "I'm considering a different spot for tonight. But I want to make something perfectly clear. You can give an opinion if I ask, but you never question my authority. Now get those men prepared to leave." I couldn't resist giving him one last smirk before moving the men.

The following day we were airlifted to another mountainous location roughly five miles away. Normally the distance wouldn't have been far for an infantry company to travel on foot, but in the rugged mountainous terrain, the slow progress would have given enemy troops an opportunity to hide or evacuate before we arrived. The commanders hoped the sudden shift in location would enable us to surprise our quarry.

Water wasn't an issue in the mountains. Streams were constantly discovered that would often flow into water basins at the base of the mountains. In fact, we had an interesting encounter while traveling along a riverbank. I was on point, with Ellis behind me. We were smelling a strong, overpowering odor. We suspected it to be a rotting corpse, a sight familiar to us. There was no sense of danger, but I told Ellis to notify the platoon that followed we were about to investigate it.

We found it was an enormous snake. Because of its size, approximately twenty feet, we assumed it was a python. We had seen death many times, but it would have been refreshing to see a living creature that had died of natural causes. That was not to be. Upon closer inspection, we saw the snake had been shot. "Damn!" I said, holding my nose. "Don't nothing die from old age around here?" We reported the finding to the platoon. Then we moved on. As the men passed, many of them expressed the same sentiment.

The water supply was good, but our food rations were running low. Anticipating heavy enemy contact in canopy too thick for a resupply chopper, we had packed more ammunition than food. After five days of chopping our way through the jungle, we were weighted down with ammunition and no food. The only platoon member with a supply of food was Hansen, who had a backpack full of C rations and only a minimal amount of ammunition. He had opted to take less ammunition and more food on the operation. My fellow squad members encouraged me to get him to share after he flatly rejected their request. I told them I would try.

At first I tried to persuade him by drawing on our old friendship, but it wasn't working. I didn't threaten him; that was not a part of my character. I just took it all. When he accused me of being just like the people I always complained about, we worked out a compromise. Hansen went over and offered to share his food with the squad. He saved face, and I could still be the good guy.

But there was a fire of unrest that was gradually rising to the surface.

It is unlikely that it would be acknowledged by military historians who portray the marines as a tight, cohesive group. However, we were different. Most of us were draftees, with little interest in a military career. We were a well-read group, informed of the civil-rights agenda and political unrest taking place back at home. So when the high-energy fighting marine infantrymen weren't confronting a common enemy, they began to bicker and polarize themselves, particularly those of African American descent.

We noticed when advancement opportunities and recognition were given discriminatorily. We were also aware that lives were often valued according to racial identity. Most officers and sergeants would at least try to give the impression of fairness. But Sergeant Nato's actions were clearly identified as a racist. So when he was given command of Second Squad, a largely African American group, we had to band together to survive.

Perhaps he didn't realize how willing I was to disobey what I considered unsound direction. Or how little his life meant to me.

We received information that our regiment was being pulled out of the operation, back to Phu Loc 6. At that point we weren't sure why.

The next morning we moved to an open area, one in which helicopters could land and transport us back. There was an ominous mood among the men when we heard we were to begin a new mission. It had been nearly two weeks since we had engaged in the fight at the Alamo, and we knew the odds favored a fight.

CHAPTER 22

Liberty Road
July 1969

▲ ▲ ▲

PHU LOC 6 SEEMED TO draw our company back like a magnet. The Communists hadn't attempted another direct assault on the base after the large number of casualties they had suffered following their latest attempt. However, they were freely moving about the area at night. The brass would pull marine units in from the bush to confront the NVA and VC, but they would simply shift their troops away until the massive troop presence lessened. Controlling troop movement became a focus. Our troops needed better mobile access between bases, and the Communist troop movement needed to be stopped or at least restricted. The solution was a managed road connecting An Hoa and Phu Lac6.

Liberty Road was a simple dirt road created by constant use. The patches of vegetation and uneven wear made it difficult to detect mines that the enemy placed at night. Therefore, the VC would constantly mine it and cross undetected.

It was decided that a compressed layer of gravel on the road's surface would enable the marines to detect disturbances that were likely the result of a newly placed mine. Much of the surrounding vegetation was cleared away.

We were informed that an engineers company would construct the road with a layer of compressed gravel. But before the construction would begin, the men from Fox, Gulf, and Hotel Companies had to clear out any enemy troops in or around the stretch of road. Fox would remain in the bush constantly patrolling. Gulf would work out of Phu Loc 6, setting two-man observation posts every one hundred yards up to the halfway point. Hotel would work out of An Hoa doing the same from the other direction. Within a matter of days, security was established, and the project was started.

The routine was set, and all responsibilities were rotated. At daybreak, the platoons would leave the base for a journey along the road. The first squad out would sweep for mines and look for ambushes. The following squads would drop men along the way in two-man positions. During the day, large gravel-hauling trucks, bulldozers, and rollers were transported from both An Hoa and Phu Loc 6, along with the materials needed. Construction would be done from both ends and would be completed when the two sides met in the middle. In addition to the observation post, a rifle squad would set up a perimeter around the work crew each day. There was also a constant presence of air support, with mortar support on standby. The marines would return to either base when the engineers stopped for the day. They would then guard the base at night.

Embankment off Liberty Road

At night, a kill team followed by four ambush squads would take over. The kill teams were smaller units with four to five men. One of the team members would act as radioman. Somewhere along the road they would separate from the column. The kill team would then conceal themselves in the bush and operate as a listening post, warning of any approaching enemy. They were also a rapid-response team for the ambushes. The ambushing squads would have more men bringing more firepower. A machine-gun team, grenadier, and corpsman would be somewhere in the column. The ambush locations would frequently change, but there were always eight ambushes and two kill teams operating somewhere on the road.

After the first days, the fighting became light and sporadic. At the beginning of the second week, Hansen was given his orders to be transported to An Hoa to finish his last two weeks at the base. Now Hansen, Walters, and Lucky were nearing the end of their tour of duty. The most promising thing for us was Lucky had never been wounded. This was a rare feat for someone who had spent his entire tour as a rifleman in our regiment. Maybe we all had a chance.

We were beginning to think this would be an easy assignment. How wrong we were. The NVA and Viet Cong were not about to relinquish nightly control without a deadly confrontation.

This particular morning, Second Platoon was to do the two-man position daytime observation post. Sergeant Nato was responsible for assigning duty for his squad members. In his constant effort to bring danger and discomfort to Ellis and me, he was not about to allow us to share a position. He instead placed me with Pepin. This was OK; I figured since Pepin's father was some sort of military big shot, he would get a less dangerous position.

Whether this was the case or just my suspicious assumption, we were given an area that provided clear vision of the immediate area. As senior of the two, I chose the specific spot. It was a point at which the road made a sharp turn to the right.

Because the terrain was sloped and the road was flat, there was roughly a four-foot drop from our position to the road. This afforded us an excellent line of vision in all directions. Beyond that bend, continuing in that direction, was a straight stretch of road, perhaps 150 yards. There was also vegetation spotted throughout the area, giving excellent cover. If the enemy was moving toward the base, we could cut them down using the straight line of fire. But we weren't there to ambush. Our job was to provide security and observe the area.

We made ourselves comfortable and settled back for what was to be a relatively easy day of security duty. This was one of the few times we could relax and talk. Pepin and I had little in common other than being male marines. Our differing social, cultural, and economic circles made it unlikely we would have come together at any point in life, so this would be an interesting exchange for both of us. We were both proud Americans but with polar differences of the country we were fighting for.

For Pepin, America is a land of opportunities. His barriers to success were within himself. He grew up around success. He knew doors would open if he prepared himself. If he was patient and connected the dots, the path would lead to a bright and prosperous future. The Communists posed a threat to his way of life and the God-given birthright inherent to any citizen of the powerful nation his ancestors fought and died for.

I was fighting the Communists because they posed an immediate threat to my life and the people around me. Otherwise, I might have been friends with them. It was not a battle for truth, justice, or divine right, but a battle to survive. I just wanted to get home and get on with my life. It was unlikely we would ever reach an agreement on the war or America as a whole. In spite of our differences, we got along well.

A conflict did ensue over a Vietnamese kid who visited our position looking for work and food. He would help set up the position, get shelter from the sun, clean up, or offer to supply us with ice or drugs. I suspected the kid was Viet Cong or at least a Viet Cong sympathizer. Knowing this, I was careful to not divulge any information and to guard my weapon and ammunition. Pepin not only hated the kid; he hated any Vietnamese. Every time the kid would approach, Pepin would respond with hostility. I would usually intervene. Eventually, Pepin struck him, knocking him to the ground. Baby-san stormed off, cursing in Vietnamese.

Around two hours before sunset, the engineers finished their work and began to return to the base. Shortly thereafter, the men on observation post and patrols went back to the base.

Pepin and I were the last to return. Once back, we found our platoon was to take on the ambush and kill team duty that night. The morale in the company was getting low. We were tired. The sergeants and officers were relaxing at the base all day while the enlisted men were being pushed to the brink of exhaustion. When we found some of the sergeants were calling home to their families, a perk we peons could only dream about, the complaining became openly expressed. This may have gotten back to the officers or the gunnery sergeant, because all sergeants were to participate in the night's activity.

Second Squad would lead the formation. We assumed our squad leader, Sergeant Nato, would put me, Ellis, Sherman, and Sally on the kill team. But Staff Sergeant Sparks, as senior commander, changed the plan. He was going to lead the kill team, and the remaining sergeants would lead the squads on the ambushes. Whatever happened that night, the sergeants would prove they were willing to take the same risk as the enlisted men.

The overly confident staff sergeant decided to take Pepin, Jackson, and Judy, the least experienced men on the kill team, where they would be exposed to the greatest danger. It was a bold move, one that was obviously done to demonstrate his bravery and tactical superiority. This was OK with Pepin; he seemed eager to prove himself. What better way than with a senior NCO? Judy seemed OK with it as well.

The squads lined up to start out for their night shift. It would be the kill team; then Second Squad, who would set the furthest ambush; next Third Squad; followed by Fourth; with First Squad taking the last position.

Pepin would point for the kill team. Staff Sergeant Sparks followed, with Jackson on radio, and Judy on tail end. I was point for Second Squad, followed by Sergeant Nato. Then there was Johnson on radio, followed by Ellis. Behind Ellis was the corpsman, then Greer. Sherman followed him, with Sally on tail end. The other squads followed with machine-gun teams mixed in. The base was on alert, and reinforcements were on the ready. It was suspected that both the Americans and Vietnamese Communists wanted to make a clear statement. With darkness approaching, we had to go before losing all natural light.

"Move out!" Sergeant Sparks bellowed. One by one we headed down the road. All ambushes had to be placed before dusk, so we had to move fast to make up for lost time. This was an unusually cloudy night, and the darkness seemed to be surrounding us. In fact, it felt like walking into a cave. Judy was the last man in the kill team, and I had to know where they split off. So I was responsible for keeping visual and verbal contact between the two groups. Due to the darkness, I tried to keep within five yards from them. But Sparks was moving the kill team too fast, and Nato was falling further behind, constantly calling for me to slow down. We were moving like an accordion. I wanted to tell him to shut up and catch up, but I wasn't about to give away my position. In the dark, noise of any kind was announcing your presence to the enemy, and Nato was shouting.

As we approached the bend in the road where Pepin and I had occupied a position that day, I found that the distance between Judy and me had widened, so I rushed to catch up to avoid losing visual contact. Now I could see the whole kill team in line. Nato had no visual of me, so he shouted my name. I spun around in anger to confront him with such force that I almost sprained my own neck.

Suddenly, like a bolt of lightning, an earsplitting burst of gunfire changed everything. An experienced pointer knows that when you have to make a life-and-death decision in the blink of an eye, you don't blink. It was instinct.

After the initial shock, I was aware that there were hundreds of red-hot projectiles coming my way, and the fight-or-flight reflex kicked in. There was no time to think so my body was acting on its own. I hit the ground hard, feeling immediate pain. That was good, because I knew I was alive. All this took a second, two at most.

Every man who turned that bend from Pepin to me was caught in the kill zone of a box ambush. It was a brilliantly staged trap, seemingly impossible to escape. The road sliced into the side of the sloping terrain. The enemy had positioned shooters on the high ground and below road level, allowing them to get their targets in a cross fire.

Sergeant Nato, who was behind me, immediately pulled the men back. He would have pulled them all the way to the base if they weren't resisting all along the way. They just didn't want to leave us. They stopped at about two hundred yards and set up a defensive position. Nato grabbed the radio from Johnson and began screaming over the airwave. "Gulf, Gulf! This is Gulf Two. They wiped out our stinger. We need mortars."

"Give the radio to Johnson," the captain ordered the frantic Sergeant Nato.

In the midst of the confusion, the composed Johnson advised against a mortar strike until they knew if there were survivors. Suddenly, two more shots rang out from the ambush spot. Again, the distinctive shots were from Communist weapons. The marines could only guess as to what was taking place two hundred yards to their front.

They had no way to know at the time that I, having been saved by nature, was still alive. The torrential rains had washed a trench where the mountain wall and road met. The ambush was sprung the moment I made the violent turn to confront Nato. The shock of that blast of machine-gun and rifle fire knocked me off my feet, and I hit the ground rolling. One roll and I was in the ditch, lying on my back.

The rounds from the shooters who had likely marked me as a sure kill were passing inches above me. I was being splattered with dirt and rocks from the rounds impacting the wall. That layer of dirt and the darkness made me difficult to spot.

I was now blinded by a cloud of sulfur and smoke, gasping for air, confused, but alive.

The trench was confining, making me feel as if I were in a coffin. *Oh shit*, I thought, *am I dead? Of course not*, I surmised, wiggling my hands and feet. In the past few seconds, I had seen my life flash before me. But that was then, and this was now. I would now have to make moves that would determine if this was where my life would end. Or if I would be captured.

First, what was the last thing I saw and heard?

Pepin was standing in front of a machine gun when the enemy opened fire. He was riddled with bullets and likely dead.

Sergeant Sparks went down. Then he called out orders in an attempt to pull the men out. That move gave his position away. Two shots followed; then his body hit the ground.

Jackson had his back blown apart, and Judy was shot in the head area. I saw him running into the enemy's position.

The enemy were to my front, and possibly above and below on the downside of the slope. *Don't move*, I thought. *They are the aggressors, so the next move is theirs. But where are the marines? Did they run and leave me? Sergeant Nato was probably pulling them back to the base.*

Then I heard movement. People were running all around. I hoped it was marines. Then he heard voices, Vietnamese voices. I tried to determine if they were at a distance shouting, or close whispering. They were searching the bodies and probably looking for me. Now I was in a total panic. I was even afraid they could hear me thinking.

Should I lie still, fight my way out, surrender, or just run? That question was answered for me when a shadow passed over, blocking out the moon and starlight. *Oh shit, someone must have seen me.* That was when I heard the familiar pop a grenade makes when the pin is pulled and the spoon flies. Running was now my only option. I had about four seconds until the explosion.

I rolled my legs back to my chest, arched my back, and then sprung forward. The thrust was so powerful that I almost fell flat on my face. I extended my arms and caught myself. Then I sprinted at a speed that would have gotten me gold at any Olympic game. The grenade exploded, and the Vietnamese began firing rounds that chased me down the road. I ducked and dodged like a frightened rabbit. My only goal was to put as much distance between myself and the Vietnamese as possible.

I might have run all the way back to Da Nang if I weren't suddenly tackled.

Someone was lying on my chest. My weapon would do me no good, so I grabbed for my knife. "It's me! It's me!" I heard a familiar voice shouting into my ear. I recognized it was Ellis.

"I knew you were alive! I knew you were alive!" Ellis kept repeating. My eyes were wide with excitement; and my heart was pounding so hard I could almost hear it. I was desperately gasping for air, while questions were coming from all around. In spite of all the noise and confusion, I could hear Sergeant Nato, about fifteen yards away, calling for a massive strike. "Hold it, God dammit!" I yelled, running toward the radio. "Judy might still be alive." Johnson snatched the radio and canceled the strike.

"We're going back up there," Nato commanded. "Harris, you take point." I didn't like it, but I realized it was the right choice. I was comforted by Ellis being behind me. Cautiously, we approached the spot I had desperately escaped only minutes before. I stopped about thirty yards short and motioned for Ellis to come up.

"Judy went off in that direction," I whispered to Ellis. "The rest of the kill team might still be on the road." Ellis crept back to Sergeant Nato to give the message. Moments later, he returned.

"He wants us to go search for Judy while the platoon goes up the road."

"Just the two of us?"

"That's what he said."

"That motherfucker is going to try and kill us," I said to Ellis. Concerned for our safety, I went over to the squad members and addressed them, ignoring the sergeant. "Ellis and I are going to be on the right flank looking for Judy. Don't shoot in that direction." I searched their faces until they gave me the look of conformation I needed. Satisfied, I turned and rejoined Ellis. The two of us crept through the brush, searching for any sign of Judy.

Ellis placed his hand on my shoulder and directed my attention to what appeared to be a man standing in the darkness. "It might be Judy," I whispered. There was just enough light to see he was facing away from us with his weapon at his side. As we crept closer, we were becoming convinced it was Judy. But he was standing motionless, and we had to consider the possibility that the enemy had placed him there as bait, waiting in silence to spring another ambush. Slowly, I approached him while Ellis scanned the area.

I was concerned the startled marine might shoot us if he panicked, so I reached out and wrapped my hand around the stock of Judy's weapon and gently pulled it away. But he never moved; he was as still as a mannequin and as white as a ghost. The gushing flow of blood from his gaping wound made him a ghoulish sight. He was unfazed by our presence. "It's Harris," I whispered in his ear. "Are you OK?"

Judy finally moved, slowly and methodically turning his head toward me to answer. "Fuck no," he said in a monotone whisper. "They almost killed my ass."

I smiled, realizing that I had asked a ridiculous question.

"They ran off and left me," Judy continued.

"Who?" I asked.

"The Viet Cong," he responded. Judy was fortunate to have been in a catatonic state. He was walking so calmly among the enemy that they didn't realize he wasn't one of them.

"You're a lucky motherfucker," Ellis laughed.

Judy was physically weak, so we had to support him as if he were a child learning to walk.

Several squads were now providing security around the road. The corpsman and several others were standing around two bodies. One of the bodies was Sergeant Sparks. His chest was gushing blood, and it seemed likely he had been shot through the heart. It likely happened when he attempted to pull the men back, exposing himself to enemy gunfire. The other body was Pepin's. His mangled body was twisted in a contorted position. His upper body appeared as if he had passed through a shredder. The condition made it evident that he was likely in front of a machine gun when the ambush was sprung.

Then there was another marine pacing back and forth, talking to himself. It was Jackson. His back looked like a rake had been dragged across it, but he was clearly alive and grinning like the Cheshire cat in *Alice in Wonderland*.

"Man!" he said, eyes as big as golf balls. "Those motherfuckers blew that radio right off my back. It just exploded." He continued to speak as if in a trance. "They were taking weapons and checking pockets." He stopped for a moment, clearly having a religious experience, and then continued to tell his story. "I thought I was going to die. All I could do was pray. Finally, I heard them leaving. Then they started shooting and throwing grenades; I just knew my ass was a goner."

"They were shooting at me," I responded.

"Did they hit you?"

"I don't think so," I said, patting myself all over.

"What about Judy?" Jackson asked.

"Over here," Ellis said, escorting him over. "Judy is now one of our bushmasters." That recognition brought a smile to the wounded marine's face. He had long sought acknowledgment from his experienced comrades. He was so inspired by the emotional support that he was able to now walk without assistance.

The men were preparing to withdraw and return to the base. Again, I was placed on point by Nato, with Ellis following. A sergeant and another marine were carrying Sergeant Sparks's body. They carried him with his arms hoisted over their shoulders in the same manner wounded marines were extracted. Pepin's ripped and bleeding corpse was transported in a poncho liner. The remainder of the squad and platoon followed.

I was moving at a rapid pace when we were fired upon from the left flank. I turned and unloaded a full magazine of rounds in that direction. Ellis fired a few rounds while I reloaded. There were no further shots from that direction. We concluded that it was a single rifleman whom we had either hit or driven away.

We continued the retreat. Suddenly, an incoming mortar round landed in the center of the column. We couldn't determine the location from which it was fired, so we just stepped up the retreat. The men carrying Sergeant Sparks's body were struggling to keep up. Eventually they dropped him. His head came crashing to the ground. They then grabbed him by the legs and started dragging his corpse like an animal carcass. The sergeant had been a proud man; seeing him handled in such an undignified manner was too much for either me or Ellis.

We pushed the two men aside and took over the body. Sherman came up to take over point. In spite of the well-known animosity between the three of us while he was alive, in death we treated him with dignity, as if his family were watching. His body would not touch the ground except when we were too exhausted to do otherwise. When we finally reached Phu Loc, we found other marines had suffered minor injuries from RPGs fired at us while we retreated, but none were fatal. We cheered the devastating barrage the artillery group launched on the enemy after we were at a safe distance. Ellis and I were uncertain of what to do with Sergeant Sparks's body, so when we looked around and saw Gunny Mac standing at a distance, we thought it would be respectful to take his friend's body to him.

The gunnery sergeant looked at his fallen comrade with a blank expression. He then looked at his subordinates with a cold, condescending glare. "Get that goddamn body out of here," he said in a clear, distinct tone. Without comment, we hoisted his body and carried it in a seated position to the base hospital.

After dropping his body off, we had a very introspective discussion while walking back to the platoon's hooch. We avoided discussing the killing and dying, as battlefield combatants routinely do, and focused on the friendship the two sergeants had. Or the friendship we thought they had. We were shocked at the gunny sergeant's attitude. Neither of us could understand how he could be so cavalier about his friend's death.

Gunnery Sergeant Mac and Staff Sergeant Sparks were more than just friends. They had a shared history, joining the military when segregation and discrimination was even more overt. They were also equally committed to their careers and shared the same values. Two black men who had overcome the odds and risen within the ranks.

They had even entered Vietnam together, just like Ellis and me. But they were the Korean War generation. A different war, a different time, a different world.

"Can you believe that fat motherfucker's attitude?" Ellis said.

"That was some cold shit," I answered solemnly.

"Maybe he thought showing emotion would make him look weak."

"Or maybe he don't give a shit. If he don't care about him, you know how he feels about us."

"You know," Ellis continued, giving it serious thought, "they might teach them that in gunnery sergeant training. Leader first, friends last."

We entered the hooch and sat down anticipating a well-deserved rest. A few of the men were engaging in low conversations. Most were sitting silently. Alameda entered the tent to make an announcement. "Listen up!" he announced. "Sergeant Nato has been promoted to platoon sergeant to replace Sergeant Sparks.

"And you, I take it," I said with disdain, "are you our new squad leader?"

Seemingly embarrassed, he apologetically answered, "Yes." In spite of Alameda being younger and less experienced, I wasn't surprised he was put in charge. That's the way the system works. I understood Alameda had no more to do with his heritage than I had to do with mine.

Alameda quickly found the job would not be easy.

"Our platoon sergeant wants us to go out on a night patrol to hunt the people who ambushed and killed our leader. We are going to show them what happens when they fuck with the marines." He expected the men to give a rousing approval, but they were silent. He hesitated before relaying his next orders, clearly expecting a confrontation. "Harris, you know the area best, so Nato wants you on point."

There was a long silence in the room as I stood up and got nose to nose with Alameda. "Is he going?" I asked.

"No," Alameda responded, flashing a conciliatory grin.

"Well, neither am I. I walked point three times tonight without question and was caught in two ambushes. Now, I'm going to sleep." Alameda was at a loss, unsure what to do next. The men sprang into action.

"I'll take point," Ellis blurted out while picking up his weapon. "Let's go." The other men grabbed their weapons and started out the door as well.

Not wanting to lose total control, Alameda called to me. "I think you have been through enough for one night, Marine. Stay back and get a good night's sleep. We'll see you in the morning. If anyone questions it, I'll tell them that was my decision."

I never commented or turned around. I just attempted to sleep.

But I couldn't. I was consumed with thoughts about the deceased sergeant, and I tried to understand why we held such contempt for each other in life. Did he fulfill his calling in life as he was driven to do? What exactly was he trying to accomplish? Did he want to save lives in combat, enrich the legacy of the Marine Corps, gain respect for African Americans in his country to stop racism and discrimination, stop the spread of Communism, or simply make his family proud? Had he done any of that?

His family would undoubtedly be proud of him. His body would be retuned with military honors. Emotions and pride would be stirred as he was eulogized for his bravery. Medals, citations, and the flag that draped his coffin would be presented to his widow as she embraced her young children. There may even be a letter of gratitude stamped with the signature of President Richard M. Nixon, for his service to his country. That citation and his proud photograph in marine dress blues would likely sit for a time on the mantelpiece of his thirty-year-old widow's home. She and her children could gaze fondly at it. Over time she would likely remarry and start a new family. Memory would fade, and that photo would be stored in a spare room where it would be one of many items on a cluttered desktop. Or perhaps it would be relegated to a box in the closet. He would enter the conversation if someone asked about her first husband who died in Vietnam.

Her children could only smile politely when his old friends said they reminded them of the father they never really knew. If he were alive, would he say it was worth it?

I would add this to the long list of life's questions I would never have answered.

With that I drifted off to sleep.

CHAPTER 23

My Right Arm
July 1969

▲ ▲ ▲

The next morning the squad went out to survey the area. The bloodbath that had taken place the night before was evident. But neither side left any dead or wounded, so there was no clear victor. The skirmish would mark an escalation in the fight for Liberty Road.

The company initiated an all-out offensive. We made constant attacks and raids around the road that discouraged the Viet Cong from mining the road. Soon Viet Cong activity began to subside. The NVA, however, who were clashing with marine units in the surrounding area, were not dissuaded. Both sides were losing men, but the NVA had no air support or ability to move their troops. They needed to move troops across that road at some point, and the logistics of going around were just not practical.

The marines were overwhelmed by a tidal wave of events. The deadly clashes that were becoming a nightly occurrence were causing to casualties to mount. It was clear we had entered the belly of the beast, and everyone was affected by the increased violence, including the medical personnel.

Tagging bodies at night was an added stress on the corpsmen. This prompted Doc Webber to make an odd request to the commanders, which would differ from protocol.

As things stood, before a body was loaded into a helicopter for evacuation, one of the dog tags from the fallen marine's neck had to be placed into his mouth and his mouth clamped shut. The identification he carried was placed in his left pocket. In the right pocket, the corpsmen placed a casualty report containing sketchy details of the cause of death or nature of wounds, whatever was applicable. The corpsmen wanted the men to carry the report partially filled out. The commanders ordered the men comply. They sent the sergeants out to relay the order. Most complied with the order as they did to orders from superiors, without question. But this was where I drew the line.

"There is no way in hell I'm going to walk around with my own death certificate in my pocket. I didn't come here to die!" I said emphatically. "The last thing I'm worried about is inconveniencing the corpsmen." The men within hearing distance nodded, indicating that I had summed up their position quite adequately. The sergeant stomped off like a spoiled child.

The operation continued. As the days passed, a feeling of impending doom hung over us like a shroud. The men were now giving each other a parting Black Power handshake each time we would leave for a kill team, ambush, or patrol. Everyone understood it might be the last contact we would have. When we returned, we would be greeted with another Black Power handshake amid smiles and cheers, as if we had been separated for years. It was the way of saying, "Hey, everybody, I'm still alive!"

Alameda was shown not to have the forcefulness and experience to control the combat hardened men in Second Squad, so Sergeant Roe was brought back in.

It was not unusual for squad members to rotate through the squad for brief intervals, sometimes leaving on a stretcher or in a body bag; other times they just weren't a good fit. But there were four members of our squad whose presence was constant. Our reputation of an undisciplined but effective force would unfortunately place us in the front when fighting was at its worst. But each possessed a unique skill that increased our odds for survival.

I was considered to have tactical and predatory instincts and would attack with reckless abandonment if cornered. The men trusted me to look out for their best interest. Ellis was insightful and a consummate thinker. He could sum up a situation at a glance, noticing things others overlooked and using it to his advantage. Sherman was a tenacious high-energy marine who never stopped moving and would never stop fighting. Most important, he questioned everything. Finally we had Sally, a big strong farm boy who didn't take no shit. He was protective, loyal, and dependable. If any of us stepped back, he would step up. Our wealth of experience would normally have gotten us advancements, but our antagonistic response to authority had halted any advancement we might have otherwise had. Roe learned to use that experience rather than attempt to control it.

It was now the third week into the road security, and the squad was preparing for a night ambush. The bend in the road where Sarge and Pepin had died had lost its uniqueness. Many others had died all along that stretch of road, so the uneasiness we felt at that spot was subsiding. It had been over four days since Second Squad had been involved in any direct contact, so we had no particular reason to believe this night would be any different.

Before leaving to set up the ambush, the brothers went around checking out with our traditional Black Power handshake with the marines who would stay on the lines. Normally everyone would concentrate on coming up with their own innovative moves, constantly trying to outdo each other. But that night something felt different. No one seemed to recognize it, but, to me, it was as obvious as a colorless flower or an odorless perfume. Something just wasn't right.

I always dismissed any thoughts of having a premonition, holding to my belief that supernatural explanations interfered with logical thinking. So I was confused by my emotions. I felt like I was a stranger to myself. One thing was certain; I didn't want to go.

Perhaps I was just facing an emotion I refused to acknowledge: fear. The other men seemed to see an absence of the confidence I always tried to display. A defeatist mood would bring disaster and could not persist.

The ever-observant Ellis moved in quickly. "Pull out of it!" he shouted at me in no uncertain terms. I was shocked by my friend's aggression, but before I could express my fears, Ellis extended his clenched fist to solicit a Black Power handshake. "Check out!" he said, flashing a reassuring smile. We would check out with the ones on the line, not each other, leaving me puzzled at the gesture, so I refused.

"What do you mean, check out? I'm going out too." But Ellis would not relent, continuing to insist I exchange the power handshake. "Damn!" I finally said, giving a macho power handshake, slamming my fist against Ellis's with powerful thumps and then pounding my chest and growling like a bear. The others joined in and began rallying together like a football team psyching themselves up for the big game. Now we were ready.

The mission was laid out. Second Squad would have the furthest position out, about two miles from the base. A kill team was drawn from Fourth Platoon. They would break away before Second Squad reached their predetermined spot and position themselves in a ravine, safely out of the killing zone. This meant that no one should pass once our squad was in place. The next ambush would be coming from the other direction and would stop short about one thousand yards.

Ellis was on point; I followed, then Roe, the Squad Leader. Donahue was behind him on radio. Next a new replacement, Kartas, then Fredericks, Sally, and Sherman on tail end. Walking down that road with its recent history of violence was like walking through a graveyard. It was expected to take about forty-five minutes to reach our destination, but perhaps the melancholy mood slowed us down. We didn't reach the spot until nine o'clock.

It was an area we were familiar with, and it was likely the enemy would also know it well. We would therefore do a routine search for booby traps while we still had light. Then the men took a defensive position, while Roe and I discussed where the claymores would be positioned for the night. The final move would be done under the cover of darkness in the event the enemy was watching.

With the exception of a few trees, bushes, and rocks, it was an open area on the same level as the road. We had to choose between the cover of the rocks and the concealment of the bushes.

The far side of the road was also open, giving the opponent few places to take cover. Roughly thirty yards behind us was a slightly elevated tree line. This was the most likely place for an ambush because of the elevation. The enemy would have known that and would likely concentrate their firepower at that spot.

The squad was low on manpower, so we decided to place two men on the high ground to guard against a rear attack. Our other positions would be parallel to the road. I was to spring the ambush, so I would take a position closest to the target. This was a clump of bushes about five yards off the road. Ellis, as usual, would be at my side.

Roe positioned the men while Ellis and I concealed ourselves. The visibility was fading fast, but before it was safe to place the claymores in the final position, I was startled by someone who hurriedly approached me. It was Roe. Leaning close, he whispered into my ear, "They're coming." Then he crept to his position. Ellis, who was only inches from me, knew what was about to happen, so no words were necessary.

The moment before engaging a foe, primal instincts kick in. The past and future are irrelevant. It is only about the here and now. Slowly, I turned my head toward the approaching enemy. I stared with open eyes, afraid to blink. My eyes darted, searching for a target. For a few seconds I heard nothing, giving me hope that it was a false alarm. Then I could hear the rustling of clothing, the shuffling of feet, the grunting sounds men make when fatigued, a revealing cough. They were close, perhaps a few yards, too far I surmised, holding my fire.

Ellis, who was against me, moved slightly, perhaps positioning himself or raising his weapon to fire. Slowly, I applied pressure to my trigger. I could clearly see my target directly in front of me. It was his time to die. "Pop, pop, pop." I fired three rounds into my target, dropping him to the ground. Once the ambush was sprung, the marines joined in. Almost instantaneously, the opponents returned fire. We were now engaging in a fierce firefight. To my surprise, I could see my target was still moving. I had only incapacitated him. Now I would have to finish the job. This time I intended to unload my entire clip into the fallen soldier, so I switched my weapon to fully automatic. Leaning forward, I took aim on my target and pulled the trigger. All I got was a click. After several more tries, I realized my weapon was jammed. Not knowing if the weapon or magazine was jammed, I released and replaced the magazine and then pulled the bolt, ejecting the chambered round. Now I could finish the kill. The process only took a few seconds, enough for my fallen target to scream out in pain. "Oh God!" I heard the man scream. "I've been hit!"

An NVA soldier would not call out to God. To my horror, I realized I had sprung an ambush on my fellow marines. "Check fire! Check fire!" I screamed. "What have I done?" I cried. At this point, the call to halt the fight was echoing throughout the battlefield. As abruptly as the fighting had started, it stopped. I was beside myself in horror. I reached over to Ellis, who was lying motionless. I assumed his silence was his reaction to the debacle that had taken place.

In my darkest moment, I needed reassurance from my oldest and closest friend. But when I touched Ellis's head, it felt as if I had touched a wet sponge. Bringing my hand close to my eyes, I could see it was covered with blood, so much, in fact, that it was flowing down my arm. The whole side of my body was saturated with blood. I could feel a warm heat radiating from his body, so I threw myself over him, trying to contain it. But death cannot be contained when the soul is called to its rendezvous with destiny. It was a force so powerful that it lifted me to my feet. Once upright, a cold chill came over me, shaking me to the bones. Suddenly I let out a deep and mournful cry like that of a wounded animal. I knew, at that moment, my friend was dead.

I was standing with a blank expression. Time, for me, was suspended. Physically, I was in the midst of the chaos. Emotionally, I was at some distant place. My weapon dropped from my relaxed hand, hitting the ground with a thud. "I can't do this anymore," I muttered passively. Sally and Sherman were now standing beside me, horrified at seeing Ellis's lifeless body, but no words were spoken.

Roe and his fellow squad leader were in a heated confrontation, each insisting the other was at fault. The corpsman had commandeered an assistant to help him attend the wounded marines.

A marine from the squad we had attacked came charging over demanding to know who had shot his fellow marine. "I did," I replied, never looking up. When the marine made a threatening move toward me, the normally demure Sally rammed him with his massive chest with such a force that it knocked him to the ground. Sherman stood over the befuddled marine telling him in no uncertain terms that a key player was dead, and it would be in his best interest to leave. The marine apologized and left as abruptly as he had appeared.

Roe called for a chopper to medevac the dead and wounded, but the men seemed to be wandering aimlessly about searching for direction. They were confused by me. My absence of emotion had created a void. They were looking for the confidence I would normally display in the heat of combat.

They weren't sure if I was afraid or lost in that inescapable emotional abyss that many combat veterans find themselves in. Sherman walked over to me, reached down, and picked up my weapon. "You'll need this," he said, handing it to me.

He then leaned into me and whispered, "Everybody is looking at you, brother; you've got to pull it together. If you're gonna have a breakdown, do it when we are in a safe zone." The statement was so profound that it shook me out of my stupor. It was as if electric shock had been applied. I was back and thinking clearly.

"The enemy knows we are here, so we need to broaden our perimeter," I suggested to Roe, who had joined us. "The chopper is going to need a large area to land, and they are probably going to try to attack it." Roe agreed, telling me that he had called for a chopper, but he was having trouble getting cooperation from the other squad leader. "You have the superior rank!" I yelled. "Tell that motherfucker what to do!"

Roe responded quickly, forcing his will over every detail.

The men quickly secured the area. Suddenly a firefight broke out in the distance, an indication that the enemy were attempting to take advantage of what they assumed to be a vulnerable force. They were wrong, and the marines quickly repelled the attack, adding several kills to their tally.

The wounded were transported to the landing zone. At least one of the wounded was in critical condition, but at that moment Ellis was the only marine confirmed dead. I carried his body, sitting it to rest against a tree next to me. The wounded and the corpsman attending to them seemed fixed on me and my dead friend. We appeared to be engaged in a conversation, as we had been routinely since we met in the induction station in Cleveland. This time, of course, the dialogue was one-way. The chopper finally arrived, and the wounded were loaded. I placed Ellis's body, which appeared to be sleeping, on the floor of the chopper. Then I turned and left without saying a word, never turning back to watch the chopper ascend to the sky.

Both squads were now in fixed defensive positions. Roe took Harris to the command post that was in the center of a large circle. Both squad leaders, the radiomen, the corpsman, and the machine-gun teams were all gathered, but no one spoke. There was an eerie silence pervading the whole area. Everyone was consumed with their own set of demons.

Although I wasn't cold, my body was shaking. I reasoned it to be anguish that I had not yet released. I cupped my bloodied hands to my face and released a torrent of emotion so powerful that it would have awakened the dead, but it was void of sound. No one, not even the man sitting next to me, knew the distress I was in.

Tears flowed from my eyes as if they were being pumped from a reservoir in my head. The tears filled my hands, moistening the dried blood that I could now smell and taste, turning my face a pale red. The moonlight would reveal the tracks on my forearm made by the liquefied blood cascading down and puddling on the ground as it dropped from my elbows. It seemed I was attempting to wash away my pain.

The blood could be washed, and the clothes could be changed, leaving no visible scars. But the hurt would be as lasting as the loss of an arm.

CHAPTER 24

Bad Luck Comes in Threes
July–August 1969

▲ ▲ ▲

THERE WERE NO FURTHER CONFRONTATIONS that night. The gods of war had given us a respite. At daybreak, the men returned to the base. Few words were exchanged. Everyone seemed to be trying to reconcile the event within their own minds. Once we arrived at the base, most cleaned up and then retreated to a private place. This was a rare opportunity to safely relax. In combat, the constant life-and-death struggle leaves little time for something as distracting as grieving.

For me, there was hope. Walters had managed to survive, and with just over three months to go, maybe he could do it as well. Exhausted from a lack of sleep, I quickly drifted off. That sleep was broken after a few hours when Johnson came to me.

"The captain wants you to report to the command tent," he informed me.

"What does he want?"

"He's the captain. He doesn't tell me anything; he just says do it."

"Maybe he is going to let us use some of that hot water in the shower."

"That is for the officers and NCOs," Johnson laughed.

"Fuck the officers and NCOs."

"Hey, man, I'm an NCO," Johnson boasted.

"Fuck you too." I laughed.

"Look, my brother," Johnson warned. "The Vietnamese aren't your only enemy out here. Watch your back." I thanked him and proceeded to the tent.

This was the first time I had been invited into the command tent, so I was suspicious.

When I walked into the neat, well-organized tent, I saw all the players were there: the captain, Lieutenant Storm, Gunny Mac, Sergeant Nato, Corporal Roe, and the squad leader from First Platoon. They were all shaved and showered with clean uniforms, looking extremely professional. I, on the other hand, was unshaven, hair a mess. Although I had changed from my bloody uniform, my boots were still bloodstained. They seemed taken aback by my appearance. I knew based on my prior appearance before officers or boards of inquiry that my appearance would provoke a reprimand. But I didn't care.

I wasn't in the mood for the in-your-face berating that officers and sergeants routinely dished out. So to get it over as quickly as possible, I did the kiss-ass greeting they were expecting. "Private Harris, reporting as ordered!" I snapped with an accompanying salute.

"Aren't you a lance corporal?" the gunnery sergeant said sarcastically.

"Oh yeah, I forgot," I said with a smile. Then I took two steps back and repeated the routine. "Sir, Lance Corporal Harris, reporting as ordered, sir," I shouted with the accompanying salute. I then went into the board-up-the-butt attention position like a basic training recruit. My exaggerated display of insincere respect seemed almost comedic. Roe was having difficulty containing his laughter. He knew I wasn't concerned about their opinion of me, and I would develop a comedic routine when retelling the encounter to the squad.

The captain, as the ranking officer, took charge of the briefing. "At ease, Marine!" he started. "We are not here to intimidate you, Marine," he said with a reassuring smile. "We just want to get your version of what took place last night."

Disregarding Johnson's warning and my own instincts that told me this was a likely setup, I told the truth. "Somebody fucked up and sent a patrol down the road after we were told to ambush it. As a result, my best friend died."

The potbellied gunnery sergeant leaped to his feet and charged at me. Standing on his toes to compensate for his noticeable height deficit, he pressed his face as close as he could without touching and began to shout. "You smartass motherfucker. You are talking to an officer in the United States Marine Corps, and you will do such with respect. Do you understand?"

I, more annoyed than fearful, attempted to speak but was, again, berated by the gunnery sergeant. "Do you understand?" he repeated.

"I understand," I said after taking a deep breath to calm myself.

The captain continued. "I'm saddened by the loss of PFC Ellis, as I am with any of the men under my command. I look at the men as an extension of my own family, and my concern runs just as deep." They all looked at the captain with compassion and sympathy. "I do realize that you and Ellis go way back," he said, offering me the opportunity to discuss Ellis, which I chose not to do. I was insulted by the captain's seemingly programmed display of concern. It was likely Ellis was just a number to him.

With no response from me, the captain continued. "Ellis showed great courage under enemy fire. He is deserving of a commendation."

I was fixed on the last comment, pleased that Ellis might get a medal. That might give a small bit of comfort to the Ellis family. I also remembered the frequent discussions the two of us would have regarding either of us getting medals. We had agreed we would only be recognized if we lost our lives. Sadly, that prophecy had come true. Then I stiffened, repeating what the captain had said. "Bravery under enemy fire? What enemy fire?" I asked.

All eyes were on me, which made me suspicious. My survival instincts kicked in, and I decided to play dumb, which generally worked.

"Things were happening so fast," I said. "I'm still not clear as to what happened."

They looked at one another. Then eyes shifted back to me as the captain continued to speak. "A recon patrol was ordered out after a ten-minute interval. Sergeant Nato passed that word to your squad leader."

Expendable and Necessary

I looked at my squad leader. Then I looked at Sergeant Nato, both of whom had blank expressions on their faces. I couldn't hold it any longer.

"There was no word about a recon team!" I blurted out. "Sergeant Nato didn't mention that. We were told we were the furthest out, and we didn't expect marines to follow."

Before I could say more or start to make accusations, Gunnery Sergeant Mac, again, began shouting into my face. "God dammit, Marine, you don't question your superiors. Shut the fuck up until your captain tells you to speak."

I was now dangerously close to telling them all to kiss my ass. Then it occurred to me that the gunnery sergeant, whom I had always considered the House Negro, might be trying to warn me.

The captain, who was nowhere around when the action took place, proceeded to describe in great detail what had happened. "As the recon team reached your ambush position, the NVA sprung an ambush from the tree line behind you. They likely hit Ellis with a short round. The recon team returned fire on the NVA, and you guys thought they were firing at you. In the confusion, you guys naturally fired back." The captain paused, waiting for a reply.

This was the first time I had heard about the enemy firing from behind, so I was trying to recall the incident to see if that was possible. We had placed two men in the tree line. Why didn't they say anything about the enemy being there? Ellis, I recalled, had clearly been shot at least once in the head, but I couldn't recall if the bullet had exited from the front or back. If he had been shot from the back and there were no enemy behind us, then he could have possibly been shot by one of our own squad members. My head was spinning as I was trying to replay the incident. Shots were being fired in all directions, including from behind. The only person I was certain didn't shoot Ellis was me.

What is going on? I thought, searching their faces. They were undoubtedly trying to blame somebody, and I had fired the shots that initiated the ambush. Everyone involved in a decision-making position was in the room, so someone here was going to take a fall. As the lowest-ranking marine in the room, the system would consider me the most expendable. I was also an African American in a justice system heavily weighted against people of color. Especially one who had shot a white American. So even if the case was called outside the military, I would still lose.

How far would they go, and who were they covering for? To make it an even greater insult, they would likely wait to bring the charges until after I had completed my combat tour. The only truth I knew was that I couldn't trust anybody in that tent, so I remained silent. The Ellis family would find little comfort knowing he died in friendly fire.

"Do you have anything to add?" the captain eventually said.

"No, sir," I responded. Satisfied that I had bought the bull, they dismissed me. I stormed out of the tent still full of questions, heading for the squad members. Somebody had killed Ellis, and I wanted to know who. But the men seemed to be in a jovial mood, and that surprised me. It seemed the story of Ellis having been killed by enemy fire had been circulated, and they were eagerly accepting the belief that he wasn't killed by a fellow marine. A mass amnesia seemed to have taken hold. Whatever the circumstances, it was an accident. So the official version was recorded. The truth, as always in combat, would remain elusive.

The following day the men were allowed to relax at the base. One of the wounded marines returned with a shopping bag full of 101s and number tens. There were also several cases of beer rations to be consumed. It was the perfect time for the men to drown their emotions in the haze of drugs and beer. The close-knit group was all there: Sherman, Sally, Ray, Butler, Woody, and Jackson. We sat about in a semiconscious state listening to Motown sounds playing on the recorder. Johnson and Donahue walked in, and the men looked at them suspiciously. It was clear they were there to talk to me, because they sat on my cot and looked directly and silently at me.

"We need to talk," Johnson finally said. I knew it was serious, so I exited the tent with the two of them, and we headed to a secluded place outside the tent. After composing himself, Johnson continued.

"Walters is dead," Johnson finally said. I lowered my head, staring at the ground as Johnson continued, voice cracking with grief.

"A communication came across yesterday. The details are sketchy, but he seemed to have been hospitalized for a time, fighting for his life. He died the same day as Ellis. Two days before his bird was to arrive, there was an accident involving an ammo truck. Possibly brought on by an incoming mortar round. He went home," Johnson went on, holding back tears. "But he was in a body bag."

"What about Lucky?" I asked in a barely audible voice.

"He is hanging on," Donahue said. "He was burned over seventy percent of his body." We sat there for a few more minutes with no one speaking. There was really nothing more to say.

"Are you going to be OK?" Johnson asked me while rising to his feet. I nodded the affirmative. "Would you rather we tell the others?" he asked. Again I nodded to him without speaking.

The two of them returned to the tent. Within seconds the men could be heard crying out in anguish. I just sat there staring into space, desperately trying to clear my mind. My story was yet to be told and might conclude in a slow and agonizing ending. I was now slipping into a spiraling funnel of self-pity. Each time I hit bottom, I would tell myself that the only way now was up. But that mind game wasn't working. Too much was happening at once. Not sharing feelings doesn't mean they don't exist.

Three of the most important people in my life had recently and tragically been taken. The realization I would never see or talk to them again was almost more than I could bear.

Each time I thought I'd hit bottom, things would get worse. I clearly understood, from what I had seen in California, that an inward escape from your pain can cause an inescapable break from reality, leading to a life of permanent institutionalization. Grief was beginning to consume my every thought, and I couldn't allow that to happen. Grief could be addressed at a future time in the proper place, like after I'd safely returned home and the daily fight for survival was done. For my mental well-being, I had to shift my focus to positive thoughts.

We were young men, an average age of twenty, full of energy and raw emotion. Young men who faced disfigurement, permanent disability, and a greatly reduced life expectancy. We had to find alternatives to violence and killing to release the raw emotion and energy that came with our youth. The solution: sex, drugs, and alcohol. All of which cost money.

Because we were now working out of a base, sex was made readily available by the ever-present Vietnamese business entrepreneurs. With the road construction operations bringing an even larger concentration of marines to Phu Lac, many villagers were becoming very wealthy. One Vietnamese family set up a portable house of prostitution, or skivvy house as they were called, just outside of the gate. There was a mama-san and papa-san for administration, a brother or baby-san who solicited clients, and a daughter who served as the prostitute. Occasionally other young women from surrounding villages would come in to help with the overload of clients. With close to a hundred marines rotating through on a daily basis, at five dollars each, there was enough money for everyone. No doubt much of that money supported the Communist effort.

Then there were the drugs. If the hard drugs had been available, there would likely have been a major drug problem. For us, the primary drug was reefer. The only problem reefer presented was the possibility of it running out. Most of the drugs came out of Da Nang or other major cities, so the further away, the greater the cost. But it wasn't bad. Two dollars for a ten pack rather than one dollar. The returning wounded and scout-dog handlers were also suppliers.

Finally, there was alcohol. Beer was plentiful. Each man was rationed two beers per day. They would often stash unused supplies or unclaimed rations. Whiskey was cheap as well. It was brought in by the entrepreneurial marines who frequently traveled in-country. It sold for about $2.50 a fifth, about double the price at the PX, but still reasonable.

Second Platoon was now doing short perimeter patrols and then serving nightly guard duty around the perimeter of the base. These patrols rarely resulted in enemy contact, so we became very lax. Prior to this day's patrol, the squad decided to have a smoke off. So the seven of us, me, Sherman, Sally, Butler, Woody, Greer, Jackson, and even Donahue, contributed to the eighty-five-joint pile. These were no average joints. The diameter and length almost equaled a manufactured cigarette. The contestants would have one minute to smoke the joint down to a quarter inch. Failure to do so would result in a disqualification. The current record of ten joints in succession was set by Ellis.

The lung condition of these twenty- to twenty-one-year-old marines following months of chain-smoking reefer and cigarettes was like that of a fifty-year-old. The average was four joints; some reached five. Woody was the smallest in the group. At 115 pounds, he may have been the smallest marine ever. Despite the odds, he decided to be the big man. He was not only going to smoke his seventh joint, but he would do it with two drags. It was the perfect betting opportunity and a challenge to the little man, who had nothing to gain except his manly pride and a good high. That was all the motivation he needed. Everyone stepped back to give him room.

He easily finished half the joint with the first drag, and then he prepared for the finish. Woody planted his feet, exhausted the air from his lungs, pinched his nose, and took a drag strong enough to change wind direction. The end of the joint turned a glowing bright red and then turned to ash. Once half the joint was gone, he lowered his head and remained motionless, appearing to have passed out in the standing position. Smoke seemed to be slowly escaping from every orifice in his head. Soon his head was surrounded by a thick, pungent cloud. "That don't count!" Sherman protested. "You have to keep the smoke in, and there is a half inch left."

As acting squad leader, I was to serve as judge, so I made the ruling. "Since there was no prior agreed-upon rule to it being a two-drag smoke, he can finish the joint in one more drag if he can hold the smoke," I officially announced. There was a slight protest, but the challenge continued. This time Woody was even more determined.

Again he exhausted the air from his lungs and took a long pull on the last half of the joint. It disintegrated like the fuse on a stick of dynamite. His frail chest swelled up like a bullfrog, and his eyes bulged and then rolled back into his head. There was some concern that he was about to explode like a steam broiler. Sensing he was in distress, Butler was about to squeeze him around the torso to grant some relief, but he was thrashing his arms so wildly that he posed a threat to anyone coming near.

The determination he demonstrated is what creates legends. Not one whiff of smoke escaped. He did, however, let out a fart so loud that it would have caused buffalos to stampede.

He then dropped to the ground on all fours, gasping for air. He had given all he had. Slowly he raised his head. His hair seemed to have grown an inch, and his skin appeared indigo-blue. "Damn!" he finally said, wiping away saliva and mucus. "That was some good shit."

"You the man," commented the doubting Sherman as he paid off his bet. Under normal circumstances the intoxicated men would have lain down for a good long sleep, but this certainly wasn't normal circumstances. "OK," I announced, "let's get this patrol over." We picked up our gear and staggered off to work.

We were a classic example of the wrong way to go on patrol. Drunks strolling the neighborhood would be the best comparison. We stopped at the first checkpoint about five hundred yards outside the perimeter. After checking in over the radio, we proceeded to the second. Then after setting a defensive perimeter, we sat down to rest.

Conditions quickly change in combat. Without warning, a faint sound of an AK-47 followed by a round pecking a chip from a nearby tree was heard. A sniper had targeted us. In the blink of an eye, we seemly disappeared into the surrounding brush. Combat veterans possess a sixth sense that allows them to react and analyze. After the first shot, we had already drawn a rough estimate of the sniper's position. The sniper had missed his best and likely only opportunity, but he was determined to get a kill. Concluding perhaps that we were hiding, he fired a second shot in an attempt at flushing us out. A seasoned sniper would have realized that our controlled reaction was a sign of experience and would have been long gone. But he fired once more at an unseen target, only to discover the quarry he was searching for had been searching for him. We were only a few yards away when he revealed himself with the fatal third shot.

Expendable and Necessary

The sniper was blasted like a treed raccoon with a volley of M16 gunfire. His body was momentarily wedged in the tree, but it was jarred loose by the high-volume rounds that caused his torso to jerk about and ripped his clothes to shreds. When he landed, a few more rounds were pumped into him by members from another patrol that joined the hunt. His head was nearly severed, and his limbs were attached primarily by tendons, making him barely recognizable as human. It would take close inspection and some imagination to determine this was likely a young Viet Cong, perhaps twelve or thirteen years of age. The young soldier had learned a valuable lesson. Unfortunately for him, he didn't live long enough to apply it.

Now sober, we continued the patrol. Another squad came to retrieve the body. Later we returned to the base without sustaining any casualties. Another typical day in combat.

The road construction continued, as did the deaths of the men protecting the work crew. The best way to avoid becoming overwhelmed by the loss of life was to focus on the men in our immediate squad or platoon. But we were touched by the loss of Preacher, who had been moved to Third Platoon. There was some dispute over whether he was killed by friendly fire or a mortar fired by the NVA, but he was just as dead in either case.

I acknowledged and regretted being hard on Preacher after finding him praying instead of fighting at the Alamo, I did admire him for his convictions. Preacher never wavered in his attempts to convert anyone he came in contact with to Christianity. "All actions," he would proclaim, "should be in the name of the Lord." Faith-based justification for killing, I concluded, was rife with contradictions.

Eventually the Liberty Road project came to an end. Whether it was worth it or not could never be answered by the men who survived. Only those who had paid the ultimate sacrifice, their life, could truly answer that. The survivors would certainly have emotions stirred anytime they rode over, walked down, or flew over it, but an "attaboy" was the most the colonel would give. The politics of combat didn't recognize peons for bravery; they usually had to die to be celebrated. The overall success was attributed to the regimental commander, Colonel whatever-his-name-was. The men were informed that they were required to secure the completed highway for the colonel to ride triumphantly down. That rankled many of us who felt he was taking credit for the blood, sweat, and tears we had shed. This was a man most had rarely seen. We were, however, motivated by the four extra beers we would be given at the completion of the ceremony.

We were ordered to get fresh haircuts, close shaves, and clean clothes. Then we were loaded into trucks and taken to drop-off points along the road. After making certain no enemy forces were in the immediate vicinity, we were placed at twenty-yard intervals in two-man positions. Patrols were also roving the area with attack helicopters flying overhead. Security was on full alert.

Down the road came a procession of armored vehicles. Stone-faced staff NCOs and staff officers glared at the men as they passed. They looked like guard dogs posed to strike. We were instructed to honor the distinguished procession with a crisp salute as they passed. Finally the colonel passed.

He looked just as the men had anticipated: arrogant, detached, and full of himself. He looked like a board had been shoved up his ass. With the men down on the road and him riding high in his vehicle, he could further humiliate us by looking down at us. But he would have looked down on us even if he were in Death Valley and we were on top of a mountain. It was hot, we were hungry, and we now had to make the long march back to the base. All the way many grumbled about what an asshole he was.

When we got to the base, the gunnery sergeant called a hastily assembled formation. Everyone was excited as we anticipated the cold beer ration. We were thoroughly disappointed.

"All right," he bellowed, "who the fuck gave the colonel the finger?" The marines were surprised and delighted, struggling to contain their laughter. The gunnery sergeant repeated himself. "I want to know, what motherfucking dickhead had the nerve to flip the finger to a United States Marine Corps colonel? Someone from our platoon did," he said. "The colonel saw it."

He searched the marines' faces for a response he surely knew would never come. "OK," he said, "since no one is willing to come forward, you will all suffer the consequences. The beer rations you were expecting will be distributed among the men in Headquarters Company." Again we gave no response. The lack of response was the collective agreement that it was worth the four-beer ration.

Before dismissing us, the gunnery sergeant made a puzzling last comment. "Whoever the man, he was more of a marine than all of you put together."

"Yes sir, Gunnery Sergeant!" the men shouted when dismissed.

Later that day I got some good news. The out-of-country R and R I had requested long ago was approved. I would be leaving for Bangkok. "The motherfuckers could have given it to me a week earlier," I complained. But I knew the delay was intentional. I had no doubt they were waiting for a break in the action. They had never given me a break. Why would they start now?

CHAPTER 25

Break Time, a Time in Paradise August 1969

▲ ▲ ▲

BANGKOK HAD BECOME THE BLACK serviceman's paradise. When given a choice of one of four R and R destinations, it was most often number one.

The next morning I picked up my orders and collected my accumulated pay. Nearly $500, just over the required amount needed to qualify for an out-of-country R and R. The officer on duty gave me the standard warning against taking drugs into or out of a foreign country. Therefore, I had to smoke as much as possible on the short walk to the supply tent where I would store my war gear. A marine could trust his buddies with everything he had, including his life. Everything, that is, but his drug stash. It is not that they would intentionally steal; they would intend to pay it back. But intentions don't have a time limit, so they often go unfulfilled. So I tucked that away with the rest of my joints and hoped they would be there when I returned. There was half-day travel time each way and five actual days and nights in Bangkok. The clock was counting down.

Then I boarded a chopper for Da Nang. Once there, I went straight to an awaiting plane. When a frontline marine rifleman is given five days out of combat, there is little if any layover time. Within hours I was at the airport in Thailand. After checking all the arriving servicemen's orders, a military liaison briefed us. Next, I, along with the other men, boarded a bus that would take us to our randomly selected hotels.

Expendable and Necessary

The ride offered an adjustment period. It took a while to accept the fact that I didn't have to concern myself with being shot at any moment. I was still in Southeast Asia, but this country was not consumed with war. The country, more specifically, the city, was consumed with creating pleasure. For the next five days, I was free to do anything my heart desired with the exception of going home. Thailand was utopia.

Stepping off the bus, I was greeted by baby-san (a little boy). "Come see me after you check in, and I'll tell you what you want to know," he yelled to me as I passed. I gave him a nod and went to the desk. After paying the thirty-five-dollar room rent, I was given a key and immediately took my clothes to my room. Not wanting to waste a minute of the precious time, I immediately returned to the lobby. Baby-san was waiting with a young Thai girl hoping to be chosen. She was an attractive girl, but I decided not to take the first available partner. It would make me appear too needy, so I respectfully declined. That was no problem. She immediately approached the next arriving potential client.

"OK, you need herb?" Baby-San asked, holding out a fifty pack. I gave him twenty dollars. "Now me take you to driver, and he take you to look at boo-koo girls," he said, motioning me along. When we reached the driver standing outside, I gave Baby-San an extra five dollars for his help.

The driver then introduced himself and offered his services. "Me drive you anywhere you want to go day or night," he said, "for thirty-five dollars." I paid him and then told him I wanted to go get a girl. The driver escorted me into the cab, and we headed to a club.

Along the way he told me what to expect. First he asked how much I gave the boy for smokes and a tip. When I told him, he laughed and informed me that the boy would have been happy with half that amount. "When we get to club," he told me, "you pick out any girl you want. Pay Mama-San sixty dollars, and the girl will live with you all week. You don't have to give girl more money," he went on, "unless you want to. Mama-San pays her." I sat back and enjoyed the short drive. Bangkok is a beautiful city. Along the way I could see servicemen and their Thai dates strolling along the street arm in arm. They were shopping, eating, kissing, playfully touching, all the behavior displayed by young couples in love, if only for a brief period. But I wasn't looking for love. Love took time, and without a future, it would likely end in pain. My future was measured in seconds, minutes, and, on rare occasions, hours. Now that I was safe, I could plan as far as five days. My needs were basic: a place to sleep, sex, drugs, and a good meal.

Finally we arrived at a seedy part of town. We went into a club filled with couples dancing and drinking with single women sitting in groups or alone. All were watching me and smiling, trying to catch my eye. The selection process, for me, was simple. Pick the one who showed the most enthusiasm. I wanted a date with enough energy to match mine. That quality would later come back to haunt me. The one I chose was a ball of energy. She rarely stopped laughing and talking from the moment I approached her. Even more annoying for me was the fact that she spoke very little English. I suspected she was sometimes laughing at and talking about me to the other girls. But after I made the selection and paid Mama-San, I understood that it was like we were married, for better or worse.

I was also in for a costly surprise. She moved in with me with nothing. She needed a toothbrush, a comb, lipstick, underwear, shoes, and clothes. I had to buy everything for her for the next five days, including food. She took a big slice from my meager resources. But she was helpful when it came to tipping advice for the service personnel. They preferred American products over money. The cleaning lady was given Safe Guard soap, and the doorman, Kool cigarettes. But her motive might have been to keep more of the money so I could spend it on her.

In spite of her constant talking, the relationship was tolerable. However, she knew exactly how much money I had with me, and she seemed determined to get me to spend it all. She ordered overpriced meals at restaurants and overpriced drinks at bars. There was no doubt she was getting a cut from the owners. But I wasn't concerned about saving money, just stretching it over the five-day period, so I overlooked it. I did, however, enjoy going to the zoo and fishing, activities suggested by the driver. This seemed to bore her. She liked to stay in the clubs. The only observable friction came when she asked about the war, which I vehemently chose not to discuss.

On the evening of the third day, we returned to the club where she worked. Motown sounds filled the room. Just as before, there were couples dancing and drinking, with the newly arriving servicemen searching for a date. This time I noticed a woman onstage dancing alone in the spotlight whom I had not seen before. She was different from the slender-built Asian women. This was a robust woman with African features and rhythm. The brothers in the room tried to disguise their fascination from their dates, but she clearly had their attention. She especially had my interest. I was mesmerized by her. I hadn't seen a sister in months. Momentarily, I forgot about being in Southeast Asia. It was like I was back in the hood. The woman seemed to possess so much confidence that none dared approach her.

Number-one girl

I forgot that I was with a date, and one who proved very possessive. "What the fuck you look at her for?" she yelled, rising to her feet. I was unmoved and continued to stare at the dancer. That angered her even more. She now seemed poised to strike me, a move that would have evoked a quick and certain retaliation. The bouncers, whose job it was to protect the girls, were moving to the area. The brothers were responding in kind. Clearly they would have joined the fray. The atmosphere was tense. The dancing sister with an uncomfortable smile tried to draw attention back to her with more provocative moves. Mama-San yelled something to the girl and defused a potentially volatile confrontation.

"Let's go!" she yelled, walking out, expecting me to follow. When I didn't, she shouted a stream of obscenities in English and Thai and walked out. The dancing sister flashed an uncomfortable smile and continued to dance. Feeling humiliated, dejected, and disappointed, I left the club.

The driver was outside waiting. He immediately ran up to me. "What happened?"

"We just broke up," I answered, giving no explanation.

The driver threw up his hands in desperation. "Do you want another girl?" he asked.

"Sure," I responded. The driver led me back into the club. I waited at the edge of the stage while the driver talked to Mama-San. After a brief conversation with Mama-San, he returned.

"Mama-San no let GIs butterfly [have two women], but she say you can pick new woman."

I smiled broadly and then pointed to the sister onstage. "I want her," I said in no uncertain terms.

The driver seemed shocked that I would even ask for her. "Noooo!" he said, eyes wide open. "She number-one girl, half Thai and half black. All soul brothers want her, but Mama-San always say no. Maybe she let you have her for one hour." An offer I quickly dismissed.

The driver pleaded for me to drop the request, but I would not relent, so the driver reluctantly took the request to Mama-San. She rejected the request immediately. In fact, she walked away from the driver, refusing to even discuss it. He begged me to make another selection. But I turned and walked out of the club, proving to be just as stubborn as Mama-San. The driver continued an attempt at persuading me on the ride back to the hotel, but to no avail.

When I returned to my hotel room, it was about one o'clock. For the first time, while lying on the bed alone on the third day of R and R, I began to question my decision. *When is my life going to get easy?* I thought. I was beginning to consider that I might be the source of my troubles. Slowly I drifted off to sleep. After an hour or so, there was a knock at the door. I suspected that, after the commotion at the club, a fellow serviceman would stop to ask questions.

When I opened the door, the girl I had dismissed was standing there, still agitated. "Look!" she said. "No more bullshit from you. I stay, or I go forever. Then you have no girl. What you want?" she said, arms folded.

"I want you to go!" I said, emphasizing each word. She flew into a rage.

She went to the drawers and threw the contents on the floor. Then she went to the closet and did the same. She did, however, keep the clothes I had brought her. At that point I'd had clearly had enough. I walked to the door and ordered her out. She could tell by my demeanor that the confrontation was about to become physical, and she was at a noticeable size and strength disadvantage. So she left, propelled by a shove from me. After one last kick on the door, she stomped away, cursing all the way down the hall. I lay back down, attempting to calm myself.

Around four in the morning, there was another knock at the door. I was set for a confrontation, believing that the girl had returned. But it was the driver, still trying to work things out. "I talk to Mama-San," he said. "She no give you money, but you can still get new girl."

"Can I get the sister?" I asked.

"No," the driver repeated several times. "She bring boo-koo money to club." He went on to explain that on rare occasions she turned tricks for a lot of money, but her job was to bring in the clients.

"Thanks," I said while shaking the driver's hand, "but I would rather just be by myself." The driver threw up his hands and left.

Finally I dozed off for the night, awakened around eleven in the morning by another knock at the door. Half awake, I stumbled toward the door. I was agitated, hungover, and prepared to give someone a piece of my mind. I jerked the door open to see one of the most memorable sights in my event-filled life. It was the dancing lady in question from the club. I stood frozen with disbelief.

She entered the room with an air of complete confidence, looking me up and down, slowly circling. Each time I turned to face her, she would suddenly stop until I would turn away, indicating that she was the one in charge, not me. When she was directly behind me, she began to quiz me in broken English, like a skilled interrogator.

"So you soul brother that wants me?"

"Yes," I answered without turning around. She continued to circle and talk.

"Why do you want me and no other girl?"

"Because you're a sister, and I want a soul sister."

"You no like Thai girls?" she snapped.

"Thai girls are beautiful, but I would prefer a woman who looks like me."

"How you know I'm half black?"

"I know a sister when I see one."

Then she continued the interrogation.

"You married?" she asked me.

"No."

"You got baby-sans?"

"No."

"You got number-one girl at home?"

"Yes."

"Then why you want me?"

"Because I may never live to get back home, and you may be as close to her as I'm gonna get."

"Where from in America?" she asked.

"Cleveland."

"Cleveland," she shouted. "Jim Brown number-one soul brother in Cleveland." I laughed at the connection. She returned the smile and then continued the interrogation. "Are you marine?"

"Yes, a rifleman."

"Oh, so you kill VC and NVA."

"When I have to," I answered apologetically. "I would rather be back in Cleveland with my number-one woman Elaine and working on my job."

The sister abruptly stopped the interrogation and flashed a broad smile. Then, to my surprise, she turned and opened the door. Instead of leaving, she reached outside and picked up a suitcase that was just outside. I must have passed the test. I reached for an embrace, a prelude to closing the deal, when she halted me with a stiff arm. "Slow down, soul brother," she said with a smile. "Me boo-koo hungry. Let's go get food."

"OK," I said, because I was hungry too. Then I went to the closet to retrieve the remainder of the money I'd stashed. It was gone. Frantically I searched, turning all my pockets out, pulling out drawers, and looking under my mattress, hoping I would discover money I had hidden from myself.

Finally, I collapsed against the wall, dropped my head, and stated the obvious. "The girl took all my money." The sister seemed as disappointed as I was. She asked for a cigarette and sat down so we could figure the next move. I went to my cigarette drawer and immediately realized she had also taken my cigarettes.

"How many days you got left?" she asked.

"Two," I answered.

There was a moment of awkward silence until the sister began to clarify my rapidly deteriorating situation.

"You have two days," she said. Then, holding up a finger each time to stress a point, she continued, "You got no money, no cigarettes, no girl, and no food." Again there was an awkward silence. Changing fortunes had taken me on such a roller coaster of emotions over the last twelve hours that I wasn't sure how I was feeling. I could only laugh. She also laughed at my situation. "What you do now, tell Mama-San?" she asked.

"No," I answered. "I probably deserved it."

At that point I was sure she would leave, so I prepared to thank her as cordially as possible, in spite of my disappointment. To my surprise she didn't. "Come on," she said, walking out the door, motioning for me to follow.

We passed other couples as we exited through the lobby. The sister was an attention grabber. All eyes followed us. The brothers would flash the Black Power salute while their dates would playfully punch them for doing so. The driver opened the door for us, and we drove off. She explained to the driver the predicament I was in with the other date having stolen my money. When he saw how well I had accepted the situation, he gave me a comforting pat on the back. He then asked if I would purchase some American whiskey for him at the base PX for the reduced price. I was happy to do so. From there, we went to another part of the city. It seemed more upscale from the parts I had seen. With no money in my pocket, I was uncomfortable. I assumed the Americans with dates were officers or staff NCOs, because they looked older and seemed much more subdued in their behavior. I certainly stood out, as did my date. I can't overstate how much an attention getter she was. They must have wondered why the hell she was with me.

The man in charge, possibly the owner or manager, seemed to know her. He gave the waiter a nod. Otherwise I might have been asked to leave. In broken English she told me to order my meal, and then she ordered hers. Immediately after ordering, she went into an office followed by the manager. Shortly after, she returned with money in her hand, some of which she placed on the table. It was obvious this was a working lunch for her, and it was just as obvious to the people watching. That only boosted my status with the people in the room. After finishing our lunch, we left the room with all eyes following. I decided to ask no questions and roll with whatever came along.

While servicemen were attracted to the sister, the Thai women showed nothing but animosity. That possibly explained why she chose to frequent parts of the city with fewer working girls. In fact, we were in an area where the locals congregated, which put me around people who didn't take kindly to men defiling their women.

When we exited the cab and approached a group of Thais sitting at a table near the center of the busy crowd, the men sitting there seemed to look at me with resentment, the children with wonder. There were several other Americans around, but none would dare approach that table, and neither would I.

The sister motioned for me to stop; then she approached alone. She was talking to the people at the table, while the driver talked to people in the crowd. They talked in their native language, so I had no idea what they were saying. I could tell by the way they looked at me and laughed that they were being told my story. In the meantime, the driver was handing two of the fifths of liquor to the man who was clearly in charge. Suddenly, the leader of the group shouted, "Jim Brown," and then flashed a broad smile and motioned me over. Although Jim Brown lived and played football in Cleveland, that was the extent of my knowledge of the man. But they must have assumed all black men from Cleveland knew each other. So I went with it. "Yes, I know Jim," I boasted.

It was easy to lie to people who spoke another language.

I was offered a seat at the table, which was full of food and Thai liquor, both of which were awful. The liquor was horrible and burned my stomach all the way down. They were impressed by the fact that I could drink it at all, and so was I. The sister came to my rescue when she began pouring my drinks from the bottles of the American whiskey I brought at the PX.

The soup consisted of meats, vegetables, and spices unfamiliar to a brother from Cleveland. I didn't ask what it was. If I had, I likely wouldn't have eaten it. When a man has no money to buy food, he has little choice. The truth is that money couldn't have brought me a seat at that table or the hospitality the people were showing me. When we left, the people embraced me as if I were one of their own. We returned to the hotel for private time, where she showed me why she was the most desired woman in the city. That evening, we went to an upscale restaurant where the owner and staff obviously knew her. She was treated like royalty.

For a period of time, she left the table. While she was gone, I was supplied with food and drinks, which I readily accepted. When she returned, she had money. It was obvious it was another working dinner. We finished the evening at a club. Surprisingly, the club girl didn't seem to be enjoying herself, so we left early and returned to the hotel. Sometime during the night, she must have left. I was concerned she wouldn't return, but, to my surprise, she returned around noon the next day.

That final day proved to be the best of all. After a quick lunch, she asked what I would like to do. "I would like to see some boxing," I stated, believing that was the one wish she couldn't fulfill. But I underestimated her. She took me to a Thai kickboxing match held in an outdoor arena. It was free entertainment with a ringside seat. Next, we went to a small farm on a river where we met an acquaintance of hers who owned a motorboat. He gave us a high-speed ride down the canal. I behaved like a child fulfilling a fantasy.

The final attraction was the one I would most remember. She took me to a snake farm that housed the exotic reptiles from the Far East. The owner's young daughter played among the enormous boa constrictors. On a dare, I wrapped a fifty-pound boa constrictor around my neck, and the owner presented me with a photo to show my friends, who would likely doubt the story. In spite of being broke, for me, the last two days couldn't have been better. Perhaps it was a testament to the phrase "The best things in life are free."

I didn't understand why she was doing so much for me when I had nothing to offer, but I could tell she seemed to enjoy those days as much as I. It is quite possible that she got little time away from the smoke-filled clubs and enjoyed getting out and mingling among her friends. But all things come to an end. The following day I would leave. Early that next day, she accompanied me to the bus stand where I would wait for the bus that drove me to the airport. While waiting for the bus that was making the rounds to all the hotels picking up servicemen, we would occasionally glance at one another and smile but spoke very little. This was a contrast to the other couples who were embracing, groping, and making promises they couldn't possibly keep.

As the bus approached, she called me her number-one marine and said she would remember me. I thanked her for everything. Then she said something that surprised me. She advised me to return home to my number-one girl, marry, and have boo-koo baby-sans. Next she repeated a phrase the brothers always used. "You owe it to yourself." I was so taken aback that I was unable to respond.

Once on board, I looked back and could see her standing alone watching the bus pull away while the other bar girls were walking away talking and laughing among themselves. For the first time, I realized how alone the Thai sister really was. She wasn't looking for a lover. She was looking for a friend. Perhaps I did have something to offer.

Shortly thereafter I was at the airport and on a plane back to Vietnam.

CHAPTER 26

Razor Back Mountains
August 1969

▲ ▲ ▲

ONCE IN DA NANG, I was transported by jeep to the helicopter landing pad. I shared the ride with another returning marine from my regiment of Hispanic descent.

"What's up?" I asked, initiating the greeting. "My name is Harris; I'm from Gulf Company."

"Oh, you're Harris," he said. "You're the O-H-Ten brother from Gulf Company." I was shocked that a marine from another company would know me, and I was about to ask the obvious question when my Hispanic friend explained. "We know who the bushmasters are." I humbly thanked him for the acknowledgment.

Once on the helicopter the noise level made it impossible for us to hold a conversation. When it landed, there was a jeep nearby. The driver asked our destination, then offered us a ride. "Gulf Company," I told him.

"Hotel," the Hispanic marine called out. The driver acknowledged us and drove off.

I wasn't sure how someone from another company knew me, and I wasn't sure how to ask.

"You know, they say you're a little crazy," the marine confided in me.

"Ten months in the bush would make anybody crazy," I laughed. "Did you say you were from H Company?"

"Yes."

"Yes."

"Oh, that's the company where a marine killed a VC with a knife."

"Yes, that was me. That's why I got R and R the first month in-country."

"No shit," I said in astonishment. "And you think I'm crazy? You know," I went on, "it's a lot safer to shoot a motherfucker than to put your hands on him. You can get ripped apart by a man fighting for his life," I said, trying to impart some hard-earned wisdom.

"I agree, but I dropped my rifle." The marine laughed.

"Oh!" I said, trying to envision the feeling of dropping your weapon in a firefight. The marine went on to explain.

"We were assaulting on line when I stepped in a spider trap [a man-made covered hole used for hiding], and my weapon flew out of my hand."

"They usually don't dig those holes too big; that must have been tight," I said.

"No shit, we were both squeezed in there."

"You were in that little-ass hole with a VC fighting with you?"

"I was fighting to get out!" he laughed. "Then," he went on, "I remembered a knife I kept strapped to my leg. I grabbed it and used it."

"Well, I'm glad you made it," I said as he exited the jeep. "Take care of yourself." We exchanged the Black Power salute, and the marine was taken to his company's headquarters.

The jeep driver, who had remained silent, turned to me as I exited the jeep and began to speak. "Sorry about your partner; I heard he was a good brother." I thanked him for his concern, and we exchanged the power handshake. Then I went to the supply tent and picked up my gear. Once I joined my squad, we talked about my R and R experience. But I kept much of it to myself. I didn't think they would believe me anyway.

The next morning we started the next mission. The two companies would be transported in a truck convoy to An Hoa, where the mission would begin. This would be the first time we would travel the full length of the road we had fought so hard to protect. Everyone anticipated emotions would be high, and we were right.

As the sun began to rise the following morning, the convoy departed on the five-mile trip. The men were silent but full of pride. Each was processing his own unique experience while the convoy moved on. The feeling was different from the ones in the past. As an assault force, our job was generally to take a position and then move on. There was nothing to bear witness to what we had done. Now we had a victory we could see and touch. It was like a part of Liberty Road belonged to us. But it was sad. The ghosts of the fallen marines were everywhere, as were the ghosts of our sworn and committed enemy. One would wonder, could they now coexist, when they could not do so in life?

There were also visual signs of what had taken place. Blood that had yet to be washed away by the upcoming torrential rains, holes dug for defensive positions, rocks and boulders that served as protection, embankments that men had hidden in. It all brought back vivid memories.

Other marines from the regiment were now guarding the winding road. One marine on the convoy called out to them as they passed. "Take care of it," he yelled. "Some good marines died for it."

"We will," the marine on the road replied, "to the death." We knew that was no idle promise.

Finally, we arrived safely at An Hoa. The company was assembled and briefed for the next objective, which concerned an army fort about eighty miles from An Hoa. The fort was built in an open valley. Moving away from the valley was a thin area of jungle surrounded by a ridgeline of steep mountains. Some areas on the crest of this long mountain range were only a few feet across. Because of the appearance, the mountain range was called the "razorbacks." To the far side of the razorbacks moving away from the base was a triple-canopy jungle.

The NVA used the situation to launch attacks on the fort. They could hide in the triple canopy, move to the ridgeline, and fire rockets at the base. They would also use the lower band of jungle to conceal observation posts. Marine recon teams were concealed in the area, and they confirmed there was a heavy concentration of NVA surrounding the base. Constant barrages from the base did little to stop the attacks. The troops were well dug in and concealed. It would take a ground assault to be effective.

Our mission was to find and then kill or capture them. At the very least, we were to drive the NVA out.

The obstacles we faced when operating in the mountains were numerous, more than we had faced before. It was August, and the temperatures could get as high as 120 degrees. We also faced the torrential monsoon rains. We would be fighting in an arena filled with blistering heat, rain, lead, sweat, and blood.

The good side was that we would have shade, hiding places, and water from the streams. The downside was that the enemy also had those same advantages and had a much better knowledge of the area. It was likely the Vietnamese had already dug a network of tunnels offering them escape and supply routes. The jungle was too thick for a supply chopper, so we would certainly be at a disadvantage when it came to getting our supplies replenished. Our first task was to capture a high ground.

A plateau approximately two miles from the ridgeline was selected as a base of operation. Offshore gunships would pound the area. After a short barrage, fighter pilots would drop the one-thousand-pound bombs. This was done to drive the enemy out of that area and to clear a spot for a light artillery base to be established. It was time, so the gunships began their task.

Miles away we, along with other infantrymen from the Fifth Marines, were assembling. Each platoon and squad was assigned a helicopter. There would be as many as twenty transport helicopters involved in the assault. Each chopper had a three-man crew: a pilot, copilot, and gunner. While we were assembling, the attack began. We were informed that the fighter pilots had begun striking in strategic spots. The work of the grunts would be up close and personal. We would be angels of death, killing anything we found alive. Gulf Company would be a part of the first wave. Timing would be critical.

The pilot gave his passengers the thumbs-up before beginning his assent. The bright morning sun was nearly blotted out by the hawklike machines. We appeared like a flock of giant birds moving in a migratory pattern. The men on board would constantly shift positions, trying to familiarize themselves with the area and direction of travel. Finally, we spotted the army base. The aerial view matched the description we were given. We were now approaching the plateau, which was now more pronounced following the bombing. Our arrival was expected; anyone for miles around could not miss the flying green dragons. We could not anticipate the reception we would get.

Once the wheels touched down, we began to exit the chopper. It looked like predatory creatures had given birth to a litter of devouring offspring. The job of the first wave was to establish an outer perimeter. We rushed into the triple canopy cutting a path with machetes, being mindful that the enemy could be hiding every step of the way. The short travel distance was difficult, and we encountered no resistance. After an exhausting four-hour push, we reached our first objective.

Command ordered the platoon to send a squad up to the top of the razorback mountain line to establish an observation post. Sergeant Nato assigned me the task.

Suddenly, I had become the squad leader again. I realized the importance of holding that strategic position. I just didn't feel I should be the one to do it. So after the usual protest, I set out with Second Squad to make the difficult climb. The sun was beginning to set, so in spite of the difficult climb, the pace had to be fast. The fear, as we scaled the vertical wall, was enemy soldiers suddenly appearing and shooting down at us. We reached the top just before sunset. The crest was narrow, never more than four feet at any point, stretching for about a mile. The drop on the far side was as steep as the one we had climbed. It was a well-worn crest obviously used by the enemy to observe the clearly visible army fort below.

The eagle's-eye view was stunning. There was enough daylight to illuminate the entire valley, and no enemy troops were visible. We reported that back to the command post. At that time, light artillery had also arrived at the mobile command post, along with hundreds of US personnel. That made the marines on the razorback a crucial part of the defense. I assigned two-man positions every twenty yards, with myself at the center and Jackson, the radioman, at my side.

We dug potholes to hold us to the side of the hill, close enough to the crest to allow us to look over the opposite side. Once satisfied we were secure, we set in for the night. Sherman left the position he shared with Sally to join me. He had concerns that he wanted to share. Because of the isolation, extended visibility, and illumination from the pop-ups routinely fired from the fort, we could talk safely.

Suddenly, we heard two distant thumps coming from the mobile artillery base. We knew the guns were finding their range. We could interpret the sound indicated a round was heading toward us, and it was going to fall short. "Jump over the side," I yelled. As we threw themselves to the opposite side of the hill, two rounds slammed into the hill. The concussion was hard enough to jar some of the squad members loose, causing them to slide down, scrambling to regain a foothold. Flames wrapped the mountain crest. It felt like the surge of heat you would feel if you opened an oven door.

"Check fire! Check fire!" I shouted over the radio. Jackson then took over the communication while I checked the condition of the squad members. They were shaken but OK. The artillerymen acknowledged the mistake and corrected the range. Once we calmed down, Sherman and I continued our conversation.

"We face more danger from friendly fire than the enemy," Sherman told me.

"I know," I responded. "I think Nato would use friendly fire to take out the brothers if he could."

"Hell yes!" Sherman shouted. "Look around you. We're a squad of brothers plus one, and he must have pissed somebody off. We've got the marine artillery to our south, army artillery to our north, and the enemy below. When the shooting begins, we are caught in the middle. That's why Nato sent us," Sherman said, throwing up his hands.

"I know. I got to stop him," I said. "But if that motherfucker is shot, they're gonna check my weapon. Then again, he might be just following orders. That's why I think hard about everything they tell us to do. If it doesn't sound right, I ain't doing it. They'll just have to court-martial my black ass."

"And they probably will," Sherman added.

"I think the best thing to do is to leave that racist motherfucker out there when he needs help," I concluded.

"That sounds good to me," Sherman said with a sly grin.

Simultaneously we noticed something in the valley below.

"What's that?"

In the valley, there was movement only we could see. It was a place obstructed from the view of the fort by distance, thick forestation, and hills. It was also blocked from the view of the mobile marine artillery base by the mountains. What had started as a single light became two, then a dozen. It looked a swarm of fireflies.

"What do you think it is?" Sherman whispered to me.

"I don't know. It could be villagers getting away," I replied softly. "Or it could be an enemy unit clearing out."

We watched a while longer in silence. The whole squad was peering down as well. Soon the lights formed a line and began to move west, moving under the cover of darkness, away from the Americans.

"What do you think we should do?" Sherman asked.

"If we report movement, artillery from the army fort will fire blindly, probably blowing us off this mountain. Or artillery from the marines behind us will try to fire over this mountain, and they sure as hell will hit us. It's all about numbers. The colonel won't hesitate to sacrifice a squad for a hundred enemy kills. That's probably why we're here. Besides, if they hit the formation, they may be wiping out a friendly village. I'm tired of being used."

"You really think they see us as expendable?" Sherman asked.

"Some do, some don't, and most don't give a damn. I'll tell them when the lights get further away. They can do what they want with it." We sat silently monitoring the movement and eventually called it in. No action was taken. They likely didn't take us seriously.

The colonel kept his headquarters at the mobile artillery base in the Que Son Mountains. Three companies would stay there and continue to search and destroy any enemy troops in the area. He sent Hotel and Gulf

Companies on long-range patrols. Hotel Company was split into platoons, with Second Platoon heading west into the mountains.

The platoon commander, Lieutenant Storm, moved Second Squad closer to the center of the formation. Nato, who was the platoon sergeant, had passed control of the squad back to Corporal Roe.

We pressed forward into the rugged terrain. For several days we searched the mountains. We went up one side and then down the other. On the third day, Lieutenant Storm rolled out his familiar map, orientating himself. "That's it," he said, looking up from the base of the tallest hill in the area. "That's where we are going to settle in for the night."

With that, we began the long ascent. Just before nightfall, we made it. We went to the far side for a spectacular view of the valley below.

We began to dig in for the night. Respect for my experience, not my rank, gave me some options. I decided to man a position with Sherman on the outer perimeter. I generally preferred danger to being in proximity of officers and staff.

The lieutenant told us the French once had a fort in that particular valley. French military strategists had probably given a great deal of thought to the decision to place a fort there.

Perhaps the French, in a need to assemble a large concentration of men, decided the valley offered the most likely location. They may have scoffed at the idea that the Vietnamese could move the artillery needed, weighing thousands of pounds, to the tops of such steep mountains. In spite of the Vietnamese's small stature, the French had clearly underestimated the tenacity, ingenuity, and sheer will of the Vietnamese people.

In the words of PFC Sherman, who never received one moment of training in military strategy, "That was some dumb-ass shit. What the fuck could the French have been thinking? They knew the NVA would take the high ground, and eventually they would find them."

The following day, Hotel Company made contact. Word had filtered to us that Hotel Company had lost their company commander, Captain Marshal. After being promoted from lieutenant, he had extended his tour and was given a company to lead. He had gained respect and recognition among the men for his willingness to join them at the front. He didn't just talk the talk. He walked the walk. Unfortunately, it cost him his life.

It was a peaceful night, and I was awake for most of it, enjoying the starlit view. I figured it would have been highly unusual for the enemy to have scaled the steep mountain to attack us.

I was resting against a huge boulder as if I were on a throne overseeing the world below. Being a man with no religious convictions, I seemed to be having what might be interpreted as a religious experience.

When the sun came up, the lieutenant ordered Sergeant Nato to have the squad leaders assemble the men in preparation for the move to the next position.

It would be another cluster of smaller mountains. The range could clearly be seen from our current position, and it would be a strenuous march.

The captain, who was coordinating the movements from miles away, insisted that his commanders keep to a strict timetable. Second Squad would start out at the lead, so Roe assigned the men to a formation. All complied except for me. I was chipping away on the boulder I'd been leaning against all night, using the pointed end of my entrenching tool, ignoring the order to join the squad.

"Move out!" Lieutenant Storm ordered, but the lead squad never moved. They waited for me. Roe clearly couldn't get me to move, so Sergeant Nato pushed the men aside, rushing over to exert his authority.

The lieutenant couldn't see us, so he was unable to determine why the squad wasn't moving. He was growing angrier by the second. Then he moved close enough to see me continuing to chip at the boulder, ignoring Nato, who was now shouting in my ear. The combat-hardened marines in the platoon never broke from their defensive positions, so there was no cluster of men. But they were stretching their necks to see what was happening. I was normally composed, but this time I appeared to have lost it. I continued to scrape away on the boulder, oblivious to the confusion around me. It was clear it might take physical force to remove me from that spot. I continued scraping and chipping at the boulder.

Finally, the lieutenant went over and stood next to me. But to the surprise of those watching, he didn't order me to stop. Instead, he pulled his entrenching tool from his pack and joined in. The gunnery sergeant had come over and was now standing uncharacteristically patient, watching us in silence. When I completed my yet unknown project, I faced the lieutenant. "Thank you, sir!" I shouted out before executing a perfect military hand salute. The lieutenant smiled and returned the gesture. Then I returned to my squad. It was a moment that only someone aware of the history between us men could appreciate.

When the men passed the boulder, they could see what I was doing. I had found closure. There it was carved in stone, on a majestic mountain peak: a legacy to my friend, the day he departed this life.

CHAPTER 27

The Rescue
September 1969

▲ ▲ ▲

THE REGIMENT PROCEEDED WITH THE difficult task of searching the mountains. Occasionally we would come into a clearing or a mountaintop from which we could see for miles, but usually the visibility would range from one to fifty meters. The jungle is a place of beauty and deception. The existence of all life in the jungle depends on a delicate balance in which fortunes shift from being predator to prey.

Each climb was a challenge. Looking up from the valley, one felt overpowered. First, nature provided physical and mental struggles every step of the way. Second and even more important, enemy soldiers posed a deadly obstacle to those who dared venture forward. Quitting was always in one's mind. But if you made it to the top, there was a feeling of accomplishment. In a sense, it was a lot like life. Then, just as in life, you look for another mountain to climb, another challenge.

Scout dogs were often used to aid us in the exhausting searches. Ours didn't yield any results. His handler attributed his behavior to heat exhaustion. So a medevac chopper was called. Eventually we found a stream running down the mountain, and Lieutenant Storm decided that was a good place to stop for the night.

Seizing every opportunity to mentally escape the situation, the men decided to have a feast. Two cans of peaches were emptied into a pot, for dessert.

Then all the extra cans of food the men had been storing were thrown together for a communal meal. It tasted awful, but no one complained.

The pattern continued, search and search with no results. Sometimes an enemy patrol was spotted at a distance, but by the time we cut our way through the thick terrain to get to the location, the enemy had left. When we found Vietnamese families living in the mountains, they were questioned and released. For our platoon it was like a mountain-climbing expedition. After another exhaustive search of a particularly rocky mountain, we set up camp for the night. The captain was beginning to accept there were no enemies in those mountains.

The following morning the company was ordered to move to the valley below and then establish a safe zone that would enable a helicopter to land and supply the troops. During the forty-five-minute descent, we would cut a path through the thick vegetation down the mountain. It was as if we were creating a maze.

Second Platoon was to bring up the rear. While waiting our turn to join the slow troop movement, Rodriquez, from Fourth Squad, slipped and broke his leg on the rocks. He would have to be taken to the valley below so a medevac helicopter could land. At first the men attempted to carry him, but he was tall and heavily built. It proved difficult to carry him on the rugged terrain. The lieutenant decided to leave a squad on the hilltop and have a helicopter brought in with a harness and pull him up. Everyone else proceeded down.

It was a steep climb down, but since it was partially cleared from more wear, it now took thirty minutes to reach the bottom. We had at least twenty to thirty minutes before the extraction, so we could use the time to rest. I took the time to disassemble and clean my weapon. Ray, the machine gunner, and Jackson, his ammo humper, and Sally sat with me.

"What do you think about this whole operation?" Sally asked me.

"Well," I answered, continuing to clean my weapon, "we saw the enemy at the start, and from time to time there is contact. They must be around. Shit, they are probably watching us right now. I just think command overestimated how many there are."

Expendable and Necessary

"But where are the bodies?" Jackson asked. "We found blood trails that just stopped. So there must be tunnels, but with all the digging and probing, we should have found something."

"That's true," I said, recalling the massive troop movement we had seen. The conversation was interrupted by the sound of an approaching chopper. We watched as it hovered over the hilltop preparing to extract Rodriquez.

Suddenly, we heard the distinctive sound of AK-47s and SKS automatic weapons in the distance. Then there was a blast from the fifty-caliber machine guns as the helicopter gunner returned fire. The marines' heads turned in the direction of the firefight. The men scrambled for cover, unsure if the fight would extend to them. I scrambled as well, trying to reassemble my M16. My basic training served me well. I snapped and slid it together while keeping my eyes on the surroundings. Once done, I checked to see if all my magazines were loaded with ammunition and advised the others to do the same. Whatever was taking place in the distance, we were sure to become a part of it. After strapping on my bandolier and placing my helmet on, I rushed to the outer perimeter.

Fourth Squad, still on the top of the hill, was being attacked. The enemy had waited for the helicopter to approach before revealing themselves. Downing a helicopter was their ultimate goal. Lieutenant Storm decided to send the remainder of Second Platoon up to join the fight. Sergeant Nato would lead the effort. The fastest way up was through the narrow path that had been hacked through the thick canopy. This would require the men to charge most of the way in a single line. This was a necessary but dangerous tactical approach.

I took point. Resistance would be strong, requiring heavy firepower in front. So Crazy Ray, the platoon's best machine gunner, followed me. Jackson carried his machine-gun ammunition and provided cover for both Ray and me. Sergeant Nato would follow Jackson, then Donahue on radio. The remainder of the squad would fall behind. They were followed by Third Squad and finally First. Butler, the mortar leader, and Woody were also sent. They were positioned in the center of the column. There was enough experience and firepower to do an effective rescue. Unfortunately the weakest link was Sergeant Nato, the man in charge. He had neither the skill nor the confidence of the men to lead such a mission. But he was the platoon sergeant.

It took less than a minute for the men to organize. I alerted Ray and Jackson to the possibility that Sergeant Nato might take the opportunity to shoot me in the back. They assured me they would keep an eye on him. Once the order to move was given, the perilous trek began. First we entered double canopy where visibility was about fifteen yards. The trees, vines, and brush took ominous shapes. I had to focus to determine if I was looking at inanimate objects or a man waiting to kill me. The further I went, the closer I got to the fighting.

Then I entered the natural boundaries of the triple canopy where the visibility was only a few feet. It was so thick it formed a dark corridor, nearly blocking out the sun. It was like a deadly maze. Each turn could lead to a dead end or an awaiting enemy soldier. I faced the lonely, silent experience of a pointer, the feeling of being watched by a thousand eyes, the feeling that death was reaching out its icy cold fingers for my shoulders. Then, ahead, I could see an opening that would lead to a clearing. Faster, faster, I rushed, running toward the light. But when I burst into the clearing, I almost lost my life.

An enemy position was trained on that opening, anticipating our arrival. I was greeted by a burst of automatic fire.

The shots were not well aimed, so they were undoubtedly surprised by my sudden emergence. I recoiled as if an unseen lifeline had been attached to my body and was now stretched to its limit, causing me to be snatched backward away from the barrage of gunfire. They were close but delivered no direct hits.

Expendable and Necessary

My next move proved to be the right move. The canopy offered concealment but no cover. The gunners would have certainly blanketed the spot I was last seen with a concentrated barrage. Instead, I immediately sprung forward and then leaped to a position roughly twenty yards away, emptying my twenty-round magazine as I made the dash, in the direction of the enemy fire. That exchange was intended to interrupt the enemy's attack. To that end, I was effective. Unfortunately for me, I was exposed for those precious seconds it would take to eject my empty magazine and replace it with a fresh clip. But I was not alone. Ray stepped into the clearing with his deadly sixty-caliber weapon. He had fire in his eyes and malice in his heart. The volume of rounds he could deliver with the touch of his finger would dispense a quick and sudden death to all living things he set his sights on. He would split trees, cut branches, and send dust flying from the ground. The smallest insects were likely scurrying for cover to escape the onslaught.

The three of us then took a position behind some trees. From there we would offer cover for the remainder of the platoon to proceed. There would certainly be other enemy positions we had not yet located. "Come on!" I yelled to Sergeant Nato, who was next in line, "We've got you covered." There was no answered, so I called again. This time Nato did answer, but it wasn't what we wanted to hear.

"We can't get through!" Nato called in a quivering voice. "Pull back so we can get more help." We were furious. Jackson was beginning to shout obscenities but was muffled by me when his shouts began to draw enemy fire. Any attempt by the platoon members to move forward was halted by the sergeant. We knew from the volume of fire coming from the top of the hill that we had to continue with the rescue. We also knew we couldn't retreat with no one offering cover. The only option was to continue up the hill. Sergeant Nato was certain to cower in that position or retreat down the hill. He would finally be able to eliminate a large number of minorities, including me.

Respect and trust would be the key to our survival. Each of us was at the top of our game. I knew our assault was anticipated by the VC, and we were likely being watched. I had to find the quickest path to the top. This would not be easy considering the enemy would nest in trees, hide behind rocks, time my approach, and then act accordingly. I had to neutralize the ambushes and expose any weaknesses they might have.

Ray, on machine gun, was the Big Dog. He was the desired target and the greatest threat to the enemy. Each time he pulled that trigger, all attention would be directed at him. But Ray was known for his accuracy and ability to dispense a high volume of fire that kept the enemy ducking.

Jackson, as ammo humper, was the unsung hero. He was the link to a perfect team merger. I would set them up, and Ray would deliver the power punch. But Jackson's job was, perhaps, the most difficult. While I would fire hundreds of rounds in the assault and Ray thousands, Jackson had to resist the natural tendency to protect himself against the enemy attack and support the pointer and machine gunner. He had to alert the otherwise preoccupied Ray of the direction I was moving in order to protect me and to make certain Ray didn't accidentally shoot me. To do this amid the chaos, he could never lose sight of me. In addition to that awesome responsibility, he must make certain that Ray never ran out of ammunition. Although he was draped with cartridge belts, making him appear as if he were wearing pleated body armor, and weighted down with heavy ammo boxes in each hand, he could not fall behind. All of this was instinctive.

The three of us were raising so much hell one would think a regiment was coming to the rescue. The enemy were scattering like rats. The marines being rescued were concerned about being accidently shot by the approaching rescue party. So when we got close, they popped yellow smoke to avoid being caught in the cross fire.

"Here!" someone called from behind the rocks. "We're over here." Slowly heads began to peer from behind hiding spots. Then bright smiles appeared.

The squad leader approached me and explained the situation. "When that chopper approached, the NVA came out of nowhere to attack it," he said, continuing to look around, anticipating a repeated attack. "Where is the rest of the platoon?" he asked.

"Sergeant Nato pulled them back," I answered angrily.

We now had a new cause for concern. The rescue chopper had left the area, and there was no way we could hold off the enemy with only three extra men. "We've got to get the hell out of here before Mister Charlie [VC] figures things out," I told them. The Fourth Squad leader organized his men. Four members from the squad grabbed Rodriquez. The rest followed me, Ray, and Jackson back down the hill.

We got about one hundred yards down before the enemy resumed their attack. The spots where enemy soldiers had been hit had blood but no bodies. It was as though everyone had vanished. In spite of the volume of gunfire, only one marine sustained a grazing wound. Another sprained his ankle on the rocks. We hoped the platoon was still at the spot where we had left them, but they weren't. Nato had pulled them back to the bottom of the hill.

The further we progressed down the hill, the more our sense of security grew. With each step I was becoming more enraged. Now anger was overtaking fear. When we got near the bottom, we passed a security position. The men were congratulating us and attempting to elicit information. I was so focused on finding the sergeant who had abandoned us that I walked past everyone without speaking. Ray was attempting to calm me down, but it wasn't working.

When we stepped into the clearing, I frantically searched the faces, looking for Nato. Johnson tried to intercept me.

"That motherfucking coward left us!" I started to yell. "He didn't even try to get up the hill."

"Wait a minute," Johnson implored. "He said he called for reinforcements. But you risked everyone's life and continued up the hill. He is going to try to get you court-martialed this time."

"That lying motherfucker," I said, pacing back and forth. "There was no time to pull back, and he knew it. He just didn't have any balls."

"Look," Johnson said, placing his hands on my shoulders. "Go back to your squad and find what they heard Nato say; then go to the lieutenant. If you attack a sergeant, they won't even listen to you."

"Where is he now?" I asked.

"He's talking to the lieutenant, giving his story."

"I can't believe that shit," I said.

"Like I said, first talk to your squad; then go to the lieutenant."

This was perhaps the first time I had taken advice from Johnson.

When I reached the squad members, they were excited to see me and quickly explained how the sergeant had blocked their effort to follow us up the hill. Jackson, Ray, and I assured them we had suspected that to be the case and graciously accepted the recognition from our peers. The more the squad members told me, the more it confirmed my suspicions that Nato wanted the brothers dead. My anger was growing.

"You probably need to go to the lieutenant," Sherman told me. "He's trying to portray you as running off and leaving us."

That was as much as I could stand. I stormed off again looking for Sergeant Nato.

The sergeant was a racist, a coward, and a liar. He had to be stopped. I always hoped to be in a position to leave the sergeant exposed so the enemy could kill him, but Sergeant Nato would always find a way to run and hide when faced with danger. Taking him out myself was becoming more implausible. I would be the first one they would suspect. Maybe, I hoped, the sergeant would hit me, and I could justify defending myself.

Just as predicted, there Nato was, trying to present a case to have me court-martialed or at least reprimanded. I went straight at him but was blocked by the lieutenant. "Stand to, Marine!" he ordered. "I want to hear what the sergeant has to say."

The sergeant was talking fast. "We walked straight into an ambush," he reiterated. "I needed to act for the safety of the men I was responsible for. To do this, I needed to have him pull back so I could set up a defense. But Harris, as usual, went his own way. This left us without a machine gunner and dangerously exposed. We did our best to give them cover, but advancing without backup was a dangerous and foolish move." He was now shouting directly at me.

"What are you talking about?" I shouted back. But my shouts could not be heard. The noise created by the evacuation helicopters starting their descent prohibited normal conversation, and evacuating the wounded was the priority. The lieutenant motioned for us to end the discussion. I reluctantly went to my squad, while the lieutenant and sergeant went to assist the evacuation. But in the blink of an eye, everything changed again.

Suddenly, as if in a magic act, the enemy appeared all around fiercely attacking the helicopters. They came from the underground like ghouls arising from the grave searching for blood.

All this time, we had been on top of a massive underground complex. It was later discovered the Vietnamese had a functioning city tunneling through the mountains. From dozens of locations, they would come up from what appeared to be trapdoors to fire at the helicopters and then disappear. Their camouflage techniques were uncanny. When approached, they appeared to become a tree, a rock, or a bush. They were masters of illusion.

It was impossible for the marines to get off a shot without hitting our own people. The pilots were having the same problem. From the air, they couldn't distinguish the enemy from marines. It was sheer chaos. The lieutenant contacted the pilots and informed them that the marines would be popping yellow smoke. Once that order was given, nearly everyone with a canister let smoke fly. Soon the whole area was engulfed in yellow smoke. Some suspected the enemy was also popping smoke. In all the confusion, one marine popped a red smoke canister, which further confused the pilots. The helicopters had become the only clear targets, and they were restricted from returning fire.

The number of wounded was rising, and a decision had to be made. The pilots were going to come down in the designated area and pick up the wounded. They would shoot anyone perceived as a threat. Everyone scrambled for cover as they came in firing indiscriminately. The scene was that of mass confusion. In a cloud of thick smoke, the Vietnamese were popping up from underground and firing. The helicopter gunners were firing down at unclear targets, and the marines on the ground were turning and firing in all directions. Unable to find a hole, I was flopping around like a fish out of water, trying to dodge bullets and see in all directions.

Then I saw one of the helicopters heading directly toward me, and the machine-gun turret was firing deadly fifty-caliber rounds in a straight-line path just slightly above my head. I rose to my hands and knees like a crab turning in circles, looking for any type of depression to jump into. Ten yards away, I saw a mud pit and dived in face first seconds before the incoming rounds. Unfortunately for me, it wasn't a mud pit I had dived into; it was an open communal latrine filled with feces and urine.

Everyone, except me, was running around trying to collect the newly wounded for extraction. I was spitting, coughing, cursing, and gasping for breath. Greer ran to me, assuming that I had been hit. "Damn!" he said, holding his nose. "That's a shit hole." Suddenly another helicopter providing cover for the helicopter being loaded began firing in our direction. Greer looked for a place to hide. There was no time to be selective, so after about a half-second hesitation, he joined me in the shit hole. "The motherfuckers are trying to kill us!" Greer screamed. In truth, the helicopter gunner was firing at an enemy soldier who was coming up on us from behind. When that man was eliminated, the evacuation was able to continue.

To everyone's surprise, there were only about six to nine men needing evacuation. Greer and I provided some comic relief when we came out of the shit hole. We looked like the Swamp Thing from the forties horror movie. Other marines ran over and dumped the contents of their canteens over our heads.

Now that the helicopters were safely flying away, we had to get out of the area as quickly as possible. Bombers were now en route with the mission to destroy the underground city from above. They had an estimated fifteen-minute ETA. Second Platoon was to bring up the rear and provide cover for the mass exodus.

The men understood the urgency, and, within five minutes, Second Platoon was also on the run. The Vietnamese were now surfacing and beginning an assault. The marines would periodically turn and return fire, but we were clearly more concerned with leaving the area. Soon someone alerted us that the bombers were spotted. Returning fire became a nonissue.

Expendable and Necessary

We needed to get to a landmark visible from above that would serve as a boundary for the pilots.

The Vietnamese were continuing to press their attack. It was clear they outnumbered us, and they were dangerously close. Then the first bomber released his payload. It landed so close that the force of the concussion knocked us off our feet. Shrapnel and debris were raining down on us, but the stunned marines continued to press on.

Johnson was on the radio, under the direction of the lieutenant, frantically trying to alert the pilots of the situation. He was yelling in an attempt to shout over the noise of the explosion and partially due to his excitement. Finally he got a response, but not before a final bomb landed. It wasn't a direct hit, but it was close enough to burn several of the marines. Again, shrapnel cut through several men. Trees, as much as twelve inches in diameter, were being hurled through the air like straws, and football-sized rocks were flying everywhere. Men were scattered, moaning in pain.

I rose to my knees and began looking around. There, less than twenty yards away, was Sergeant Nato, lying on his back appearing mortally wounded. Seeing it was the sergeant, I looked for someone else to help, but everyone was already being assisted. The task was now to collect the dead and wounded and then place them in an open spot where they could be medevacked.

With none of the others going to help Nato, I crept over to him. It would have appeared to the uninformed that I was going to risk my own safety to assist my fallen sergeant. But anyone even vaguely aware of our situation knew it was more likely I would seize the opportunity to finally kill my archenemy if he wasn't already dead. When I reached Nato, I noticed the sergeant was moving his head. The sergeant looked at me with a blank stare, perhaps concerned about my intensions.

I inspected him with my eyes to evaluate the extent of his injuries. Blood was flowing under him, but he was not calling out in pain. He just looked directly at me. His foot also appeared to be shattered. Then I began to smile. "Is your foot crushed?" I said. There was no response from the sergeant, only a blank stare. "Is your spine cut?" I whispered, still smiling.

"Ain't that a bitch? That is even better than you being dead. I won," I said, laughing out loud. Then I turned and left him lying there. Several other marines eventually went over to him. One was a stout Caucasian marine who had recently joined the company. He actually picked the sergeant up and carried him in his arms.

The wounded marines, some of whom had mortal injuries, were moved to an area further away. Once they were at a safe distance, the bombing resumed. A medevac chopper would come to do another evacuation. Sergeant Nato was thrown in with the rest. It wasn't clear if he was paralyzed, but it was clear he was too injured to return.

"Is that blood?" Ray asked me, referring to his own back, which he could feel was soaked. I looked him over and then told him it was just water from the water canister he was carrying on his back. After closer inspection, I pulled a piece of shrapnel out of it that was clearly the cause of the rupture. "That water can saved your life," I said, handing the nickel-sized piece of jagged steel to Ray. Ray kissed the shrapnel and stuck it into his pocket, vowing to take it home as a souvenir.

Then the marine who had cared for the sergeant came over and spoke to the two of us. "That was a good job," he said with a salute. "We're going to kill all those goddamn Commies."

"Who the fuck are you?" I said with disdain.

"They call me Recon," the marine answered. "I just joined the company."

"Well, go join them now," I said, motioning him away. Feeling dejected, the new marine turned and left.

"You should give the white boy a break," Ray said with a smile. "If that gung-ho motherfucker can stay alive another month, they'll put him in charge of all of us."

"I know," I replied. "That's why he needs to know where I stand right away." We joined the company, who were to meet up with the regiment.

CHAPTER 28

An Underground City
September 1969

▲ ▲ ▲

WHILE THE BOMBING CONTINUED, GULF Company continued to patrol the surrounding mountains. The command decided the naval and air-force pilots would collapse the honeycombed mountains; then the marines would return to search and destroy the ruins. The only complaint about the lull in action came from Recon. Butler, who was in charge of the mortars, talked to me about the new man.

"What do you think of the new guy?" he asked.

"He's pumped up for war," I answered.

"You know, he seems to act without thinking. He needs to be controlled."

"Sergeant Bazarr is the platoon sergeant now. Maybe he'll check him."

"I hope so. I would hate for him to run into a mortar drop zone," Butler said.

"I'll bring it up whenever I get his ear."

"Thanks," Butler responded while walking away.

The platoon was ordered to move out. We would eventually divide into squads so we could cover a larger area. Fourth Squad took lead. Then, as expected, Recon volunteered to walk point. Second Squad followed. His overzealous nature kept everyone on edge. Suddenly, he stopped and crouched down in a defensive position.

As a matter of procedure, he should have waited for the squad leader to give instructions, but the new marine was eager for a fight. Recon suddenly took off running. His squad responded, trying to catch him, with the rest of the platoon in pursuit. To everyone's horror, he ran into a cave, obviously chasing something or someone. His squad took a position at the mouth of the cave, and the remainder of the platoon guarded the area. Sergeant Bazarr approached his squad leader to get information. He had none to give.

Moments later, Recon emerged from the cave. He was dragging a young pregnant Vietnamese woman dressed in Viet Cong PJs. His squad leader was at a loss for words. Sergeant Bazarr wasn't. "Good job, Marine," he said, patting him on the back. Recon was smiling broadly. I had a different reaction and voiced it loudly as he approached. "Good job, hell. He just ran into a cave without telling anybody what was going on. That could have been a trap."

Sergeant Bazarr might have agreed in principle, but he wasn't going to express it. He favored the aggressive approach of the new marine. "The situation required an immediate response," Bazarr responded. Then he told me to take control of the prisoner. I threw up my hands and then ordered her accompany me.

She looked at me for sympathy but got none. I was skeptical, pushing her along rather roughly. As we approached the men in our squad, she was crying in deep sobs, holding her stomach and cupping her genital area. She complied with commands given to her, but she repeatedly shouted, "No-com-beick; No-com-beick." ("I don't understand; I don't understand.")

Growing annoyed, I turned her over to Sally, who took responsibility after a slight protest. Immediately, she played on his gentle nature. He protected her as if he were the child's father. "Here, Mama-San," he said to her, giving her water and assisting her to a seat. All the while she smiled affectionately and massaged her stomach. I was suspicious of her claim not to speak English. I pulled Sally out of her hearing distance and explained the plan as it was given to me.

"We are going to keep her here until a chopper arrives to medevac her, so just keep her quiet."

"Why are we going detain her?" Sally asked.

"Because she is VC," I snapped, surprised at the naïveté of the experienced marine. "They are going to interrogate her."

Johnson was now approaching, speaking to me as he got near.

"Lance Corporal Harris, the lieutenant wants all the squad leaders to report to the CP [command post] immediately."

"Cut the John Wayne shit, and I'm not the squad leader," I snapped back.

"He told me to make sure you came too."

"Why?"

"I don't know. He just wants you to get briefed with the rest of the leaders."

"They must be about to pull some shit on me."

"Not now, OK?" Johnson said, throwing up his hands.

Lieutenant Storm addressed me upon my arrival. "Harris, you are going to take over Second Squad."

"Why me?" I responded.

"Because I said so!" the lieutenant yelled.

"That's why your ass is stuck as a lance corporal," the gunnery sergeant added. "You don't know when to keep your goddamn mouth shut."

Lieutenant Storm went on to explain the situation. "Fox Company went into those hills after the saturated bombing. It looked as if the roof had been peeled off a complex. They found heavily fortified rooms. It is believed that they had a hospital, a large command post, and maybe an R and R center. There were possibly hundreds of camouflaged openings for entrances and exits." That made sense to us. It explained why the enemy seemed to disappear and why we never could find any bodies.

The lieutenant went on. "Now that they have been routed out, the mission is to hunt them down. We will return to those mountains later. Beware," he warned, "we aren't sure of their troop strength. We may be heavily outnumbered. Harris, take the prisoner to the base of this hill," he said, pointing to a spot on a map. "A chopper has been dispatched to extract her. She is your responsibility. Sergeant Bazarr will be flanking you with Third Squad; he will be your backup. Remember, he is the ranking man, and all calls are ultimately his. By the way, Recon is going to be assigned to you." I rolled my eyes and then went to inform the squad of our assignment.

After binding the prisoner's hands, we moved to the designated pickup area, which took about twenty minutes. The open area was about two hundred yards across and twice that distance on both sides. The terrain was thick, and we could see a narrow stream cutting through. I positioned the men deep in the tree line to wait for a helicopter. Suddenly, a call came over the radio, and Kartis, the radioman, gave it to me. Sergeant Bazarr was on the line. "Be informed," he told me, "H Company ambushed a platoon of NVA on the hill to your west, and they are headed in your direction. Take them out. We are going to shift our position in case they try to cross further downstream."

I positioned the men and ordered Sally to secure the prisoner deeper into the tree line, concerned she would alert the NVA of the ambush. Then we waited in anticipation of the appearance of the fleeing enemy soldiers. I was hoping for easy kills, like shooting ducks in a pond. Within a matter of minutes, movement was spotted. All eyes were trained at the spot. Soon we were able to distinguish it as a person. Immediately I contacted the command post. I had to get conformation that no friendlies were operating in the area. It was quickly confirmed. Sergeant Bazarr was then contacted, and he headed for our location. My squad waited and watched as the soldier went back into the tree line. Shortly thereafter, other soldiers appeared on the edge of the tree line. They also went back. The men were holding their fire, waiting for more targets. Sergeant Bazarr arrived and asked for an update. He supported the wait-and-see approach. In a hushed conversation, we assessed the situation. All possibilities had to be considered.

Was it a reconnaissance patrol looking for our positions? Did we miss an opportunity? Had the enemy decided to follow the tree line rather than expose themselves? If so, in what direction were they now traveling? Or were they mustering their forces for a mass crossing?

As we stared at the opposite tree line, another soldier appeared, then another, then another. They were creeping forward, not looking back, indicating they were going to cross. Now there were over thirty heavily armed

NVA regulars heading straight for us. "Pull your men back!" Sergeant Bazarr ordered as he headed up a retreat. "I'm calling a strike on the area."

Sally and Fredericks were holding the prisoner about thirty yards inside the tree line to keep her from knowing what was taking place. They were to join the exodus as we made our rapid retreat, but there was a problem. When they tried to bring her to her feet, she supposedly went into labor, falling to her back and spreading her legs as if she was giving birth. Sally was frantic.

"Get the prisoner up!" I said as I approached. "We've got to move now!"

"She's giving birth!" Sally panted.

"Bullshit!" I shouted. "Get that bitch up now. We've got to move!"

"I'm not bullshitting; she's giving birth!"

"Then she'll drop that motherfucker on the trail," I said in anger. "Drag her!"

"I can't, man. I just can't!" Sally pleaded.

I had no such reservations. I knelt beside her and grabbed her hair with my left hand, slamming her head to the ground. Then I came down with a powerful blow, striking her in the nose and upper teeth. The force was so hard that two teeth were pushed to the roof of her mouth, and her nose burst like a ripe tomato. I halted her gag reflex by cupping her mouth and nose with the same hand that had caused the damage. Blood was oozing from between my fingers. She was choking on it. She grasped my wrist, trying to free my grip, to no avail. Satisfied she needed no further encouragement, I released my grip. Miraculously her labor subsided, and she sprung to her feet and broke out in full stride.

We continued to run away from the target area. As we did, we could hear the first blast of the bombing pattern. It was dangerously close, with shrapnel falling on us. Once safely away, we held our position. In time, we were given the all-clear to return to the pickup spot with the prisoner. We found that the enemy forces had been killed or dispersed. Shortly thereafter, the evacuation chopper arrived to extract the prisoner. Her lively movement and her ability to jump on the helicopter unassisted made it clear that the premature labor she had displayed was only a delay tactic. Once on the helicopter, she stared directly at me. If looks could kill, I would have been a dead man.

When the helicopter was safely away, the squad joined the platoon. Second Platoon was now ordered to search for Viet Cong who were living in plain sight. They were likely the inhabitants of the relatively large villages in the mountainous area, but unless they attacked us, they were to be treated as friendly. To segregate the Viet Cong, a curfew was set. Anyone out during that time would be treated as hostile. We targeted a village that housed about thirty people. Most of them were very old or very young.

First and Second Squads would go into the village and maintain positions. We would hit anyone attempting to enter or exit after the curfew time. Sergeant Bazarr would be there, and this would serve as the command post. Butler was also there with his mortar section, and Ray with his machine-gun squad. Third and Fourth Squads would set ambushes in the surrounding area. They would hit anyone moving around after curfew. The squads in the command post would also serve as backup, if needed.

A new replacement had come into the platoon. His name was also Harris. He was Caucasian, so everyone knew we weren't related. During orientation, he was told to look to the brother with his surname when arriving in the bush for guidance. He was also warned not to pick up my bad habits. This was both an insult and a compliment to me, but it was also sound advice. So when the newly arriving marine joined the platoon, he did just that.

Just like anyone coming into combat, he was terrified. I did my best to reassure him while cautioning him that his life was in very real danger. On finding that the new recruit was to be assigned to Ray's machine-gun squad, I advised him that Ray was an expert at what he did and to pay close attention to what Ray did and said. Ray decided to test the young marine and sent him out with the experienced Third Squad on an ambush.

That night Ray, Butler, and I sat in the command post located in the center of the village. I had placed the men from my squad around the perimeter, and Ray had positioned the gunners. Butler would be called into action as needed. The area was heavily patrolled by VC as well as NVA. Based on our past experience, we were predicting there would be contact. We shared our concerns in a hushed conversation. Ray was now feeling uneasy about having sent the new man out on an ambush. If there was to be contact, that was where it would likely occur. Once the darkness completely enveloped the camp, we went into complete silence. Unknown to us, a Viet Cong patrol was headed toward the village. They were about to have a deadly clash with Third Squad, a clash that would end the silence.

The order of gunfire told the tale: M60, M16, AK-47, then SKS. A marine machine gunner sprung an ambush with his M60. Then the squad joined in with the M16s. Next, and almost simultaneously, the Vietnamese force responded with their AK-47s and SKSs. After the initial blast, there was a smorgasbord of gunfire. Second Squad was quickly sent out into darkness to assist. We immediately made our presence known. The fighting was fast and furious with orders being given in both English and Vietnamese. As the shouting subsided, only the English commands could be heard. This indicated we had overpowered them and were rousting captured prisoners. Johnson, who was operating the company radio, was frantically trying to establish contact. But it was obvious that we were preoccupied with staying alive. Finally he got a response. "This is Gulf Three stinger, and we have the situation under control." The ambush was successful.

Even through the darkness, we could see what looked like a slaughterhouse. Three dead enemy soldiers were piled together, and three others were bound and gagged. It was estimated that at least four had escaped, and several marines had received superficial wounds. I along with the Third Squad leader was concerned other Viet Cong patrols might be in the area, so we decided that it would be safer to secure the prisoners, wait, and return the following morning. Everyone was on alert. Few, if any, got sleep.

As soon as there was daylight, we returned to the command post. The dead were transported like deer carcasses. The hands and feet were bound with a pole threaded between them with a man carrying each end. The captured men had the look of defeat. Their eyes were trained on the ground, looking up only when addressed. When eye contact was made, they had expressions that conveyed both sadness and fear. The second Harris arrived, he looked for me, eager to tell his story.

"Man!" he said, resting his arm on my shoulder. "I killed two of them. The squad leader told me to open fire when a target was directly in front of me. So when I was told they were coming, I just listened intently. Soon I could hear them. The sound got closer and closer. Before long it looked like shadows were moving closer. My heart was pumping, and I fought to resist opening fire. Suddenly they were in front of me. I squeezed the trigger on that machine gun, and a couple hundred rounds popped out before I released it." He then illustrated how their bodies twisted and turned as the bullets ripped them apart. I listened respectfully, my way of acknowledging the new man had been initiated into the "club," a unique club made of people who had killed without consequence. What the newly inducted marine had yet to learn was membership had a cost. The images he so vividly described would haunt him for the remainder of his life. That would come later. For now, I just congratulated him.

The captured prisoners were extremely lucky. Captures at night are rare. It's just too dangerous. One of the prisoners was separated and guarded by two sergeants who gave closer supervision. His mannerisms and dress indicated he had the senior rank. His uniform was neat and pressed. His hair was neatly trimmed, and even more astonishing, his shoes were shined. How could he have shined shoes in the middle of the jungle? After brief questioning, it was discovered that he was an officer. I was watching from a distance, alarmed at the sergeants guarding him. They seemed too trusting.

The captured officer must have felt the catastrophe was his fault. It was likely he was seeking redemption. To accomplish this, he seemed to be assessing the situation, looking for an advantage. His eyes scanned the weapons that were lying about. I suspected he would make a mad dash for a weapon and gun down as many marines as he could before being killed. What was even more alarming was that one of the sergeants guarding him untied his hands.

I went to Roe, who was also a sergeant, to tell his peers of my concerns, which he did. The guarding marine told him, in a hushed tone, that the .45 on his hip wasn't loaded. The second guard would have shot him dead had he made any attempt to go for it. The NVA officer never fell for the ploy.

He was probably smarter than the both of them. Roe continued to be unsure of his counterpart's ability to contain the sly prisoner, continuing to watch from a distance.

I was more interested in the other prisoners being guarded. They weren't NVA, but VC. They were dressed in the traditional black pajamas worn by the VC and closer to my age and rank. I kept a short distance from them and the four marines guarding them, just close enough to hear what was being said. The prisoners were understandably frightened, but relieved. They had survived the initial contact, the critical stage when caught in an ambush. That is the moment when your only objective is to kill those on the opposing side or force them into subjugation. Many times unarmed or uninvolved persons, or even allies, are killed in the fray as each does the deadly dance alternating between being predator and prey. Some might argue that destiny had already predetermined the outcome. Others might argue that each man is determining his fate from moment to moment. Whatever their philosophy, all are relieved when the shooting stops.

Viet Cong prisoner of war

One of the prisoners seemed extremely young, no more than sixteen or seventeen years of age. Being at the mercy of men who had sworn to kill them was a heavy burden. He was facing a future that could be exhausting, painful, or limited, and it showed on his face. The others were a year or two older but just as worried.

The captured tried to establish common ground with their captors. Humanizing themselves would lessen the likelihood of being brutalized. But the language barrier limited them to repeating, "Marines number one!" over and over. There would be no interrogation, so the guarding marines did attempt to interact cordially with the prisoners. Love of women and song was the key. One pulled out a picture of his wife and showed it to the young Vietnamese, who had probably never seen an American woman.

"Number one," said the smiling Vietnamese, "number one." The proud marine kissed his wife's picture before returning it to his pocket. The marines then tried to connect through the universal language of music. The Vietnamese couldn't master the words of the Motown sounds, but eventually, they got the rhythm. When The Miracles was selected, they likely had no idea how prophetic the choice had been. It was truly a miracle how the group's songs had brought these sworn enemies together.

About thirty feet from us was the grim reminder for all to see. There, piled up like discarded rags, were the dead bodies. This wasn't unusual. Some marines almost tripped over them. The villagers would show more than a casual interest, but it was obvious that they didn't want to be associated with an identifiable enemy. So they would only pause momentarily as they passed. I did noticed one observer fixated on the bodies. It was a small Vietnamese boy, about six or seven. He stared intently at the bodies as if in a trance.

At first I was sympathetic. This just wasn't something for a child to see, so I went over to chase him away. To my surprise, the child seemed not to notice me. I shouted several times before getting his attention. He acknowledged my presence by pointing at one of the bodies and then slowly turned to me. The young boy looked well beyond his years. Speaking in a low, melancholy tone, he said, "Me papa-san." This child was looking at me, one of the men he likely held responsible for killing his father. I knew it didn't matter to the young boy if I was individually responsible or not. Whatever the child's past attitude toward Americans, he now had a purpose in life: to kill Americans. He would likely return one day with a purpose.

The child had also exposed his hand. There was no doubt he was VC; he could have been captured on the spot. Instead, feeling no immediate threat, I shoved him away. "De-de mow!" I shouted, shoving him violently toward the jungle. He gave me a look of hate and anger and then slowly turned and walked away. The marines guarding the perimeter allowed him to leave. I watched the young boy disappear into the jungle, knowing only death would stop him from returning to fight in the future.

Three unarmed Viet Cong came into the village to surrender by the time the choppers arrived. The pilot informed us that he had picked up other surrendering Viet Cong. The entire regiment was reporting an unusual number of prisoners. There was a reason for this. The army, which was the principal force in the area, was out defending its fort. They brought enormous troop strength and overwhelming firepower. Marines, on the other hand, were an assault force. We broke off into small groups and meticulously continued to search and destroy. This proved a more effective tactics in fighting VC.

But the North Vietnamese Army was undeterred. Their greatest asset was unity, direction, and purpose. They had a history to avenge, and they would not stop until they had taken control of the whole country. When we were told the NVA had received orders to fight to the death, no one would expect anything less.

The final phase of the operation was for us to go back into the mountains and join the search of the underground caverns. The ground we walked on was like a roof. The bombs had blasted away the top layer, exposing what looked like a modular office. I was ordered to explore many of the passages. We were like ants in a complex anthill, or rats in a maze. Everything was blown apart, making it difficult to visualize how it originally appeared. It was obvious, from the equipment that lay in disarray, that it had once been a hospital. There was an area for bomb and booby-trap making. Much of the unfinished ordinance was thrown about. We were amazed at what the enemy had accomplished.

VC digging a tunnel

A young boy stood around during the search. The fact he didn't leave when approached caused me to be suspicious of him, suspecting he might be hiding something. So we thoroughly searched the area around him. All I saw out of place was a basket of white powder with a greenish hue that sparkled in the dim light. I was about to tip it over when the boy ran over to stop me. Concerned it

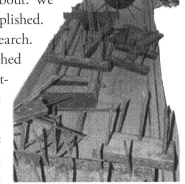

recovered booby traps

might be a booby trap, I stepped back. The boy slid it a few feet to show me it wasn't. I then tried to determine what it actually was. Sherman and Greer came over and tried to assist me. It took a few tries, but the boy finally communicated that the substance was for pain.

"Goddamn!" I said with a sly grin. "That's about fifty pounds of coke. We're rich!" We were jumping up and down like people who had won the lottery. Sherman was more reserved, trying to determine how we could get it to the United States, or at least distribute it. Woody, who had just walked in, realized immediately what he was seeing. Before we could keep him quiet, he shouted, "Holy shit! That's a basket of drugs." That outburst alerted everyone in the area. First the corpsman came in; then he shouted for the sergeant. "Sergeant Bazarr, there are drugs in this room."

We were about to reach into the basket and grab handfuls to stuff into our pockets when the lieutenant, who had also entered the room, ordered us to stop.

"That's the property of the United States Marine Corps!" he shouted. "Step away." With a great deal of trepidation, we did as ordered. If there had been any possibility of me becoming a permanent squad leader, it was erased. Under the close supervision of the lieutenant, the drugs were packed up for transport.

When the chopper arrived, there was a new sergeant. He was immediately given Second Squad. This Hispanic sergeant was older than the others. They found he had been disciplined and busted down two pay grades for alcoholism and insubordination. This made him a perfect fit for Second Squad.

Command had also sent orders that didn't go over well with the battle-hardened marines. Command needed information, so we were to make all attempts to capture rather than kill. If anyone made a kill, he would be subject to an inquiry. After locating an open area, we stopped for the night. This area was large enough to be used the next morning for a chopper to land and provide us with much-needed supplies.

CHAPTER 29

Stalking a Fox
September 1969

▲ ▲ ▲

EARLY THE FOLLOWING MORNING, THE chopper arrived. On board were supplies, letters, and a Kit Carson Scout. These were captured Vietnamese prisoners who had been repatriated and now assisted the US forces. The methods used to turn them might be questionable, but it was clear they were willing participants. Their input as scouts and interpreters would be invaluable to us when confronting the captured Vietnamese.

There was a noticeable change in the platoon, both in the newly arriving personnel and in considered old-timers. After candid conversations with people whose opinion I valued, I needed to reevaluate myself.

I, who was usually outgoing and interactive, was becoming withdrawn, isolated, and as some suggested, unpredictable. How the hell could you be expected to be predictable in such an unpredictable situation? I would concede to becoming withdrawn and to ceasing contact with people back home. As a result, I rarely received mail; however, being labeled withdrawn didn't bother me. As my rotation date approached, I had to focus on surviving. The withdrawal wasn't caused by a period of idle thought. I was consumed with analyzing the surroundings and anything or anybody that would interfere with my chance of survival. With death and danger all around me, I had little choice. I was tired; nothing I would ever face would be more physically exhausting than fighting daily for my life.

And the isolation wasn't all my doing. Most of the people with whom I'd had close associations were either dead or convalescing in hospitals. I didn't more friends. Well, that's not true. My friends were what kept me alive. I just didn't want to watch any more die. I would try to listen. Starting with the scouts.

Although I had never met the scout, I believed the KC Scout was someone I could talk to, so I approached him. The officers and staff sergeants were more inclined to interact with the scouts, perhaps because they understood their importance. The enlisted men were generally less accepting. Some resentment was over the favoritism the scouts were shown. They generally traveled with the staff officers and sergeants; therefore, they were kept away from the fiercest fighting. From a strategic prospective, they were, perhaps, more valuable than the frontline rifleman, but not to the rifleman. Some of my fellow riflemen dismissed the scouts as cowards because when captured, they switched sides. Some couldn't get past the fact that, not long ago, these men were trying to kill them.

Experience was teaching me not to judge until you walk in someone's shoes. The choice between being captured and dying was one I hoped I'd never be forced to make. So after a few anxious moments, I developed a cordial relationship. We both were experienced enough to realize each had a vested interest. The scout needed to develop a rapport with his captors, and I needed to understand the enemy, to gain an advantage. I learned a great deal about Viet Cong strategy from our conversation, and the knowledge would serve me well.

Sitting at a distance was Sergeant Bazarr, who was wrestling with his own inner demons. The sergeant was driven to be written in the annals of Marine Corps history.

Because he was a sergeant, his accomplishments might be recognized quicker than the men under him. So with the constant clashes with the enemy, it was likely he would gain that recognition. Unfortunately for the men, it was their lives he would be willing to risk for the sake of glory. However, unlike Sergeant Nato, he was an opportunist rather than a racist, so all lives were at risk. All under his command would be advised to follow the creed of the bushman, "Look out for yourself." The common ground was that we were professionals, and there was a mission to be accomplished.

Our company was to search an area of about two square miles. The four platoons were separated, with each given a half-mile quadrant. Sergeant Bazarr was in command of Second Platoon, which I was a part of. The intelligence report predicted movement in Second Platoon's search area, so the scout was sent with us to interrogate any potential prisoners. The men were doing a thorough search in dense terrain that had pockets of open space. The men were growing weary as the noon hour approached, so the sergeant decided we would stop for a break. A defensive perimeter was established, and Second Squad was to provide two observation posts one hundred meters out. Greer and Woody were on the left, Sherman and Sally on the right. The squad leaders, radioman, and corpsman were in the center of the position planning strategy. Although the new sergeant was officially in charge of Second Squad, the lieutenant and gunnery sergeant weren't confident in his ability; therefore, I was included in the discussion.

In less than ten minutes, Greer returned, reporting to have spotted an enemy soldier. Sergeant Bazarr returned with him to investigate, taking me along. When we reached the observation post, Greer pointed out what he believed to be a Viet Cong sitting in the tree line about 150 yards away.

"What do you think?" the sergeant said to me.

"Well, he is older, but not old; I think he's a Viet Cong," I whispered.

"Can you hit him from here?"

"I'm not sure, but Fredericks is our best shooter; maybe he could make a clean shot."

"I can't risk it. He may get away and warn his people," Bazarr answered.

"Well, Sarge, an unarmed older man would be the perfect ploy. His people might be right behind him."

"I don't want him killed anyway. We need him alive," the sergeant answered.

"Well," I said, "there is cover around. If we follow the tree line and get behind him, maybe I could get a small team close enough to snag him."

"Then that's what we'll do. Who do you want?" Bazarr asked.

"Fredericks is the best shot. I want him on point. I'll be behind him with Kartis next to me on radio. Put Sally on tail end. If you want him alive, I'll need the scout for an interpreter."

"OK," he said before ordering Woody to go and get the men requested.

It took less than three minutes for them to return. They were quickly briefed by the sergeant while painting camouflage on their faces to match their uniform. I felt no need to add anything. They trusted I would do everything within my power to keep them alive, and I trusted their combat skills.

Cautiously we moved through the tree line, aware of the possibility that a large Viet Cong force could be waiting to cross the open area. We also had to be quick. The Viet Cong we were stalking might make a break for the tree line at any moment.

We approached on his right flank. It was convenient, and he was primarily looking in the other direction. If he saw us, he would take off, and we would lose the opportunity to kill or capture him.

The heavy vegetation offered concealment, but it also restricted our vision. Finally we reached a point about seventy-five yards from him, remaining undetected. The soldier seemed to be contemplating going into the nearby bombed-out village. Sally leaned toward me and whispered into my ear.

"I got a good shot; can I kill him?"

"No!" I said emphatically.

"Come on, man. I ain't killed nobody yet, and I've been hit twice."

"I know, but they made it a point that they wanted him alive. This is what I want you to do. Position yourself behind this mound and draw a good bead on him. We are going to run out and grab him. If he runs toward the tree line or turns to fire on us, take him out."

That brought a wide grin to Sally's face. He was anxious to get payback for his wounds. I told Kartis to stay back with the radio. He was our lifeline in the event we needed reinforcements. Then Fredericks, the scout, and I crept up on the VC from behind. He was in grass that seemed to be a foot high spotted with clear patches. We understood that patience is a hunter's greatest asset, so we took measured and deliberate steps. Our prey seemed relaxed, as if he were taking a stroll through his backyard. This worked well for us, enabling us to move at a quickened pace. As the VC walked toward the open ground, he began to lower his body, making himself a smaller target. To make ourselves less visible, we did the same.

We stalked him like a cat does a bird. Periodically, he would look around, like any animal looking for predators. We were now within twenty-five yards, close enough for a quick sprint. Then something got the Viet Cong's attention; perhaps it was just animal instinct, but when he made a sudden move, Sally fired off a round. He dropped like a deflated balloon. "Check fire, check fire!" I called to Sally as we sprinted toward the fallen soldier. But he was not there. Right before our eyes, he had vanished.

In a state of panic, we searched the area where he was last seen. We were digging, patting, scratching the ground, frantically searching for spider traps, tunnel openings, or anything he could hide under or behind. "He's got to be here. Fan out and find that motherfucker!" I shouted. While the men searched the ground, I scanned the surrounding area, pivoting in a circle. Sally ran over to me apologizing as he approached, but there was no need. I was focused on the imminent danger we were facing. There was a tree line surrounding us and what appeared to be a bombed-out village on its perimeter. If troops weren't already hiding in the tree line, the gunfire and shouting would have drawn them to us. The village was also a problem, as it offered hiding places.

"Fredericks, go to the village," I shouted. "The rest of you keep searching; we're going into the tree line," I ordered, pulling the scout with me. The scout was as terrified as I was. He knew if the Viet Cong was a pointer, there would be a fighting force behind him waiting to attack.

As soon as we entered the tree line, I stopped. I had become so overwhelmed by the impending danger that I had overlooked a detail that could cost me my life. I was visually separated from my forces with a well-armed former enemy soldier. A soldier who might turn on me just as he had turned on the Viet Cong. At the very least, it would be an opportunity for him to escape. I pushed the scout back into the opening, not bothering to explain my actions. Perhaps having my weapon trained on him might have given him a clue. When Sally saw the scout being shoved by me, he raised his weapon again, hoping to seize another opportunity to get his first kill. Now I had another problem to add to my list of concerns, being accidentally shot by the overzealous Sally.

Then, in the distance we heard Fredericks cry out. "Dung lie, dung lie!" Fredericks had found the soldier near the village.

"Get him up!" I yelled.

The frail old man had slithered from the spot he had fallen toward the village and concealed himself under a board. Fredericks had spotted the slightly elevated board and kicked it over, exposing the shrewd soldier, who had practically bored himself into the ground. He appeared to be weak and ailing, but that was deceiving. To accomplish what he had done required tremendous dexterity, contortion ability, and a remarkable skill at avoidance.

Fredericks should also be recognized for his skill. Perhaps he had called upon his childhood hunting skills or recent combat experience. Whatever the case, he had proven his worth. Fredericks had stalked a fox. As the first to locate the prisoner, he was the first to attempt to get him to cooperate.

Fredericks did his best to frighten the man. "Get up, motherfucker!" he repeatedly shouted, using his toughest posture. Under different circumstances, it would have been comical. The war had hardened the blue-eyed all-American young man, but not enough to give him an intimidating presence. The old man just looked at him with a puzzled expression. He was continually claiming to be hurt and not to understand English. Growing impatient, I told Sally to go over and drag him.

The old mad fought them all the way, but not in a physically threatening way. He would scuffle, grab objects, and claw at the ground. Every few feet Sally would lose his grip and then try again. It was obvious the old man was stalling. I called on the scout, who knew what he was expected to do.

The scout walked over and proceeded to viciously brutalize the man. He beat and kicked him until he was nearly unconscious. Then he pulled his .45 from its holster and chambered a round and aimed for a point between the soldier's eyes. Anyone familiar with the weapon knew the destruction a round from it would cause. The blunt projectile doesn't cut bone; it shatters it. Still, the prisoner wouldn't cooperate.

The scout then fired two rounds, one on each side of his head only inches away; then he pointed his weapon directly between his eyes and applied a slight pressure on the trigger. The sound alone had likely burst the prisoner's eardrums; still he would not cooperate. The scout turned to me for permission to kill. Everyone's life was in imminent danger of a counterattack. Each second delay might cost our lives. The prisoner now had a defiant gaze in his eyes. In spite of the threats and physical abuse, he would not submit. Like a caged animal, he was aware the ones outside the cage were also afraid. He was determined to delay our retreat.

The others were circling the captive, but his attention was fixed on me. Our eyes met. We were both predators, and as predators, we knew one of us had to make a move. Disregarding my orders, I was going to kill him. I brought my weapon up in a sweeping motion, grabbing the stock with my left hand, applying pressure to the trigger. The men recoiled in anticipation of seeing a man's brains being blown out of his head. At the last moment, the prisoner leaped to his feet and began to scream for mercy.

"Chu hoi! Chu hoi!" the prisoner screamed, eyes as big as fifty-cent pieces. "No more bullshit, Marine!" he pleaded in English. "No more bullshit." At that point it was questionable if I would stop the actions that had already been put in motion. Fortunately for both of us, I paused. I was looking the prisoner directly in his eyes, and I didn't want that moment to be permanently placed in my memory. I took a deep breath and, to the relief of everyone, lowered my weapon. "Let's go," I ordered, hustling them along.

The prisoner not only offered no further resistance; he was being helpful as we moved to rejoin the platoon. But he never took his eyes off me and continued to attempt to solicit support from the people around him. "Soul brother number one," he would say, "me no VC." Sally would continually slap him on the side of the head and order him to shut up; eventually he did.

We returned to the platoon without further incident. Sergeant Bazarr took control of the prisoner and immediately began to behave as if he had done the capture. Donahue contacted the company command. Once the captain was on the line, he handed the handset to Sergeant Bazarr. The sergeant began to boast of the capture, reassuring his commanding officer that his men would likely bring other valuable prisoners in as ordered.

"Excellent job," the captain could be heard saying over the radio. This brought a broad smile to the face of the sergeant, who craved recognition. "That should get him a promotion," I said to Sally, resulting in a cold stare from the sergeant.

The captain went on to tell the sergeant that, with night approaching, it wouldn't be safe to attempt to transport the prisoner to the company command post, and a helicopter extraction wouldn't be safe. As he spoke I was shaking my head no, hoping the sergeant would pose an objection to the order. The sergeant agreed with the captain and signed off. Then he admonished me for attempting to interfere.

"He's dangerous, Sarge," I told him. "He shouldn't be with us on an ambush." Sergeant Bazarr wasn't listening and again voiced his displeasure with me. But I wouldn't back down.

"That's my decision, Lance Corporal. Now join your squad; we're going to move to another position to set an ambush."

"Sarge, he can understand everything that was said," I said, referring to the prisoner.

"I don't give a shit. What the fuck he is going to do?"

"Well, he can escape and tell the enemy what our plans are or kill a few of us."

"You just do as I said, Marine," Sergeant Bazarr scoffed.

"I'm not questioning your authority, Sarge. I just want you to know that old man is as slick as I've seen. He's hard-core VC. Shit, he disappeared right before our eyes."

"Well, he won't disappear from me," the sergeant said with confidence. "By the way, you shouldn't have beaten him so much. He can barely walk."

"Sergeant. That old man can walk, run, jump, hell, he can probably fly. He's just putting on an act."

"This is not a debate, Marine. Go and join your squad and prepare to move out."

Begrudgingly, I did as ordered. The prisoner was tied and closely guarded as we moved to a more advantageous position. All along the way, the prisoner stumbled and appeared weak and disoriented. He was obviously playing to Sergeant Bazarr, and it worked. The sergeant repeatedly slowed the march and ordered the marines in his charge to assist the prisoner. Finally, just before dusk, we stopped at a spot that looked to be advantageous for us.

It was a position inside a tree line, next to an open area that could be used to land a helicopter, which was planned for the following morning. The rest of the surrounding area had dense vegetation, offering perfect cover and concealment for an enemy force. It wasn't the perfect place strategically, but it was the best under the circumstances.

Great care was taken to secure the prisoner. We established a perimeter about twenty-five yards in diameter. At the center of the perimeter was a tree, at the base of which the prisoner was placed. His back was against the tree with his hands tied behind him. His hands were not touching, to prevent him from using one hand to untie the other. His feet were tied, and he was secured at the waist. The sergeant was confident this would make it impossible for him to stand. We placed twigs and leaves on and around him so that any movement he might make would alert us. He was blindfolded and his mouth taped shut. The corpsman was placed in a position directly in front of him. His only job was to watch the prisoner. Most of the men could observe him from their positions. Even I felt confident the man couldn't escape.

As the gray evening turned to night, we set up in two-man positions and prepared to place our claymores. I shared a position with Greer. This was a good match for me. I got along well with the Motown brother who had an uncanny ability to make people laugh. I did, however, notice a dark mood in Greer. Having gone through bouts of depression myself, I brushed it off as a passing thing. Greer would be the one placing the mine in front of our position, and I would watch his back. As we began to walk out, we had a brief, hushed conversation. "I'm going home, bro," Greer said to me.

"So am I," I responded, surprised at the comment.

We were to set the claymore thirty yards out. I stopped at fifteen to search for enemy movement in the darkness while Greer continued. I calculated it would take about two minutes for Greer to place the claymore and return. When that time passed, I became concerned. I waited another minute and then moved up to investigate. Before I could reach him, I heard a loud explosion. There was a ball of fire followed by a scream. I dropped to the ground and was narrowly missed by hot, jagged shrapnel. Then I jumped up and continued toward Greer. When reaching Greer, I found him thrashing around screaming in pain. "My hand, my hand!" he screamed, blood spouting everywhere. Within seconds, Sally and Sherman arrived. Concerned an enemy soldier had tossed a grenade and was waiting nearby, I told them to take Greer back while I scanned the area. When we reached the perimeter, Greer was going from shock to hysteria.

The men tried to place a tourniquet on him to stop the blood that was gushing from his hand like a squirt gun. The corpsman came over. Upon seeing him, Greer immediately began to scream for drugs. "Give me some good shit!" he cried through clenched teeth. "I need all the morphine you got!" The men offered to retrieve the corpsman's drug supply, but he knew that wasn't a good idea. For certain, some of it would disappear in transition. He instructed one of the marines on applying pressure to the wound while he retrieved his medical supplies.

Sergeant Bazarr was contacting the company commander during all the commotion. We now had a severely injured marine and a Viet Cong prisoner to deal with. But our problems were about to get worse. The corpsman was in a state of panic, rummaging around on the ground on all fours. "Oh shit! Oh shit!" he kept repeating. "He's gone!"

The unthinkable had happened. The prisoner had escaped. The platoon went into a state of panic. Sergeant Bazarr was on the radio seeking advice from headquarters. The new sergeant was giving orders, but the men weren't listening. The other two sergeants were checking on their men and imploring me to assist the new sergeant. I suggested that Roe, who was second-in-command, send out two-man listening posts to give us advance warning in case of an attack, which he did. Greer was continuing to cry for drugs, while the clearly shaken corpsman was finally administering them. Fredericks, who had made the initial capture and who knew best of the cunning ability of the escaped prisoner, was searching the face of each man. "That motherfucker could be standing right beside you, and you wouldn't know it," he said. "You better look at the people around you."

The consensus at that point, however, was that the man had escaped during the confusion. We now had to concern ourselves with an enemy soldier on the loose with enough information about us to place our lives in grave danger. Sergeant Bazarr pleaded for a medevac, but it was not to be. The captain determined an extraction would be too dangerous. On such a particularly dark night, the lights from a descending helicopter would pinpoint our location. But with the noise we had already created, it was almost certain the Vietnamese already knew our position, and there were signs of strong enemy presence in the area. We were therefore ordered to maintain radio silence and wait for first light for an evacuation.

We had already anticipated the order, and a plan was already in motion. A perimeter was established with listening posts outside the lines. Greer was now heavy drugged and silent. There was a possibility Greer's injury was self-inflicted, but he never said it, and neither would we.

It was a long and anxious night in which none slept. We would whisper opinions among ourselves on line that night as to who was to blame for the escape. But no one openly pointed the finger of blame, and the issue was never revisited.

The following morning Third Platoon moved closer to provide more security, and a helicopter arrived to take Greer out. He was unconscious during the extraction, and it wasn't explained if he had lost all or part of his hand. Once he was taken out, we turned our attention to the task that lay ahead, patrolling the valley.

The terrain in the valley was constantly changing. One day it was open with visibility for miles, the next triple canopy where you could only see a few feet. It was the ever-present problem of tunnel complexes that was of greatest concern. But we weren't trained as tunnel rats, so headquarters decided tear gas was the best option. Personally I would have preferred a flame thrower.

This was the same nonlethal gas used by police to control riots. It causes a burning sensation to the eyes, nose, mouth, and skin. As unpleasant as it is, it's unlikely anyone would choose coming out of hiding and risk being shot. But it was our only option, and Sergeant Bazarr never questioned orders. So when a few dozen canisters were delivered, we knew we would eventually get the opportunity to put them to use, in spite of the fact none of us were experienced in its usage.

Several openings in the ground were detected, so Sergeant Bazarr ordered gas be used. The first mistake was for us to release an overconcentration of gas. We released six gas grenades in each opening. Immediately the gas shot up from the ground like smokestacks. We were in awe of the strange sight until the wind shifted. We were literally engulfed in a fog of pain. To make matters worse, we had neglected to remove our gas masks from our packs. Until that moment we had never needed them, so most had them buried deep in their backpacks. Some scrambled to dig out their gas mask. Others searched for pockets of fresh air. We were running into each other, reminiscent of a scene from a cartoon. If the enemy was watching, they would have been laughing too hard to attack. It was not our finest moment. Eventually, the smoke cleared, and we hoped to put it into the past.

The search was directed to an area that was much less dense. It wasn't long before the kill teams that traveled in front of the platoon spotted enemy movement. They returned to report their finding to Sergeant Bazarr. He motioned to Roe, Donahue, and me to accompany him up to the kill team. The kill team had spotted two enemy soldiers. All agreed it was likely they were the advance for an enemy patrol. That patrol would make a prime target. "Roe," Sergeant Bazarr said, referring to his senior man, "I want you and Harris to take a position in front of them. Then, when they pass, I want you to jump out and cut their throats, and then pull their bodies off the road. The enemy patrol will follow, and we can cut them down."

Roe, who seemed to feel it was an honor to be chosen for such a distinguished mission, responded with a broad smile. I had the opposite reaction. "Fuck that!" I immediately blurted out. "We don't even know if there is a spot to do such a grab. And how are we going to keep them silent with the enemy passing so close? Why don't we just let the main force get into the kill zone and shoot them?"

"Because I told you to do it as I said," the sergeant snapped back.

"Damn, Sarge," I complained, "why don't you pass this shit around and stop calling on me all the time?" Then I remembered the vow I made to myself to be more cooperative, and I remained silent. Besides, he was also sending his good buddy. The two of us quickly moved into the trees and then scouted a spot to ambush the anticipated enemy. Roe sat down his weapon and grasped his Ka-Bar, preparing for the attack.

"What the fuck are you doing?" I asked.

The puzzled Roe repeated the orders we had just been given.

"You don't take a knife to a gunfight," I told him. "Have you ever seen a man fighting for his life?"

"No," replied the puzzled Roe.

"I didn't think so."

"Why?"

"Because if you had, you would realize how stupid that order was."

Roe didn't reply. There was no need to. We waited for another twenty minutes, with our rifles in hand. Once satisfied the enemy had changed direction, we returned to the platoon. Both of us were relieved.

When we got to the platoon, Sergeant Bazarr informed us of new orders. We were to serve as a blocking force, which we were happy to do. This would allow us time to stay in one place. The constant patrolling of such difficult terrain was exhausting. Once we found a strategic position, we dug a few trenches and foxholes and then waited for the enemy to come our way. This gave us all an opportunity to engage in a conversation with the KC Scout.

In combat, this sort of exchange of ideas is rare. When a prisoner is captured, the focus is on gaining control. Prior to the capture, the focus is to kill them. With this repatriated Vietnamese soldier, we could tell him why Americans he'd never met hated him so. It went like this.

The American government had developed a template for teaching hate. Those targeted were dehumanized through caricatures that accentuated distinguishing ethnic facial features in unflattering ways. Or it could be done by describing them in degrading and dehumanizing terms. African Americans, Indians, and other minorities were keenly aware of this. The same was done with Communists. That explained why the brothers could hold a civil conversation with the scout. We had something in common. Although the Communist probably didn't know that.

So there we were, me, Johnson, Woody, Sally, Sherman, and Butler, the lone Caucasian, trying to hold a conversation with a man from the other side of the world. He may as well been from Mars. How do you initiate a conversation with a man who had been sworn to kill you? Forget about the familiar salutations: what's up, hey, morning, my man. None of these work on someone who is totally unfamiliar with American customs or language. Commenting on food and the weather seemed too trivial. And asking about his family, considering they were fighting for the other side, was insensitive. Politics was certainly a no-no. It took the straightforward style of Woody to cut to the chase.

"How did you get captured?" he asked. There was a long pause, causing us to suspect he wouldn't answer. This would have been insulting to Woody, who, in spite of his small stature, had no qualms about expressing his anger. After taking a few moments to collect his thoughts, the scout told an insightful story in broken English.

"Me patrol with NVA," he explained. "Then boo-koo marines surround us." The emotion was so strong that he stood up. Then, using a combination of English and Vietnamese, with his arms flailing wildly, he continued. He was ducking and crouching as if he were fighting an invisible foe. "Marines and NVA buck-buck. Marines kock-a dile boo-koo NVA. Then tee-tee NVA. Me no dinki-dow, so me chu-hoi." At that point he began to laugh as we all did.

What he said was, he was on a NVA patrol, when they were ambushed by marines. The fighting became fierce. Soon the marines got the upper hand. When he saw the NVA were dead, he surrendered.

I said I would have died rather than surrender. "Not me!" Woody announced. "I'm going to stay alive as long as I can."

"It's not that I want to die, or that I'm particularly brave," I said, defending myself. "I just don't want any torture involving rats."

Johnson couldn't resist ribbing me. "Oh yeah," he said, stroking his chin, "I remember how you acted when Louie got those rats to come around." When everyone except me laughed, Johnson realized that he had revealed a secret best kept quiet. But the curiosity of the men who hadn't joined the company at that time had been piqued.

"What do you mean, brought the rats around?" Woody asked.

Johnson began to choose his words wisely as he continued with the story. "Harris and a brother that was in the company were on a listening post on Operation Taylor Common. The spot had been used for weeks, and rats were coming around to eat the discarded food. Well, Louie thought it would have been funny if Harris woke up with rats running over him, so he placed food all around."

"That motherfucker!" I shouted, jumping to my feet. "Why the fuck didn't anyone tell me he had done that?"

"You tried to kill him for not helping, man; we sure as hell couldn't tell you he caused the rats to be there," Johnson said. It took a few minutes for me to calm down. Then Butler wisely changed the subject.

"Have you ever been tortured?" he asked the scout. The scout shook his head no, and then he continued to explain. "They buck-buck me like this!" he said, pounding his fist into his hand as a demonstration. Then he demonstrated how they kicked him. "But they no torture me," he finally said with a laugh. We all joined him in laughter. No one was quite sure why. A cordial and lively conversation continued for hours. We talked about the differences in clothes, jobs, and entertainment. We laughed at the similarities in women. Male-female relationships seem to be the same regardless of cultural and geographic differences. The most amusing subject was music and dance. It seemed to the American brothers that it was impossible for anyone not to follow the lyrics and rhythm of the soulful sounds so popular in America. But when the Vietnamese tried to teach us a popular song from his culture, we were just as inept. An officer and occasionally a sergeant would come close, but the group would become conspicuously quiet. Perhaps the higher-ranking marines were suspicious that we were talking about war and policies and felt they should monitor the conversation. After a few moments, the intruder would sense they were unwanted and leave. As the sun began to set, we took our positions on the lines. My job that night was to rove around the perimeter checking on the men. It turned out to be an uneventful night. This was not the case, however, the following morning.

As the sun rose, First Squad sprung an ambush on a small Viet Cong patrol. There was a sudden burst of rifle and machine-gun fire from marine weapons. Only a small and sporadic burst from the Communist weapons could be heard. Second Squad went to assist, but when we arrived, we found the situation was already under control. They were now waiting for a helicopter to do an extraction.

There was one dead and two wounded Viet Cong soldiers. For the victors, it was a routine day. For the victims, their lives were forever changed or ended. One of the wounded was in a semiconscious state. It was likely he would die shortly. The other wounded soldier was only slightly better off. He had several wounds in the upper body, but the primary bleeding was in the groin area. It looked as if he was urinating blood. In all likelihood, this teenage boy's sex life had ended. In spite of this, his expression was one of fear rather than pain. He watched the marines pass him, seeming to anticipate that one of us would raise his weapon and kill him at any moment.

The wounded Vietnamese's clothes were ragged and dirty, and his odor revealed his hygiene was nonexistent. The weapon he carried was outdated and rusty. He had about fifteen rounds at best. The marines, on the other hand, had been recently supplied. Our clothes were clean, our weapons well oiled, and we were overburdened with ammunition. It was no wonder he was afraid. I wondered if he would eventually become repatriated and become a scout like the man we had interacted with the night before.

Waiting for the chopper was a welcome respite. For a brief time, I could feel safe for the moment. I smiled to myself, contemplating the fact I only had a little over two months remaining. I just might actually make it. With the exception of Johnson the radioman, I had been in-country longer than most in the company. That was somewhat of a miracle. When I considered I'd not been wounded, it was not just a miracle, but a divine miracle.

Again I smiled at having referenced such a religious term as *divine miracle*. Anyone who knew me, even in passing, knew I held no religious beliefs. Why pray for answers and divine intervention when everything you needed to know was all around you? You just had to pay attention. And when you pay attention, you can see life for what it really is, one big food chain. Life is just humankind's ability to master their environment and to overpower other predators with technology that has them sitting on the top. Now to the task at hand.

Second and Fourth Squads were ordered to separate from the platoon and search for a Viet Cong patrol that had been spotted. We quickly picked up the trail. The trail led into thicker vegetation. It was easy to follow, but the dense terrain blotted out the sunlight, and as darkness fell, the visibility lessened. Our ranks began to close. Soon the man in front was no more than an arm's length away. We continued to push forward. In time it was so dark that it didn't matter if our eyes were open or closed. Eventually we were guided only by sound. There was no choice but to stop.

We had traveled so long in total darkness that none was sure of the surroundings. Sitting in total darkness, we listened for any sounds. Occasionally we could hear tussling sounds that indicated movement. In a jungle with mice, snakes, birds, and other animals moving about, that wasn't unusual. There was also the possibility of a stream being nearby. But those were friendly sounds. Hostile sounds would be Vietnamese voices or the sound made by the chambering of rounds in a weapon.

So we sat in silence, grouped tight enough for each to feel the man beside him. Any movement was heard by all. We sat in total darkness anxiously awaiting daybreak. It was possible but not probable that some of the men fell asleep. Whatever the case, their secret was safe. Daybreak was delayed in the dense growth. Slowly, specks of light began to appear. Gradually our vision was beginning to be restored. As the morning moved forward, the sounds of movement increased. The jungle was coming alive. We could clearly hear what we suspected to be a small stream. We were anxious to taste the cold mountain water.

While chopping and pushing our way through, we noticed how entwined in the growth we were. We also realized the sound of the stream seemed to stop. The biggest surprise was yet to be discovered. About twenty yards from us was an area that had been cleared. Not with machetes or shovels but from bodies compressing the vegetation or shoving it aside. It was obvious that people, and what appeared to be a large number of people, had been in the area. The rustling sounds we had heard throughout the night were likely a large enemy force. A further search indicated that the force was likely traveling a parallel route. Had we continued another twenty yards, we would have had a deadly confrontation. Our silence was our salvation. Any noise such as talking or coughing could have sparked a fierce firefight. The prospect of a confrontation in such close quarters in total darkness brought chills to us. We were shaken but alive.

The squad leaders contacted the platoon, who informed us that because we were so embedded in the dense terrain, it would be impossible to locate us. We had to move to a more open position. The fastest route was to travel the path already cleared by the enemy. It was also the most dangerous. The enemy might double back at any time. We did shift to the east and eventually exited the triple canopy. Finally we met with reinforcements. That brought a collective sigh of relief.

CHAPTER 30

North and South
September 1969

▲ ▲ ▲

WE DID A CURSORY SEARCH before concluding the enemy force was moving in an easterly direction toward E Company. It was now their problem. G Company was airlifted back to Phu Loc 6. When we reached the regimental headquarters, we were told we would provide security for the base until the next operation, which would start in one week.

It was likely we would make occasional enemy contact on the daily patrols, and there was still danger from the constant shelling at night by the Communist forces operating in the area. But on the days and nights we guarded the perimeter from inside, we felt relatively safe. In addition, we could get a shower, a cot to sleep on at night, at least two hot meals a day, beer, reefer, and a chance to visit the prostitutes who were doing business just outside the gate. Hell, it was like a vacation.

Butler, Judy, and Sherman decided not to waste a moment of the safe time. The following morning, after posting Woody as lookout, they got an early start on the reefer stash, filling the tent with secondhand smoke while I slept.

Woody proved inept as the lookout and burst into the hooch about three steps in front of the lieutenant. Fanning reefer smoke as he entered, he looked around the smoke-filled room calling for me, who was still asleep, to join him outside. I anticipated a berating from the lieutenant for allowing the men to smoke on the compound. To my pleasure, the lieutenant chose not to bring it up.

He was there to inform me of the government's plan to reissue the MPCs (Military Payment Certificates). They were now going to exchange all currency for newly issued certificates, making money possessed by unauthorized persons worthless. "Tell the men to exchange all the old currency immediately," he instructed me. "By the way," he said, "Sergeant Roe will be taking the squad back. You'll serve as his team leader until further notice." If he expected a reaction or any sign of disappointment from me, he didn't get it. I was more concerned about how we could take advantage of the monetary situation.

Everyone knew there would be a rush by the Vietnamese to exchange the certificates. Those who obtained the certificates legally like barbers, laundry workers, and local people who performed some legitimate service on the base would have no problems. It was those who operated on the black market like prostitutes and drug dealers who could potentially lose all their wealth.

The marines were eager to assist the enterprising Vietnamese who were consistently overcharging them, for a surcharge, of course. When H Company returned, villagers were flocking to the base hoping to make an exchange.

Outside the gate there were skivvy houses every one hundred yards. The most efficient was just outside one of the gates. There, in clear sight of the guard towers, they set up a house of prostitution. Before long, the majority of the marines had made the sojourn. Staff sergeants and officers were likely having women secretly escorted to them, so they had no need for the skivvy house. They rewarded the discretion of the men they commanded with silence. Within days a path was worn from the removable opening in the fence to the front door of the house.

The skivvy house was to provide privacy and concealment. The hastily built structure was constructed with leaves and sticks. There were two rooms and a courtyard with two cubicles in it. The line would start outside; then they would enter the first room. Rank had its privileges, so marines of higher rank were allowed to wait in the inside room.

The first room was a five-by-five-foot entrance where the line would form. A baby-san (boy) would usher the men through the process. From this room the client, when called, entered a larger room approximately twelve by fifteen feet. In this room the financial transaction took place. It was five dollars per session, three dollars if the new MPC was used. Papa and Mama-San would take the money, and a young female baby-san would direct them to an area with two rows of benches. As the clients were serviced, they moved over until they reached the chair just outside the entrance to the courtyard. It was the final station for the next man up. The prostitute, whom everyone assumed to be the daughter, would usher in the man sitting on the chair when it was his turn. Mama-San would occasionally enter the courtyard acting as security. Each of the two cubicles had a mat on the dirt floor. One of the baby-sans would do a periodic cleanup on the unused one. No one knew if this was a nuclear family or a created business; it really didn't matter.

It was a professionally run operation with the prostitute, or "sick little girl" as the Vietnamese called them, somehow making each man feel he was special. This was not easy considering she must have serviced at least fifty men each day. There was no doubt this was a dysfunctional family. The parents, if they were actually parents, were clearly exploiting the children. The damage to the family unit was likely permanent. However, this was war, and everyone's actions should be viewed in that context. No one remains the same when they are experiencing something so different, including the marines. If you looked closely, you could see the pain in the Vietnamese eyes. The unity was there, and it showed when a marine displayed any hint of a sexual advance toward the underage daughter. She was clearly off limits.

Occasionally the family members would give each other a smile or a hug, revealing signs of comfort, understanding, grieving, and compassion. The same interaction loving families demonstrate. The only sign of a weak link was the youngest boy. The daughter servicing the client tried to get a reassuring hug from her younger brother, and he pushed her away in disgust. There was no doubt that he would be admonished later. This family was, most likely, providing for their future and supporting an extended family.

This young girl was making the greatest sacrifice. Only time would tell the damage she would suffer. But, for that moment, her painted smile faded.

The downside was obvious to everyone. These people were likely Viet Cong keeping count of the large concentration of American forces. That knowledge would have deterred the NVA from assaulting the base. So the next few days were routine and uneventful. Security patrols and observation posts during the day, with guard duty and listening posts at night. If his family wasn't supporters of the Communists, there would certainly be reprisals against them when the war was over.

On the third day an ARVN unit came onto the base. The commander of the Vietnamese unit held a brief meeting with the Fifth Marines regimental commander in which he requested assistance from the marines. They were going into an unfamiliar area, and they needed a unit that was familiar with it. Our company was selected. The platoon commanders met with the platoon sergeants. After a discussion with the sergeants, Roe was ordered to deliver the conclusion of the meeting to his squad.

He was obviously uncomfortable as he went directly to Second Squad, who were sitting in a group. "I need to talk to you, Harris," he said to me. In spite of the friendship we had developed, tension was always in the room. Roe quickly reminded me that he was just the messenger.

"The commander told his staff to select a man for a high-priority assignment," Roe stated, choosing his words carefully.

"What the fuck does that have to do with me?"

"Your name came up."

"Then it must be some bullshit job."

"No," he said. "The Vietnamese commander needs a marine to go on a patrol with them. They need a pointer."

"Bullshit. I bet they are planning to have one of those motherfuckers shoot me in the back," I protested. "That way, there won't be any witnesses."

Me on point

"They wouldn't do that," Roe assured me, "but they would court-martial you for disobeying an order. Especially one that comes from the top."

"You mean God wants me to walk point?" I said sarcastically.

After a quick laugh, Roe advised me to be careful and then left.

I went back to the hooch and gathered my gear while the men questioned me. When I explained my assignment to the squad, they were equally suspicious.

"Sorry, brother," Woody said, seemly concerned. Then he added, "You think you can get some drugs from the ARVNs?" I began to laugh and playfully punch Woody, wrestling him to the ground. "Hey, man," Woody said, "maybe they know how good you are." I rebuffed any notion the lifers would acknowledge me for anything before exiting the hooch and heading for the helicopter.

I boarded a helicopter with the ARVN platoon, and we took off for the patrol and ambush. The soldiers were very friendly and professional. They also had a much more relaxed leadership style. All the annoying bravado the marine leadership displayed was noticeably absent. The respect was for ability rather than rank. I thought that was a novel idea. They attempted to engage me in conversation, but it was difficult for both sides. I quickly found they had a much better grasp of English than I of Vietnamese. I decided to look and act professional but, most important, pay close attention and watch my back. These were some crazy fools who liked to take pictures of decapitated kills.

The chopper landed; I took point. We would occasionally switch off, but it was clear this was my primary responsibility. During breaks the ARVNs would engage in quiet conversation among themselves, often looking in my direction, but I wasn't particularly concerned. A marine, particularly a black one, was an oddity to them. I began to understand how the scout felt when he traveled with us. I was still bothered by the fact that I was sent out in the first place. What was the motive? During a ten-minute rest, I tried to sort it out. Was I such a thorn in the gunny sergeant and lieutenant's side that they actually wanted me shot?

Then maybe there is no broad conspiracy. The officers and sergeants were professionals. There may have been some racists and crazies among them, but the majority may just have wanted to maintain the status quo.

Times were changing faster than the military. It would be up to future generations to resolve that.

Having reconciled that issue in my mind, I needed to concentrate on my immediate situation. Could I rely on these men around me, when I didn't know shit about them?

The patrol continued. As darkness approached, the ARVN lieutenant looked for an ambush site. He picked a spot just outside a village and ordered the men to cluster there in a mass command post. *Hell no*, I thought when I saw what he was doing.

I approached the officer. "This spot's no good," I told him. Surprised and insulted that a low-ranking enlisted man would question his judgment, he ignored me. I would not be deterred. This shocked the Vietnamese soldiers. They had never seen an order challenged. This time I spoke clear, unbroken English. "If you place us outside that village and we spring an ambush, we'll be in the open, and they'll cut us down." Had this been one of his men, the Vietnamese commander would have likely knocked his subordinate to the ground. Instead he stood eye to eye and toe to toe with me.

The men watched to see who would blink first. Had the Vietnamese officer ordered his men to subdue me, they certainly would have done so, but there would have clearly been a struggle. Then they would have had to bring me back to the marines bloodied and bound. Things may not have gone well for them.

After a few tense moments, the commander asked for suggestions. Without hesitation I came up with quite a few. "Any patrols familiar to this area would be heading for that village. We could take over the village before they do and wait. If you choose not to go in the village, get us out of this open area. Send men to the far side of the village to protect us from a rear attack. Send out some listening posts, put machine guns in the rocks, and place positions in the tree line or have them build some sort of embankment for cover." Again, the commander paused, but he followed some suggestions.

The ARVNs positioned themselves in two-man positions for the ambush. I was in the rocks. To my surprise the soldier assigned to share my position discretely thanked me. He explained it was the first time the young commander had been sent to the field, and, in spite of his inexperience, none would have dared question his decisions. They needed someone outside his authority who would challenge him but couldn't override his decisions. *That would be me*, I said to myself.

The patrol had been long and exhausting, so I was happy to give the first two hours of duty to my Vietnamese partner. Immediately, I went to sleep. But it wasn't a peaceful sleep; it never was. For me nightmares were the norm. The memories of my past deeds would flash through my mind. Those split-second decisions, the many brushes I'd had with death, almost being captured. All of this was causing me to twist and turn, moan and groan, as if I were fighting an unseen opponent. Nightmares were likely my subconscious keeping me on alert for a fight that could happen at any moment. A kind of a radar. Regardless of the depth of my sleep, I would immediately wake up if someone came within arm's length.

So there I was, lying on my back, face toward the clear sky on a moonlit night, when I found myself staring into the face of a Vietnamese soldier.

It was the most frightening moment I had yet to experience. I believed, for a moment, that I was looking into the face of a North Vietnamese soldier, my mortal enemy. We were so close I could smell his breath. I was helplessly frozen with fear. I tried to raise my weapon, but the soldier's knee was on it. Believing that, at any second, I would be violently beaten or killed, I attempted to beg for my life. After a few seconds, the Vietnamese soldier spoke.

"You OK, soul brother?" he whispered. That was the moment I remembered I was on an ambush with a friendly South Vietnamese unit. I must have been holding my breath or simply let out a tremendous sigh of relief, because a rush of air came bellowing out. The Vietnamese wouldn't take his knee off my weapon until he was sure I was thinking clearly. Scared shitless was the best description of what that moment was like. Before allowing the Vietnamese to go to sleep, I had to ask a profound question of him. "How can I tell the difference between a North and South Vietnamese?"

I wasn't asking on a whim. It was a life-and-death situation, and I needed a definitive means of distinguishing the two sides. Who better to make that distinction than a representative of one of the two parties in question?

The Vietnamese soldier, in a sincere and definitive tone, told me. "The enemies come from there," he said, pointing to the front. "Friends," he said, pointing to the ARVN soldiers, "are over here."

I wasn't sure if the soldier was making fun of me or not. Maybe he was, but what he said was true. The uniforms weren't that different, particularly at night. It was like trying to tell the difference between someone from Michigan and someone from Georgia. In fact, it was even harder. There was no regional accent to aid me. In addition, I couldn't understand any of them. Now an ambush would be even more terrifying. I might be advancing or retreating with the wrong side.

The absurdity of my participation was irritating. I had fought with North Vietnamese soldiers who had switched sides. Some of the South Vietnamese soldiers I was fighting with had family in the North. If the soldier who woke me had been born in the North, he would have been coming to kill me rather than wake me up. There may have even been North Vietnamese around me who had infiltrated. After all, they had been fighting for decades. Who knew who was who after all that time? The only person I trusted was myself. To top it off, I was fighting in a civil war that had nothing to do with me.

I came to a decision. If the shit hit the fan, I will shoot anybody who pointed a weapon in my direction. For the rest of the night, I stayed awake. Fortunately for all concerned, there was no enemy contact. At daybreak, a chopper extracted me and returned me to Phu Loc 6.

CHAPTER 31

We Are Who We Are
October 1969

▲ ▲ ▲

When the chopper landed at Phu Loc 6, I found Gulf Company had left, so I was given an informal briefing from a sergeant from Fox Company.

He told me NVA forces had, again, begun using the recently constructed road on a regular basis. It seemed while the cat's away the mice will play. In response, the colonel (the Six) decided to give a heavy show of force, moving three companies of marines to the area, and Gulf Company had already marched to their assigned location. It all seemed futile to me. The enemy would just wait until we left and then return. But I knew such a large concentration of marines would make it a relatively safe action, so I welcomed it. I boarded a truck convoy headed for An Hoa that dropped me off along the road where the platoon was setting up. "Fly you out, fly you in, and then drive you; must be nice," Sally said sarcastically, referring to the fact they'd had to walk.

There was a new gunnery sergeant waiting to brief me. In fact, there were other personnel changes. Lieutenant Storm had completed his tour and moved on. Gunny Mac had been transferred, and another gunnery sergeant had taken his place. I was prepared for the customary intimidation speech, but to my surprise, it didn't come. The new gunnery sergeant informed me that Roe had been transferred, and I was now the permanent Second Squad leader. "Congratulations, son," he said. "If you prove yourself a leader, you might receive a promotion to corporal."

If he was looking for gratitude from me, he was disappointed. I just stood in silence waiting for the gunnery sergeant to finish. Once dismissed, I went away grumbling. "A motherfucker that just got here thinks I have to prove myself to him. Not being shot is all the proof I need. Big deal, I'm now the most experienced and lowest ranking squad leader in the company. That just means my people will get shit assignments, and I can't do nothing about it."

When I told the squad members what had happened, they were happy about it. "Now we won't have to train another asshole," Sherman joked.

"You mean you weren't the squad leader?" Marshal asked. The reality was having stability was good for us as a unit.

After a couple days of nonproductive patrols and ambushes, Gulf Company was trucked back to An Hoa for an anticipated two-day break. For hardened combat veterans who take rest wherever they can get it, it was a two-day mini version of R and R. For me, it was two days closer to returning home.

Back at the base, the men of Gulf Company spent time getting high, taking showers whenever possible, and eating good meals at the chow hall. The platoon as a whole was extremely skilled at pilfering supplies from the chow hall. It wouldn't have been possible, however, had it not been for the mess sergeant's willingness to overlook the missing bottles of hot sauce, steak sauce, Tabasco sauce, and other condiments.

While it was not uncommon for enlisted men to engage in illicit activities and occasional displays of insubordination, I was one of the few squad leaders who condoned it.

My squad would never be held up as poster children for the Marine Corps, but we always got the job done. Perhaps the willingness of the officers and staff to turn a blind eye from time to time was their way of showing us respect for our skills. Respect was better than a medal.

Later in the day, the lieutenant sent Johnson to gather all squad leaders for a briefing. In my first briefing by the newly appointed lieutenant, I was characteristically late, but it wasn't my fault. As low man, I was the last to be informed. "How short are you now, Marine?" the lieutenant asked when I came into the room.

"Five weeks, sir," I replied with a broad smile. "Five long weeks." The lieutenant congratulated me before spreading out the map on the table.

"This area," he said, drawing a circle on the map, "is where we will be going next. The enemy has a concentration of Viet Cong operating there, and it is suspected they have a supply route somewhere. This river," he said, tracing a winding river, "has to be crossed. The only place with a completed bridge is here," he said, using his pointer. "The river actually cuts through this village." He pointed again. "Therefore, that village and that bridge are key to the operation. The company will operate in the area, and the platoons will separate and set up command posts. Second Platoon will cover the area around the village. One of the four squads will actually be positioned on the bridge. I would like one of the squad leaders to volunteer his men," he said, looking around. "Otherwise, I'll pick one at random."

To everyone's surprise, I volunteered. My motive was suspect, given this was the first time I had volunteered for anything, but, when there was no protest, Second Squad was given the assignment. "Can I get mortars and a gun team?" I asked. "We will have a clear line of sight, so we might need the firepower."

"Good idea," the lieutenant agreed. "I'll send Ray and Butler with their people. We have a new corpsman. I'll send him too." After reminding me to be on the lookout for saboteurs, the lieutenant dismissed the squad leaders and platoon sergeants. On the way back to the men, I was smiling like a cat that swallowed the canary.

When I reached the men, I called them together. Showing them the map, I explained the mission as it had been explained to me. Looking at the terrain, Sherman expressed concern at the physical challenge of patrolling and the need for foxholes at night due to the lack of solid structures to offer cover. I agreed. "I guess the officers and staff get to stay in this village," Sally grumbled while pointing to the key position.

"Nope!" I said, smiling.

"Then who does?"

"We do," I answered. The men couldn't believe it, so Sherman wanted it confirmed.

"Do you mean," he said, listening closely for the answer, "we are going to just stay in that village on the bridge all day?" I nodded yes. The others were slowly beginning to figure it out. Then Sherman asked, "How long?" When I told him a week, he jumped for joy. The two new squad members still had questions, so I explained.

"There is no one to guard the village or the bridge from." I smiled. "It's their village, and they sure as hell won't blow up the only crossing they have. And outside the village is the best spot to land a supply helicopter. We'll get our supplies first.

"With all that military presence, Mister Charley will get as far away from here as possible. They are even going to give us a machine-gun team and a mortar section, so Ray and Butler will be hanging with us." Everyone was extremely happy to know all the old-timers would be there. "The band is getting back together." I laughed.

"Wait a minute," one of the new marines called out, "won't we be an obvious target for a mortar attack?"

"They need that bridge," I reminded him. "Besides, there will be marines swarming that area. This will be one of the few times someone will be there to protect you." I laughed again. "Enjoy it."

Now they were beginning to understand the opportunity we had been given, and they rejoiced along with us as we pondered the possibilities. Once we collected our gear, we hurried to the landing zone before the assignment could be changed. When we arrived, the transport helicopters were waiting.

Two choppers carrying Second Platoon landed near the village. We disembarked and rushed into the village and then across the bridge. It was a friendly village, so we didn't expect or encounter resistance. After we did a check of the individuals' papers and a thorough search of the huts, the people were allowed to return to their normal routine. Second Squad members immediately dug foxholes to provide shelter in the event of an attack. Elevated positions were selected for lookout points. We also built a low hutch with reinforced walls. The machine-gun teams and mortar sections positioned themselves as well.

Expendable and Necessary

While Second Squad secured our area, First, Third, and Fourth were establishing strategic positions in the surrounding area. All roads leading into and out of the village were covered. The feeling-out process between the men and the villagers took about a day. By the end of the third day, the villagers knew the chain of command and the personalities of the men who had dropped into their lives. We were equally observant. We contacted the village elder who called the shots, and we learned the families and extended families and the chain of command among the young boys who could connect us with the goods and services we required. Soon Baby-San made his presence known.

He was an aggressive young boy with a swaggering walk of confidence, about eight or nine years old. He wore a loud flower-print shirt, soiled black pants, and a panama hat cocked to the side. He walked up to greet me. "How you do, soul brother?" he said with a wide smile that showed all of his tobacco-stained teeth. While speaking, he gave the clenched-fist salute. I knew I was about to be presented with a business opportunity, so I decided it would put me in a better position if I acted uninterested. I acknowledged Baby-San's presence and then walked away. The young man and his entourage ran behind me. The fact that our position was stationary enabled us to act as a supply depot for the squads patrolling the area. We had to bargain carefully.

"How much?" I responded.

"Two C rats for one ten pack."

"No, me give MPCs for one oh ones," I insisted.

"OK, one ten pack for one C ration."

"No way," I said, walking away. The young boy stomped away in the other direction.

The two new marines standing near were perplexed by my flat-out rejection of the offer made to me. I explained to them that the kids were trying to collect nonperishable goods for the Viet Cong to use in the field. I made that clear to the squad members, but it was likely some would use food for bartering when they ran out of money.

Later that evening, I called for a meeting. Baby-San and two of his crew were there. Sally, Ray, Butler, and Sherman also attended. The purpose was to establish a set agreement for goods and services. The average marine earned about $160 per month. Half of that was generally set aside for future R and R, so we had to be careful not to deplete our limited resources. After a lengthy discussion, a compromise was made. The cost was double the price of goods purchased in Da Nang, but the remote location justified the markup. But we had a bargaining chip. We could exchange the old, useless MPC many Vietnamese were holding for the new certificates that were in circulation at a greatly increased exchange rate.

A ten pack of joints was two dollars. A fifty pack of number tens was five dollars. Beer, which was difficult to obtain in the bush, went for two dollars a can. That was considerably more that the twenty cents it sold for in the bars on base. The most difficult item to obtain was ice, which made it the most expensive. A six-by-ten-inch square block of ice would go for five to ten dollars, if you were lucky enough to obtain it. One block of ice, when wrapped in a towel, would cool about four beers before melting. It was much cheaper to do drugs than to drink beer. We could also obtain pornographic magazines, writing materials, and playing cards. The squad members could purchase the items and sell or trade with the passing marine patrols.

The kids from the village could also perform services such as cutting hair, washing clothes, and replenishing our canteens from the water storage containers (Water Buffalos) that were brought into the villages.

For the most part, we had established a boom town. Because we were a security detail, we weren't required to patrol, so we spent our time relaxing, socializing, getting high, gambling, and listening to music from tapes and radio. Of the twenty marines, fifteen were a part of the criminal enterprise. Three kept to themselves due to religious convictions, and two had not yet gained enough trust to be included in the inner circle.

Trust was usually developed from the life-and-death experiences of combat. With the lull in fighting, the new men had yet to prove themselves. One of the responsibilities confronting me was to put their minds at ease, so on the third day I held an extended conversation with the new men.

"What do you guys think so far?" I asked. They looked at each other, uncertain how to reply. After some urging, they opened up.

"Lance Corporal Harris, I'm scared," one said.

"You should be," I replied.

"Why aren't you scared?"

"I am," I said, laughing.

"I don't get it. If this is enemy territory and we are surrounded by VC, shouldn't we be on guard?"

"What makes you think we aren't?"

The marines looked around at the squad members who were sitting around laughing, talking, and getting high. So I explained what I thought they already knew.

"We are out of range of the enemy's long-range artillery. If they got close enough to fire mortars, one of our patrols would pick them off. At this very moment, our people are watching us. That's why we built structures to hide behind and in while getting high. The squad members you don't see are on guard duty. In fact, you two will be going on duty soon. There are listening posts and machine-gun teams concealed all around in case the enemy gets through. Each day and night, those positions are moved. If something does happen, you'll find how skilled the men around you are. So relax," I said in conclusion. "This is as good as it gets." The men left seeming more at ease.

I went to the primary observation post to check on the men. This post had been meticulously built by Butler and Jackson. They had done such a good job camouflaging it that one could walk past without knowing it was there. It was a spot from which they could observe most of the village. It was also a volatile position, the most likely target in the event of an attack. Therefore, the men were equipped with a set of binoculars, a high-powered rifle, and a radio. They knew to clear out immediately if they heard an incoming round.

Upon entering the door, I was confronted by a thick cloud of reefer smoke. I had to fan it away to see clearly. There were beer cans scattered around with soul sounds playing on the tape player. "It's a good thing a lifer wasn't coming in," I said to Woody and Butler, who were tussling over a pair of binoculars.

"We saw you coming," Butler assured me.

The distraction allowed Woody to take possession of the binoculars. "Check this out," he urged me while passing the binoculars to me. He directed my attention to a particular location in the village and a person who seemed to be stooping. I studied the figure for a moment and then began to describe what I saw.

"It looks like a woman exposing her wrinkled butt. Goddamn!" I said, passing the binoculars back. "She's taking a shit."

"Let me see!" Woody responded, snatching the binoculars.

"Are you motherfuckers so horny that you're getting a hard-on watching an old woman shit?" I laughed. "I better keep an eye on the water buffalos and chickens." Butler seemed embarrassed, but Woody was undeterred and continued to watch.

"You know, man," Butler said to his old friend, "we do need some women out here."

"I'm not a pimp," I countered.

"I know, but maybe you can send a patrol out and bring some hookers back."

"Are you kidding me? You want me to organize a pussy patrol?"

"Me and Ray don't have enough people in our squads to organize a patrol, so we hoped you could maybe get some riflemen to volunteer."

"So you and Ray have already discussed this?"

"Sure, and we already have the volunteers lined up."

"Any woman who is of the age of consent is VC, and there is no way I'm bringing the enemy in. But when the Baby-San hustler comes through, you and Ray come over, and we'll see what we can work out. Before we so blatantly bend the rules," I cautioned, "I have to check for spies in the woodpile." I was referring to the fact that some of the men might report everything to the lifers. Butler agreed, and I continued my inspection of the lines. In spite of the relaxed attitude within the perimeter, the men on line were alert and professional, at least while I was there. The morale was high, but at each stop, one theme was consistent, the need for a woman. There seemed to be no need to be concerned about an informant. Even the conservative radioman, Donahue, shared the liberal attitudes of his fellow squad members. And after a long conversation with the new corpsman, I decided they could all be trusted.

Later in the day when Baby-San and his entourage passed through, I waved Baby-San over. Initially all of his crew came, but I insisted I deal only with him. Reluctantly he sent them away, and we talked.

"Marines need boom-boom girls," I told him.

"You mean sick little girls?" Baby-San replied.

"I don't like calling them sick little girls," I insisted. "We don't want them sick, and we sure as hell don't want little girls."

"OK," Baby-San laughed, "they're boom-boom girls. Me take marines to boom-boom girls."

"No, you bring girl into camp."

"How many girls you want?"

"One."

"One, me no can get one girl for so many marines. They buck-buck her [beat her]."

"If you bring a squad of VC boom-boom girls in this camp, I'll kick your ass," I warned him.

"Boom-boom girls are no VC. Me kock-a dile VC [kill VC]," Baby-San said, pounding his fist in his hand to prove his point.

"Fuck that. You bring one boom-boom girl to that gate; then she gets strip-searched before entering. If she has a weapon on her, she'll be shot, and so will you!"

Baby-San decided to avoid an argument he couldn't win. He began to negotiate a price.

"Twelve dollars for one marine," he offered.

"No way, three dollars for one marine," I countered.

"Ten dollars, one marine," Baby-San shouted with his arms folded.

"Four dollars, one marine," I came back.

"No way!" Baby-San said.

I decided to attempt a bulk deal, hoping Baby-San would lack math skills. "Sixty dollars for twelve marines," I announced.

Baby-San wasn't good at math, but he was smart enough to insist I show him how much it was for one marine. After a prolonged math lesson, Baby-San made a final offer of sixty dollars for ten marines, payable up front. After those ten, it was to go up to eight dollars for one marine. I finally agreed, and Baby-San shook my hand and left. I then went over to Butler, Woody, Sally, and Sherman, who were sitting near. I was beaming with delight at the deal I had set. The squad members were equally excited and pleased with my bartering skills. "That's leadership at its finest," Sherman shouted as they all searched their wallets.

That joyful moment quickly passed when we realized we only had seventeen dollars between us. Sally had the most with ten. "Goddamn," Sally shouted. "You mean we only have seventeen dollars between us? Well, I got mine," he said, putting his money back in his pocket.

"It's all or nothing," I reminded them. "We have to come up with the whole sixty dollars before she gets here."

"Well, I don't like that deal," Sally continued to protest, "It's not my fault you guys spent your money on drugs and beer. You didn't share that with me."

"It's not our fault you don't drink," Sherman scoffed. "Harris just made a bad deal."

My rapid fall from grace was upsetting. But I understood. Butler, who proved to be the mediator, reminded us that there were other marines in the area. So while I went my own way, mumbling something like, "To hell with all of you," they went out to solicit the remainder of the money from marines on the listening post and machine-gun positions.

After about a half hour, they returned. Unfortunately for us, it was five days to payday, and the marines lived from paycheck to paycheck like most working people. They were able to collect another twenty-one dollars, which gave them a grand total of thirty-eight. Now they were just twenty-two dollars short of the front money, but it might as well have been a million.

"I can't believe those boots [new marines] didn't have money," I said, shaking my head. "They didn't even buy any drugs or beer."

"I asked, but they seemed scared to join in," Woody interjected.

"Scared of what?" I asked.

"Scared the lifers might find out."

"I can't say I blame them," I responded.

"You're a lifer." Woody laughed.

"I'm not a goddamn lifer."

"You're the squad leader; that makes you a lifer."

"Fuck you!" I said, bringing an end to the discussion.

"Wait a minute," Woody said, urging me on, "they might give you the money if you ask. You're their squad leader, man; they want your approval." Sally, Sherman, and Butler agreed; soon they were all urging me on. Reluctantly I went out to approach the boots. Within five minutes I returned waving the remaining twenty-two dollars. The two boots followed directly behind me, smiling and eager to be included. They were like high-school boys preparing for a date. This might have been the first time in days some of them had washed up and brushed their teeth.

As promised, Baby-San arrived with the evening's entertainment. She was an attractive woman who responded to the strip search as if it were a performance. Her sophistication and Americanized appearance indicated she was likely a bar girl from one of the major South Vietnamese cities. In truth, the oversexed marines would have been satisfied as long as her teeth weren't stained from betel nut and her body parts were washed. So Woody and Butler's closed-in hooch served as a cheap hotel. Some if not all of the marines had been holding out, because after the first prepaid sixty dollars, they kept coming, some on a return visit.

I was constantly patrolling the lines to make sure each position was manned by at least one man.

My primary concern was that she might grab an unattended weapon and kill a few marines. Therefore, Sally served as security guard, enforcing the strict "no weapons in the sex quarters" rule. The marines understood and were compliant, but they were reluctant to part with their Ka-Bars. Sally reminded them that a distracted marine in the heat of passion might easily get his throat cut, and they took his word for it.

It turned out to be a blissful night of passion for all. They lived up to the creed of the Romans: "Eat, drink, and be merry, for tomorrow you may die." Fortunately, no one died that night, or the next when she returned charging six dollars per turn. When she got down to four dollars with no takers, she knew she had drained all the cash and moved on a very wealthy woman.

While the men outside the village weren't enjoying the pleasure amenities that Second Squad was, they were enjoying the continued break in combat action. In all likelihood, the lack of enemy contact indicated the VC had been using another route or were simply waiting for the marines to leave. An extended break in action, as always, brought an end to the operation.

The following morning, the lieutenant came through and confirmed it. He assembled me, the rifle squad leader; Ray, the machine-gun team leader; Butler, the mortar section leader; and Donahue, the radioman, together to give us the news.

The exit strategy was outlined, and the village was to become the landing zone for the extraction of all the marines. The company would gradually assemble and converge on the village where we would board the chopper. There was only room for one chopper at a time, so the platoon sergeants and squad leaders would be responsible for moving their men in a predetermined order. Satisfied the men understood, the lieutenant left. The remainder of the evening was uneventful. Sally and Sherman went with me to mingle among the villagers. We noticed a large gathering of the villagers.

In short order, we realized it was the start of a funeral procession. We decided to be considerate of the mourners and keep a respectful distance. It was an interesting event for us. Most, if not all, had never seen a Vietnamese funeral. With all the death we had witnessed since coming to Vietnam, this was the first time I had seen someone who had died from natural causes.

We were filled with questions. What was their religion? Did they have a religion? Who officiated over the funerals? How was the body prepared? Did they have mass graveyards or mini resting places for the individual villages? None approached the mourners for answers, so these questions would go unanswered. We were struck by the fact that, if not for the decorative colorful clothing and unfamiliar relics, it was identical to the funerals in the

States. Given the fact this was a war zone, we were suspicious of the casket being hoisted out of the village. It would be an opportune time to smuggle a Viet Cong soldier or weapons right past us. I felt there were many other less conspicuous ways of doing this, so we allowed the procession to pass unchallenged.

The following morning, as planned, marines from the outlying area began converging on the village for transport. With them came dozens of kids begging for food and money. Security for Second Squad meant not only protecting the withdrawing marines from attack, but keeping the kids from pilfering. Fortunately, the choreographed exit was going smoothly, while I continued to prowl like a mother hen.

Finally we were down to the last platoon. Only two lifts remained; our squad would be on the very last one. The tension was mounting. Everyone knew if there was to be an attack, this would be the most opportune time. The next marines to board were sitting with their backs against a brick wall that protected us from the mincing force from the wind generated by the whirling helicopter blades. Some chose to wait until the final moment to scoop up the heavy combat gear they traveled with.

As the final chopper began to descend, Jackson and I braced ourselves. Jackson noticed Baby-San approaching. The marines grouped together in preparation for the departure. He tapped my shoulder, alerting me of Baby-San. Because of the connection Baby-San had with us, we suspected he was coming to say his final good-bye. We felt protective of the little deal maker, whom we considered a friend. There was no way his forty-pound frame could withstand the powerful gale winds. We both yelled for him to stop, but he continued to approach. The chopper was now on the ground. Both of us ran toward him, trying to catch him before he would be blown off his feet.

But Baby-San's attention was fixed. He never looked over at us. The marines were so braced for the helicopter that they didn't notice him reach down and scoop something up. It appeared to be a grenade that was lying next to Marshal's, one of the new marines, unattended gear. He was now fumbling with it as he ran toward the helicopter. Jackson and I both spotted him and gave chase. I was both taller and faster than the little guy and quickly caught and passed him. I couldn't allow him to reach the chopper.

I caught Baby-San with a hard right hook, the force of which was doubled because Baby-San ran full speed into it. His head snapped backward, but his feet continued to run forward. It was obvious that he was immediately knocked unconscious, because he made no attempt to break his fall, and his head slammed into the ground. Jackson was now standing beside us, poised to fire a bullet into his brain. I now had my left knee on his chest and my Ka-Bar raised poised to strike. A blow from the fourteen-inch blade of hardened steel would surely have severed the young boy's head. But Baby-San was lying flat on his back, spread-eagle, with his eyes rolled back into his head. Fortunately for him, he didn't move.

It was confusing to onlookers, who were standing motionless with blank expressions. None questioned why we had attacked this young boy. All questions were answered when Jackson reached down and took the grenade from Baby-San's hand. The marines preparing to board or the waiting to board the helicopter were the likely target. "Arrest that motherfucker!" I shouted. The squad members quickly scooped him up. Marshal, the marine whose unattended grenade was snatched, ran up to me attempting to apologize. I gave him a look that was somewhere between disgust and sadness before handing him the grenade and turning to walk away. It would have been hypocritical to blame Marshal when I had invited a saboteur to enter our camp. The kid was likely waiting for an opportunity to kill us. He had gained his opponent's trust so he could attack when it was to his advantage. I shuddered to think of how terribly wrong things could have gone. Baby-San was still unconscious as they dragged him into the helicopter. Soon after, Second Squad boarded the final bird. In spite of my vicious attack on Baby-San, I didn't really hate him. If I did, I would have killed him rather than take the chance of subduing him. I had seen only what I wanted to see in Baby-San; I should have striven to see beyond that. "He is who he is, and we are who we are," I said to myself as the village faded out of view.

Once we arrived at An Hoa, we got a shave, a haircut, a hot meal, and, more important, a safe night's sleep. Now down to my final four weeks, I was really feeling good. But I would have felt even better if they had allowed me to finish out that time at headquarters. When I returned from my brother's funeral, I had requested duty at the base and was denied. Maybe now I could get a chance. Surely I deserved some of the good life. I looked around feeling OK. I wasn't in the bush, but I wasn't safe. It was a typical military installation, barbed wire surrounding the perimeter with observation posts at designated intervals. There were portable buildings that served as offices and tents used for housing, all of which were surrounded by sandbags. And we had tanks and artillery installations. This was a good place to be.

I remembered the chaplain who had informed me of my brother's death. A job as his assistant was open. I would even become a Catholic for a month if it would keep me from being shot. I knew there were white marines applying for the position, but maybe the chaplain could set his prejudices aside and just consider time in combat. After all, his job was to show compassion. I was feeling positive as I approached the chaplain's tent.

The chaplain did remember me but was not moved by my reasoning. He informed me he was reviewing a request from another marine requesting to be transferred to his charge. This marine, according to the chaplain, was undergoing tremendous mental pressures, and he was moved by the fact that the marine had served nearly four meritorious months in combat. *What a load of shit*, I thought.

As I walked away, I felt a familiar tap on my shoulder. It was fear, my constant companion, demanding attention. Fear was good; it kept me alert. But fear is an emotion in anticipation of an event. It was the event I needed to focus on. At this time there was no event on the table. For my own sanity, I needed to brush that fear aside. The only sure thing at this point was that I had been lucky to have survived this long. But luck would run out over time. I could have been told I was going home to a tomorrow that never came. Maybe this would be my year of miracles.

In the distance I noticed Johnson sitting alone on a pile of sandbags. I knew Johnson had a week less than me, so he was the one person who could understand how I felt. I went over to join him. Johnson was so consumed in thought that he didn't notice my approach. "You got a joint?" the normally by-the-book marine asked me when I sat down. This surprised me, but I never refused a fellow marine a joint.

I felt something was wrong, but I really didn't want to know, so for a while we just sat in silence consuming mind-altering drugs. Finally Johnson spoke. "We are going back into Arizona." I didn't flinch. I hoped Johnson would break out in laughter and say he was joking, but he didn't.

"How do you know?" I asked.

"I'm with the CP. I hear what's going on."

"When will they tell us?"

"Today, most likely; offshore artillery is softening them up as we speak."

"What else did you hear?"

"Not much. I'm too far down the ladder. I do know they are going to have us assault from the outside rather than drop us in the middle of the enemy like before."

"Do you think we'll have a better chance?" I asked.

"A better chance for what?"

"Fuck the gung-ho kill-VC shit. Do you think we'll have a better chance of coming out alive?"

"It's a choice between being dropped into the middle of a hornets' nest and fighting your way out, or starting from the outside and fighting your way in. I don't know which is best. I know that being with the command post, it will be better for me, because I won't be the first in. You guys will catch it either way."

"You got a point," I said, rising to walk away. "Hey, man," I said, turning back to Johnson, "was that the big plan you always talked about?"

Johnson smiled and gave an affirmative nod with his head. "Remember, my brother," he said, "you didn't hear anything from me." I smiled, gave him the customary Black Power handshake, and then left. I needed private time to think before addressing my squad. I could not address them with self-doubt.

Actually, my doubt wasn't with myself. I was doubting the whole damn war. When will Americans learn you can only conquer people who believe you can? The strategy was flawed. The NVA and VC would never give up

Arizona, or this country. It was their house. We were trying to take it over a room at a time. We fought and died taking over a room. Then we moved to the next room, and they returned to the one we had just left. So it was still their house.

No matter how much we bombed them, they were still there. It was like trying to wipe out ants by stomping on the ground. Ants are interesting in drawing analogies. I remember watching ants devour an earthworm. The worm thrashed about killing hundreds if not thousands of ants before succumbing to the attack. That worm became a food source for thousands of other ants, so who was the winner?

Of course, we are not insects. But the will to survive is inherent to all living creatures. Whether it is for food, to protect, or to defend, we will kill to survive. Humans are animals at the top of the food chain. For us war has been accepted as justification to kill without consequence. I am human.

While I doubted the operation, I never doubted the men I was about to ask to follow me into hell. I knew any seed of doubt could lead to our downfall. To succeed, cooperation was a must. There were no second chances. Therefore, I hid any fears I harbored with boldness and spoke to them with confidence.

"I know you may have gotten wind of something coming down. Well, so have I," I said, pacing in a circle. "I'll give it to you in a word: Arizona. We're gonna go into the devil's house and do what we do best, kill. I know every man in this room. I've seen what you can do, and I trust you all with my life. I'll do all I can to gain your trust in me. Remember this, unlike the lifers, I'm not sending you anywhere. I won't be in a planning room, on the radio, or behind a tree telling you to attack. We are going in together, and we'll come out together. I will be within your sight at all times, so I'm asking you to trust that I'm as concerned about your lives as I am about my own. Whatever happens to you will happen to me. I've been here for a year, and I only have a few weeks to go before going home, and there is no way I'll let anything get in the way of that. The one thing I can do well in life is survive. If that means killing, then that's what I'll do. Nothing, I repeat, nothing, be it animal, vegetable, or mineral, can stop me from getting from point A to point B. Any motherfucking thing that gets in my way will be destroyed. And nothing gets past me. I don't give a shit if it is a five-hundred-pound gorilla. I'll slaughter him, then grind him up for hamburger and eat it. That's right," I said, licking my lips, "its feeding time."

"It's about time," Sally said, showing his allegiance. "We've got to kill some more motherfuckers. I've been with this brother most of my time in-country. We party hard, and we fight hard. It's time to fight!" Sally's endorsement meant everything to me and the men.

"Kill, kill, kill," the men chanted, growling, pounding their chests, playfully wrestling, and giving high fives and Black Power handshakes. The scene was surreal.

Hearing the commotion, the captain, lieutenant, gunnery sergeant, and staff entered the hooch. They seemed to believe they would be received as honorary guests at a pep rally. It was quite to the contrary. We viewed ourselves as a force within a force. The lifers were perceived as attempting to steal the thunder. When Sally, Butler, Sherman, and I, the senior squad members, went silent, the festive atmosphere subsided. After a short unifying speech confirming the return to Arizona from the captain, they left. As soon as they exited the hooch, we resumed our pep rally.

Word of the attack on Arizona quickly spread, and the whole base was buzzing. Few knew or truly understood the dangers ahead, and those who did skillfully masked their fears. Personal stories were exchanged and sometimes embellished. Some prayed, wrote letters, sang, danced, drank, and did drugs. Soon other members from the company would come and go. From the outside, one would assume this company of frontline marines was having a celebration of life. In truth, the fire burning beneath the calm was the realization that some of the men present might die. Each man had postponed reality to reach an inner peace. For now, each man chose to do his own dance with death.

I was no exception. Sitting alone, I searched for purpose and inspiration. I found it in the things that mattered most. I had not compromised my principles. I had a family back home, a woman waiting to build a life with me, a job, and a new car. There were friends around me who depended on me, and I could depend on them. I had reefer, beer, warm food, a clean shirt, a place to shower, a sanitary place to shit, and a safe place to sleep. Today I was content with plenty to live for. I would deal with tomorrow when it came.

CHAPTER 32

Show Time
November 1969

▲ ▲ ▲

THE MEN EVENTUALLY DOZED OFF consumed in their own private thoughts. Sometime before sunrise, about five, Johnson came into the tent. "The lieutenant is calling all squad leaders for a briefing," he informed me. I hadn't been asleep; in fact, I was fully dressed. The men were also awake and quickly prepared to leave.

The four squad leaders joined the lieutenant, who had been recently briefed by the company commander along with the other platoon leaders. The gunny sergeant, platoon sergeants, and section leaders were also present. It was a diverse group, culturally, ideologically, and socially. For now, they would act as one.

Following the standing blackout orders at combat bases, the room was illuminated by a single kerosene lamp, visible only when the door opened. The dim light made the inhabitants barely visible. It had the appearance of a den of nocturnal creatures preparing to prowl. The lieutenant laid out the mission.

"Our company will be a part of a regimental search-and-destroy operation into the area the men refer to as the Arizona Territory. It is, as you know, a part of our area of responsibility," he said drawing a rectangle on a map. "I have not personally been into the area, but some of you have," he said, searching the room. "Those who have been there can surely tell you it houses a large concentration of NVA and VC forces. We suspect they use the area for the training and staging of troops and as a base for launching operations. They have gotten far too comfortable. This is our area of control, and we are going to take away that comfort." The other squad leaders cheered their approval. After an accepting pause, the lieutenant continued.

"This will be a sweep limited to five days. Several companies will be transported to this area," he said, plotting a line on the western side of the territory. "In fact, they have landed and are digging in. They will serve as the blocking force. Our company along with Fox, Hotel, and Echo will act as the assaulting element. Golf has been given the honor of being the center position. Our platoon will be the first in." The rousing cheer he expected was slow to come. Those who had been in Arizona before were particularly concerned. We knew the NVA and VC needed to hold the territory for strategic purposes. They would not retreat from a fight. The lieutenant quickly addressed those reservations. "I will not allow my leaders to show doubt," he said emphatically. "The men must believe in you before they can believe in themselves. Doubt will cause hesitation, and hesitation for even a split second could mean the difference between life and death." There was silence but no dissention, so the lieutenant continued.

"Offshore artillery has been pounding the area for three days," he went on. "We are now doing saturation aerial bombing. There are periodic pauses in the bombing to allow a window of opportunity for surrenders. There have been civilian and VC surrenders, but the hard core, and certainly NVA, will hold out.

"They know we are coming, gentlemen, and they'll be waiting. Remember, we are fighting for the South, and we are in the South. So assume the Vietnamese you encounter are friendly unless you can clearly identify them as hostile. Your platoon sergeant will give you more specifics," he said as he turned to leave.

Sergeant Bazarr, as platoon sergeant, would have the moment he lived for. All the squad leaders would report to him. So with his kerchief, handlebar mustache, and flamboyant style, he provided more details.

"Just as the lieutenant reported, this will be a short, limited operation," he began. "There will be heavy firepower on standby. An air attack can be launched in a matter of minutes as well as heavy artillery. One of our responsibilities will be to locate specific targets for them. Immediate targets can be hit by our own mortar section. Everyone is there for us. They will transport us in, back us up, and supply intelligence. But we are the key, and our job will be up close and personal. The company and platoons will be broken into parts. Sometimes a family has to be broken apart, then come together for the common good. The smallest unit will be kill teams drawn from individual squads. They will be moving to the front and flanks of the main body, so it is imperative that their locations are well coordinated with the company communications. Harris," he said, addressing me, "the first team will come from your squad." I knew any objections or reservations would be ignored, so I offered none. Bazarr gave the redundant rally-for-freedom call and then instructed us to pray together.

I refused to participate in what I considered smoke and mirrors. I wasn't looking for divine intervention or a miracle. I wanted aerial reconnaissance and a detailed account of the enemy's positions. If God had that, he should speak up. And the call for "unity and the fight for freedom" made me laugh. Richard M. Nixon was our president and commander and chief. That man would have reinstituted slavery if he could. A better rallying call would have been, "Let's pull together by focusing on our common enemy so we might all live to see tomorrow." But I knew I was likely the only one in the room who felt like that, so I stood silently waiting for him to finish. "OK," Sergeant Bazarr finally said, "return to your squads and brief your people." The men complied.

When I returned to the hooch, the men were ready. We were under a tight schedule, so I had to brief them as they packed war gear. Within minutes we were rushing to the helicopter pad. G Company was the last company transported from An Hoa. On the short ride, the men began to paint their faces with camouflage paint. When we landed, the immediate area had been secured, so there was no imminent threat. We could, therefore, immediately begin our three-mile forced march to our area of entry.

Along the way we passed other marines who were also part of the cast of killers being assembled. Some were embedded on the edge of streams that offered both cover and concealment. Facial paint and tactically applied vegetation allowed them to disappear into the surroundings. They could cut down any retreating Communist troops.

Eventually, the platoon reached the edge of the tree line, which bordered the shallow river where other members of G Company lined the riverbank. The timing was perfect, because darkness was approaching. The marines on the riverbank were backed up with mortars and machine guns. Long-range artillery was on standby. With that amount of firepower, there was little concern of a nightly attack from the Communist troops. It would have been futile.

Second Squad would not be on duty that night, so we could rest. As the sun set and the surroundings began to fade to black, the life force within us was alerted. We could no longer see the man beside us. But we needed no visual confirmation; the energy force so powerful we could feel one another's presence.

The young lions would sleep tonight and awaken the next day hungry and thrusting for blood. In truth, we got little sleep. We just sat in silence waiting for the sun to rise.

Sitting in the darkness the night before the battle was like being in an unlit auditorium. The trees and bushes stood in silence like an audience waiting for the curtain to rise.

Day One

Finally the black was turning to gray; the sun was rising. It was awe-inspiring. Everything appeared fresh and new, like the first day of creation. The sunlight and sweat accented the physiques of the young warriors at their physical zenith. They had the look of determination and confidence and the eyes of predators poised to assert their dominance.

I motioned them close for a final briefing. Butler, who led the mortar section, also came forth. He was an important component and needed to be a part of the discussion. I started by telling them what to expect.

"In a few minutes, artillery will begin to blanket the area we'll invade," I said. "First, Second, and Third Platoons will assault on line. Fourth Platoon will make up the command position. Each platoon will send a kill team out prior to the sweep. So the teams will have to be in deep to avoid being hit from behind." I paused to allow any questions. There were none, so I went on. "Second Platoon will be in the center, and the platoon's kill team will come from our squad." The men were anxious about having to take such a vulnerable position but remained silent, hanging on to each of my words. So I continued.

"We will form a five-man kill team. Sherman will point, I will be directly behind him, and Donahue will be behind me on radio. Sally will be on the right flank and Kartis on the left. Jackson and the new men will move with First Squad for now."

"Then you're gonna be with us on the kill team, brother?" Sally inquired.

"Of course I am," I assured him, insulted that he would expect anything different. "Now remember," I said sternly. "We have to be far enough in front so as not to get caught in the fight. We'll have to be quick or dead. If one of you falls, we are going to have to drag you."

"Won't they try to hit us when we run toward them?" Sherman inquired.

"Hopefully they will have pulled out; that's what the artillery bombardment is for," I answered. "But Butler can give more details on that." Butler then took over the briefing.

"Long range will begin soon. When they stop, the mortars will start a pattern. We'll drop twenty rounds in their lines. We already have the coordinates. I guarantee their heads will be down. When the last two are fired, you guys are gonna charge in. Time it so the last hits right before you enter the tree line. Their heads will be down waiting for more to drop. That will be you guys' opportunity to get by them." Butler withdrew and joined his people.

I continued with my briefing. "When we are far enough in, Donahue will call it in, and they will begin the assault. At that point the enemy will be concentrating on our main force, and we will be in a position to feed information on the enemy's movement. Donahue will then become the key. He has to keep them informed of our position at all times, so we need to protect him, and if he goes down, Kartis will take the radio. I want Sally and Sherman to be free to fight. Any questions?" The men were concerned, but they understood their roles, so they exchanged power handshakes and began to move forward.

We moved forward to take our positions. For the moment, all the attention was directed toward us. The marines on the line parted their ranks as we passed, giving a supportive smile or a clenched-fist salute. We were the starters and would, therefore, set the pace. Some facial expressions were sad, and rightfully so. The first into battle are generally the first to fall. The men might possibly be viewing the walking dead. The kill team, however, could not allow ourselves to harbor such a thought.

It was too late to think about it. Time had run out. Once we started in, the only way out was through. We were totally focused. As we knelt on the bank waiting for the equivalent of a starter's pistol, every fiber of nerve in our bodies tingled.

Unknown to us, the "dogs of war" had already sprung into action. Miles away at a command post, the top dogs, who coordinated the action, gave the OK for the big dogs to launch the weapons of mass destruction, long-range heavy artillery.

It started with white phosphorus rounds to calibrate range. Then a blanket of high-explosive rounds. The immediate area across the river was pulverized. When that bombing pattern ended, Butler began his reign of terror, twenty rounds.

The drop was uniform: poof, poof, poof, poof, and then boom. Once the first mortar landed, four more were propelled. "We'll leave at eighteen," I yelled, calculating the time it would take to cross the shallow river. The internal clock had started, sixteen, seventeen, eighteen. "Now," I shouted.

We charged forward like racehorses breaking from the starter's gate, or ferocious animals who discovered the cage was unlocked. By the time we reached the halfway point of the river, the last rounds were landing. When we entered the tree line on the opposite bank, hot shrapnel was still raining down. Perfect timing, for any enemies who lay in wait still had their heads down. The ground beneath us was scorched, and the vegetation was ablaze. We were literally rushing into a wall of fire and trusting we would not get burned. Soon we had broken through the tree line and were in the open. Now, with an unrestricted path, we could run at full speed. We ran as if we were in a foot race with one another. Each man knew he must put as much distance between himself and the wall of assaulting marines as he could.

Then a sudden a burst of enemy gunfire rang out. We were in the open and could only lie as flat as possible. We listened closely for the distinct sound of an incoming round. Not hearing it, we knew we weren't the ones being shot at. "Gulf, Gulf," Donahue shouted over the radio, "we are in and approaching checkpoint one." This was the conformation the marines waited for, and the full assault began. The kill team was by no means out of danger. We still had to make the three-hundred-yard sprint to the grassy knoll that was identified as checkpoint one. Only then would we be out of the assaulting marines' kill zone.

We entered the area and discovered a village. A quick search revealed it had been abandoned. We relayed the information and prepared to move to the next checkpoint, which was on high ground and could be used for an observation post. The information at hand indicated it to be a much larger village, so there was a greater likelihood of people being present. Cautiously, we entered. I would take a moment to assess the situation and discuss things with the team. The map revealed the heavily wooded spot to be about two hundred yards in diameter. We could immediately see many well-worn trails, but no evidence of fortified positions. This was likely a farming village, but the inhabitants would be Viet Cong sympathizers.

The team was beyond the fierce fighting taking place behind us, and the enemy was to our front. A deceptive calm encircled us. We were in the eye of the storm.

Kartis was positioned at the edge of the land island. He was responsible for alerting the team if a retreating enemy force was coming our way. Slowly the remainder of the team entered. They followed but stayed off the well-worn trails that led toward the center of the village. Soon we maneuvered close enough to the village to see people rushing about. It was quite possible that a Viet Cong unit was present, and they might have much greater numbers, so extreme caution was exercised to avoid detection.

Families were gathering their belongings for a hasty departure, making it evident that they were aware of the approaching marines. They would have been shocked had they realized we were already there.

I sent Sally and Sherman to get a closer look while Donahue informed the command post of the situation. Within minutes, Sally and Sherman returned to alert me of a single armed Viet Cong soldier approaching. "How close?" I whispered.

"Thirty yards," replied Sherman.

From the lessons learned from repeated clashes with Viet Cong guerillas, they had perfected the art of springing a spontaneous ambush. It took raw nerve, opportunity, and gaining an advantage by exploiting every action or mistake your opponent made. "Get off the trail," I instructed, which they did by taking strategic positions on opposite sides of the trail. Donahue turned off his radio and moved a greater distance from us. The trail on which he traveled circled a sturdy bush, which made the perfect spot for me to crouch and conceal myself. All eyes were on the approaching soldier, now within twenty yards. He was a young man, perhaps in his midtwenties, carrying a stack of papers. His hair was neatly cropped, and he was wearing civilian clothes, khakis, and a soiled gray shirt. The primary concern was the .45 strapped to his waist. Had he changed directions, gone for his weapon, or noticed us, we would have immediately shot him dead. But he was so focused on the papers in his hands that he didn't seem to notice his surroundings. I had a clear shot at twenty-five yards, but the sound would have alerted other soldiers who might be in the area. I needed him to get close so I could push the barrel of my weapon into his chest to muffle the sound.

Unfortunately, my vision was obstructed by the bush, making it difficult to know exactly where he was. The closer the soldier got, the more I was at risk of exposure. Now he was only five yards away. If I waited any longer, the soldier might have run into me. So I stepped from behind the bush. My weapon was waist-high with the barrel pointed at the soldier, finger on the trigger, and the safety off. The Vietnamese stopped in midstride. He had the look of surprise and confusion, the look one might have when stumbling across an intruder in his home. The fact his weapon was still holstered saved his life.

We stared into each other's eyes. The snake had stumbled upon the mongoose. It would be a moment neither would forget. Under normal circumstances, it might have been a cordial encounter between two strangers. We likely had more in common than in difference. Just another chance meeting. But chance meetings, like luck, are a controlling factor of life and destiny. Our lives started from chance meetings between our parents, who were conceived from generations of chance meetings. However, in this case, providence, kismet, or politics had deemed the two of us could not coexist. The one condition that prevents a bloodbath between mortal enemies, each with an equal history of violence, is for the scales to be tipped, giving one an overwhelming advantage.

In this case, the advantage was mine. The Vietnamese offered no resistance, and his life was spared. With Sherman and Sally coming from the soldier's rear, his escape options were diminishing rapidly. He could have called for assistance from his allies jockeying for position in the area, but he surely would have been killed, or at the very least, beaten mercilessly. Our deceptive calm masked a ruthless aggression that could be unleashed in an instant. He wisely chose to connect with us on an emotional level. "Soul brother," he said to me, flashing a broad grin.

"Viet Cong," I replied with a sly smile. Before the prisoner could say another word, I pressed my finger to my lips, a signal to remain silent. There was no need for further communication.

Slowly, the prisoner raised his hands. Once his pistol holster was cut from his waist, he put his hands behind him, where they were tied, and his face was blindfolded. At that point, the situation was defused and the threat level lowered. The incident would now become an interesting footnote in each of our life stories, a tail we could repeat in our later years to the grandchildren.

But the trophy still had to be tagged and bagged, so he was searched thoroughly, and a gag was placed in his mouth. To assure he wouldn't make a sudden dash for freedom, a rope with a slipknot was placed around his neck. One jerk from Sally, who held the end, and his air supply would have been cut off, rendering him helpless.

Cautiously and rapidly, we made our way to the outer perimeter, where we notified the command post of the situation. Within fifteen tense minutes, the platoon reached us. The lieutenant took control of the prisoner and eased some of the restraints. After a quick interrogation by the KC Scout and an inspection of the papers he carried, he was identified as a Viet Cong tax collector. He could later provide valuable information.

The open area was an ideal spot for a landing zone. The prisoner and others captured in the sweep along with wounded marines from the company were extracted by helicopter. The sweep continued with First Squad taking over the point and my squad joining the platoon on line. There were no further major battles that day, only minor skirmishes. The NVA and VC had most likely broken their forces apart.

Our regiment, unwilling to yield any ground, went into defensive mode. There were sporadic firefights throughout the night, sometimes at a distance, and sometimes within yards. The enemy would constantly probe our lines to assess troop strength and vulnerabilities. It was as if we were in the lion's den and the hungry lions were circling in an attempt to drive us out or find a way in. There was little sleep on either side of the divide as both sides were planning their next move.

The commotion caused by the invading humans had likely disrupted the natural order for all living creatures that inhabited the jungle. They too were on alert as much as the marines and Vietnamese who listened intently for footsteps and looked for shadows.

The first day had passed, and we were into the night. While there were wounded marines in Second Platoon, none had been killed. The regiment as a whole didn't fare as well. Those of us who survived the day let out a sigh of relief, but we all knew a new day would bring new challenges and new adventures. For now, we would just take one day at a time.

Day Two

The sun would rise, and the sun would set, but it was not a factor in determining when we would eat or sleep. Opportunity was the only consideration.

However, it did affect visibility. So when the sun rose, we continued the assault. Fourth Squad would now take the point and the kill team position for the platoon. They left about twenty minutes before the remainder of the platoon.

The men who were on the first line of the assault would attempt to stay shoulder to shoulder, like fishermen casting a net, as long as the terrain permitted. The forces in the middle offered backup and reinforcements. They were the ones responsible for collecting the dead and wounded from both sides. Rear forces were on guard for a counterattack. Sometimes they were hit with more force than those in front. So there were no safe zones, just fighting from a different vantage point.

As the day progressed, resistance from the Vietnamese against the regiment was minimal. In all likelihood, the small pockets of resistance were a distraction to allow the larger forces to escape. Eventually they would be pushed together, and a battle of attrition would ensue.

Sometime around noon, Fourth Squad made contact. Four distinct shots from a Russian-made weapon rang out. That was followed by a volley of gunfire from American-made weapons, making it obvious that the marines had gained the upper hand. Sergeant Bazarr ordered Second Squad to assist. We rushed forward, but the firefight had ceased before we arrived. When we got within twenty-five yards, we could hear what sounded like a fistfight.

When we reached them, we saw what appeared to be four marines wrestling with a wild animal. The squad leader had his weapon trained on the group, trying to get a clear shot. We could now clearly see that it was an enemy soldier they were attempting to control; however, with the black attire and ferociousness exhibited by the man, one could have easily mistaken him for a black panther. And like a wild animal, this man would have to be physically bound or killed. He was attacking his captors with any appendage he could wrestle free. The marine holding his right arm temporarily lost his grip, and the prisoner scratched a large gash on the marine's arm. Angered by this, the marine held the arm and pulled the finger back, breaking it with a snap. The only reaction from the prisoner was to become more aggressive.

Disregarding the squad leaders warning to keep my distance, I moved closer for a better view. It was a jaw-dropping shock when I saw it was a woman. In fact, it was a young petite woman, possibly in her late teens, who only weighed about ninety pounds. On the rare moments they could grip her head to prevent her from biting, I could see that she was an exceptionally beautiful woman. "You powerful macho marines can't hold that little-ass woman?" I ridiculed. Whether or not she could understand English well enough to be insulted by my comment, she clearly didn't like it.

I didn't realize that I was facing something for the first time: a person who had overcome all fear of the consequences of her actions. With a sudden burst of strength, she broke free and lunged for me, nearly ripping my shirt off before they could regain control of her. "Hold that bitch!" I yelled after a high-pitched, uncharacteristic scream.

"Was that you?" Sherman laughed. I would only answer with silence. I did, however, maintain a safe distance. A fifth marine grabbed her head to restrain her from biting. But she could still work her mouth, and the tenacious prisoner continued to fight with the only thing she had control over, her voice.

Most of her speech was in Vietnamese, but a few American terms like "fuck you," "dog motherfucker," and "son of a bitch" came through. Then there were a few choppy sentences. The one repeated most was, "Me get away and kill all you asses." She could not even be compared to a wild animal. A wild animal fights its captors to escape. She wasn't trying to escape. She was trying to kill us. She was hate and violence in human form. Whether from fear or respect, the battle-hardened marines were only concerned with restraining her. They finally managed to bind her hands and feet and then thread a pole between them with a man on each end. It looked like hunters carrying their game back to camp. Still she tried to fight. "How did you get her to give up her weapon?" I asked the squad leader.

"She didn't," the astonished squad leader laughed. "The bitch ran out of bullets."

Eventually more marines arrived. With them was a KC Scout who was having a busy day interrogating prisoners. He spoke to her in Vietnamese, to which she replied by yelling and spitting. When the captain arrived, he directed the questioning through the scout. She was unimpressed and proved just as verbally abusive and assaultive toward him.

The scout did determine she was a much-sought-after sniper who had killed at least six marines. This made her a valuable prisoner.

First Platoon would stay with the command center to await a chopper to pick her up. Two wounded marines were also extracted.

"Damn," Sherman said as we proceeded with the sweep. "That is one badass bitch."

"Would you call her a bitch if she was standing beside you untied?" I asked him.

"No way," he replied. "I would say, 'How do you do, ma'am? I'm happy to meet you.'" We laughed at the newfound respect we had learned that day for what was considered the weaker sex. Then we continued to push forward.

The topography of the region dictated the speed of the sweep. We were exposed when in the open plains, but we could travel at a quickened pace. The patches of vegetation contained many hidden dangers, so when entering, we had to move slowly and exercise extreme caution.

By midday we had gone through two friendly villages. So after thoroughly searching the third, we were about to exit the dense growth into an open plain over five hundred yards across. The fifty-member platoon stepped out of the dense growth and stared intently at the distant tree line. The situation was relayed back to the captain, who was responsible for strategy. An air or artillery strike would have naturalized the threat of an ambush, but it could be a friendly village in the thicket, and many innocent lives would be lost. He ordered Second Platoon to assault on line and return fire only if fired upon. Sergeant Bazarr ordered the men out.

With his typical flamboyant style, he ordered the men to form an on-line assault. I was only a few feet from him. A proximity neither of us relished. "Move your men out!" he ordered, waving his arm in a sweeping motion.

"Don't do that shit!" I snapped at him, concerned a sniper was looking for an authority figure to pick off.

The tree line was the perfect cover for the NVA to spring an ambush on us. Our best strategy was to make quick, sporadic motions when approaching a potential ambush, hopefully causing the opponent to react prematurely. But we were making the approach in tall grass, which would conceal booby traps, making it necessary to make slow and deliberate movements. This made it a highly intense crossing. We listened intently for a triggered booby trap or a sudden ambush. The only sounds were Sergeant Bazarr bellowing out orders and waving his arms.

The concern wasn't if something would happen, but when. Once the moment came, it was somewhat a relief. A rocket-propelled grenade was launched from the tree line and was coming straight at us. The time between when the rocket was launched and when it reached us was less than three seconds, a big window when caught in an ambush. We were on the ground before it landed. The round traveled less than five feet over our heads, leaving the trail of white smoke before exploding in the ranks of the second wave of marines. The perpetrator's position was revealed. But before we could return fire, two other rockets were launched.

The brave but foolish Sergeant Bazarr stayed upright, and the concussion from the explosion threw him facedown. Hot shrapnel and debris were raining down on us, as we were now under a full rocket attack. "Stay low!" the squad leaders ordered their men.

"Assault on line!" Sergeant Bazarr shouted while jumping to his feet, countermanding those orders. A sharpshooter, who could now clearly identify the one in charge, fired two rounds at the exposed sergeant. One round hit him on the shoulder, knocking him to the ground.

Bleeding profusely and totally out of control, the sergeant again ordered the men to assault. "Kill those motherfuckers!" he shouted from the ground. "Kill all those motherfuckers." In spite of being the lowest ranking squad leader, or perhaps because of it, I canceled the order. "Fuck that shit!" I yelled out. "Stay down! Roe is in charge now!"

With all the confusion, Roe had forgotten he was the next in line, but he was in panic and not quite ready. Butler, who controlled the mortar section, knew what to do. His people were already blanketing the area with high-explosive rounds. With the enemy taking cover, the conditions for an assault had improved. Sergeant Bazarr, however, was not ready to relinquish command to Roe. He had gained enough strength to order another command. "Drop your gear and assault!" Again, I differed.

"Second Squad assault, but don't drop your gear!" I yelled. The other squad leaders also ordered their men to assault, and the platoon moved in unison.

Roe had gained his composure and now directed the platoon, ordering the corpsman to stay and administer medical attention to the fallen Sergeant Bazarr. The men were fearless in their effort to drive the enemy out, and the attackers were just as determined to hold their position. There was a heavy exchange of automatic and semiautomatic fire from both sides.

Initially, the cover and concealment combined with the element of surprise gave the advantage to the Vietnamese. But they underestimated the level of skill and aggression they would evoke from the exposed marines, who had no choice but to move forward. The sound level from the weapons was deafening. The sulfur smell had the men gasping for air, and the smoke burned our eyes, but we never wavered in the charge.

The riflemen, under the direction of their squad leaders, were on the front line. Crazy Ray was close to me at the center of the formation, the perfect vantage point for him to direct his machine-gun teams, who were constantly moving. The men from E Company would move up to replace any fallen marines from G Company. It was a textbook assault. Quickly, the advantage shifted toward us. The closer we got into the tree line, the less resistance we encountered. The enemy was obviously making a hasty retreat. Once inside the tree line, it was like a turkey shoot. The retreating Vietnamese took as many dead and wounded as possible, but they clearly suffered the greater losses.

We were now only about twenty yards in, and the greatest threat was the marines outside the tree line firing blindly into the heavy vegetation. All squad leaders and anyone near a radio were calling for a cease-fire.

The message was received, and the firing came to an abrupt halt. Johnson then entered the heavily vegetated area along with the command post. The captain issued the orders to the lieutenant, who passed it to the platoon sergeants and, finally, the squad leaders. First and Second Squads would do a thorough search of the area. Third and Fourth Squads would go back to retrieve the dropped gear and then assist in the medevac of dead and wounded. First, Third, and Fourth Platoons would set up an outer perimeter. E Company would continue to chase the enemy east. With that, First and Second Squads began the search.

We searched using a combination of caution and zeal. Two members from First Squad were slightly wounded by booby traps, but there were no further casualties. We found plenty of blood, but no bodies or weapons. We did find foxholes, trenches, fortified positions, and food stockpiles. This was clearly a base camp that had accommodated somewhere around 150 hard-core NVA troops.

When Third and Fourth Squads returned, they discovered all the gear left behind was gone. All the personal items, like toothpaste, toothbrushes, razors, shaving cream, pencils, paper, cigarettes, address books, letters, combs, socks, towels, candy, medical kits, and poncho liners that could be used to make shelter from the torrential rains, had fallen into the hands of the VC. All personnel who had lost the names of friends and loved ones back home were advised to contact them and alert them to the possibility of being targeted by a Vietnamese letter-writing campaign. Because Sergeant Bazarr was already being flown to the medical station, I was denied one of the few pleasures allotted a junior marine, proving his sergeant wrong.

The second day was coming to an end. Protected by the marine platoon assigned to guard the outer perimeter, our platoon would finally get a peaceful sleep. It felt as if we had stormed the castle of the enemy and were relaxing in their kitchen, eating their food. Sherman, Sally, and I sat with our feet up, reflecting on the day. "We are some badass motherfuckers," Sally said with a broad smile.

"Goddamn right," I agreed as we drifted off to sleep. Whatever tomorrow would bring, the day had belonged to us.

Day Three

Each man had taken a turn guarding the perimeter. I would occasionally prowl the lines making sure those on guard were alert. Considering the stress we were under, we were relatively rested. So when the sun began to rise, we gathered our gear and prepared to move on. In all likelihood, the enemy would be reoccupying the compound within hours. And perhaps it would be the VC who had pilfered Third and Fourth Squads' gear.

Leaving a position we had fought so hard to get gave us mixed emotions. We understood that we were an assault force, not an occupying one, but it is somewhat disheartening to risk your life to take something and then give it back. But so goes the nomad life of a marine.

The NVA that had been driven out was headed west. Fox Company would now take pursuit. Gulf Company would continue southwest. The operation had scattered the enemy, which was considered a success to some degree. But to be effective, we would have to separate our forces. In addition, we were now headed into the mountains and could no longer move on line. So the company broke into its four platoons and moved into the mountains like a four-fingered hand. As we traveled, small bands of Viet Cong would be encountered. Resistance was isolated but consistent. For now, marines were clearly the more formidable force. That advantage was seized upon when a band of VC made a tactical blunder when taking refuge on a small hill that we managed to surround. Once the VC were trapped, an air strike was called. It was a slaughter. Any of the Viet Cong who tried to escape the net were shot dead. We acknowl-

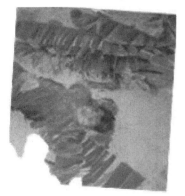

edged the bravery and tenacity of our foe. We watched in awe at the boldness of one VC resister spotted through binoculars. He actually tried to shoot down an attack chopper with an outdated rifle. When the chopper gunner fired a several-hundred-round blast from his powerful fifty-caliber machine gun into his body, he literally exploded.

When the attack was over, we went in to survey the human carnage.

The visual could only equal the bronze sculpture *Gates of Hell* done by Rodin, in which he depicted convulsed forms tormented by pain and death. The smell of the burning flesh and dismembered bodies caused even the most hardened veteran to turn in disgust. It was a sight we would likely never forget. There was no further need for a thorough inspection, and the men exited as soon as possible. We suffered casualties as well, but the greater loss was clearly from the Communist side. I try not to think too hard about it.

From there we continued with the physically exhaustive search through the mountains. Finally, we stopped near a stream. We had the high ground, so we were relatively safe. After checking the squad members' positions, I was able to allow myself a moment to relax. It was also important to keep Marshal, who seemed to be deceived by the momentary calm, on his toes while guarding the line. "Enjoy the break, but stay alert," I cautioned him.

Then I left to be alone and ponder our next move. We were now deep into the Arizona and about to enter the fourth day. I knew life could take a drastic turn at any second, but it wasn't necessary to remind the men of it. Whatever was to happen, we would have to deal with it.

Day Four

Now in the fourth day, even I was beginning to feel more at ease. The enemy surely knew we were there in full force, so perhaps they had decided to pull out.

Second Squad was now on point, and I decided men out front. It wasn't long before I realized he was too inexperienced constantly turning to me for direction. This wasn't the place for school, so I moved up the wily Sherman, who was now my most skilled pointer. The move paid off. Sherman stopped and called me up. After directing the men to move off the road, I went to Sherman. "Look," Sherman said, directing my attention to the well-worn trail, "fresh cracks crossed the road heading

Sherman

in that direction." The two of us went alone about fifty yards down the road, where we saw other tracks that were made in the soft mud.

"If all these people are moving around, why don't we see them?" Sherman whispered.

"I think they are flanking us," I said.

"You know, they could be watching us now," Sherman whispered.

"They probably are," I answered. "Let's move back before they pick us off."

We returned to the squad and relayed our suspicions over the radio to the lieutenant, who went to confer with the captain. Roe came up with First Squad for a meet. "This looks like a main road," I told him, "so it is probably leading to a village. But with all this rain, we can see that a lot of people have left, and they seem to be moving to our flanks."

"The lieutenant thinks it was likely a small force, probably VC in the village, and they knew we were coming, so they are pulling out. If they have been watching us, they probably don't have enough firepower to take us on," Roe said.

"What is the next move?" I asked.

"I don't know yet," Roe told me. "I'll pass it to the lieutenant and get back with you." Roe slipped back into the jungle to confer with the platoon commander while Second Squad held our position. In about fifteen minutes, the lieutenant contacted us over the radio. He told me to continue into the village and search. The remainder of the company would search the flanks.

I was apprehensive about taking a single squad into the village, suspecting there may still have been a large force waiting. But the closer we got, the more tracks revealed troops were coming out of, not going into, the village. Soon firefights began breaking out around us, confirming that assessment. My squad continued into the village, where we found villagers waiting. We approached cautiously, holding our fire, since they didn't appear as a threat.

There were, perhaps, eight to twelve villagers. The ages ranged from ten to sixty. We quickly searched each of them and then placed them in the center of the village. I made several attempts at communicating with them, but none acknowledged understanding English. Americans generally assumed that most Vietnamese encountered spoke some English. But in this isolated village lying deep in-country, perhaps the people hadn't encountered English-speaking people. In fact, they didn't seem to be afraid, were not overly curious, and were cooperative. In any event, a KC Scout was en route to serve as an interpreter.

The squad continued to search, and in time the tension between us and the villagers began to ease. The lieutenant eventually ordered the squad to remain in the village for the night, an order with which we were glad to comply. Once the men had taken a defensive position for the night, I sat with Sally and talked. The sun was gradually setting.

"Does it seem like there are more villagers now?" Sally asked me while looking around at what now seemed to be fifteen to twenty villagers.

"You know, there does seem to be more of them," I said.

"Did we shut off the village?" Sally asked.

"No, there was no need to. They could just be returning home from the field, but check the lines," I told Sally. "And don't let any more people in."

Soon Sherman came over to me holding some papers. "Look at what I found under a basket," he said, passing them to me. They were three-by-five papers with writing in Vietnamese that looked like they were done on a crude printing press.

"Show me where you found them," I said to him, which he did.

We searched more thoroughly, this time using the villagers in the event of a booby trap. Then, under the watchful eyes of the villagers, we made an even more startling discovery.

"What does this look like to you?" Sherman said. We both looked closely at a large paper, about nine by twelve inches, with a crude drawing on it.

"It looks like a person holding a head, and the one holding the head looks like a child's drawing of a Viet Cong."

"That is probably a marine's head he's holding," Sherman said as we turned to the nervous Vietnamese, who stared intently at us.

"We need a scout to interpret this shit," I said as we went to the radio operator. When he notified the lieutenant of the urgency, he located one who was with the nearby First Platoon. A squad of marines brought him to us just before sunset. After inspecting the materials, he confirmed our suspicions and clarified the reason for the increased presence of villagers.

The leaflets posted a bounty for the marines. We were the cash cows the impoverished villagers had dreamed about, and they were drawn into the village like moths to a flame. Now that their intentions were known, the once-friendly villagers with the glistening nervous sweat and the shifting shadows were now ominous figures. They had the appearance of hungry ghouls, watching and waiting for an opportunity to attack and drag their prey into their underground  haunts. It was now too late for reinforcements, and that made for a tense night. All the men were informed of the situation.

"Don't fall asleep next to a buzzard," I warned. But the villagers were in equal if not greater peril from us. They had gorillas in their midst who would bring down a reign of terror in an instant. All creatures, both big and small, were on watch. The night had a thousand eyes, and each was a predator. I remained awake, weapon in hand.

As soon as the sun came up, the violence began. Every villager was considered a prisoner of war. Most of them were beaten, tied, and forced to the open ground, where a helicopter transported them back for interrogation. We destroyed the village, burning everything to the ground. Any standing tree had USMC KILL NVA or VIET CONG MUST DIE burned on it.

This was a prelude to what was to come. We were about to enter the fifth and final day, and it would be the last day to make a statement. No one doubted there would be bloodshed.

Day Five

As we moved to join the platoon, I tried to mask my anxiety with a smile and a reminder that it was the last day of the operation. The men knew what I wasn't saying. The end of this operation would bring the start of another. But information, like medicine, is easier to swallow if taken in small doses.

"Harris!" Roe called as we approached. "Our platoon is point for the company, and Second Squad will point for the platoon." I nodded in compliance and then motioned for Sherman to take point. Sherman responded with an angry glare. I understood that I had used him and Sally in excess, but they were what I needed the most. So Sherman moved out, with me following and the other squad members in line.

We were now leaving the mountains and entering ever-changing terrain. First it was the grasslands, which gave more visibility, some concealment, but little cover. If fighting were to break out, we were at an increased risk of getting in cross fire with other marine units. As we entered the jungle, the vegetation was getting thicker. We would have less visibility but better concealment and cover. Fighting, however, would be close up and likely a high causality rate. The enemy was also in constant motion and most likely traveling in the thick vegetation. Again, there was no question of if we would make contact, but when. The men were mentally prepared for anything. You could see it in their every move.

Once we were about two hundred yards into the brush, where the visibility was about twenty-five yards, Sherman spotted movement, and I moved beside him to observe. I had the radioman report the situation, and the lieutenant ordered the squad to enter and search.

The men crouched and cautiously moved in. Any sounds we might have made were masked by the bustling movements of the villagers who were going about their daily routines. Silently and skillfully we approached like a pack of wolves stalking unsuspecting prey. We weren't spotted until we were within a few yards of them, much too close for the villagers to react. They froze like deer caught in headlights.

It was just a small village of about twelve people, perhaps two or three families. Two of the men were likely over sixty, with several older women. They had no other men of fighting age among them. There were one or two women in their early thirties. If a weapon were in either of their hands, I would definitely have been afraid. But they were unarmed, so I had to treat them all as friendly. The people made little movement. Their eyes were trained on us while we circled them. Slowly they raised their hands and took a submissive, nonthreatening posture. The people in this isolated village had lived their lives with the violence around them and were likely taking refuge in the thick canopy.

To survive they had to be deeply involved and thoroughly informed. That information and insight could tip the balance between life and death for us. Therefore, they were important captives. The men wanted to attack and beat information out of them, which might have been wise in this case. If it's a choice between being feared and being loved, to gain compliance, it's best to be feared. But one must be careful that the fear doesn't become hate. I harbored no illusion. I knew I could not solicit truthful information from them given the interaction between the marines and Vietnamese in Arizona over recent days.

The events of the past year were beginning to affect me. What was happening to me and the naïve young men barely out of their parents' charge whom I had befriended? Was violent antisocial behavior going to be our norm? It was no surprise that when your daily goal is reduced to fighting for survival, you will become a little less human as the days go by. But were we being pulled into a psychotic quagmire we could not escape? This was one of the few instances in which the decision rested with me. So before we were reduced to being purely predators, I decided to make one more try at humanity by confronting my enemy with compassion.

"Papa-San," I sternly said to the village elder, "me don't want no bullshit. Where VC?" At first Papa-San was about to pretend not to understand, but he wisely decided against it. Papa-San looked me directly in the eye and with grandfatherly compassion and sincerity lied. "Me no see VC, two maybe three days," he said. I was sure he was lying, but I had no way to prove it. All the villagers joined the charade, laughing, smiling, and calling the marines number one and the VC number ten. I got on the radio and informed the command that we had searched the people and found no weapons. I also told the lieutenant that Papa-San claimed not to have seen VC, which I doubted. The lieutenant ordered us to move on, and the second wave of marines would further interrogate the villagers when they arrived. I mustered the men, and we prepared to leave, with the villagers cheering us on and wishing us a speedy victory. I made one more appeal to Papa-San. First I gave the old man some C rations to be distributed to his people; then I held a mutually respectful conversation with him.

"Papa-San, if there VC or NVA, tell me now," I said.

The old man again repeated, "No VC, marines number-one soul brother."

"Should we be careful, Papa-San?" I asked one more time. Again, the old man assured me there was no danger. With that, we moved out with Sally on point with me behind him. Crazy Ray, who would normally travel with the company command, was again with us, traveling in the center of our formation. After leaving the village, we entered denser terrain. Soon the ever-changing terrain was beginning to clear. The stumps indicated it had been manually cleared. We knew we were approaching a major village. The closer we got, the more apprehensive both Sally and I were becoming. Not because of what we could see, but what we didn't see.

We were in a major village that contained about a dozen hooches, but no people. The structures were straw, which rendered them useless for stopping bullets, but they made perfect cover. The only visible item that could stop a bullet was a large rock that sat conspicuously in the center of the village. Sally stopped beside one of the hooches and turned to me for direction. I walked up to him while urging him forward. The two of us were now nearing the center of the village with the remainder of the squad following. Suddenly our fears were realized.

A burst of automatic gunfire broke out. Sally and I were caught in a kill zone. The shooters were likely firing from a machine gun mounted on a tripod or an elevated position, because the rounds were coming down at our feet. The squad members who had not yet come into view began scrambling for cover and position. Whether it was fate, fortune, or divine intervention that placed the rock in the center of the village, it saved our lives.

We slammed hard into one another as we both dived for the rock. "I've been hit!" Sally screamed in pain. "I've been hit." His screaming seemed to energize the attackers, who were now firing directly at the rock, breaking chunks off of it. Sally was in excruciating pain and began thrashing about while I tried to hold his head down.

"Keep your head down," I repeated to Sally while calling for Ray to get the shooters off of us. Soon the squad, and Ray on the machine gun, were engaged in a fierce firefight. Each time Sally would cry out in pain, the attackers would turn attention back to the rock, which was getting smaller. That prompted a confrontation between us.

"You gonna have to stop hollering about that foot!" I warned.

"Shit, man, it hurts to lose a piece of a foot," Sally continued to scream.

Oblivious to the fighting raging around us, we continued to discuss the foot.

"I don't want to hear no more about your foot," I yelled at him. "Not until we get from behind this rock. I'm going to cover you while you break for that tree," I said.

"I can't run with just one foot," Sally pleaded.

"You're just going to have to use the other one twice as much."

"Fuck you," Sally snapped. "Hey, man," he said, then suddenly smiled. "I'm going home."

"What?" I said, surprised he would change the subject at such an inopportune moment.

"I only got one good foot. They gotta send me home now," he said, still smiling.

"Congratulations," I said to my old friend. "You got your ticket home." Then I got an ominous feeling. "You hear that?"

"What?" Sally said.

"Nothing."

"What do you mean, nothing?"

"The rag man's not shooting."

"Good."

"Bullshit," I insisted, "they might be flanking us to get around this rock. We gotta go now."

Before I could give the traditional one, two, three, go signal, Sally was up and hopping for cover. I jumped up, let go with a quick burst of gunfire toward the flanks, and ran to catch Sally. As fast as he hopped, he only needed one foot. Once we were out of the cross fire, the other marines also began to fire to the flanks, and a firefight ensued.

Sally, who had not yet mastered the art of running on one foot, slammed into a tree and nearly knocked himself unconscious. I reached down to help, but before I could, Sally sprung to his foot, still in a state of euphoria, hopping unassisted all the way to the waiting platoon. "I'm going home!" he hollered. "I'm going to see my girl, Sally, my mom, my dad," and he continued to name all his family members and friends. I laughed, remembering that his nickname came from his constantly talking about his girlfriend, Sally. We had called him Sally so long I had nearly forgotten his name.

"This is probably the last time you'll be called Sally," I laughed.

"I sure do hope so," he replied. "From now on it's Herman Dank Smith."

Then Sally revealed the compassionate side of him that would become his legacy among the men he served with. "I'm sorry," he said to me. "I was only thinking of myself. You've been here a long time, brother. I just wish you could be going home too." I was feeling guilty for yelling at Sally and attempted to apologize, but Sally wouldn't let me. "Forget that," Sally said, stopping me in midsentence. "You did what was necessary to get us out. Now you've got to get yourself through and help the brothers. Keep strong," he said, giving me the power handshake.

The corpsman, assisted by members of Fourth Platoon, arrived with a stretcher. Under normal circumstances, it might have appeared strange to see a severely wounded man attempting to comfort a man with no visible signs of trauma. But in war, where compassion, humor, and violence are woven throughout, few sights are strange. In fact, they too envied the wounded man. Sally had escaped the house of death, and the fate of the men assisting him was yet to be determined. My friend was taken to a spot to be extracted, and I returned to the squad.

On the walk back, I began to take the ambush personally. My decision may have caused my friend to become disabled. Sherman came running toward me. "The villagers," he said between gasps for breath, "were not around when we returned. I think they set us up." That conclusion was confirmed by Roe, the platoon sergeant, who had more information.

"First Platoon hit the people who ambushed you," he said as he approached me, radio in hand. "The description sounds like the villagers you talked to." I was humbled by the news and lingered somewhere between self-doubt and anger.

Roe made an attempt to comfort me. "Our standing orders were to treat the people as friendly unless they took action against us. If you took any other action, you could have been brought up on charges. Like it or not, that is the way we have to do it. Hold it!" Roe said, pausing the conversation to respond to an urgent radio message.

I joined the other squad leaders who had arrived for a meeting of the minds. Roe moved to a quiet location to continue his radio exchange.

The squad leaders were complaining about the constraints we were working under. We had to take direction from men making assessments through radio communication, positioned in secure locations.

What we didn't know was that the captain, who was en route to our location, had given the orders that would release us from the shackles of restraint that bound us. Roe called the squad leaders together for a hasty briefing. It was the news we wanted to hear.

"The planners believe the pockets of villagers are VC under orders to slow us down and relay information of our movements. We have yet to encounter friendlies," he told the squad leaders. "There is likely a large NVA unit around, and they are the big prize. The VC are just table scraps. We need to get those pesky motherfuckers out of the way and go after the big meal. We are the Devil Dogs, and we are hungry. Anyone claiming to be a noncombatant must prove it. From now on there are no innocent bystanders. Tell your people to take them out."

Agreement among the squad leaders rang out like a hungry lion's roar. Each man returned to his respective squad, where we relayed the new orders. Any princes of peace among us would now renounce the calling and conform their deeds to the horror of war. Guardian angels encouraging compassion were now grounded. In truth, we were about to engage in a contest in which the only winner was the common enemy to both sides, death. Everyone else would lose something: life, limb, or a piece of their humanity.

The company divided into platoons and then squads. Second Squad, as did our peers, attacked the next village mercilessly. The few Vietnamese who escaped death did not escape the violence. They would be savagely beaten regardless of existing injuries. If it moved, it died, including the livestock. Many who attempted surrender were shot, just to render them incapacitated.

We set fire to, scattered, defecated on, or urinated on any potential food source, such as rice or grain. Anyone seeking shelter would have it blown up or set on fire.

The VC were not submissive victims. They fought back like trapped alley cats every step of the way. But it was now survival of the fittest, and they were overwhelmed by the formally repressed violence coming their way. Those of us in the first wave didn't get a hard look at the death and destruction we inflicted, but it was massive. The bodies were so riddled with bullets, it would have been impossible to determine who the shooter was. When a target fell, we moved on. When any of our own fell, we would hold the position just long enough for the second wave to arrive and attend to them. The battlefield was soaked with blood. Everyone following that first assault team gave the same assessment of what they saw. It was hell.

In fact, it appeared as if the gates of hell had swung open and the advocates of death were released. Second Squad made up the stars leading the pack. We were now encountering fortified enemy positions. Any hesitation on our part could mean swift and sure death, so there was no hesitation. Angered by the deception of the villagers, I abandoned all reason, rushing to the front of the pack. Armed with youthful recklessness, physical prowess, and a medley of weapons, we were like a pack of wild dogs that would continue to kill until we ran out of prey or were somehow stopped. That would happen soon. Unknowingly, we were entering the mouth of a dragon. A regiment of hard-core VC was just ahead, and they were not about to back off.

Command was frantically trying to get the information to us, but the squad was in such frenzy that we weren't listening to communications. I paused my charge to reload. That's when the captain personally rushed forward to within twenty yards of me. This put the company commander in a position of grave danger. But he was, perhaps, the only voice I would have listened to at that moment. "Stop!" he ordered while alternating conversations over the many handsets given to him by the radiomen surrounding him.

His lieutenants joined him shortly, and they set up a hasty command post. I was close enough to hear the valuable information they were assessing. It was the first I heard of the massive force in the tree line just beyond the open field in front of us. I could also hear the captain calling for an air strike and instructing his lieutenants to order a frontal assault when it was over. The lieutenants returned to their platoons to prepare their troops. The impatient enemy troops opened with a burst of machine-gun fire, perhaps in an attempt to get the marines to reveal ourselves. I smiled at the sight of the captain frantically dodging for cover. I was about to call for Ray to return fire when the captain stopped me. "We don't want to reveal our gun," he said sternly. I believe he just didn't want to draw fire in his direction "Marine!" he called while tossing me a bright-orange plastic panel. "Get one of your people to put this in front of that embankment." He was referring to the one-foot mount about fifty yards to our front that stretched roughly one hundred yards across. I understood the importance of marking a visible boundary for the air strike that would arrive soon. I also knew I couldn't live with myself if I had sent a friend to a certain death, with the enemy taking aim at anyone entering what was clearly a kill zone. So I reached down and grabbed the panel in my right hand, held my weapon firmly in my left, and made the fifty-yard sprint for life.

This was perhaps the first time I had volunteered for anything since entering the Marine Corps. I immediately realized this wasn't a well-thought-out decision. The exposure made me as easy a target as a deer in a wheat field. My death was likely a forgone conclusion from both sides of the battlefield. If I were religious, I would have called it a miracle the NVA shooters hesitated. Perhaps they assumed someone else on their line would take the easy shot, or they might have been waiting for more targets to emerge. Whatever the case, that delay gained the precious seconds I needed.

But I wasn't going to make it easy. I was attempting to make myself as difficult a target as possible, maneuvering like a fullback dodging phantom tacklers. When I reached a point about twenty yards from the embankment, the tension and deadening silence were shattered by an explosion of gunfire coming at me like a horizontal rainstorm of bullets. There was an enormous volume of rounds coming at me. It was dense and concentrated. If there was a record for the biggest number of people trying to shoot one man, it would have been shattered that day.

The rounds coming at my torso were so close that my clothes rustled from the air vacuums they created. The crisp, high-pitched sound like a mosquito flying into the ear canal indicated the rounds were missing my head by fractions of an inch. If any of the projectiles from the fifty-caliber machine gun had even clipped my skull, my head would have exploded like a watermelon being dropped from a bridge. I went down hard and then rose from the ground. Onlookers appeared to be witnessing a second coming. I rose to my knees, stumbled forward, and then leaped over the embankment as if I were attempting to fly. Anyone watching had to have been in shock and awe. They had witnessed a condemned man escaping a firing squad.

My fellow marines launched a ferocious counterattack. The two sides fought like two pit bulls. The fighting didn't let up until the smoke and debris began to restrict their vision. The momentarily lull allowed the two sides to assess their next move. As the thick veil of sulfur created from the volumes of rounds fired from rifles, machine guns, rockets, and mortars cleared, the otherwise beautiful sky revealed itself like heaven opened for viewing.

Contrary to forgone conclusions of those witnessing the spectacle, I was very much alive, lying on my back looking up at the sky. Apparently I had slammed my head on the ground at some point and was momentarily knocked unconscious. "Damn!" I shouted, looking to the heavens. "I must be dead." Dazed and confused, I tried to put the events together. This wasn't the first time I had been caught in a kill zone, so I knew the drill. Move my limbs to see if they were attached and working properly, then check the crotch, heart, and head for damage. There were cuts, scrapes, and bumps, but I was otherwise OK. Now I could assess the situation and decide to fight or flee.

As my head continued to clear, I remembered diving over what I at first thought to be an embankment into a trench. It was likely dug by the NVA as a defensive position. It was about three feet wide and three feet deep. *They did a good job*, I thought. *I'll just camp here for a while.* I positioned myself in an upright position with my back to the marines and my front facing the NVA. *Anyone attempting to crawl up on me will get one to the head*, I thought, smiling to myself.

The silence was beginning to concern me; I needed to pop my head up to take a look. *I'll do it on three. One, two, three, four, five.* By the time I reached fifteen, I knew it wasn't going to happen. Both sides were waiting for a target, I concluded. My head would be like a pop-up duck at a carnival. *This is the safest place. I'm like a baby in its mother's womb. Let them wait. I'll come out when I'm good and damn ready.*

The silence was again shattered, with the marines opening up first. Now another fight raged for about thirty seconds with the dominance constantly shifting. I sat like a biased referee cheering for his favorites. Then the shooting from the NVA began to subside. I heard running coming in my direction. Bracing for a fight, I listened intently. They were coming from behind, so I knew it was marines. Then two bodies leaped into the trench. One landed on me. It was Woody, and he began to scream and fight like he had landed on hot coals. I held on to him to keep him from possibly rising up and exposing himself to a shooter. Butler was to his right.

When I released my grip on Woody, he scooted away like a frightened child. "What the fuck is wrong with you?" I asked him.

"I thought you were dead."

"Well, I'm not dead, so what were you fighting for?"

"I thought you were dead."

"And?"

"I didn't want to be lying on top of a dead man."

Butler, who found the episode amusing, was laughing at the both of us. Woody, who still wasn't convinced he wasn't looking at a ghost, moved close to me, attempting to look into my eyes.

"Boo!" I shouted, teasing him, causing Woody to recoil.

"Don't fuck with me, man," Woody shouted, as he began to pat me down.

"What are you doing?"

"They had to hit you somewhere."

"Look, man, I'm not dead, and I'm not hit."

"Then whose blood is this?"

"Sally's."

"Oh, I forgot," Woody said.

Convinced, at last, that I was OK, he smiled, and the three of us exchanged the power handshake. "He charged out here like John Wayne," Butler said, referring to Woody. "Then he starts screaming like a little girl."

"Fuck both of y'all," Woody snapped over our laughter. During this entire episode, bullets were being fired just inches above our heads. We just sat with our backs against the wall, oblivious to the danger around us, talking and laughing like three typical teenagers waiting for a bus.

"Oh, I forgot," I said, digging into my boot and pulling out a blood- and sweat-soaked joint.

"You been holding out," Butler snapped at me.

"I've been saving it for a celebration," I said, defending myself. "It's not going to get no more special than what just happened."

"Let that motherfucker dry out," Woody commented in disgust. "It's gonna taste like your foot."

"It'll dry while I smoke it," I said, lighting it up. "It's my foot, anyway." After I had taken a couple drags, Butler took a turn. Then I reached for it again, but Woody intercepted it.

"I risk my life for you," Woody said in his customary cantankerous style, "and you gonna hog the joint." In spite of his small stature, Woody had the lung capacity of a man twice his size. Two hits and it was gone. We looked at each other as if we were survivors on an island who just realized they were out of food. Motivated by either guilt or the desire for more self-medication, Butler pulled out the emergency joint he had in his helmet. One hit each; then we passed it to Woody. Again he boxed it, letting go only when it burned his fingertips. The two of us stared at Woody, knowing he had a stash somewhere on him. Then the sound of an approaching aircraft killed our high.

"You hear that?" Butler said, motioning for us to be quiet.

"Oh yeah," I said. "That's air support. When they fire into that tree line, we'll make our break."

"Where is the panel?" Butler asked me.

"Oh shit," I shouted, "about two feet on the other side of this trench." Butler stressed the need to get away from the marker and began to pull himself out of the trench. "Too late," I yelled, pulling him back down. The three of us sat helpless, frozen from fear, staring up at death as one of the Marine Corps Phantoms, with its deadly rockets visible, dived straight at us. At the last second, it pulled up.

"We got to move out," Butler yelled. "That other jet is making a dive. Let's do it on three."

"Fuck three!" I yelled. "We're going now." Like jackrabbits getting flushed from their holes, we popped up and ran for our lives. We got about twenty yards from our company before the NVA opened up. The marines immediately responded, which made the situation even more volatile. It wasn't until we reached the lines and took cover that our breathing became regular again.

Coordination between the spotters on the ground and the pilots enabled them to hit with deadly accuracy. The riflemen watched while the big guns took over. We viewed it like patrons in a theater watching a war movie. We had no popcorn or candy, but Butler asked Woody about the joint we had discussed a few minutes earlier. The smell of gunpowder would have masked the reefer smell from the lifers. Woody reluctantly informed us that, in his haste, he had dropped it as well as his pack of Kools. So we sat and drank the warm water from our canteens, smoked the Camels we had saved as a last resort, and continued to watch the show.

Once the planes and helicopters were done, the mortar section launched an attack, and E Company went in to finish any survivors off. The lieutenant called the squad leaders together. He informed us we would set up a safe zone for the medevac helicopters to land, and the dead and wounded would then be extracted and flown back to the base. When that was done, G Company would be returned to the base. Our job was done. The jubilant men let out a cheer. The surviving gladiators were exiting the arena.

CHAPTER 33

At Last
November 1969

▲ ▲ ▲

IN COMBAT, LIFE'S FORTUNES CAN change in an instant. Especially when traveling in a low-flying aircraft over hostile territory. So there was an expected uneasy silence among the marines taking the flight to Phu Loc 6. Once the helicopter touched down and the marines exited, the euphoria began.

We were assigned tents in a safe area, with cots to sleep on. We would be given a turn to use the showers. Our rank, however, would guarantee there would only be cold water remaining when our turn came. We would be allowed to use the outdoor latrines, where we could leisurely relieve ourselves, without having to dig a hole and carry a weapon in our free hand for security. The chow hall would be stocked with warm meals, and the accumulated beer ration would be distributed. For a bushman, we had it all.

Typically there would be a two-day break between operations. So we had at least twenty-four hours to celebrate being alive.

Early the following day, the squad leaders received orders to go to the supply tent and pick up new uniforms for their men. The lieutenant was there, along with the platoon sergeant, beaming with delight. He eagerly announced that the battalion commander would be addressing the men in a ceremonial formation. We hadn't participated in a traditional formation since boot camp, so we would spend the remainder of the day practicing.

The lieutenant informed us that the commander was coming to congratulate the company for our accomplishments. Medals would be awarded to three of the marines in our regiment. The lieutenant quickly added that none of the men in our platoon were among the recipients. He told the squad leaders that the Marine Corps Band and possibly photographers would also be coming. So the entire area would be on high alert. He finished by telling us not to tell the men about it. He wanted to be the one to give them the good news.

I called Sherman over to help carry the uniforms back to the tent. The men rushed in when the clean uniforms arrived. Seeing the new uniforms, they were full of questions. I answered before they could ask.

"The colonel is coming in for a photo op, so we've got to dress up and act like we give a shit," I said sarcastically.

"You think we'll get some in-country R and R?" Sherman asked.

"I doubt it," I answered.

While the other squad members groaned their dissatisfaction, Sherman continued to ask me questions that I would likely have no answers to.

"Is the Marine Corps Band coming?"

"Yeah, with those bright-ass uniforms. But I can't hate," I added. "I wish I could play an instrument."

"Shit, I hope they don't draw mortar fire."

"There will be fighter jets and security rings surrounding the whole area. They're not gonna let enemy gunners anywhere near the battalion commander, the Marine Corps Band, or the photographers," I assured Sherman. "The closer we are to them, the less chance of us being shot."

The men agreed and continued to complain. Later they exited the tent and went to the parade field to practice.

The lieutenant played the role of the colonel, in an undressed rehearsal. After about two hours of practice, we were able to skillfully execute the traditional movements required. The actual ceremony would take longer. In fact, we would have to stand in a rigid stick-up-the-butt position the entire time. The only consolation was watching the fear on the faces of the band members, as they anticipated being shot at any moment.

After rehearsal we got haircuts and finished of a few cases of the accumulated beer ration.

The following day we put on our new uniforms. Then we assembled at 1130 hours for the scheduled noon formation. By the time the band played a few selections and the colonel congratulated the men for our brave accomplishments, we had been standing over two hours. It was a hot and humid day, and fatigue was quickly setting in. We would remain in the hot sun for another hour while he inspected each man's person. But he wasn't really looking at us; he was only looking in our direction.

I followed the colonel's every move with a cold, hard stare, trying to solicit a reaction, any emotion that would indicate he could step outside the commander role and see me as a man. As he passed, our eyes did cross, but the colonel remained detached. To add insult to injury, he announced there was another search-and-destroy mission into the Arizona Territory being planned. "We're going to finish those Commie bastards off this time!" he bellowed.

The rousing cheer from the marines he might have expected turned out to be an uneasy silence. The formation was dispersed, and the men separated, grumbling our displeasure. The lower the rank, the more humiliated we felt. We were offended at the way the officers seemed to look down on us and the way some of the sergeants, who were supposed to be our role models, followed behind those same officers like obedient children.

From a distance the men congregating in pockets, engaging in animated discussions, might appear to have been motivated to action. In truth most were anything but inspired by the pompous spectacle they had been forced to be a part of.

The conversations were more like, "That arrogant, self-serving son of a bitch, what the fuck does he mean, we're going back? He wasn't there in the first place."

Another marine would add, "His ass wasn't dodging bullets, rockets, and grenades for the past five days. He didn't have to look into the faces of the enemy minutes after we took their lives. He didn't gag at the overbearing smell of death and burning flesh."

I gave my own prospective. "I only have three weeks left on my tour," I said while walking away. "I don't give a shit about killing; I give a shit about dying."

Expendable and Necessary

Walking alone, I noticed someone racing toward me. My emotions were high, and I was in no mood for anything but good news. In fact, it was. Johnson was bringing news that would change everything.

Johnson was so excited he could hardly contain himself. "We're going home; we're going home!" he shouted, running in a circle.

"What are you talking about?" I yelled, running after him.

"You, me, and Butler, we're all going home," Johnson shouted again, waving a sheet of paper.

"You better tell me something more than that, dammit!"

"President Nixon ordered a troop withdrawal," he said, holding the list in my face. "Anyone with a month or less on their rotation date is being pulled out. We're on the list."

```
                                                          LtrO 106-69
                                                          14 Sep 1969

Effective during November transfer following personnel. Authority: CMC ltr DFB1/2C-
tl of 26Aug69.

From:  2d Battalion, 5th Marines              ULTIMATE DUSTA

MOON T E              Cpl      246 02 35/0331    CO HqBn HQMC (MCC 011)
KINER W H             LCpl     205 20 20/3041    CG MCDEC QUANT (MCC 012)
DAY R P               LCpl     245 83 39/0341    CG MCB CamPen (MCC 014)
KOWALCZYK F M         LCpl     245 88 10/0351    -do-
MCBANE W E            LCpl     243 69 23/0311    -do-
TORRES H M            PFC      245 27 51/0311    -do-
VILLARREAL R          PFC      246 89 98/0311    -do-
DAHMS B H             Cpl      231 20 25/3371    CG MCRDep PISC (MCC 016)
MORRIS R L            PFC      247 58 92/0311    -do-
BUTLER J W            LCpl     241 36 00/0341    CO WpnsTrngBn (Edson Range Area)
                                                    MCRD CamPen (MCC 038)
LAPOINTE L W          Cpl      238 89 45/0311    -do-
LOOMIS G R            PFC      240 99 63/0311    -do-
CARTER R W            Cpl      245 87 44/0311    CG 2dMarDiv FMF CamLej (MCC 122)
DEVITT M J            PFC      242 79 51/0311    -do-
GOODE W H             Pvt      236 75 98/2511    -do-
HALL G                Cpl      240 62 45/0311    -do-
HARTZELL M E          PFC      243 09 62/0311    -do-
SEEVER R L            Sgt      223 97 31/3371    -do-
SMITH E M             Cpl      241 97 99/0351    -do-
JOHNSON W E           PFC      244 40 17/2511    CG 5thMarDiv CamPen (MCC 128)
ROYAL D E             PFC      241 43 92/2511    -do-
SEITZ D W             Sgt      227 17 17/2533    CG 2dMAW FMFLant CHERPT (MCC 142)
BROWN D L             LCpl     242 38 35/0311    CG ForTrps FMFPac 29 Palms (MCC 150)
FLANNERY W M          LCpl     240 39 31/0341    CG ForTrps FMFLant CamLej (MCC 151)
MITCHEM H J           Pvt      226 36 68/3051    -do-
ACOSTA M H            Cpl      242 73 56/0351    CG/CO nearest MarCorActy for Furas
                                                    (MCC W99)
ARANDA A              Cpl      243 47 71/0331    -do-
BOOHER E A            PFC      247 74 00/0341    -do-
BULLOCK J H           PFC      246 70 32/0341    -do-
CASCIANO J E          PFC      246 70 25/0341    -do-
COLBERG S A           Cpl      240 36 51/0341    -do-
CURCIO J M            LCpl     241 42 94/0351    -do-
DIEDEN L W            LCpl     247 18 54/0331    -do-
DOMER G W             LCpl     244 57 91/0311    -do-
ELLIS R L             PFC      247 84 37/0331    -do-
FRANKLIN D O          PFC      246 89 05/0311    -do-
HARDRICK R G          LCpl     245 65 04/0341    -do-
HARRIS R              PFC      247 84 33/0311    -do-
HEARD J W             LCpl     246 03 38/0341    -do-
HUGHES M              PFC      239 83 65/0311    -do-
```

While I read the short list, searching for my name, Butler looked for his. Johnson found his on another sheet. The three of us were so elated, all we could do was wrestle around on the ground like children in the playground. I was annoyed but not surprised at the callous disregard for accuracy the persons compiling the list had shown. There were deceased persons listed to rotate home, like Ellis, who had died months earlier, and inaccuracies in military rank, as in my case. It was likely there were other mistakes, so I was understandably skeptical of the accuracy of the list.

What the hell, right or not, I was going to celebrate.

While each of us was holding a jubilant and animated conversation with each other, the jubilation was tempered by our private thoughts.

Although we worked well together, our individual military occupations were one of the many subcultures in our unit. Each of us would be leaving the men who shared our own specialized skills. We would leave behind friends who trusted and depended on us, with whom we had a shared life's experience, which had changed us all forever.

Johnson was the company's radio operator. His proximity to the officers made him feel special. I had to constantly remind him that he wasn't. Although I will admit that he was the best at what he did. His baritone voice, confidence, and composure would serve him well if he decided to become a disc jockey on returning to Detroit. The radiomen were the fabric that held it all together.

Before leaving to join his fellow radio operators in the communications tent, he gave me the power handshake. Then he added, "By the way, the colonel was pissed at the way you eyeballed him at the formation. The gunny or the lieutenant might be getting back to you about that."

"Fuck 'em," I replied sarcastically. Johnson could only throw up his hands and shake his head while exiting the tent.

Butler was a mortar team leader. His skills had gotten us all out of many tight spots. To me he was more than a mortar man. He always went above and beyond without regard to risk. He and Woody had left their mortar tube, picked up a rifle, and run to my aid only days earlier. He was my friend. We acknowledged each other before he walked away in another direction, seeking out the members of his mortar section whom he had so skillfully led.

Now I had to say good-bye to my fellow riflemen. The lead dogs of the pack. We were the first to go in and the last to come out. That life-and-death dance was one we all knew well. Risking our lives for one another was routine, not an act of valor. We knew who the heroes were.

When I entered the tent with the news regarding my release, the men showed the true meaning of friendship. They were cheering for me. They were almost as happy to see me go home as I was. I was one of them. If I could survive, so could they. I'll never forget those men or the others whose lives were shattered or lost. I fought as hard for them as I did for myself. My recent promotion to squad leader meant little to me. I felt greater pride when I was recognized as a leader by consent rather than appointment. Their respect assured me a level of self-esteem that can never be taken away.

One by one the men came to show their respect. They shared stories of the times we had spent together. Stories that switched the mood from being melancholy to a burst of jubilation. The scene was becoming surreal. I felt as though I were being eulogized. Then I was leaving their world for good, and this was likely the last time I would ever see these men. Perhaps that's the bizarre nature of war.

If world leaders knew what these warriors knew, they would understand the importance of balancing power and peace.

I woke the next morning to the men being mustered for a briefing before leaving for another mission. It was sad to see them leaving without me, knowing that many of them might never return.

But they were more concerned for my well-being and future. I even managed to get a few hastily scribbled notes that I will always cherish.

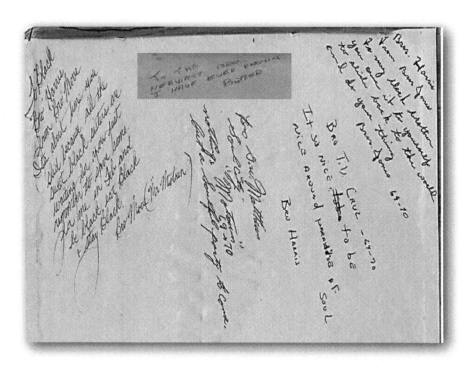

Johnson, along with others on the list, volunteered to be on the first wave of marines transported to the First Marine Division MAF Transient Facility in Da Nang.

Me, Butler and Friend

After our orders and identity were confirmed, we were finally allowed to board the aircraft carrier that would transport us to California. Those marines with six months or less remaining on their enlistment obligation would be given a discharge from active duty option.

Butler, one of my few surviving friends, and I would leave the following day.

We found that the enlisted men below the rank of sergeant who had boarded a day earlier were assigned mess duty while on board. Some were required to serve at officers' tables. I was put on laundry detail, washing the dirty underwear and uniforms of officers and NCOs. It was another clear indication of how we were viewed by those in positions of power.

First we were used as expendable commodities in war; now we were being used as subjugated servants. I suppose having the authority to command proud warriors may have boosted the ego of those officers. But if you want to learn about the horrors of war, talk to the participants who don't have power.

The ocean crossing was a relaxing journey in which we could just sit, talk, and make new friends. We no longer needed to worry about the perils of war.

While I spent some time with Butler and others, I would mostly spend many hours in solitude. The three-week ocean crossing allowed time for a mental withdrawal from war. A time to pause and look to the future.

The life I'd lived for that past year was over, and new challenges were on the horizon. I had to determine how to apply the lessons I'd learned, now that decisions would be life altering, rather than life or death. I knew now that I alone was responsible for my future; there would never be a person, belief, or idea, no matter how uniformly accepted, that I wouldn't question. I would always look for opportunities to overcome the obstacles that would be placed in front of me. Death was the only barrier I couldn't overcome.

I would still witness sickness and healing, death and destruction, success and failure, joy and pain, laughter and tears. But events would be stretched over years or decades rather than days, hours, minutes, or seconds. I would have more time to weigh my choices and perhaps make better decisions. I may later regret some of those decisions, but I can't deny having made them. Everything you do reflects who you are.

War gave me a crash course in friendships. A lesson that would transcend war. I learned to recognize a true friend. They're the ones who will be there when you need them with no strings attached.

Recognizing your enemy is more difficult. They can be cleverly disguised. The true question is, why are they your enemy? Does the fault lie with them, you, or something neither of you had anything to do with?

Your most valuable asset is your character; that is what people will remember after you're gone. Be consistent; people will either accept or reject you for who you truly are.

For me the war is over. It was one hell of a year. May it rest in peace.

Ralph Harris

EPILOGUE

▲ ▲ ▲

AFTER A BRIEF RESPITE UPON returning to civilian life, I returned to my job at the General Motors facility, where they honored my Military Leave of Absence agreement. I then enrolled in junior college under the GI Bill. Next I married my neighborhood sweetheart and friend, Elaine. After completing junior college, I continued my studies at Cleveland State University.

When General Motors offered me a diemaker's apprenticeship, I quit college to pursue my trade. After working at several plants across Ohio, I acquired employment at a plant in Grand Rapids, Michigan. After thirty-seven years of GM employment, I retired as a lead diemaker and a three-term local 730 executive board member for the United Auto Workers.

Elaine made a rapid transition from high school graduate to teenage bride. She then gave birth to two daughters while finishing junior college. After graduation she worked at several medical laboratories around Cleveland. When we moved to Michigan, Elaine enrolled in a private college. After earning her bachelor's degree, she got a position in research and development at Amway Corporate Headquarters, where she worked until her retirement.

Our older daughter, Saheedah, managed to overcome the challenges posed by a debilitating genetic disorder, sickle-cell anemia, and a divorce to receive her master's degree. She is now a social worker and single mother successfully raising and inspiring her two daughters, Jordyn and Nia.

Yasmeen, our younger daughter, attended and graduated from Grambling State University, one of the historically black colleges. After graduation she married a fellow student, Marcus Youngblood, and they settled in North Texas, where they are raising their son, Jaxon, and daughter, Ivy. Yasmeen is employed as an educator in the Dallas school system. In 2012 Elaine and I moved to North Dallas; shortly  thereafter Saheedah and her daughters made their move to Texas. Our families now live within twenty minutes of each other. Elaine and I see our daughters and grandchildren nearly every day. We take yearly vacations together and celebrate all birthdays and holidays together. We have even created holidays to justify having a celebration.

I cherish these moments, because had I not survived that year in 1969, my children and grandchildren would never have existed, and the memories I hold so dear would never have taken place.

I hope we as a society realize that when one of our young men or women dies in combat, it affects not only those who are currently in their lives, but also generations to come, and that is a loss to us all.

Made in the USA
Columbia, SC
08 September 2017